D1518937

African Spiritual Practices

A Comprehensive Guide to Yoruba, Santeria, Voodoo, Hoodoo, and the Orishas

Free Bonus from Silvia Hill available for limited time

Hi Spirituality Lovers!

My name is Silvia Hill, and first off, I want to THANK YOU for reading my book.

Now you have a chance to join my exclusive spirituality email list so you can get the ebooks below for free as well as the potential to get more spirituality ebooks for free! Simply click the link below to join.

P.S. Remember that it's 100% free to join the list.

 9 Types of Spirit Guides and How to Connect to Them

 How to Develop Your Intuition: 7 Secrets for Psychic Development and Tarot Reading

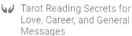 Tarot Reading Secrets for Love, Career, and General Messages

Access your free bonuses here

https://livetolearn.lpages.co/african-spiritual-practices-paperback/

Table of Contents

Part 1: African Spirituality

Unlocking the Power of Orishas, Yoruba, Santeria, Voodoo, and Hoodoo

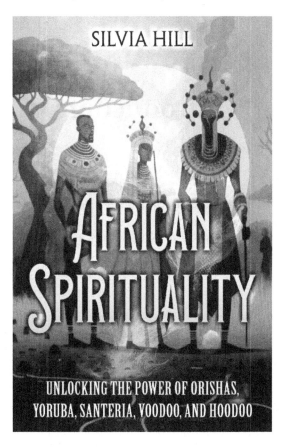

Introduction

African spirituality isn't just a fascinating topic filled with interesting mythology, magical rituals, and spells. Learning about it can help you better understand your heritage and culture's rich history. In this book, you'll discover the interesting and ancient world of African spirituality and have all your burning questions answered. The first thing covered is the diversity in African spirituality, its history, and its origins leading to various practices within African spirituality. Learning about them and their historical background can give you a clear idea of African religions, beliefs, and traditions.

Every religion and faith is usually defined by its deities, and African spirituality is no different. Although all their deities play prominent roles, none is more significant than their supreme god. You will not only learn everything about this chief deity, but you'll also discover why he is highly revered in all practices.

If you are familiar with African spirituality, you have probably heard the term "Orishas" a couple of times. These beings play an influential role in African spirituality and all its related practices. In this book, you'll step into the vast and rich world of the Orishas. You'll learn who they are, where they come from, their characteristics, and how they can help you. The book will cover in detail everything you want to know about the Orishas and more.

You can't learn about deities and supreme beings without learning how you can honor them. In this book, you'll learn how to create your own private altar to honor your ancestors and the Orishas. If you are new to the world of altars, don't fret. The book will provide you with step-by-step instructions on how to set up an altar of your own.

Magic and rituals are an intrinsic part of African spirituality. For some people, this may be the most interesting section of the book, and you will not be disappointed. The book will first introduce you to some magical practices, including the well-known Voodoo doll. In the last part of the book, you'll apply everything you have learned to practice various spells, rituals, and baths.

African spirituality isn't just an interesting topic you can read about in your free time. It can become a way of life easily integrated into your daily lifestyle. The book will give you helpful tips so that African spiritual practices easily become a part of your daily routine.

This book will act as a helpful guide, especially if you are a beginner. We made sure to make it as simple as possible to avoid confusing the reader. Although the book is extremely informative, you will not feel overwhelmed by the information provided as it's all presented in an interesting manner. You won't need to look elsewhere as this book includes everything you need to get started, including various methods and helpful instructions.

Prepare yourself for an enchanting journey into the world of African spirituality. This page-turner will be a handbook you'll return to whenever you need help or have a question.

Chapter 1: African Spirituality Basics

Before religions like Islam and Christianity arrived in Africa, the African people had their own beliefs, ceremonies, practices, and festivals, which they referred to as African spirituality. African spirituality, naturally enough, originated in Africa and is derived from the continent's ethnic identity. Each religion that has branched out from the spirituality of Africa is linked to its country's culture and history. For instance, the Zulu religion is based in southern Africa, and the Yoruba religion originated in southwestern Nigeria.

African spirituality originated in Africa and is derived from the continent's ethnic identity.
https://www.pexels.com/photo/a-man-in-maroon-robe-holding-a-burning-stick-8243596/

African religions are incorporated into the people's daily lives because, in African spirituality, all beliefs and practices impact every area of the people's lives. There is a belief that African spirituality is holistic, and spiritualists view certain parts of people's lives differently. For instance, if someone gets sick, they don't consider it simply an ailment of the body. They believe there may be an imbalance in other aspects of the person's life that makes them sick. Taking a holistic approach, questions are asked about the state of family relationships or their relationship with one or more of their ancestors. In fact, the ancestors play a significant role in African spirituality by giving advice to the living, honoring them, and bestowing good fortune on them. However, these gifts come with a price, although it isn't a high one. Sometimes the ancestors make simple demands, like regular maintenance of their shrines.

This begs the question, are these ancestors considered gods? African spirituality is different from other religions because there isn't a fixed concept of a deity. The role ancestors play in the African people's lives differs from one group to another. Some people hold their ancestors in similar regard to deities, while others don't share the same belief. Either way, the African people revered their ancestors. They see them as something more or higher than regular human beings who have the power to bless or curse them.

The ideas of polytheism and monotheism don't exactly exist in African spirituality, as this type of thinking may seem a bit simplistic when describing such a complex belief. Spiritual beings, deities, and gods exist in the world of African spirituality. This makes it difficult to put this belief into one single category. However, some African spiritual beliefs believe in the concept of a supreme being. For instance, the Yoruba believe in a supreme god called Olorun or Olodumare. They believed that Olorun created the universe with the help of other deities called the Orishas. Orishas receive prayers from the people and deliver them to the supreme deity. They help him with other earthly functions as well.

African spirituality is built on the belief that the spirit of the Creator is in everything, including living beings and everything that exists in nature.

Certain elements define African spirituality:

- The Spirit of Being
- The nature of existence
- Cyclical existence
- The interconnectedness of things

- Order and balance
- Social and spiritual hierarchy

African spirituality is diverse. Over the years, various religions have passed through Africa, mainly Christianity and Islam, which changed and impacted the region's culture and did allow African spirituality to evolve throughout time. Over the years, contact with other countries and cultures from all over the world has helped African spirituality grow, and it has been able to adapt to these changes. African spirituality didn't dismiss these religions' beliefs or wisdom. On the contrary, it allowed itself to expand by incorporating their views and wisdom. For instance, you may find verses from the Bible or the Quran on African amulets. On the other hand, these religions resist accommodating African beliefs.

Like other ancient cultures, African spirituality was passed down through oral methods like songs or stories. Therefore, their beliefs weren't collected in a single religious text like the Bible. This made it easier for African spirituality to be influenced by other religions and beliefs. This kind of adaptability is how African spirituality manages to deal with modernity. As a result of its flexibility and diversity, African spirituality has spread to different regions around the world, like Europe and the United States. There are communities in various countries that practice African spirituality, like Yoruba, along with other spiritual beliefs from different cultures. This allows for diversity in African spiritual customs and beliefs.

All types of African spirituality share some common beliefs. One of these beliefs is the concept of the afterlife. They believe that death isn't the end of one's journey as there is life after death but in a different realm. This is where their ancestors exist and where the spirits of the dead can live on. This makes death desirable as they spend eternity with the ancestors they revere. Another belief in African spirituality related to death is the concept of reincarnation. Reincarnation is the rebirth of the soul. Since the soul is eternal and doesn't die, unlike the body, it can begin another journey through rebirth. In other words, the soul is reborn as another human, an animal, a spirit, or a vegetable. That said, the details of how a soul comes back to life vary from belief to belief. For instance, the Yoruba people, specifically in West Africa, believe that a person can be incarnated if they had unfinished business before they died or weren't buried properly. Accordingly, the newly reincarnated person is frequently named after the deceased person.

Since Africans believe in the afterlife and regard death as a happy occasion, their burial rites and preparation of the deceased for the afterlife are significant. Although not all ethnic groups share the same burial traditions, they still all hold this occasion in very high regard. For instance, a group in Kenya called the Abaluya buries their dead naked. Since they regard transitioning to the afterlife as a form of rebirth, they prepare their dead for this moment by burying them naked like a baby. An appropriate burial is vital for the spirit's transition to the afterlife. If a deceased person doesn't get an appropriate burial, their spirits are doomed to wander the physical world and aren't allowed to transition to the next realm. These spirits will never be at peace, and they punish everyone for it by wreaking havoc, causing serious diseases, and becoming evil.

Sometimes, an inappropriate burial rite can be done on purpose as a punishment to the deceased. If the deceased wasn't a good person or didn't lead an honest or kind existence, they are usually given an incomplete burial. All followers of African spirituality desire nothing more than to cross this realm to go to the next and become highly revered ancestors. Therefore, an incomplete burial is a perfect punishment for bad people. Arriving in the afterlife doesn't necessarily mean the deceased is safe from judgment. They are often judged for everything they did when they were alive to determine if they should be rewarded or punished. This belief is meant to encourage people to be good to one another. The people of Yoruba were among those who believed the deceased were either punished or rewarded in the afterlife. However, there are groups in Kenya who believe that an afterlife is a place in another realm where you continue living your life; your spirit continues living in another realm. There is no punishment or reward.

Now that you have familiarized yourself with the basics of African spirituality, we will focus on the different African practices in the next part of the chapter.

Yoruba

The Yoruba religion is one of the oldest beliefs in the world; it even predates Christianity by centuries. It is based on songs, legends, myths, and proverbs taken from West African culture. Yoruba culture originated in West Nigeria about 5,000 years ago, and most of its followers still live in Nigeria. However, there are a few groups that live in Togo and Benin. The people of Yoruba worship the supreme deity and the creator Olodumare, and they refer to themselves, the worshippers, as children.

They are also strong believers in the Orishas and the concept of reincarnation. In the last few years, West African culture has seen a resurgence in countries like the United States, the Caribbean, and Canada. In fact, it's estimated that about 500,000 people in different cities around the United States practice the Yoruba religion.

The Yoruba people are one of the largest ethnic groups in Africa. There isn't just one ethnic group in Yoruba culture, but multiple groups. They are diverse people who share the same culture, history, and language. According to Yoruba mythology, the people of Yoruba all descend from their divine king Oduduwa. Like every culture and religion, the Yoruba have their own creation myth and believe that Olorun was the creator of the universe.

After various religions came to Africa, the practice of the Yoruba religion decreased significantly. Yet, about 20% of the people of Yoruba still practice their ancestors' religion. Not all groups follow the same practices, though. For instance, some groups worship a male deity, while others worship a female deity.

There are a few main gods in Yoruba spiritual practice. The first is Olodumare, who is the creator and the sky god. His worshippers call on him by offering prayers which the Orisha usually receive. They can also call on him by pouring water on kola nuts. Olodumare's divine messenger is called Legba or Eshu. Eshu's job is to deliver the sacrifice left by worshippers at Olodumare's shrine. All worshippers pray to Eshu. Another deity is Ifa, who is the god of divination. He interprets Olodumare's wishes and delivers them to the believers. When the worshippers find themselves struggling and needing help, they often pray to Ifa.

Ogun, the god of war, metalwork, and hunting, is one of the most important gods in the Yoruba religion. According to Yoruba practices, when someone is supposed to give a testimonial, they have to swear to tell the truth by kissing a machete that is sacred to Ogun. The last significant deity in Yoruba's spiritual belief system is Shango, the god of thunder. Shango, the god of thunder, is the final major deity in Yoruba spiritual belief. The people of Yoruba believe that lightning and thunder occur when Shango throws a thunderstone to earth. According to their beliefs, this isn't an ordinary thunderstone; it has special powers. This is why religious leaders roam the streets after thunderstorms looking for this magic thunderstone.

There are several festivals in the Yoruba religion. Honoring the supreme god and the Orishas is one of their main events. Other celebrations include offering sacrifices to their deities so the gods bless them with a good harvest and plentiful rain. During the obligatory festivals, participants reenact different myths and folktales from Yoruba mythology and have a great deal of fun. It is considered a sign of disrespect to the gods, spirits, and ancestors if followers don't attend the festivals and celebrate them.

The Yoruba people are firm believers in reincarnation, and they regard it as a positive experience and even a privilege that is only bestowed on good and kind people who lead honest lives.

Santeria

Santeria originated in West Africa among the people of Yoruba. However, it is considered an Afro-Cuban religion. Through the years, it spread to different countries around the world, like Cuba, Haiti, Puerto Rico, Brazil, Trinidad, and the United States. Santeria is often referred to as Regla de Ocha or the Lucumí, which are the names that their practitioners prefer. The word Santeria is Spanish and loosely translates to "devotion to the saints." This name is appropriate as the practitioners of Santeria refer to their gods and Orishas as saints.

This spiritual practice consists of more than one religious belief. In fact, it is a blend of various cultures and faiths. Interestingly, many of them are extremely different and even contradict each other. As mentioned, African spirituality is diverse, and Santeria is the biggest proof of this diversity. This practice has borrowed elements from different cultures and spiritual faiths worldwide, like Yoruba, Catholicism, and Caribbean traditions. It is also influenced by several African cultures like Senegal, Bantu, and Guinea Coast.

This belief is different and fairly complex because it blends two different faiths with each other, the Orishas of Yoruba and Catholic saints. Santeria has even associated each of their Orishas with a Catholic saint. It's not only a spiritual practice; magic also plays a major role in this belief. Practitioners of Santeria also practice magic. However, their magic is closely related to their understanding and interactions with the Orishas.

Voodoo

What is the first thing that comes to mind when you see the word "voodoo"? Most people, even those unfamiliar with African spirituality, have heard the word voodoo more than once in their lives. If you heard about voodoo from a movie or a TV show, then you probably associate it with black magic, zombies, or devil worship. However, this is an unfair stereotype which is why voodoo is considered the most misunderstood religion. Unfortunately, voodoo has a very sinister reputation. It has been linked to witchcraft and evil spells in the last couple of centuries. With the popularity of some aspects of this practice, like the voodoo doll, most people's idea of what voodoo is has been manipulated by the media. This has put its practitioners in a very precarious position, constantly defending their beliefs and dealing with other people's distrust.

There is no need to be afraid of voodoo. It's time to unlearn everything you know about this practice and approach it with a fresh perspective. You should first be aware that voodoo has nothing to do with demonic worship and isn't a branch of witchcraft. It is a spiritual belief that is no different from Yoruba and Santeria and is not associated with anything evil. The religion originated in Haiti and later spread to different African regions and blended with Catholicism.

Voodoo, which is also spelled *vodou* or *vodun*, is one of the oldest religions in the world, with origins dating back 6,000 years. When voodoo became a part of the modern world, it borrowed elements from Catholicism and African magical and religious rites. It isn't easy to define voodoo or to put it in a category because of its dynamic nature. You may even find two temples in the same village, each with its traditions. That said, there are still some similarities between voodoo traditions. Many of its African elements are borrowed from Yoruba, the Kongo people, the Ewe people, and Fon. Similar to other beliefs, voodoo has changed over the years, yet it still maintains many elements of African spirituality. The people still worship their ancestors and perform transcendental dancing and drumming. Voodoo is practiced in different countries around the world: The Caribbean, Haiti, and New Orleans.

If you watch any movie that features voodoo, you will notice that it is portrayed as something closely related to dark magic with the purpose of harming others. This is clearly a misconception, but what has brought it on? Well, this isn't merely a Hollywood creation. There was a specific incident that took place in 1791 in Haiti. A group of people came upon a voodoo ceremony and believed that what they witnessed was people making deals with the devil. This story is still alive today, with many people acknowledging it. In fact, some people believe the 2010 earthquake that struck Haiti resulted from this deal with the devil that cursed the people of Haiti.

The voodoo followers believe in one supreme deity, which they call Bondye. The deity shares similarities with the Catholic god. They also had their own version of the Orishas, which were gods who were not as powerful as the god they called Iwa. The people who believed in the Iwa made an offering of food and other pleasing objects. These offerings are made when followers need Iwa's assistance. When they want to talk to an Iwa, they hold ceremonies and ask it to take over one of the people there. The followers also use voodoo dolls to attract an Iwa. However, the concept of poking voodoo dolls isn't associated with the voodoo spiritual practice.

Hoodoo

Since voodoo and hoodoo have similar spelling, you may think that they share some similarities. However, the two practices don't have many things in common. Voodoo has its own religious leaders, and its followers usually perform specific practices. The followers also highly revere certain deities and spirits. On the other hand, hoodoo couldn't be more different from anything that voodoo represents. Unlike voodoo and the other practices mentioned here, hoodoo followers don't worship any specific deities. They can worship any god they choose or even choose not to worship any. There is also no hierarchy associated with this religion, and its worshippers don't have to follow a specific structure.

Hoodoo isn't a religion that everyone can practice since only Black people are allowed to practice it. It began as a way to help Black people overcome the trauma they had experienced as enslaved people. To this day, Black people practice hoodoo to protect themselves from all the dangers they encounter daily.

African spirituality has a rich and fascinating history. This belief is very tolerant of other religions that it meets along the way. It borrowed elements from many religions, which allowed for a diverse belief system to evolve that many people gravitate toward. There is still much more to discuss about African spirituality. This chapter has only scratched the surface. In the next chapter, you'll learn about the supreme deity Oldumare and the creation myth.

Chapter 2: Olodumare, the Supreme God

With few exceptions, every culture in the world has come up with its own myth about creation. It's a fundamental and universal question: how did the world come to be? Because people don't believe that the world just appeared out of nowhere, someone must have created it. When they couldn't find an explanation, many cultures decided to come up with their own interpretation. African culture is no different; it has created its own myth to help explain how the universe and mankind came into existence.

Priests in their temple.
Creator: Dierk Lange, CC0, via Wikimedia Commons:
https://commons.wikimedia.org/wiki/File:Obatala_Priester_im_Tempel.jpg

Most creation myths have the same elements. They are usually supernatural stories that revolve around the culture's mythology and include multiple religious' themes. These stories explain how the earth, humanity, and the universe were created. Usually, one or more deities are involved in creating the universe. The most dominating themes in these stories are usually one of the following: creating the universe out of nothing, two parents' deities separating, or a land appearing from an infinite ocean.

You can learn so much about a culture from its creation story. Although the events in these stories aren't necessarily real or factual, they still reflect the culture's beliefs. However, some of these beliefs are expressed on a symbolic level. The African creation myth will help you better understand your culture's history and learn about the supreme being, Olodumare, and his role in creating the universe.

The Myth of Creation

In the beginning, before mankind came to be, the universe looked nothing like it does today. There was only darkness, except for a translucent layer that stood out in the darkness. It was a small land that laid the foundations for the universe's birth. Inside the translucent layer were space, air, water, and light. This layer was the home of Olodumare. He created light and ordered it to spread over the universe. Although there was light, the world was still empty, leaving room for plenty more creations, something that Obatala was beginning to realize.

There was only the sky up above, wild marshlands below, and water. Olodumare was the supreme god who ruled the sky, and his twin sister Olokun was an Orisha spirit and the sea goddess. Although both siblings were twins, they were, in fact, estranged. One day, the god Obatala, who was also one of the greatest Orishas, reflected on the state of his existence and the world around him. He was bored and restless with his existence in his heavenly home. Obatala believed that this world could be more than it was. He decided to create another world but wanted to get Olodumare's permission first. Obatala went to Olodumare and told him that he wanted to create a dry land with fields, mountains, forests, and valleys so all living creatures could live on it. Olodumare liked Obatala's idea and granted him instant permission.

Obatala was very excited to start creating his new world. However, he didn't know where to start, and he had a few questions that he wanted answers to before he headed off on his new adventure. Obtala wasn't stubborn; in fact, he was rather intelligent. He was aware that he wasn't all-knowing and saw no shame in consulting someone who had more knowledge than him. Obatala sought the advice of Orunmila, the god of prophecy and Olodumare's oldest son. Orunmila told him that he would need a long golden chain to help him reach the world below. Obatala went to a goldsmith to make him the chain. The goldsmith agreed but said that Obatala must provide the gold. He went to all the gods, asking them for gold, and they were all happy to help him. He delivered the gold, and the goldsmith created the chain for him. Orunmila also told Obatala that he would need a black cat, a white hen, a palm nut, and a snail shell that he must fill with sand from the heavens, put them in a bag, and carry them on his journey down below. Orunmila helped Obatala to obtain all these items. With the help of the gods and Orunmila, Obatala was ready for his journey.

Orunmila advised Obatala to take another Orisha to help him, so he chose Oduduwa. Now they were both ready for the trip. Obatala used the golden chain to climb down from the heavens. However, he realized that the chain wasn't long enough, and he still had a short distance to go. Orunmila helped Obatala from heaven and told him to begin using the items in his bag. He was first instructed to throw the sand in the snail's shell on Earth and then release the hen. The hen scattered the sand, and it began forming the land. Obatala and Oduduwa finally descended on the earth and called the place where they landed Ife. The land kept expanding thanks to heaven's sand and the hen.

Obatala and Oduduwa spent some time in Ife with the black cat to keep them company. Obatala planted the palm nut, which immediately grew into a palm tree. Palm nuts dropped from this tree on the ground, and they all grew immediately. Now Obatala had his own forest of palm trees all around him. He then wanted a place to settle, so he built himself a hut. Obatala lived in the hut with the black cat. He had a daily routine, and he was enjoying his new life. But after a few months, Obatala became lonely and bored. He decided that he wanted to be around other beings like him so he could interact with them, and they would keep him company. Obatala was a talented sculptor, so he used his skill to make clay figures of beings like him. He began sculpting, but after some time, he grew tired, so he took a break and drank some wine. He got drunk, but he continued creating his clay figures. After he was done, he asked Olodumare to breathe life into them so they could come alive.

The next day, Obatala was shocked to find that the beings he created when he was drunk were all deformed. Obtala was ashamed of what he had done and vowed never to have a sip of wine again. He decided that he would become the protector of the deformed to make up for his mistake.

After seeing what Obatala had created, Oduduwa decided to create his own beings, but he wanted them to be better formed than those that Obatala had created. He sought Olodumare's help. Oduduwa created mankind with the help of the supreme god. Oduduwa loved human beings, so he decided to live among them and become their king instead of going back to heaven. His children and grandchildren populated Yoruba and created more kingdoms.

Olodumare

Olodumare was the lord of the heavens, and he ruled over 17,000 divinities that existed in the pantheon of Yoruba. It is clear from the myth of creation that neither the world nor human beings would have existed if it weren't for Olodumare. He gave his permission to Obatala to create the world and helped him and Oduduwa to create mankind by breathing life into them. Although Obatala and Oduduwa did most of the work, none of it would have happened without the supreme god lending a hand. Olodumare was the supreme god/being of Yoruba. According to the people of Yoruba, he was one of the first beings to exist, and he created heaven and earth, day and night, and the four seasons. The fate of mankind is in Olodumare's hands, but he is a fair deity. When someone makes a mistake, the Orishas usually handle their punishment. Olodumare judges people differently, though. He doesn't only look at their actions, but he also considers their personality, character, and inner feelings. Olodumare knows each person's true self, so he looks into their hearts before he judges their actions.

When a person dies, their soul must stand before Olodumare and be judged. He judges mankind based on their morals. If the person has been good in their life, they receive rewards from Olodumare. Olodumare rules over heaven and earth, so he judges all beings in both worlds, including the Orishas. His will must always be done, and no creature in heaven or on earth can go against it. He is the one in control of everything in the universe, which is why all beings abide by his will.

Olodumare and the Orisha aren't the same, and one main thing sets them apart. Olodumare is a supreme being, not just a regular deity, unlike the Orisha. He represents the natural force of life, a higher form of humanity, and a pure concept of human nature. Although both Olodumare and the Orishas play major roles in the Yoruba religion, Olodumare has a more significant role. He is a more complex being, and no mortal is able or allowed to see Olodumare.

Unlike other deities, there aren't temples in which to worship Olodumare. There also aren't any priests devoted to this supreme deity. According to the Yoruba religion, all priests highly revere Olodumare and give him offerings. There is a group of priests called the Oracle of Ifa, who have the required skills to understand and interpret Olodumare's words. Olodumare also communicates his will to the devoted followers of Orisha Orunmila, who is also the god of wisdom.

Death wasn't a concept in the Yoruba religion, as it didn't exist at first. People didn't die, but they kept growing until they became huge. They then began shrinking until they became weak and old. According to legend, mankind grew tired of living such long lives, and since death didn't exist, the region became overpopulated. They prayed to Olodumare to liberate them from these long lives, and he answered their prayers by creating death. Just like Olodumare breathed life into mankind, he created what can take life away - death. He is the creator of everything and is revered for his knowledge and wisdom. Since he is the supreme god, no deity is wiser or more powerful than him. He isn't a passive god who just watches mankind from the heavens. Olodumare plays a significant role in the destinies of all beings in heaven and on earth, yet he never directly interferes. Olodumare often depends on the Orishas to handle mankind's prayers or concerns.

Olodumare resembles the concept of god found in Judaism, Christianity, and Islam. This deity has been around since the beginning of time – possibly even before, since he has no beginning and no end. He is and will always be present. Although he lives in the sky, Olodumare is everywhere and the source of life. All that was, all that is, and all that will be, comes from him. The simple human brain can't comprehend or conceptualize the concept of Olodumare.

At night, when the world goes to sleep, Olodumare is the one who is in charge and handles all the hopes and dreams of his creation. Olodumare wasn't born since he didn't have any parents. Most gods in other cultures are often illustrated so that people can understand and have an idea of what they look like. However, there aren't any images of this deity, just like there aren't any shrines or devoted priests. This means that Olodumare isn't worshiped directly - even sacrifices aren't made directly to him. The Orishas often act as the "middle man," receiving the people's prayers or sacrifice instead of Olodumare. In fact, Olodumare prefers to keep a distance from mankind. However, there are some of his followers who directly worship him. When a person is in trouble, they call on the Orishas for assistance. However, sometimes the Orishas refuse to help or may lack the ability or power to assist in a particular issue. In this case, the people will have no other choice but to call on Olodumare directly.

Olodumare didn't always keep his distance from mankind. In fact, once upon a time, the earth was in very close proximity to Olodumare and the sky. However, mankind offended Olodumare by eating from the sky. He decided to keep his distance from them and the earth. This is why the sky is now far away from earth.

As the creator of everything, he is also considered the source of mortality and virtue. When a child is born, Olodumare bestows upon them his knowledge. He is the most powerful being with superior knowledge, yet he has the capacity for good and evil.

Olodumare is a just and fair god, but he doesn't suffer disrespect or bad behavior lightly. According to a Yoruba myth, at one time, Olodumare wasn't happy with how the Orishas were behaving. He didn't want to destroy them and decided that punishment and teaching them a lesson was the better option. He prevented the sky from raining and let the Orishas suffer a drought so they could learn from their mistakes. The Orishas were struggling and sought Olodumare's forgiveness. They tried to call on him and reach out to him, but he was too high in the sky and couldn't or wouldn't hear them. One of the Orishas, Oshun, transformed into a peacock and volunteered to fly to heaven and beg Olodumare to return the rain. However, on her way up, she lost her feathers and became a vulture. She kept flying until she reached him. Olodumare appreciated the sacrifice and what she had endured on her trip to meet him. He brought back the rain, and as a reward for her sacrifice, he made Oshun his messenger. To this day, there are still people in Yoruba who worship Olodumare.

Olodumare, Olorun, and Olofi

Olodumare means the almighty and supreme, Olorun means the owner, and Olofin-Orun means the lord of heaven. According to the Yoruba religion, Olodumare was the creator and supreme god. Olofin came before him, and he ruled over everything that existed in the universe. Olofin was also responsible for the Orishas and had power over them. The Orishas aren't allowed to take action with matters concerning the earth without going to Olofin first. Olodumare, Olorun, and Olofi are all manifestations of the deity. They represent three stages, the universe, the creation of man, and everything that takes place on earth.

Olofin and Olrun are Olodumare's other names. In Yoruba mythology, these three names represent different aspects of the same deity. The concept is similar to that of the Holy Trinity in Catholicism. In fact, the followers of the Santeria wanted to come up with a concept similar to the Holy Trinity. It's basically three individuals/beings who have the same essence.

Olodumare

This is the spiritual manifestation of the deity. In this stage, he is the creator who breathes life into all living things.

Olorun

This manifestation of the deity spreads supreme energy that facilitates the continuation of life on earth. Olorun is often represented by the sun, which also emits energy responsible for all life on earth.

Olofin

The people of Yoruba use this term to refer to their king, the manifestation closest to the Orishas and mankind. It represents the manifestation of the god on earth. According to the Yoruba religion, Olofin is their patriarch. When he wants to come down to earth, he often transforms into energy. He is the keeper of all secrets related to creation.

Olodumare in African Spirituality

Olodumare and his manifestations play a huge role in the practices of African Spirituality, Yoruba, Santeria, Voodoo, and Hoodoo. Voodoo is a monotheistic religion which means that its followers worship one god. This god is Olorun in Yoruba culture. Olodumare is highly revered and regarded as a supreme deity in all faiths. In the Yoruba religion, followers don't offer sacrifices to Olodumare, but they offer them to the Orishas. In Yoruba and Santeria, there aren't any symbols or statues of Olodumare. However, he was still highly revered. In Santeria, Olodumare is in first place on their religious hierarchy.

It is obvious from everything mentioned so far that Olodumare was a good deity. He supported both Obatala and Oduduwa to create the world and mankind. Instead of destroying the Orishas, he opted for punishment to help them learn their lesson. He is fair and just and looks at the person's character and heart before he punishes mankind. It makes sense for Olodumare to be highly revered among different religions in African spirituality.

Olodumare created the universe and breathed his life into mankind, making him the most significant being in all African religions. Now that you have learned about the supreme being Olodumare, you'll enter the world of the Orishas in the next chapters. They have a prominent role in African spirituality and aided Olodumare in creating the universe.

Chapter 3: Who Are the Orishas?

The Yoruba people of West Africa are among the most populous and widespread African ethnicities. Their culture is rich in art, music, and traditions. The Yoruba people also have a unique spiritual system known as Orisha worship. Orisha worship, sometimes called Orisa, centers on spirits known as Orishas. These Orishas are manifestations of nature and forces that help keep the balance of life on Earth. Moreover, they are the only conduit through which God's energy flows and the only way humans can communicate directly with him. Each Orisha has different responsibilities, characteristics, and personality traits. This chapter will delve into Orisha's origin and its significance in African spirituality.

. Orishas are manifestations of nature and forces that help keep the balance of life on Earth.
Omoeko Media, CC BY-SA 4.0 <https://creativecommons.org/licenses/by-sa/4.0>, via Wikimedia Commons: https://commons.wikimedia.org/wiki/File:Orishas_in_Oba%27s_palace,_Abeokuta.jpg

Who Are the Orishas?

In the African diaspora, Orishas are a group of deities that have found significant representation among the descendants of enslaved Africans. African culture is filled with stories of spirits, gods, and goddesses. These are the powerful forces that make up the Orishas. Orishas are found to exist in many different cultures throughout Africa. They represent natural forces and can be found everywhere, from rivers to trees to rocks. Although most people do not commonly know them outside of Africa, you can meet them wherever you go. These beings are described in various ways, which is indicative of their omnipotence.

Orishas are divine beings believed to guide the world and provide guidance to followers. The Yoruba people believe in a pantheon of different Orishas responsible for different realms in life. Some Orishas are responsible for health and healing, while others oversee love, money, and social justice. Orishas are believed to have both positive and negative characteristics, and followers can tap into the Orishas' powers to help with different areas in their lives. Orishas are also referred to as gods and goddesses, the chief difference being that the Orishas are seen as nature deities who govern and control the forces of nature. The Orishas are seen as ancestors who were kings and queens of the ancient Yoruba civilization. Orishas are worshiped as supreme deities of the Yoruba people. Their shrines are found in houses, vernacular shrines, and churches. Orishas are associated with specific aspects of life, such as love, war, fertility, music, and many other parts.

The Orishas are also known as spirits who have survived in various forms throughout Africa. They have been worshiped as gods and goddesses. Still, they have also been recognized as natural forces and energies that regulate life on the planet. This is a very old practice and can be traced back to the beginning of human culture. It is easy to dismiss spiritual practices as outdated and irrelevant, but they are still alive today. If you are looking for a unique spiritual practice, Orisha worship may be a good fit for you.

What Religions Believe in the Orishas?

Although Orisha worship is most commonly associated with the Yoruba people, many African and Latin American religions believe in the Orishas. In fact, they were originally the objects of a Hindu spiritual practice before being adopted into the Yoruba people's beliefs. Orisha worship is most popular in Brazil, Cuba, Puerto Rico, and Haiti. However, you may also find practitioners in other parts of Latin America and in western African countries like Nigeria and Ghana. Orisha worship is also commonly associated with Santeria, a combination of Yoruba beliefs with Catholic and Animist practices.

You might have heard of the Lwa. Also called Loa or Loi. Lwa spirits are part of the African diasporic religion of Haitian Vodou. Much like the Orishas, Lwa are deities whose identities are derived from traditional African religions. As opposed to Yoruba gods (Orisha), the Loa are spirits of voodoo. The Orishas are gods in their own right and answer only to the divine being and creator, Olodumare.

The Importance of Orisha in African Spirituality

The Yoruba people have had a profound impact on the world. Not only did they create beautiful art and music, but they also developed spirituality and rituals that would influence other cultures and religions. Orisha worship is the most prominent spiritual practice that came from the Yoruba people. The worship of Orisha spirits from the Yoruba religion is called Orisha-Ifa. Orisha-Ifa is an ancient spiritual practice that the Yoruba people have practiced for hundreds of years. Orisha-Ifa is based on the philosophy that everything in the universe is interrelated. The Orishas are spirits and energies that keep the balance of life on Earth. Orisha-Ifa is a way to communicate and tap into the Orisha spirits to help with life.

The Orishas are responsible for helping humanity and providing guidance to the people that worship them. However, the Orishas only help people who try to communicate with them. People who worship the Orishas are expected to make sacrifices to them to show respect. Followers must also maintain a strong, honest code of moral conduct and follow strict guidelines to receive help from the Orishas.

The Orishas and Spirituality

Spirituality is a word that is often associated with religion. But spirituality and religion are not the same things. Religion is often defined as a belief system connecting people to a higher power (as in a god). Spirituality, on the other hand, is a journey to find meaning and purpose in life. It's about finding one's own connection to a higher power. Orisha worship is the spiritual practice of the Yoruba people, but it's not a religion. The Yoruba people do not believe in one true god but in many gods that can be found worldwide. Orisha worship is a way to tap into a higher power and get guidance and advice on how to best navigate life.

In Practice

Because the Orishas are deities that represent natural forces and principles, through their stories and teachings that illustrate how humans should live to please them, they serve to reinforce social norms. Orishas also play an important role in healing. People who practice Ifa usually visit Ifa priests to consult them about their problems. During the consultation, the Ifa priest will advise on how to solve the problem or how to cope with the situation if that is not possible. Orishas also provide inspiration when a person is feeling depressed or in need of motivation. Orishas inspire people to live a life connected to nature and the universe, and they will be healthy and live a fulfilling life.

Orisha Beliefs

The Orishas can be both benevolent and malicious. They rule over different parts of life, and their moods can change depending on the day. Orisha worshipers must take these mood swings into account when communicating with them. Orisha worshipers also believe that a parallel realm of spirits exists alongside humans. There is a set of rules and limitations in this realm, and humans can tap into these spirits to help with life. Depending on where an Orisha is coming from, they can either help or hurt humans. An Orisha coming from a negative place can harm humans if left unchecked. But an Orisha coming from a positive place can help humanity immensely.

In Practice

Orishas represent natural forces and principles, such as fate, fertility, love, war, or healing. They also serve to reinforce social norms through their stories and teachings that illustrate how humans should live to please them. Orishas are similar to the gods of other religions in that they are immortal, superhuman entities that can be either beneficent or malevolent toward humankind. However, the Orisha consciousness does not exist independently of human consciousness. Every Orisha has a human counterpart, called an Orisha-head, through whom they can live and contact the physical world. This human counterpart can be a living person or someone who has died. Orishas are often associated with colors, foods, and numbers. They have distinct personalities and temperaments and can be either hot-tempered or cool-headed. They can also be either white or black, good or evil.

How to Worship the Orishas

The best way to worship the Orishas is to tap into the powers of each Orisha. To do this, you first invite an Orisha into your body by drinking a libation (usually a type of alcohol). When you drink an Orisha libation, you can expect them to come into your body within 30 minutes. After you invite an Orisha into your body, create a ritual to invite them into your life. You can do this by burning incense or by lighting candles. You can also write down what you want to accomplish in life or which Orisha you want to invite into your body.

Exploring the Classification of Orisha

The classification of Orishas was serious for the Yoruba people because it helped them logically organize the deities. It also gave the people an idea about how to interact with them through the Ifa system. The Ifa system is a complex system that uses various symbols and colors to understand the world and communicate with the Orishas.

How Many Orisha Are There?

There are hundreds of Orishas, and their number is continuously growing. However, when the Orishas were first brought to Africa, they were part of a small group of deities. With the evolution of the Ifa tradition, the number of Orishas grew. As the Orishas were worshiped, they were given new names and were associated with different aspects of the natural world and human life. Orishas were also combined with each other or with others to create new deities. More deities were added to the pantheon as time passed because people needed new Orishas to worship. New deities were also created to represent natural phenomena that were not previously part of the Ifa tradition.

The number of Orishas varies between and within the sources. According to the Orisha religion, there are 400 - 1,440 Orishas. Different communities and scholars have given different numbers, but they all agree it is very high. According to the Encyclopedia Britannica, there are more than 600 Orishas. The encyclopedia claims that it is impossible to know the exact number of Orishas because the Orisha religion is an oral tradition passed down from generation to generation.

What Are the Different Types of Orishas?

The different types of Orishas are complex questions, and there isn't a single answer. The question often depends on whom you ask and what source you are looking at. According to the Orisha religion, the classification and the number of Orishas are not fixed. The types of Orishas change over time, and the people who interact with them also change. So, it is impossible to say that there is a single correct classification of Orishas. However, there are many Orishas who are commonly known and worshiped. Some of the most important gods and goddesses are Oshun, Ogun, Yemaya, and Eshu. Oshun is the goddess of love and beauty, Ogun is the god of iron, the forge, and weapons, Yemoja is the goddess of the sea, and Eshu is the god of communication, luck, and chaos.

The dark or hot-tempered Orisha is a god or goddess who is connected to the concepts of disorder, chaos, and destruction. These Orishas are associated with the sun and the color red or black. The dark Orishas are often feared and misunderstood by those who don't understand the Orisha religion. They are often considered evil, but actually, they are concerned with destroying evil.

- **Eshu:** Male deity (red and black)
- **Ogun:** Male deity (dark green or blue, and black)
- **Shango:** Male deity (red and white)
- **Oya:** Female deity (red)

They symbolize fire, volcanoes, and the masculine principle. As well as representing the destructive powers of the Earth, they can also be both kind and frightening. Volcanoes and earthquakes are closely linked to these deities. Transformation, death, and rebirth are also important powers of the darker Orishas.

The white or cool-tempered Orisha is a spirit connected to the concept of justice, peace, and order. They are concerned with the imposition of order, which is why they are often connected to the kings and queens who rule over these kingdoms. White Orishas are associated with water, the moon, and lighter colors like white. They are usually kind and loving. They are usually the Orishas of priests because the priests are concerned with the order of the spiritual world.

- **Orunmila:** Male deity (white)
- **Obatala:** Male deity (white)
- **Erinle:** Male deity (green, yellow, coral)
- **Yemoja:** Female deity (white and blue)

They are the creators of the Earth, and all of nature, with Eshu being the creator of the human species. White Orishas focus on the positive things in life. They dislike negativity and sustain their power through love, joy, and peace. These deities are also closely connected to the Earth's natural forces, like water, wind, and the feminine principle.

Understanding the Terminology of African Spirituality and Orishas

When it comes to African spirituality and orishas, there's a lot that can be confusing for those who are new to the topic. You likely need a bit more help understanding a few of the core concepts. We understand that this can be a little bit frustrating, especially if you're interested in learning more about them. After all, who wouldn't want to learn more about something that intrigues you so much?

How Does One Work with the Orishas?

Orishas are the spirits of nature and human life. They are both the giver and the taker of life. They are the guardians of our world and our lives and are always ready to help us. The best way to work with the Orishas is by communicating with them and making offerings of gratitude or requests for their assistance. Orishas love to be acknowledged and thanked for their presence and assistance. They also love to be acknowledged for the gifts that they have given us. If you want to work with the Orishas, it is best to meditate regularly to open a channel of communication and to start to learn about their names, symbols, and characteristics. Regularly reading about the Orishas is also very helpful in furthering your connection to them.

Ashe

When presented with the entity of Ashe, Orishas can carry out their missions using the positive energy that is present in the world. As a result of their energy and power, Orishas can give blessings, create miracles, and dispel misfortune in the world. Ashe can be compared to the concept of divine power and energy found in many religions. Orishas use this power to create miracles, promote changes, and dispel evil.

Ebbo

Ebbo is an offering and sacrifice to the Orishas. It is a gift to show them respect, gratitude, and love. Ebbo can be any gift that you feel comfortable giving to the Orishas. This can include items like food, beverages, incense, animals, flowers, and more. Ebbo is practiced regularly by those who work with the Orishas. It is a way to show your respect, love, and gratitude to the Orishas and other spiritual beings helping you.

Can Orisha Get Offended?

Yes. But we can't generalize and say that all Orishas get offended. We have to look at the specific Orisha for the answer. Each Orisha has its own special personality, likes, and dislikes. They are also living entities that are capable of feeling emotions just like we are. Just like we get offended, so do the Orishas.

How Can I Make Sure Not to Offend an Orisha?

If you don't want to offend an Orisha, there are a few ways to avoid doing so. First, you want to determine which Orisha you are interested in working with. Once you have decided which one you want to work with, you want to learn as much as possible about them. Then when you've done the background homework, you can start to ensure that you don't offend them. One thing that you can do is to make sure to always be respectful of Orisha. Show them the love and gratitude you want others to show you. Suppose you have a specific Orisha that you want to work with. In that case, it is important to understand that they have their own personalities, likes, and dislikes.

When Am I Ready to Connect with a Certain Orisha?

As with most things involving spirituality, there is no "one size fits all" method when connecting with an Orisha. However, some general guidelines can help you along the way. Look for signs indicating when you are ready to connect with a particular Orisha. Some of them include your purpose in life, how comfortable you feel with yourself and others, what you want to achieve, your level of confidence as well as your beliefs. For example, if you are unsure of who you are or what you want out of life, then it would be best to wait until you can figure those things out first. On the other hand, if you are clear on what you want and where you want to be in life, then it could be a good time to start connecting with Orisha. It all depends on where you are on your journey.

What Signs Do Orishas Give?

To see signs from an Orisha, look for any corresponding behavior that matches the description given in prayers. For example, suppose you are praying to Yemoja. In that case, you may notice that you have a strong maternal instinct or that your body feels lighter during menstruation as a sign of your devotion to this goddess.

The most common signs of an Orisha include:

- A strong sense of community or belonging
- An increased interest in spirituality or religion
- A feeling of being protected or safe
- A sudden and overwhelming need to do good deeds or help people in need

Do I Need to Be Initiated into an African Religion before Attempting Communication with the Orishas?

There is no requirement for initiation into an African religion. If you are sincerely interested in contacting the Orishas, it is best to do so while mentally and emotionally calm. The only requirement is that you have an open heart, willingness, and desire to learn about and respect the Orishas. Most people who work with the Orishas do so on their own after feeling the call of the spirit in some way. Others are initiated into a religion by a trusted friend or family member who shares a close bond with the Orisha they want to commune with.

Many become familiar with traditional African religions to cultivate spiritual awareness, practice gratitude, and deepen their connection with nature. In addition, some people find it helpful to use traditional practices as a form of prayer – seeking guidance from the divine but still remaining in control of their practice by making daily choices aligned with their personal beliefs and values.

Chapter 4: The White Orishas

There are many Orishas — some say there are hundreds of them. However, most of them can be grouped into four main families. The Red Orishas (warrior spirits), the White Orishas (peaceful spirits), the Blue-Green Orishas (nature spirits), and the Black Orishas (royal spirits). In the Yoruba religion, each deity has a distinct role and responsibility regarding natural elements like water, earth, fire, and air. This chapter will examine the most prominent white Orishas, exploring their main characteristics. Some suggested deities in this category are Orunmila, Obatala, Yemaya, Osain, Oshumare, Oshosi, Oshun, and Olokun. Collectively, they are known as the white Orishas because their colors contrast the colors of other Orishas. And most especially because their characteristics represent purity and peace above all things.

In the Yoruba religion, each deity has a distinct role and responsibility regarding natural elements like water, earth, fire, and air.
Omoeko Media, CC BY-SA 4.0 <https://creativecommons.org/licenses/by-sa/4.0>, via Wikimedia Commons: https://commons.wikimedia.org/wiki/File:Orishas_in_Abeokuta.jpg

Main Characteristics of the White Orishas

Several deities can be classified as white Orishas due to their association with light, purity, and peace. These gods have very different roles from the others within the Yoruba culture. There is an Orisha for everything from love to war, agriculture to hunting and fishing. An Orisha's role is to link heaven and earth, maintain balance in all things, help a person through difficult times, and bring comfort. The white Orishas are considered more benevolent than other Orishas. They can be male or female, though most white Orishas are female. They can take many different forms but are usually depicted as beautiful young women with long flowing hair wearing white dresses, white cloaks, or white beads around their necks. They are often shown to be wearing white robes that shroud their faces in shadows so that they cannot be seen clearly by mortal eyes. They may also wear masks or carry calabashes filled with water or sacred liquids. Their presence can be felt through music, nature, or even in the air itself. White Orishas are also represented in artwork such as paintings, sculptures, and carvings on wood or stone. They appear as guardians of children, heroes, and healers in stories and myths. The white Orishas help people in need by offering guidance, strength, and understanding during difficult times.

Because the white Orishas guard the balance of creation, they inhabit all things and watch over the world at all times. They often appear in visions to those seeking guidance or protection and can be invoked for blessings during rituals and ceremonies. In addition to providing protection against evil, the White Orishas also bless their followers with success.

In order to choose the right Orisha for you to connect with, you'll have to consider all of the different types of Orishas out there. However, if you want to be in touch with Orishas, you should start by getting to know them a little better.

The White Orishas

Each deity has its own individual characteristics. Understanding these groupings helps you better understand the role of each individual Orisha so you can choose the one that best suits you. While some of them may share commonalities, there are subtle differences in how they are perceived. However, just like any other culture or belief system, the main characteristics of these spirits can be narrowed down to a few key points. Next, we'll go over the main characteristics of some of the main white

Orishas and explain why they are unique compared to other deities from this religion.

Orunmila (Orúla, Ọrúnla)

Orunmila is the god of knowledge, wisdom, creativity, and justice. He is often illustrated with a staff in his hand, a crown on his head, and a book in his hand. Orunmila is one of the oldest Orisha. Some myths claim that he existed even before the creation of the earth. He is also credited with being the creator of the Santeria Ifa, a set of symbols used when reading the divination system known as Ifa. This deity's name translates to "Owner of the compound" or "Owner of the house."

For modern-day spirituality, Orunmila is a balanced and gentle spirit. He is a great deity to call upon if you need help with a creative project or want to excel in a field that requires knowledge. He can provide you with the guidance and creativity you need to make your dreams a reality. Orunmila is a helpful and patient Orisha who is also extremely generous. He does not have a temper and is rarely angered by other people's actions. He can also help you win any challenge, competition, or situation where you need a bit of luck.

How to Greet Orunmila

Orunmila can be best described as a balanced yet assertive energy. Greet Orunmila with white, yellow, and green, and ensure you are in touch with your emotions and are without judgments in your heart. He is a great source of wisdom and guidance, leading people toward the right choices. Orunmila is the spirit of knowledge, so he is a great deity to call upon if you want to expand your knowledge in a specific field. He can help you grow and understand your strengths and weaknesses. If you need luck, Orunmila can also help you in that area. He can also ease any feelings of anxiety, granting you the ability to cope easily with stressful situations.

Symbols and Ebbo (Sacrificial Ritual)

Orunmila's symbols are a crown, a staff, a book, and a rooster. Orunmila's rooster is a symbol of his connection with the sun. His staff symbolizes Orunmila's abilities with knowledge, abundance, and justice. The staff is an ancient symbol that can be traced back to ancient civilizations. A crown Ebbo is used to call upon his status and the knowledge he holds. A holy book can be used to access the divination system known as Ifa.

Obatala (Oxalá, Ochalá)

Obatala is the god of creation. He is also known for being the Orisha of purity and is often depicted as being very clean and polished. Obatala was one of the first Orisha to emerge. Some myths claim that Orunmila was created from a virgin coconut tree that sprung from a flood. Because he is one of the first, many people consider him a great deity to call upon when starting a new venture or project. It is believed that he can help you create a smooth and successful transition into a new situation.

How to Greet Obatala

The best way to describe Obatala is that he is extremely pure. He keeps everything around him clean and well-organized due to his strong desire for order. Aside from being patient and helpful, Obatala is also a very kind and generous Orisha. He rarely gets offended by other people's actions and doesn't have a temper.

Symbols and Ebbo

Obatala's symbols are a staff, a white crown, and an iridescent white gown. The staff symbolizes Obatala's connection with the sun and the principles of justice. The coconut tree symbolizes Obatala's abilities with creation and new beginnings. It is believed that this tree sprang from the flood, which was the first beginning of the world. Obatala usually receives white animals as offerings, such as pigeons, hens, and goats. He prefers bland food offerings, for example, milk, rice, and white bread. Alcohol should not be included.

Yemaya (Yemoja)

The Orisha Yemaya is the goddess of the ocean. This Orisha symbolizes fertility and growth, representing the ever-changing tides of life. She is considered the mother of the universe and is believed to be the primary force behind creating life. Swans, turtles, and crabs are her sacred animals, and she is associated with the colors white and blue. Yemaya's characteristics include being gentle and compassionate but also having a certain level of toughness when the situation calls for it. She is willing to help anyone who asks for it and expects nothing in return. She is also the guardian of women, babies, and young children. Yemaya performs many rituals relating to the sea, including healing rituals. Additionally, some of her ceremonies are focused on finding lost items.

Her colors (blue and white) symbolize purity, honesty, and simplicity. Yemaya's primary characteristics are her gentle nature and selfless compassion for others. She is also a symbol of fertility and growth, representing the ever-changing tides of life. Her association with the ocean comes from her ability to produce life even in the most extreme circumstances. Yemaya is capable of great things but is also very demanding and expects a lot from people.

How to Greet Yemaya

When greeting Yemaya, remain calm but ready to take action if necessary. Yemaya is not one for small talk, so it would be wise to keep any greeting short. You can start by facing her Ebbo and gently pressing your palms together. After that, you should bow your head to show respect and gratitude. You can say "Ashe" ("be blessed" in Yoruba). After the greeting, you can move on to your request. The ritual can end by thanking her, but without the bow.

Symbols and Ebbo

The symbols that represent Yemaya are the shell, sea sparrow, conch, coconut, ebony, cedarwood, water lily, and swan. All of these items are associated with the sea. The Ebbo that is given to Yemaya consists of anything related to the sea.

Oshun (Osun)

Oshun is the goddess of love, the river, and sweetness. She is the Orisha of the sweet orange in Caribbean and African cuisine. She represents water, a symbol of fertility and abundance. Hence, she is associated with love and marriage and is the protector or nurturer of humanity. Oshun is a motherly figure and also a seductress, as she represents femininity and the unbridled sensuality that comes with it. Her fertility derives from the sweetness of her personality, while her association with love and marriage comes from her connection with the river. Oshun is associated with white, red, and yellow. These colors represent the purity of her heart and her connection with love, fertility, and the river. The Orisha Oshun is strongly associated with the number five and the elements of water, earth, and air.

How to Greet Oshun

Goddess of love, sweetness, and the river. Therefore, when greeting her, it is important to embrace the symbolism of each of these things. When greeting the Orisha, you want to do so with respect and love. Therefore, a great way to greet her is to give a gift. This can be anything from flowers to a nice piece of jewelry.

Symbols and Ebbo

Oshun is strongly associated with the crescent moon, white, the number five, and water, earth, and air elements. Therefore, these items can be used to summon her for blessings and assistance. Using a crescent moon to summon Oshun is as simple as wrapping a white cloth around your body. This will help you tap into her energy and allow her to help you with your problems and issues. Wrap the white cloth around you and use white decorations when summoning her too. And don't forget the number five. Place five things in your summoning area, or have five people present during the ritual. Because water, earth, and air are her elements, as are sunflower, pumpkin, or cinnamon, sprinkle water in the summoning area - specifically outside in the open air.

Osain (Osanyìn)

Osain is the god of the forest, the harvest, and the hunt. He is associated with the color green, red, white, and yellow and the number eight. He is also the Orisha who rules over all of the wild animals. Osain is a fierce warrior who protects his followers and destroys evil spirits. He is a fearsome warrior and a gentle healer. Summon him to heal any ailment, be it physical or mental, and bring you great fortune.

How to Greet Osain

When greeting Osain, it is best to remember that he rules over the forest and is strongly associated with those colors. Therefore, when greeting him, it is a good idea to use forest-specific items and have his colors wrapped around you. This is the best way to greet Osain and get his attention. You don't need to do much because he is known for his rational temperament.

Symbols and Ebbo

Osain is strongly associated with his colors and the number eight. Therefore, these are the perfect symbols to use when summoning him. Clay is a symbol of Osain and can be used to help cleanse your space and remove negative energy before a ritual. Then use eight items for his Ebba, such as plants or twigs.

Oshumare (Oshunmare)

Oshumare is the god of creation and purity. Together with the moon, Oshumare is the patron saint of marriage, sickness, and death. In addition to creating the Earth, Oshumare informs the other Orishas of their responsibilities on the planet. He has the greatest amount of power over the oceans, seas, and all water sources like rivers and lakes. As such, Oshumare is often consulted during the process of divination and when one wishes for knowledge and wisdom. Oshumare is also consulted when one wishes to have a child or trying to conceive.

Oshumare is said to be very wise and kind and has a lot of knowledge to share with those who seek advice from him. He is said to be a passive Orisha, meaning he does not like fighting or having those around him engage in conflict. In fact, Oshumare is a very peaceful Orisha and is the creator of peace and happiness in the world. He is considered a healer and is said to have the power to heal any physical or mental illness that one may experience. He is often illustrated as a smiling Orisha.

How to Greet Oshumare

When greeting Orisha, remember that Oshumare is a very peaceful Orisha who does not like being surrounded by loud noises or feelings of aggression or hostility. Be calm, take off your shoes, sit down and wait for him to appear. Oshumare may appear in the form of bright light, as a reflection in the water, in a mirror, or in any other peaceful setting.

Symbols and Ebbo

Oshumare is associated with the sea, the moon, and the color white. As such, these are the main symbols associated with Oshumare. Some of the most common Ebbo of Oshumare include seashells, pearls, oyster shells, seaweed, white fabrics, and candles. Oshumare can also be offered white rice, egg whites, white bread, white flowers, coconut, and water.

Olokun

Olokun is the Orisha of wealth and the ocean. Olokun is a fierce spirit living in the ocean and is also associated with the color white. Olokun can also be considered an androgynous spirit who can be both male and female depending on the situation. While on earth, this deity takes the male form. Olokun is a greedy spirit who must be appeased with offerings and sacrifices. Wealth, greed, and ferocity are their most prominent characteristics. They are the source of all riches, which they can give to anyone who appeases them during the ritual. Colored blue and white, they are deep and mysterious, like the seas and lakes they rule over.

How to Greet Olokun

If you are interested in Olokun, you can offer white items or white flowers as a gift. Olokun is also associated with white foods such as rice and salt. Offers need to be in abundance and practiced near the sea or ocean. You can also offer them a white candle during your invocation.

Symbols and Ebbo

The symbols of Olokun are their purity and the color white. Olokun can be associated with the number three. The Ebbo of Olokun is salt and a white flower.

Oshosi (Oshoshi)

In addition to being known as the master of the forest, Oshisi is the god of fortune and prophecy. Oshosi may have originated in the Yoruba people of southwestern Nigeria, where he is the chief Orisha of the forests, hunting, and war. In south-eastern Nigeria, Oshosi is a very popular Orisha. There are many festivals in which he is celebrated and worshipped. One of these festivals is Oshogbo, which takes place between the months of July and August. As well as being the Orisha of the hunt, he is also associated with killing animals for food. Since he is a food provider, he is strongly associated with farmers, families, and wealth. Oshosi is a fierce warrior and is the patron of fighting and sports, making him aggressive in nature.

How to Greet Oshosi

You can greet Oshosi by lighting a candle or incense in the forest or woods. If you seek prosperity, you can offer him something sweet, like honey or flowers. Oshosi is the god of the forest, so he will be pleased to see a tree inside his shrine. Another way to greet Oshosi is to offer him food, such as a goat's head or a roasted pig.

Oshosi Symbols and Ebbo

The animal's blood is needed for Oshosi's rituals, together with honey and mahogany leaves.

Oshosi's main colors are white, yellow, and blue. Oshosi's main symbol is the tiger, representing his ferocity and strength. His Ebbo mahogany bark or leaves, honey, and gold coins.

These are just a few examples of spirits from the Yoruba traditions. Many other spirits and deities from these cultures are just as interesting and powerful. But the White Orisha is a spirit of healing and purity. Any one of these deities can help bring light and positivity into your world. They are also a spirit of service and can help you to serve others in your life.

Now that you know who some of the White Orisha are and what they represent, remember that no Orisha is better than another. All Orisha represent different aspects of life and have different gifts to share. So when choosing one, find the one that best suits your personality and needs. Once you have done this, you can start observing Orisha's energy and learn more about what they can offer you.

Chapter 5: The Red and Black Orishas

The Orisha faith is one of the oldest religions in the world, with roots that reach back to 400 BCE. Over the course of history, this unique and diverse faith has spread to many different regions and has been practiced by many people. Its popularity has spread throughout Cuba (Santeria), Haiti (Voodoo), Brazil (Candomble), and Nigeria (Yoruba). The deities of this faith are constantly evolving to incorporate new beliefs and deities. The Orisha Osanyin and Orisha Shango are two Orishas gods of passion, and each has a distinct personality and role within the faith. Their followers often wear different colors, including the more virtuous white discussed in the previous chapter.

The Orisha faith is one of the oldest religions in the world, with roots that reach back to 400 BCE.
Rept0n1x, CC BY-SA 3.0 <https://creativecommons.org/licenses/by-sa/3.0>, via Wikimedia Commons: https://commons.wikimedia.org/wiki/File:Shango_staff,_oshe_Shango,_World_Museum_Liverpool.JPG

Just like their lighter counterparts, these Orishas can be seen as forces of nature, spirits, or incarnations of natural energies. This chapter will explore the origins of this category of Orisha and its connection to the Yoruba religion. The Orishas are usually known as the Red and Black Orishas, as their primary colors are red and black. They often manifest as complex or compound deities with distinct personalities and unique characteristics. Each deity represents a specific element, force, or natural phenomenon. These entities can be found in almost all Afro-American religions in one form or another. They are often referred to as spirits, gods, saints, angels, devas, or totems. They have different roles but serve the same purpose: bringing balance back into our lives so we can live a healthy and happy life.

Main Characteristics of the Red and Black Orishas

Understanding the Orisha categories is crucial. While each Orisha has its own personality, some are more wrathful than others. But despite their tendency to anger easily, they also have a positive side to them. They can help you solve problems in your life if you work with them in the right way. These Orishas represent the energy of new beginnings and passion for life. They help followers embrace change, release anger and fear, and find their inner strength during difficult times. They all have their own distinct characteristics, rituals, and origin stories. Red Orishas are spirits that were born from fire and light, while black Orishas come from darkness and water. The color red is used to describe these deities because red is associated with blood and life flow. This indicates that red Orishas are associated with healing and protection. Similarly, black Orishas are connected to witchcraft, sorcery, and the dark arts. Most deities in this category have fiery temperaments, are war-like, and are aggressive with their power. Understanding the different Orishas can help you determine what type of assistance you need from the divine.

Ogun

Ogun is the Yoruba Orisha of iron and the lightning bolt. Ogun is considered to be a warrior god, and he represents strength, power, and fearlessness. He is also associated with the color black and death. However, Ogun is not evil; he simply represents the power of death and destruction. In Africa, Ogun is often seen as the opposite of Yemaya, an

Orisha who protects and gives life. As well as being the protector of iron, Ogun is also linked with thunderstorms. This connection makes him an ideal protector of crops in areas where thunderstorms are common. In Trinidad, Ogun is believed to be a messenger between the dead and the living. He is also responsible for bringing lightning bolts down from the sky to show that someone has died or been struck by lightning. Ogun's pivotal role is as a judge. He determines what happens to people after they die by weighing their sins against their virtues and deciding if their souls deserve eternal punishment or eternal reward. Black and red are sacred colors for Ogun because they represent both his destructive abilities and his heavenly quality of protecting those who need them most.

How to Greet Ogun

To honor Ogun properly, always show respect for all life and nature, both on your own behalf and on behalf of those that you love. Take two steps back from the Orisha and bow low. Raise your right hand and say, "Mo w nibi" (I am here). Then take one step forward and bow again. After this, you should place a small offering on the ground next to you.

Symbols and Ebbo

Like all Orisha, he has many symbols that can be used to represent him. One of the most common is iron, which represents strength, power, and protection. It can also be used to represent money, success, and victory. As an Ebbo for Orgun, worshipers mark symbols onto clay or wood, or they can be either painted or stitched onto clothing. Symbols such as an axe, spear, or shield relate to his powers, and are used to pay homage to his ability to protect and heal.

Esu (Eshu)

Esu closely resembles the mythical Aztec god Huitzilopochtli. Since these cultures existed at different times, historians believe that Esu was a shared deity between the African and Latin American regions. The similarities between these depictions and rituals lead many experts to believe that Esu is one of the oldest and most influential red Orishas within African spirituality. This deity is an intermediary between humans and the supreme being known as Olodumare. In Orisha cultures, Esu is the god responsible for regulating disease and death. As such, he is often shown as a skeletal figure who wears a crown made of human bones. Esu is often accompanied by a dog and a horse and is associated with red and black. This helps people understand his role as a deity who controls the spread of disease through animals. Esu is also depicted as a bird who has the ability to travel between the spiritual and physical worlds. This has helped inspire legends that describe Esu as a mythical creature with strong magical abilities. Esu can help people struggling with health issues, disease, or addiction. He also serves as a guide who helps people transition smoothly through the different stages of life.

How to Greet Esu

People who wish to greet this deity should start by facing south. Next, they should say "Babalu Aye Esu" three times and then bow three times. When you feel the need for protection against health issues or death, you may perform this ritual during the San Lazaro ritual, or at any other time you feel the need for such protection.

Symbols and Ebbo

Ritual foods that can be offered to Esu include palm oil, beans, cornmeal, popcorn, and farofa, a flour made from manioc. Four-legged birds and animals are also offered as Ebbo sacrifices. Other artifacts used in his greeting rituals include a broom, a needle, and a knife. The broom is a symbol that is used to cleanse the spirits of the dead out of homes. The needle and knife are used during ritualistic cutting that can help heal and protect individuals from disease.

Babalu-Aye

Orisa Babalu-Aye is a black Orisha associated with witchcraft, sorcery, and the dark arts. This deity is often depicted as a shadowy figure who uses his powers to manipulate and harm people and is often accompanied by a dog and a rooster. This helps people understand his role as a deity who uses witchcraft to spread pain and suffering but also healing. Babalu-Aye is also associated with the number nine and the colors black, purple, and yellow. He promotes cures for illnesses and healing for those who are close to death, but some believe him to be capable of bringing disease to humans. Babalu-Aye is most commonly worshiped by those who believe they have been given bad luck or misfortune in their lives. He is also invoked when someone's life is about to end, especially if it happens unexpectedly. His other purpose is to help people make their own decisions rather than having them made for them by others.

How to Greet Babalu-Aye

When greeting Babalu Aye, you should stand with your hands in your pockets, with your head slightly tilted towards the ground. This shows respect and humility towards this deity. You should also avoid saying words like "no," "don't," or "stop," as they can offend this deity. Next, you should say "Alápa-dúpé," meaning "One who kills and is thanked for it." This ritual can be performed at any time when you want to tap into Babalu-Aye's witchcraft powers. On the day of celebration for this Orisha, people visit the ocean or a river to cleanse themselves of negative energies.

Symbols and Ebbo

Offerings are also made to this deity appealing for help in healing loved ones. Babalu Aye is associated with the number seven. This number is considered lucky and is often used in amulets and jewelry to protect those who wear them. The symbols of the Orisha Babalu Aye are the snake, a bowl of herbs, and the number seven. The Ebbo of this Orisha is tobacco and water.

Osanyin

Osanyin is one of the most mysterious Orishas. He is not well known outside of the Yoruba people, and even within the community, his worshipers are hard to find. Osanyin is the god associated with plants, healing, medicine, vegetation, and the harvest, which makes him an essential part of the Orisha faith. Osanyin means 'the hunter' in Yoruba. Originally, he was a hunter, and it was through the experiences he had in the forest that he became an Orisha. He is also associated with healing. As a result, Osanyin is often illustrated with medicinal plants, leaves, and herbs in his clothing. His colors are red, green, and black. Red represents passion and creativity, while black is associated with transformation. And green because of his role in providing food and his deep connection with nature. He is often seen as a deity of fertility. Various saints' feast days can be related to celebrating his significance. These celebrations relate particularly to Saint Joseph and his Americanized syncretism. These days, people make offerings to their plants and trees, appealing for strong and healthy growth. Osanyin is a hunter who prefers a solitary life away from large groups of people. But he is revered for his ability to see through deception or lies and to expose those who are hiding secrets.

How to Greet Osanyin

There is nothing to worry about when getting in touch with Osanyin because he has a patient personality, but he can be very stern if he feels someone has misused his powers or if he sees his followers doing harm to others. He is very intelligent and can solve any problem with careful thought. Besides being practical, he is also playful. He is most often receptive to single people, both male and female, and the elderly due to his desire to protect those who might feel vulnerable. When greeting the Osanyin, you must be humble, respectful, and kind. Men should wear blue clothing, whereas women should wear a blue headscarf or blue jewelry. Many people also like to use blue flowers when worshiping Osanyin. To show your respect, you should kneel on the ground and bow your head before you speak to him.

Symbols and Ebbo

There is no fixed understanding of these symbols when it comes to Osanyin and his worship. The interpretation of his attributes and significance can vary among different groups of followers and may also differ depending on where they live. But some of the common symbols for Osanyin are the drum, horse, leaves, and birds, as is a green hand, which is called an Odu Ifa. This symbol represents his role as a healer and his connection with nature. The Ebbo for Osanyin is cassava bread, palm wine, and pepper.

Shango

According to Shango folklore, he was born into slavery but rose up against his master in an attempt to gain freedom. Shango was first worshiped by the Yoruba people of West Africa, and today, he is one of the most popular Orishas among practitioners of Santeria. Shango is considered a very temperamental deity. He is known to have a quick temper, but he is also quick to forgive those who are sincere in their apologies. He is also quick-witted and a natural leader who knows how to get things done efficiently. He is fearless and takes risks. He is also very generous and loving, which makes him a compassionate deity. He is also known for being a great healer who uses his powers for good. Because he is associated with thunder and lightning, he is often depicted with lightning bolts or a sword as his emblem. Associated with the colors red and white, this deity of fire and passion represents life flowing through all living things. Often associated with fertility and new beginnings, this Orisha is commonly depicted as a large bearded man carrying a sword or a staff. As a war deity that symbolizes strength and power, he brings change, transformation, and a new order. On the day of Shango's celebration, people clean their houses and make offerings to their ancestors.

How to Greet Shango

Shango is a non-physical god who can be invoked by anyone who sincerely desires to connect with him. Shango's purpose is to protect people from evil spirits, and he is said to have a very long reach. Therefore, worshipers need to show respect when greeting him by bowing down and making offerings such as food or drinks.

The best time to greet Shango is at dawn when the first rays of sunlight are starting to peek over the horizon. If you cannot greet him at this time, you can do so any time after sunset until midnight - just make sure you are respectful when doing so.

Symbols and Ebbo

If you wish to pray to Shango, you should carry objects representing his symbols, such as items connected to lightning bolts, thunderbolts, and storm clouds. You can also wear a representation of one of his symbols, such as a feathered costume or a helmet adorned with horns. When praying to Shango, ensure you are respectful of others around you. You should also keep your thoughts positive so that Shango can help you achieve your goals.

Ebbo is a small bottle of rum used in voodoo rituals, usually filled with rum, herbs, or other ingredients.

Oya

Oya is from a class of deities in the Yoruban and Afro-Caribbean religions. In the Yoruba religion, she is one of the hottest-tempered deities, married to Shango. In other cultures, including Haitian Vodou and Candomblé, she is known as Iansã. In Yoruba, Oya takes the role of the goddess of fresh water and is associated with spring water and wells. She takes on different roles in other cultures, such as healing, fertility, and wisdom. Oya's image shows her as a young woman wearing a headdress with two horns that resemble those of a cow or calf. She also holds plants and animals in her hands to symbolize her ability to heal and protect nature.

Some depictions have her holding a pitcher full of water to symbolize her role as the giver of fresh drinking water for humans and animals alike. Some statues show Oya pouring water from one container to another to demonstrate her ability to move from place to place without ever getting tired. At times, Oya can be fierce, protecting people from storms and floods, but she can also be nurturing and protective when needed. As

Orisha of childbirth, Oya also provides guidance for pregnant women and new mothers.

How to Greet Oya

To greet Oya, you'll need to first ground yourself by walking or sitting in silence for a few minutes. To be prosperous and abundant in all areas of your life in the future, you'll need to ask Oya to remove all obstacles in your way. Afterward, it's time to offer food, drink, or money as a form of thanks.

Symbols and Ebbo

A significant aspect of Oya's worship needs to be understood: she cannot be bargained with or bargained out of. This means that if you want something from Oya, you must offer something of equal value in return. She is called the "mother of nine," which comes from her nine stillborn children. Plants and trees often grow from mounds of earth, so when given over as offerings, Oya interprets them as giving life to the world. In addition to Ebbo and images, there are also ritual items for use in worshiping Oya, such as paper money, shells, candles, and tobacco leaves. The Oya Ebbo is a special offering given at all times of the year to the Orisha, who is believed to be present everywhere all the time. It includes food, drink, and other items that symbolize life and nature, such as growing plants or blood.

Different cultures have adapted and adopted religions throughout the world to fit their unique lifestyles. A prime example of this is the Orisha faith of African spirituality, which blends ancestral traditions with new beliefs. The Orisha faith has a diverse group of deities known as the Orishas. As a result, there are many variations in how these deities are worshiped and what they represent. These deities are seen as intermediaries between humans and the supreme being. Each Orisha provides a specific type of assistance to help people cope with everyday struggles or deal with stressors in their lives.

These deities represent natural forces, human principles, instincts, or even different aspects of human personality. They are manifestations of the Supreme Creator and intermediaries between mankind and the divine. In essence, Orishas are messengers from God to humanity. As we go about our daily lives, they provide us with guidance and help us make sense of our existence on this planet by teaching us about love, faithfulness, sacrifice, and other passionate aspects of life. Some of these might be confusing for us at times but nonetheless are essential to understanding human nature.

Chapter 6: The Orisha and Ancestor Altar Setup

In this chapter, you'll find all you need to know about setting up an altar when you want to contact your Orishas. You'll get practical instructions, including where to best place your altar, what to use for decoration, and how to cleanse, maintain, and more. However, before you dive into all this, you'll read about the benefits of having this sacred place and whether or not it's necessary to do it in the first place.

Some practitioners swear that altars provide lots of opportunities to develop their practice.
Mauro Didier, CC0, via Wikimedia Commons:
https://commons.wikimedia.org/wiki/File:Un_autel_de_santeria_d%C3%A9di%C3%A9_%C3%A0
Oshun, orisha de l%27amour CUBA. TRINIDAD culte de Santeria . Autel d%27Oshun.j
pg

Advantages and Disadvantages of Setting Up an Altar

You might wonder whether or not you need to set up an altar for your spiritual practices. Some practitioners swear that altars provide lots of opportunities to develop their practice, while others skip this step because they don't need a dedicated altar. So, to answer this question, it really depends on what feels right for you. There are pros and cons to building an altar to honor your ancestors or spiritual guides.

One of the things about having an altar is that it helps you focus your energy and get closer to your ancestors or the Orishas. However, depending on the strength of your spirituality, you may not need to have an altar for this. If you have a strong intuition and can focus your energy and intention during your worship time without the need for anything special, you probably won't want an altar. And if you are highly creative, you'll be able to perform acts of spiritual practice from anywhere. For some people, decorating an altar is a way of expressing their artistic abilities and helps them communicate their ideas, beliefs, and emotions.

For those who prefer practical solutions, decorating the altar for a particular purpose (like honoring the Orishas and ancestors or asking them for guidance and protection) is just too time-consuming. For example, in the case of an altar for Orishas, you'll need to take the time to learn their symbolism and corresponding associations. Otherwise, you won't be able to adorn your altar correctly to communicate with these ancient divinities. And if you aren't skilled at crafts, you'll probably have to buy most of the decorations, which can also be costly. You may be focused on spiritual development and not on communication. Or you may not spend too much time in front of an altar. In either case, you probably won't need to invest that much time, money, or energy in creating a dedicated space for your practice.

When it comes to space, not having enough of it is one of the most common reasons for people not creating an altar. The number of people living in urban settings turning to unorganized religions is growing quickly. Living in a small, rented apartment often doesn't leave enough space for dedicated altars, especially if you aren't living alone. You can always sneak a few symbols and items onto your nightstand, but that kind of defeats the purpose of having a sacred space. Everything you place on an altar should be placed there intentionally. Putting or leaving random objects on your altar can mean that you may not get the results you want from your practices.

People who are used to being part of a large religious community often set up an altar to keep feeling like they belong. Building an altar will be the best option if you feel the need for centering and grounding during your practices. Having this space will allow you to learn more about symbols. After all, you'll need to keep most of them in your head if your altar has to double up as something else and you have to decorate and redecorate it. For example, the Orishas all have different symbols and offerings. So, unless you're working with only one (some choose to work only with the Supreme god), you'll need to change your symbolism for each one.

Another good reason for making an altar is to redirect negative influences in your life to positive actions. For example, simply building a space where you'll be able to connect with your guide can allay your fears of being influenced by evil or dark forces. Then again, you may choose to brush off this influence by simply implementing other healthy habits into your life.

Some say that building an altar is relaxing and helps them break away from the stress of everyday life. It's also said to be inspiring. Yet others claim that it's not as motivating as having the magical energy permeate every corner of your home. And if you choose not to have an altar and practice your craft wherever it's more convenient for you, you'll be able to do just that. Eventually, you'll have cleaned and filled every part of your home with good spiritual energy. Every place you go to will help you stay calm and keep you wanting to grow spiritually and improve your practice.

As you can see, there is a positive side to creating an altar and not setting one up. How you choose to organize your practice will be up to you. If you opt to build an altar for your ancestors or the Orishas, you can learn how to do it in the continuation of this chapter.

Creating an Orisha Altar

Before you decide to set up an altar for an Orisha, choose an appropriate place for it. Where you put your altar depends on several factors, including your personal preferences, whether you practice alone or with a group, and how much space you have for it. For example, if you're a private person and practice alone, having an altar in your bedroom will give you all the privacy you need. And if you have a small space, you'll want to keep your altar hidden away from doorways and windows, which can be sources of negative energy. On the other hand, if you're setting an altar where an entire family or household will practice, it makes more sense to do so in the living room or a room all members frequent. Once you've chosen the place for your altar, you'll need to cleanse the entire space. Smudging is one of the most common practices for clearing out negative energy. You can also choose purifying incense, a cleansing spell, or literally sweeping the place clean. The latter is recommended even if you opt for smudging because clutter and dirt attract negative energy, and you'll want to keep this away from your altar. Before cleansing a space, open your windows to let the negative energy out and positive vibes flow into your space. Depending on how you want to do it, you can recite prayers during the cleansing or put on some relaxing music if you like. Make sure that the altar itself is already in the room when you're doing the cleansing. That way, you won't have to repeat the process.

You don't need to buy a specific piece of furniture for your altar. You can work on whatever you have with the largest flat surface. Tabletops are usually the best option, but old dressers or nightstands work just as well. Just don't keep anything in them that's unrelated to the altar's purpose. You can also use your floor if you don't have another surface to work on - you'll put a cloth on your altar anyway, so it doesn't matter.

After cleansing the space, you may put the base of your altar into place. If you're using an item that was already in the room, you can skip this step. You can move on to selecting what you want to put on the altar. This depends on your purpose, so make sure you work out which Orisha you want to honor and start collecting the symbolic items needed. As you remember from the previous chapters, each Orisha has its preferences for offerings. Consult the respective chapters for the correct Orisha and symbol correspondences. Whichever Orisha you choose to honor, ensure that whatever you place on the altar matches the Orisha perfectly, as some items may be taboo for some of the divinities. Some of the items to include on your Orisha-dedicated altar are:

- A cloth in the color associated with the Orisha you're working with
- Symbol of the Orisha
- The representation of the four elements through candles, crystals, etc.
- Larger candles that burn for several days
- Offerings for the Orisha

- Incense (optional)
- Spell work, ritual tools (optional)

Place the symbol of the Orisha right in the center of your altar. If you're making an offering, you may place it in front of the symbol. The pictures or representations of the four elements should be placed around the surface's edge at equal distances from each other and the center. Any other items you choose should be set according to the intent of their use. Take each of them into your hands, and let your intuition decide where you should place them.

Altars need to be cleansed after each use, especially if you've used them for spiritual communication. Sometimes messages can pick up negative energy on their way to and from the gods. If you don't cleanse the altar and your space after working on it, you should do it before you use them again. You can do it the way you did before setting up an altar, or you can choose another method; it's entirely up to you.

You might also want to create a ritual that lets you use the energy of your sacred space all the time. Whether it's through prayer, journaling, meditation, yoga, or any other method, the best way to take advantage of your altar is to stay connected to it.

Creating an Ancestor Altar

Before reaching out to the divinities, set up an altar for your ancestors as well. After all, their energy should be easily available to you to harness. This will also make it easier for you to develop this practice. It can help you lay the foundation for reaching a higher level of spiritual energy, such as the power of the Orishas. Apart from being the source of wisdom, your ancestors can also act as protectors, healers, and guides on your life's journey. They can facilitate decision-making in and out of magical practices. Ancestor altars are personal representations of your connection to the spirituality of those who lived before you. Through them, you can build a line of communication with your ancestors, which is especially important if you don't know them personally. Because, in this case, you won't know whether they'll help you before talking to them.

The initial steps of the preparation process (cleansing, finding the best place, and setting up the altar) are the same as with an Orisha altar. You may refer to how it was described in the previous section. After completing them, you should decide which ancestors you want to work with and which ones you would rather not welcome at your altar. Setting up pictures or items that used to belong to them should help signal to them who is welcome, but you may want to reiterate this with a quick spell. You can also recite the names of those whom you wish to exclude.

If you haven't had any personal connection with your ancestors, don't worry. While having a picture or personal items helps, you may choose to represent them otherwise. Do a little research on them through your living relatives and add items you know they've cherished. If you used to know the ancestors you'd be working with, you should include objects reminding you of your time with them. This can be a meal you had together, a game you played, or a picture of a place where you've created memories with them. This will help revive the connection that's often lost when a soul passes on and leaves the world of the living.

You should also make tools for protecting yourself from disruptive spirits. Not all of them will listen when you list them as excluded and will try to contact you anyway. If you feel as if a bad spirit is still around after your session, don't use your altar until you've thoroughly cleaned it.

Apart from reaching out to your blood relatives, altars can also be used to communicate with historical figures you've found inspiring and whose wisdom you feel can improve your life. Contacting a chosen mentor or teacher is also a possibility, and it also contributes to spiritual growth.

Here are some items to place on your ancestral altar:

- **A Cloth:** White is preferred by many, but you can also use a cloth in your ancestor's favorite color, just as you do with the Orishas. If you need your ancestors' help with healing, you can use colors associated with the organ you're having problems with. Or, you can simply use a piece of fabric that has a personal meaning for you.

- **A Glass of Water:** This is recommended for added protection but can also serve as a tool to harness and channel natural energy.

- **A Symbol of Your Ancestor or Spiritual Guide:** If the spirit is unrelated to you. You can invite anyone you identify with, even if you need healing from a personal or family trauma.

- **Candles:** Depending on your experience level, establishing communication may take some time. So, for starters, it's a good idea to get 7-day candles. These are great to re-light if you have to stop what you're doing to tend to your everyday activities or sleep before going back to spiritual communication. They are also larger, which makes them a better choice than tea lights. Ideally, the candles should be your only source of light as you'll use them to attract the ancestral spirit. Yet another reason you should get larger ones.

- **Offerings:** This is optional, but if you need more extensive help, your ancestors will definitely appreciate the gesture of being offered food and drink. Particularly if it's their favorite selection. The offerings symbolize their soul's nourishment and help attract the spirit to your sacred space.

- **The Symbols of the Four Elements**

- **The Intention You Want to Manifest:** This is also optional. If you don't feel the need to write down your intention and place it on the altar, you don't have to. However, beginners find it easier to keep their minds focused on their intention when they have it written down in front of them.

Before you set up the altar, you must reflect on your reasons for doing it. While this reflection period may also be included before creating an Orisha altar, it's even more necessary when you're trying to reach ancestral spirits. Since you'll be communicating with people you've had a connection with (even if it's only on a spiritual level), your personal reasons truly matter. And not just for achieving your goal. If you don't understand why you're doing something during the setup process or you're doing something that isn't in line with your values, it probably won't help you make a meaningful connection.

The best way to set up an altar for your ancestors is to simply listen to your gut. This is the source of the spiritual energy you'll use to make a connection with your ancestors. Besides, your ancestors and you likely shared common values. If your gut tells you that creating an altar in a certain way is a good idea, your ancestors' intuition would have probably told them the same thing. If they would have liked you to set up, you're already a step closer to spiritual growth.

Chapter 7: African Magical Practices

African magic has a nefarious reputation, especially through the media and Hollywood's lens of it. People may have the misconception that African magic, also known as Hoodoo, is dark and evil. Some even refer to it as black magic.

Magic is just like any other tool; it can be used for both good and evil.
https://pixabay.com/es/photos/mu%c3%b1ecos-vud%c3%ba-mu%c3%b1ecas-brujer%c3%ada-vud%c3%ba-3380821/

The vast majority either view magic as fake or evil. However, there are some people who are aware of magic's existence in the world. They know its power and, more importantly, view it as a neutral tool.

At the end of the day, magic is just like any other tool. It can be used for both good and evil. African magic is no different from any kind of magic practice or any other tool for that matter.

In this chapter, you'll be exposed to Hoodoo in greater depth and learn about natural ingredients you can use in your craft. You'll also learn how and when to use these ingredients to help you with your activities.

Voodoo, Hoodoo, Conjure-Work, and Rootwork

People often confuse Voodoo, or Vodou, with Hoodoo. As you may know by now, Vodou is a religious faith that is practiced by Haitians, Caribbeans, and some Africans in West Africa. Hoodoo, on the other hand, is a spiritual and magical practice. It is practiced by many Africans, including African Americans from New Orleans.

Both Vodou and Hoodoo Are African spiritual practices. This means they are closed practices, and only Africans can use them. Some minor Voodoo and Hoodoo practitioners welcome outsiders into their indigenous practices, but they have to undergo an initiation process. This is considered rare, so not every outsider can count on entering this world.

Being referred to as closed practices means they are related to indigenous people. African countries and their people were colonized for centuries. Africans held tightly to their spiritual beliefs when they were fighting off colonizers and being held captive. During these terrifying times, Voodoo believers prayed to the divine lwa while Hoodoo practitioners practiced their rootwork to free themselves and their people.

So what are conjure-work and rootwork exactly? The word conjure is used interchangeably with Hoodoo. These two words signify the same thing, African magic. The word conjure is self-explanatory since it implies working with a spirit. Hoodoo relies on working with spirits of the earth, air, water, sky, and different Lwas. There are spirits all around us, and Hoodoo comes in contact with them.

The spirits are seen as creative and mischievous. Some spirits will help you or guide you. Others are malevolent and carry evil energies. Usually, in Hoodoo, practitioners work with helpful spirits who will assist the conjurer.

In the Hoodoo realm, the word rootwork is often used. This word refers to every part of the plant, not just its roots. This means that a practitioner may use the petals, stems, leaves, seeds, and roots.

Today, Africans remember their ancestors' bravery and endurance, so they practice these beliefs to honor their ancestors and express gratitude. Moreover, Hoodoo is more of a way of life for any practitioner. This is why it is inappropriate when an outsider practices either of these spiritual faiths without an initiation process.

Whether you are here as a native practitioner, an initiate, or a curious person, there is a lot to learn about Hoodoo and its numerous rituals, magical spells, and recipes.

Oil Magic

In Hoodoo magic, oils are seen as a medium of transportation that facilitates the spirit's journey from its realm to this one. Oils also have numerous properties, but mainly they are used to bring spirits in to help activate the spell. You can use as many oils as you like, so long as they match the spell. Hoodoo practitioners usually create their oil mixtures and store them.

There are various uses for oils. You can work it into candle magic and anoint your candle with it. You can also use your oils for baths or apply them to certain body parts. There are oils that are placed in specific areas in your house for cleansing and protection.

Magical Oil Recipes

Money Oil

This oil's purpose is to draw more money into your life. You can use it to manifest creating more money or receiving more money through your business. It is also used to free oneself from debt. It can help you get money back from family members or anyone who has taken your money and is not giving it back. You can use this oil with candle magic or rituals. To make it, you need the following:

- 1 tiny bottle
- 4 drops of Vanilla
- 1 drop of Vetiver

Love Oil

This recipe contains ingredients that target romantic love, so do not use it for platonic relationships. You can use this oil to attract someone into your life. For this to work, the person you are attracting should be a person of interest to you. This oil mixture can be used with candle magic. To create this recipe, you'll need the following:

- 1 bottle
- 1 tsp of grapeseed carrier oil
- 6 drops of rose essential oil
- 1 drop of ginger essential oil
- 5 drops of patchouli essential oil
- A pinch of dried ginger root
- A pinch of dried patchouli
- A pinch of rose petals

Break Spells and Banish Bad Luck

This oil recipe is used to free yourself from a spell, bad luck, jinxes, and black magic. It is best that you create this recipe and keep it at your house. You'll know if you are experiencing a negative impact of a spell when you do not feel like yourself, lose sleep, and feel drained and tired. This mixture will require the following:

- 1 jar
- Sunflower oil
- Poke root
- Rule Sandalwood

You can come up with your own measurements for this recipe. When you are done with this recipe, leave it out in the sun for a month. You can anoint yourself with this oil when it is ready to be used.

Dip your finger in the oil and trace the cross symbol above your brows, heart, hands, and feet. Make sure that you follow this order. You may anoint your private parts if the spell includes your sexual energy. If you anoint your private parts, then make sure you do so before you mark your feet. When you are done, trace the cross on the back of your neck.

When you have finished, walk away until you reach the edge of your property or a crossroads. Do not look back when you are walking away. When you reach your property line, shake off your misfortune. You can visualize yourself being relieved of everything that has been holding you back. This recipe is used with Voodoo dolls and gris-gris, which you'll read about in the coming chapter.

Banish Obstacles

- Small skeleton key
- 10 drops of fresh orange juice
- Scraped bits of dried orange peel
- 2 drops of orange food color
- 10 drops of fresh lemon juice
- Scraped bits of dried lemon peel

Protection and Cleansing

This oil mixture recipe is used to cleanse yourself or your space from unwanted energies. This mixture is also used to cure oneself of illnesses and eliminate bad energy. It is also used to ward off evil energy. To create this mixture, you'll need the following:

- 1 bottle
- 5 drops of rosemary essential oil
- 15 drops of lemon essential oil
- 20 drops of clove essential oil
- 10 drops of eucalyptus essential oil
- 10 drops of cinnamon essential oil
- Add black salt (optional)

You may add black salt if you are creating this mixture to cleanse your house. However, if you want to bathe with this mixture, then do not use black salt.

Candles

Candle magic is known relatively well and is practiced in different spiritual beliefs. Hoodooists also practice candle magic in their own way. Hoodoo practitioners believe that candles are light threads that connect them to the creator, spirits, and supernatural forces.

Candles are connected with protection, restoring balance and justice, wealth, good luck, love, and health. Hoodoo has assigned certain candle colors with certain intentions. The idea is that specific candle colors vibrate with certain concepts.

Candle Colors

- **White**

White candles are associated with purity and healing. This means you can purify a place or energy using a white candle. You can also use it to heal yourself mentally or spiritually.

- **Yellow**

Yellow candles have various functions. You can use them to have your prayers answered. For instance, it would be a good idea to use a yellow candle when you are waiting for a sign or confirmation that your prayers were heard and about to be answered. You can also use them when you want to lure attraction into your life. These candles are also used when you are dealing with a friendship issue. You may want to attract good friends in your life or have a problem with one of your friends.

- **Orange**

Orange candles are mainly used when you are curious or anxious about the future. Let's say that you were following a fixed plan, but for some reason, it was interrupted. You can find out what the future holds for you now through an orange candle.

- **Pink**

Pink candles are mainly used for romantic relationships. Whether you are attracting romance to your life or maintaining a romantic relationship, they are also used for beauty and allure.

- **Red**

Red candles are similar to pink ones as they are associated with romance. They are also used for love on a broader level. You can use them to manifest love into your life, which is not necessarily romantic love. You can manifest love from others or sustain self-love. They are also used to bring in good health and passion.

- **Brown**

Brown candles are linked to restoration. Brown is associated with soil, earth, and tree bark. Naturally, brown is connected to renewal and revival energy. They are also used to win any kind of legal battle.

- **Purple**

Purple is associated with royalty and power. This is why purple colors are connected to ambition and power. You can use purple to find your own power or if you are seeking powerful placements in the material world.

- **Green**

Similar to brown, green is also associated with nature. You can use it for harvesting or giving your plants powerful positive energy. Green candles are connected with money and wealth, so you can use them to receive more money in life. Green candles are also used to attract good job opportunities.

- **Blue**

Blue candles are used to bring joy and happiness to one's life. They are also used to attract unity and people with good intentions into your life.

- **Black**

Black candles are mainly used for protection. This means that you can use them to shield yourself from negative energies and send unwanted energies back to the sender or the source.

Mixing Candles

You can be very creative with your candle magic. You don't have to stick to one color; you can include multiple candle colors for the same spell. For instance, you can use black and green to break your bad luck streak with money. You can use black and white candles to purify yourself of negative energy and return it back to the sender. You can use black and red to break or shield yourself from a love spell. You can use white and pink to heal your romantic relationships. You can combine as many colors as you like, so long as your spell is clear and makes sense.

How to Cast a Spell with Candles

Now that you know what candle colors correspond to, it is time to learn how to cast a spell. First of all, set your intentions. You need to be clear on what you want in or out of your life. You might have a general idea but feel lost when it comes to casting a spell. This is why it is important to thoroughly consider what you want to attain from your spell.

Once you are clear on what you want from your spell, write it down. Think about the candle colors that correspond with your intentions. Get the right candles and carve your wish on them. Try to come up with a short sentence that reflects your intentions. You can carve anything on your candles. It can be a symbol of one of the Lwas, a number, a name, or a sentence. You can anoint your candle with certain oils and herbs. This is optional, but you should know that herbs and oils strengthen your spell. Make sure to pick the right herbs and oils that vibrate with your intentions, just like the candle color.

Exercise 1

Situation #1: You want to bring in friends with good intentions.

- **Use:** Yellow and Blue candles.
- **Write:** I attract friends who have my best interest at heart.
- **Anoint:** (optional)

Situation #2: You want to attract a powerful position in your career that will grant you a lot of wealth.

- **Use:** Purple and green candles.
- **Write:** I am a (insert powerful position), and I am wealthy.
- **Anoint:** (optional)

Cowrie Shell Divination

There are various things found in nature that can be used as divination tools, and you can add cowrie shells to the options available. These shells have been part of divination ceremonies that date back centuries ago and were first used by Yoruba people in West Africa as divination tools.

The cowrie shells are seen as portals or gates to the spirit world. They are a way to hear from the ancestors. The system is simple; one must ask the ancestors a question, shake and toss the shells, and receive an answer from the ancestors. This divination tool does not give complicated answers; it gives a simple yes or a no.

There are different ways to interpret the shells. There are practitioners who use four shells and others who use 16. This chapter will mainly discuss different ways to interpret readings with four shells.

1. Alfia

The Alfia arrangement is made up of four upright cowries. This is considered to be a very loud "yes." This can be the answer that the practitioner seeks or fears the most; it depends on the question asked. Alfia also tells the interpreter that they are blessed with divine assistance. The practitioner may toss the shells again to see how long this 'yes' will last.

2. Etawa

Etawa has three upright shells and one upside-down shell. This is not a strong "yes," but it points towards a "maybe yes" kind of response. This means that the practitioner should consider other areas or examine different factors before making a decision. The interpreter may throw the shells again to get a clearer response.

3. Ejife

This arrangement has two upright and two upside-down shells. This is also another clear "yes" sign. Ejife is considered the ideal "yes" because there is a perfect balance between the "yes and no" or the light and dark. As an interpreter, you do not need to toss the shells again.

4. Okanran

Okanran has one upright and three upside-down shells. This reads as a clear "no." This reading has a sense of strong opposition because three shells are upside-down. This reading also notifies the reader that they should work on whatever they are asking about because there is more work that should be taking place.

5. Oyekun

Oyekun, or four upside-down shells, read as "no." This is a feared result because it indicates that the reader has negative energies surrounding them. They should seriously consider cleansing and ridding themselves of these negative parasites that are draining them of their energy.

Enhance Psychic Powers 114

There are various ways to enhance your spiritual gifts, and one of these ways is getting yourself into a magical spiritual bath. To do this, you'll need the following:

- Anise Seeds
- Holy Water

- Fluid clothing dye
- Florida Water
- White Flower
- 2 white candles
- Vision Oil:
  - 1 bottle
  - 1-star anise
  - Pinch of cinnamon
  - 1 bay leaf
  - 3 drops of frankincense essential oil
  - Pinch of yarrow
  - Pinch of mugwort

Instructions:

Fill your bathtub with warm water. Grab a mug, add 1 tbsp of anise seeds, and pour boiling water until the cup is filled. Let it sit for 10 minutes, and strain the herbs. Fill a bowl with water and the anise water to it. Add a bit of fluid, clothing dye, and holy water into the bowl. Add Florida water as well.

Now take the flower and place it on top of your third eye. Pray and ask the spirits to guide you and open your eye. When you are done, separate the petals from the stem and place them in the bowl. Place your palms into the bowl and pray that your third eye is cleansed from any blockages.

Place two white candles next to your bathtub and sink into the tub. Now, pour the bowl over your head and recite your prayers again. When you have finished, put a bit of vision oil onto the bottom of your feet.

Magic and Freewill

Dabbling with magic means that you are using your energy and integrating with spirits and nature's divine power. This is serious work that involves powerful power sources. Of course, this is great news because you can bring a lot of joy and fortune into your life. However, with great power comes great responsibility. You must be careful if you are casting spells on other people, specifically manipulating their free will. This is not encouraged, especially if you are a beginner. You need to read more and hear from other practitioners. There is nothing wrong with practicing magic, but be careful and approach with caution.

African magic is a vast realm. You do not have to own much to successfully practice conjure work. You can integrate anything into your craft, so long as it comes from mother nature. You can use any oils and store them in your house for any kind of spells. You can also do the same with candles. Remember that you can get creative with your craft so long as you are using it morally. Speaking of which, it is important that you use this craft if you are part of the culture. As explained, Hoodoo is tightly linked with the Africans' ancestors. So if you are not African or an initiate of the practice, then this practice is not for you. However, if you feel connected to conjure work, then seek conjurers who may be able to help you with your initiation process.

Chapter 8: Gris, Mojo Bags, and Voodoo Dolls

In the previous chapter, you were introduced to some better-known African magical practices, but you cannot be properly introduced to Hoodoo without first learning about gris-gris, mojo bags, and voodoo dolls.

Voodoo dolls are used to channel a person's spirit

Guy Donges, CC BY 2.0 <https://creativecommons.org/licenses/by/2.0>, via Wikimedia Commons: https://commons.wikimedia.org/wiki/File:Voodoo_doll.jpg

These talismans have been around for centuries and are powerful and effective. This is why Hoodoo practitioners use them and often carry either gris-gris or mojo bags everywhere they go.

In this chapter, you'll learn about these three talismans and their origins. You'll learn how to create them and how to use them effectively.

Gris-Gris

People often confuse gris-gris with Mojo bags or use them interchangeably. Both of these bags might be similar in the way they look, but they have different functions.

Originally, the gris-gris bag was used by Africans and Arabs. Its sole purpose was to ward off bad spirits and evil energies. The typical gris-gris bag used to have holy Arabic scripture on it. It is also used to carry stones, coins, herbs, flannel, and feathers. Muslims also used to put sand in it to attract a helpful jinn or spirit to shield them from any evil.

Over the years, non-Muslims were introduced to the gris-gris bag, and it soon became a popular item. As a result, the Arabic writings were removed and replaced with other enchanted writing. Today, the gris-gris bag contains different elements influenced by various cultures and beliefs. There are five main elements that should be included when making your own protection bag.

1. Color
2. Odd numbers between 3-13
3. Contents should match your intention
4. Anoint the bag with essential oils
5. Smudge the bag with your own breath, candle smoke, or incense

Colors

Color symbolism is essential when you are making your bag. As you know by now, every color vibrates with a certain energy. Remember that a gris-gris bag's purpose is to protect you from unwanted happenings. For instance, if you want to protect your health, you might choose brown for longevity and pink for health. You can be creative with the colors *as long as you know what your intention is.* Here is a list that you can refer to:

- **White:** Purity and peace
- **Gray:** Security, intelligence, and sadness

- **Black:** Death, protection, evil, mysterious objects, people, or events
- **Red:** Passion, energy, love, danger, and anger
- **Gold:** Wealth
- **Silver:** Technology
- **Turquoise:** Protection, healing, envy, spiritual life, and femininity
- **Blue:** Security, masculinity, intelligence, trust, and fear
- **Green:** Fertility, money, and jealousy
- **Yellow:** Happiness, creativity, and instability
- **Orange:** Bravery, Friendliness, confidence, and success.
- **Pink:** Health, compassion, and femininity
- **Purple:** Luxury, spirituality, and moodiness
- **Brown:** Longevity and the outdoors
- **Beige:** flexibility

Gris-Gris Bag Content

Nowadays, people put whatever they need in a gris-gris bag, so it is really up to you. The idea is to include things that you believe will help you. Most often, practitioners put in herbs, symbols, pictures, plants, bones, fabric, keys, hair, or nail clippings. Remember that you are creating this bag to protect yourself from harm, so pick out the objects that will shield you. If you want to include herbs in your bag but do not know which ones to choose, you can refer to this list:

- **Penny Royal:** Removes hexes and curses. Protects travelers on their journeys
- **Mistletoe:** Shields you from nightmares and protects you from harmful spirits. (If you use this herb, then it is best to hang the gris-gris bag over your bedroom door for best results)
- **Black Salt:** Absorbs negative energies
- **Frankincense:** Gets rid of evil spirits
- **Copal Tears Resin:** Purifies your space
- **Mandrake:** Protects your house. Hang over a gate or the doorway
- **Saltpeter:** Reduces men's libido

- **Valerian:** Protects you in your sleep
- **Skull Cap:** Protects your money and increases it. Protects your relationships
- **Spearmint:** Protects children

Gris-Gris Bag Instructions

You do not need much to create a gris-gris bag. Firstly, pick out a piece of fabric or anything from which you can make a satchel. Your bag could be made out of fabric or leather if you want to create a traditional bag. Try to incorporate relevant colors in your bag, so dye your leather or pick a piece of fabric with the right colors.

Spread your fabric and insert relevant content. You can put herbs, seeds, plant parts, odd numbers, pictures, written spells, or anything else that you wish to carry with you. When you are done, fold your bag and tie it up with string or rope.

Now, anoint your bag with protective essential oils like tea tree, peppermint, or sage. You don't have to drown your bag with oil; just lightly dress it. Keep your intentions in mind as you anoint the bag. Finally, smudge the bag with sage smoke, incense, candle smoke, or your breath.

Mojo Bags

Similar to the gris-gris bag, mojo bags also ward off evil. However, that is not their only function. Think of mojo bags as physical manifestations of your desires. In other words, they channel your dreams and carry them into the physical realm. Usually, mojo bags are stitched to the inside of your clothes so that it is close to you and always on your person.

Mojo Bag Samples

Gambling

Ingredients:

- 1 green bag
- 1 lucky charm
- 1 lucky hand root
- 1 silver dime

- Ginger root
- 1 Pyrite stone
- 1 whole nutmeg
- Anoint in Hoytt's Cologne or Frankincense essential oil

Steps:

Spread your green bag and put in the aforementioned ingredients. As you do so, visualize your winnings and try to feel the thrill and excitement of winning. Visualize how your ingredients will help. For instance, the lucky hand root guarantees a good outcome for you. The silver dime is also a lucky charm. The ginger root gives you a lucky streak. The Pyrite stone draws money toward you. Finally, the nutmeg guarantees winning, especially by tossing the dice. When you are done, tie your bag with a rope and a lucky charm. For the final touch, anoint your bag with Hoytt's Cologne or Frankincense essential oil.

Respect in the Workplace
Ingredients:

- 1 purple bag
- Snakeroot
- Jasmine essential oil
- Rosemary essential oil
- Rock root

Steps:

Unfold your purple bag and put the snakeroot and rock root. Mix Jasmine and rosemary essential oils and anoint your bag with them. These two oils are known to boost confidence, which will, in return, help you earn respect professionally and everywhere else. Finally, tie your bag and keep it on your person when you are at work.

How to Create a Mojo Bag

Color is important when picking a bag. So be mindful of the colors you choose. More importantly, pay attention to what you'll put into the bag. Normally, anything can be put into the bag, herbs, oils, trinkets, stones, rocks, sand, crystals, or anything else. As long as the content matches your energy, your mojo bag should work.

Do not forget to anoint your bag when you are done stuffing it with herbs or stones. It is important to anoint your bag with oils or liquids that will help you achieve your desires. Here are different liquids and oil blends that you can use to dress your bag with the magical power of essential oils.

Protection Liquids

- Holy water
- Florida water

Protection Oil Blends

- 1 bottle
- 3 drops of Geranium oil
- 15 drops of Myrrh oil
- 10 ml of Olive oil
- 9 drops of Sandalwood oil

Love Oils

- 1 bottle
- 5 drops of Blue Spruce or Cypress oil
- 10 ml of Coconut oil
- 2 drops of Ginger oil
- 10 drops of Orange oil
- 5 drops of Clary Sage oil
- 2 drops of Nutmeg oil
- 10 drops of Ylang Ylang oil
- 1 drop of Rose oil

Prosperity Oils

- 1 bottle
- Green Aventurine crystals/chips
- 2 ounces of distilled water

- 2 milliliters polysorbate 20
- 15 drops of Spearmint oil
- 15 drops of Peppermint oil
- 10 drops of Ginger oil

Voodoo Dolls

Almost everyone is familiar with Voodoo dolls. The general idea is that Voodoo dolls are used to hurt an individual. This notion is far from the truth, and it paints Voodoo dolls in a bad light. The truth is that Voodoo dolls are used to channel a person's spirit. Through this channel, the practitioner can heal or bring fortune to this person. Also, please note that you can create a Voodoo doll of yourself; they are not only used on other individuals.

To channel an individual's spirit into a Voodoo doll, you'll need a personal item from this person. Usually, these items include but are not limited to hair, nail clippings, blood, teeth, and any form of bodily fluids.

Once the link has been established, the practitioner can begin performing healing sessions. These dolls are usually made from fabric and stuffing. They can also be made from corn husks, tree parts, or tree parts.

Practitioners use colored pins to address something specific in this person's life. So, they might use green to address money or red for love affairs and so on. Speaking of colors, different colors channel various themes with Voodoo dolls. So, be mindful when you are choosing your fabric.

Voodoo Doll Colors

- **White:** Channels purity and positive energy. Spiritual, mental, emotional, and physical healing
- **Black:** Banishes evil spirits and negative energy
- **Red:** Brings power and love. Draws in a love interest
- **Purple:** This color is used to communicate with souls in the spirit realm. It is also used to receive wisdom from the spirit world and navigate the psychic realm.
- **Green:** Draws in professional success and increases fertility.
- **Blue:** This color is used to bring tranquility to said person's life.

It is also used to channel love and peace.

- **Yellow:** Brings in confidence and success.

Voodoo Doll Instructions

The best thing to do before making your doll is to gather your ingredients first. This will help you be more focused and organized. You'll require the following:

- Fabric
- Stuffing
- Needle
- Thread
- Picture of the person
- Bodily fluids or hair, nail clippings, etc.

Now that you have gathered your supplies, you can begin creating your doll. Spread out the fabric and cut it into the shape of a doll. Make sure that you have enough fabric so that you have room to stitch it together and stuff it with cotton. Stitch the beginnings and endings of the doll and leave room in the middle to create a hole. Stuff this hole with cotton and bodily fluids, nails, or hair. Stitch the hole and make sure it is secure. You can stitch a picture to the doll or tape it to the doll.

Cleanse your working space and doll with sage. When you are conducting your ritual, make sure that you are in the right mindset. So, if you are bringing healing energy to the Voodoo doll, make sure that you are grounded, dressed in white, and have incense or sage smoke in the room. Protect the doll from bad energies with a salt circle.

When you are summoning this person's spirit, have candles or oils around you. You can also play the drums or have a drum track around you as you are summoning this person's spirit.

Cleansing

In the spiritual realm, cleansing is a necessary step that must be completed. Whether you are practicing Hoodoo, folk magic, or any kind of magic, you need to cleanse your tools. That said, your Voodoo dolls, gris-gris, and mojo bags need to be energetically cleansed.

Why should you cleanse them? These tools absorb energy and manipulate it. So the amount of energy they consume and deal with means they need to be cleansed so that they can be used again. Using any of these objects without properly cleansing them first is not wise.

Gris-Gris Bags

As mentioned before, these bags are specifically made to ward off evil. This means that they are charged with intense energy to protect you from negative ones. In other words, whatever energy they shield you from, they absorb it. So, your gris-gris bag has absorbed large amounts of negative energy.

If you are in tune with your tools, you'll know when they need to be cleansed or recharged. Other times, you'll feel like it has simply stopped working. In this case, you need to sage your gris-gris bag and anoint it in holy water. If your gris-gris bag works again, then you have done your job. However, if it does not, then this means that it absorbs intense energy, and its content needs to be removed and replaced. You do not need to get rid of the bag itself, but cleansing it is vital. Replace the old content with new ones and reuse your gris-gris bag.

Mojo Bags

There are two types of mojo bags, one that banishes bad energy and one that draws in good energy. This means that these two bags will have to be cleansed differently. Energetically cleaning the mojo bag that protects you from evil will resemble the gris-gris bag cleansing method. If you feel that your mojo bag has absorbed too much, you'll need to bathe it in sea salt and smudge it with sage. These two ingredients are known as powerful tools that banish evil energy and clear the air.

Mojo bags that attract good energy do not need to be intensely cleansed. This means that you can spray it with holy water or use sage oil. You can also cleanse it with sage smoke or incense. You can also get creative and mix sage oil, sea salt, and water together and spay the bag to cleanse it.

Voodoo Dolls

Voodoo dolls carry heavy energy, so they must be properly cleaned. There are many ways to do this, but the best method is to do multiple cleansing rituals to ensure that the doll is properly cleansed. Cover the doll in earth soil, then let it soak in both sunlight and moonlight. When this is done, wash your doll with salt and holy water. For the final touch, put some sandalwood oil in the diffuser and smudge your doll with it. Then smudge the doll with sage smoke. These are a lot of steps. You do not have to do all of them. However, if you feel like it needs to be intensely cleansed, you can go through all these steps just to be sure.

These talismans have been painted in a bad light, especially Voodoo dolls. However, as you can see, you can use them to bring in the good and protect yourself from the bad. It is a natural instinct for humans to feel fear and to want to protect themselves from the seen and unseen. This is why carrying a gris-gris bag with you is vital. It is fairly easy to create, and you can take it with you everywhere you go.

The same applies to mojo bags. Not only do these bags protect you from evil, but they also bring in good fortune to you. If you want to heal someone or yourself, you can use a voodoo doll. Voodoo dolls can channel a person's spirit if created properly. Be mindful when you are creating your talismans, and remember to cleanse them.

Chapter 9: Sacred Rituals, Spells, and Baths

This chapter has a few simple spells, rituals, and baths for people who are just starting out in their African spirituality journey and want to learn more. These practices can offer you protection, guidance, prosperity, and much more. Most of them can also be tailored to suit different needs and preferences, and you can use them as described here or add your own spin by centering them more around your own spiritual values. By using different symbolisms and correspondences, you can invoke a different Orisha - and not just the one described in the particular practice. All you need to do is look up the corresponding associations in the previous chapters, apply them, and you'll be able to obtain the results you need.

These practices can offer you protection, guidance, prosperity, and much more.
https://www.pexels.com/photo/woman-in-black-dress-holding-a-lighted-candle-5435271/

A Candle Ritual for Obatala

Obatala is one of the most commonly invoked divinities in all African spiritual religions. Obatala will help you fend off disruptive forces during your practice or day-to-day life. With this simple ritual using a seven-day candle, you can harness his Ashe and achieve your objective. Make sure to add plenty of white elements to enhance the ritual's purifying nature.

You'll need the following:

- A white, seven-day candle
- A representation of Obatala
- A piece of white fabric or yarn
- A white cloth
- Cascarilla - fresh or dry
- Milk
- Coconut (shavings work best)
- Yams
- Any other white food you want to use

Instructions:

1. Clear your altar of anything you won't need for this ritual. You want to remove every item that can serve as a distraction.

2. Cover the altar with the white cloth and place the white candle in the center. Put a symbol representing Obatala next to or in front of the candle.

3. If you're using fresh cascarilla, tie it in a bunch with a piece of white fabric or yarn.

4. If you're using dry cascarilla, chop the leaves and sprinkle them around the candle. Tie the piece of fabric or yarn around the bottom of the candle before spreading the leaves around it.

5. Prepare the white foods, rice, milk, coconut, yams, and anything else you might be using, in separate containers. Place them on the altar in front of the candle and the symbol.

6. Take a few moments to relax, then light the candle, close your eyes, and call on Obatala by reciting the following spell:

"I call on you, Obatala, asking you to please lend me your divine power,

Empower me with patience and wisdom.

I wish to be strong and wise,

So my soul can pursue its destiny.

May I stay compassionate and caring,

And following your example, treat others with great integrity."

Traditionally, the candle is meant to be left burning for seven days and nights. However, this is not recommended because of safety issues and because it's impossible to focus on any spell for that long. Instead, you should choose to burn the candle for regular periods of time over the course of seven days. Whenever you have a little time to work on this during the day, light the candle, and recite the spell. When you are finished, extinguish it until you have time to relight it again. The food should ideally be served raw, but you can also cook them into all-white meals and put some aside for the offering.

Oshun's Nurturing Ritual

Oshun is known for being kind and caring, and she may bring you fertility and plenty in many other areas of your life, like art and work. The goddess can also provide protection and even help cultivate relationships. Tools can include the sunflower and pumpkin, and the color of the tools used in the ritual are all associated with her power.

You'll need the following:

- A representation of Oshun
- 1 pumpkin
- Sunflowers, fresh if possible
- 1 yellow candle
- 1 pencil
- 1 piece of brown paper (paper bags or other recycled materials work best)
- Honey
- Yellow jewelry (optional)
- Yellow fruits (optional, depending on the season)

Instructions:

1. Set the yellow candle in front of the symbol of Oshun on your altar and light it.

2. Close your eyes, relax, and focus on your intention. First, recite it in your mind a couple of times, and if needed, repeat it out loud as well.

3. Place the honey in a bowl beside the candle. Follow up with the yellow fruit and jewelry if you're using them.

4. Open your eyes, place the pumpkin in front of you and carve a circular opening on the top of it.

5. Write your intention down on a piece of paper.

6. Place the paper inside the pumpkin, then take the candle, tip it, and pour the wax on top of the paper.

7. After the pumpkin has been sealed with the wax, repeat your intention.

8. Snuff out the candle.

9. If you have the ability to do so, take the pumpkin to the nearest water source and offer it to Oshun.

If you feel the need to reiterate your intention or need more time to harness Oshun's power, you can relight the candle any time you want during the next five days.

A Prosperity Offering

Even though Oshun can help you get rich, there are other Orishas who can also do this for you. You can choose to invoke the one whose Ashe you need the most according to the area of life you want to prosper in. For example, Olokun may provide material abundance, while Oshun will grant you spiritual wealth. The ritual is based on Oshun's correspondence. If you're working with another Orisha, you'll need to apply the tools associated with the respective deities.

You'll need the following:

- A representation of an Orisha
- 5 oranges
- Honey
- A pinch of ground cinnamon
- 1 large yellow or white candle
- 1 large white plate

Instructions:

1. Set the candle in front of the symbol of the Orisha on your altar and light it.

2. Place the oranges on the plate and drizzle them generously with honey.

3. Recite your intention out loud to ensure Oshun can hear what you need.

4. Sprinkle the cinnamon on top of the oranges.

5. Leave the oranges on the altar beside the candle for five days.

6. When the five days are up, you may dispose of the offering and put away the candle.

As mentioned after the previous ritual, the candle shouldn't be left burning continuously. Snuff it out anytime you leave it to do something else and light it again when you can keep a watch on it. Use fresh oranges so they can stay out safely at room temperature during the five days.

A Prayer for Olokun

The best time to make an offering to Olokun is around the time of the traditional harvest celebrations. However, you can also make this offering at any other date throughout the year if you require her protection or guidance. Doing it in the open air will let Olokun know when she is needed much faster.

You'll need the following:

- A representation of Olokun
- Charcoal
- A piece of white cloth
- Yemaya incense powder
- Cowrie shells
- Fruit, meat, grains, or other offerings of your choice

Instructions:

1. Spread the piece of cloth on your altar and place the representation of Olokun on it in the center of the altar.

2. Pour the charcoal into a small bowl and sprinkle some incense powder over it.

3. Light the powder and place the shells in a basket.

4. Place everything you've prepared for the offering around the basket.

5. Light the candle and recite the following prayer:

   "I honor you, Olokun, the queen of waters.

   I will praise and serve you as long as you keep water on the Earth.

   Let the vast waters be calm, so they bring peace to my soul.

   And I'll respect your water kingdom. Ashé, ashé. "

6. Relax your mind by focusing on the flame of the candle. You can also close your eyes and meditate for a couple of minutes if you find it easier to calm your mind this way.

7. Work on manifesting your intention until the incense burns out, then thank Olokun for the blessing she may bestow on you.

The Yemaya powder can be substituted with another incense powder. Live sacrifices are not recommended in modern practices, so if you offer meat, make sure to use only the cooked part of an animal you have already prepared as a meal for yourself.

A Sour Bath for Overcoming Difficulties

The purpose of this bath is to acknowledge that while your current life experiences may be difficult, good times are still waiting in the wings for you. Immerse yourself in this sour bath made from bitter herbs to see the negativity in and around you and how you can change things to work more in your favor. The seven drops of ammonia represent the seven evil forces in African spirituality.

You'll need the following:

- A cup
- Some tea light candles
- Seven drops of ammonia
- Half a cup of vinegar
- Flowers with red or purple petals
- Fresh or dried bitter herbs, such as dandelion, yarrow, horehound, wormwood, and stinging nettle

Instructions:

1. Just before sunset, start filling up your bathtub with hot water. Adjust the water temperature to how you usually have it.

2. Place the tea light candles around the bathtub's rim and light them.

3. When the water in the tub has reached the desired level, turn off all the other lights in the bathroom.

4. Toss all the ingredients into the water, then enter the tub between two candles.

5. As you immerse yourself in the water and inhale the bitter scent of the herbs, focus on the areas of your life you feel might be harboring negativity.

6. If you require additional guidance, you may also ask Orisha for assistance in chasing away the bitter experiences.

7. Aim to spend seven minutes completely immersed in the water, so make sure to dip your head under from time to time.

8. Once the water starts to grow cold, exit the tub through the same gap between the candles as you got in.

9. Scoop some of your bathwater and other ingredients into the cup before draining your tub.

10. Let yourself dry naturally so the healing effect of the herbs can soak into your skin.

11. Put on dark clothes, and take the cup with the bathwater outside.

12. Stand facing west and hold the cup over your head while saying:

    "I have now given the Orisha their due. I now ask them to hold onto me. With this water, I cast out all my problems from my head and life. Ashé, ashé!"

13. Toss out the water from the cup, head back indoors, and spend some time recouping your strength.

14. Drink lots of room-temperature water after the bath to replenish the fluids you have lost while soaking in hot water.

If you want to avoid blocking your drains, place the herbs in a reusable tea bag or cheesecloth. You can include this bath in your regular beauty and healthcare practice. For the best result, apply shea butter or other natural moisturizing agents afterward and avoid using electronics after your bath. Spend your time journaling or meditating instead.

Energizing Bath

This sweet bath is very similar to the previous one, except this one is taken at sunrise to purify and energize you. The ingredients, milk, eggs, and honey, will nourish your body and invigorate your mind anytime you feel the need for some pampering.

You'll need the following:

- A pair of tea light candles
- 3 cups of milk
- Honey
- Powdered cinnamon
- Flowers with all-white petals, such as roses, lilies, white chrysanthemums, and daisies
- Whole nutmeg and powdered nutmeg
- Five different fresh or dried herbs that are invigorating, such as angelica, hyssop, allspice, and comfrey,
- 1 raw egg
- Cocoa butter or shea butter (optional)
- Your favorite perfume
- An empty cup

Instructions:

1. Before sunrise, fill up your bathtub with hot water. Adjust the water temperature.
2. Place the tea light candles around its rim and light them.
3. When the tub is full enough, turn off all the other lights in the bathroom.
4. Crack the egg and toss it in the water. It may start to cook a little bit, but this is normal.
5. Throw on the flowers, herbs, cinnamon, and nutmeg, and pour in the milk and the honey.
6. Add a few drops of your favorite perfume, and gently stir the water to distribute the ingredients evenly.
7. Enter the tub through the gap between two candles.
8. As outlined in the previous ritual, when you enter the water, focus on the good things you already have going on in your life.
9. Consider all the good experiences you may have on that day as well. It's a good idea to express gratitude to the Orishas for these blessings.

10. Aim to spend seven minutes completely immersed in the water, so make sure to dip your head under as well from time to time.

11. Once the water grows cold, get out of the tub through the same gap between the candles you have entered.

12. Scoop some of your bathwater and the ingredients into the cup before draining your tub.

13. Let yourself dry naturally so that the effect of the herbs can soak into your skin.

14. Put on light-colored clothes, and take the cup with the bathwater outside.

15. Stand facing east and hold the cup over your head while saying:

    "I welcome all the beautiful things in life that are waiting for me on my journey!

    As I cast this water where it's needed, I ask the Orishas to bless me with health, love, prosperity, and happiness! Ashé, ashé!"

16. Toss out the water, head back inside and get ready to welcome the blessings you've invoked.

Once again, place the herbs in a reusable tea bag or cheesecloth to avoid blocking your drains. You can incorporate this bath into your regular beauty and healthcare practice. If you don't have time to meditate, journal, or perform any other self-care routine before heading out for the day, don't worry. Avoiding electronics and stressful situations right after your bath can still help you remain calm and relaxed throughout the day.

Chapter 10: Daily Practices with the Yoruba Calendar

Now that you're familiar with the Yoruba culture and ritual practices, you can put your knowledge into practice. The pivotal point of any culture and spirituality is being able to form a connection between it and your practical life. There are so many Yoruba practices and rituals that can be incorporated into your daily life, and the best way to do that is to first understand the association of each practice and event and then include them into your life one at a time. This chapter will act as a guide to teach you the daily Orisha rituals you can practice and how you can practice African spirituality more often.

So many Yoruba practices and rituals can be incorporated into your daily life.
Cliff from Arlington, Virginia, USA, CC BY 2.0 <https://creativecommons.org/licenses/by/2.0>, via Wikimedia Commons:
https://commons.wikimedia.org/wiki/File:Staff_and_sheath_for_Orisha_Oko,_Yoruba_peoples,_O yo_region,_Irawo_village,_Nigeria,_Late_19th_to_early_20th_century,_Staff_iron,_wood_(292363 5450).jpg

The Yoruba Calendar

The Yoruba calendar, also commonly referred to as the Kójódá calendar, has been used by the Yoruba people for centuries. Originally, this calendar year began after the last moon of May or before the first moon of June. Traditionally, a Yoruba week is divided into four days dedicated to the Orisha. In contrast, the modern version of this calendar has the week divided into seven days to align with the Gregorian calendar. Whether you want to incorporate Yoruba practices according to the four-day week or the seven-day week is up to you. However, you should be aware that each of these days has its own rites and practices that should be followed.

Days of the Week

For the seven-day week in the Yoruba calendar, each day has a particular meaning associated with it. According to this classification, each day of the week is to be associated with a certain part of your life. So, the rituals and rites you perform on this day should coincide with the specific meaning of the day. Listed below are the practices usually performed each day:

1. **Sunday/Ọjọ́-Àìkú**

Sunday, or Ojo Aiku, is considered the day of rest. According to Yoruba legends, this is the day on which the mother of Esu Odara was buried by Orunmila. On this day, the world's people requested immortality (aiku) from Oludumare. Orunmila, who was a close confidant of Olodumare, refused to appease him. So Oludumare was unable to grant immortality to the people of earth. This is why life has to come to an end. However, it is believed that offering a sacrifice to Oludumare on this day can prevent premature death.

2. **Monday/Ọjọ́-Ajé**

Ojo Aje, or Monday, is the day that the concept of money or wealth was brought to this earth by the Orishas. And so Mondays are associated with all things money-related. As a result, many Yoruba believers consider this day to be the best time to start a business or discuss their finances.

3. **Tuesday/Ọjọ́-Ìṣégun**

Tuesday is considered to be the day of victory. Many Orisha heroes won great battles and defeated their enemies on this day. So Tuesday is considered to be the time when all evil forces can be overpowered. Many Yoruba people use this day to begin anything that will lead to a better quality of life.

4. Wednesday/Ọjọ́rú

Ojuru, or Wednesday, is the day of confusion or calamities. This is the day that all disruptions, problems, and calamities entered this world. On Wednesdays, most Yoruba people pray against any forms of evil, problems, and confusion.

5. Thursday/Ọjọ́bọ̀

Ojobo, or Thursday, is the day people's ancestors visit their families. You will notice that most Yoruba festivals begin on this day, making it the week's most important day. Many people also believe that this is when the souls of the departed visit their homes.

6. Friday/Ọjọ́-Ẹ̀tì

This day is considered to be the day of failure. Its meaning is also synonymous with postponement. The Yoruba people believe that whatever is scheduled for a Friday gets postponed or, worse, *fails*. This is why most Yoruba people avoid beginning any business ventures or journeys on this day.

7. Saturday/Ọjọ́-Àbámẹ́ta

Saturday, or the day of three suggestions in the Yoruba calendar. This day is considered to be similar to Ojo-Eti or Friday. You shouldn't start anything on this day to avoid three types of negative incidents. It is also advised that you don't bury a person on this day unless they're an elder.

Traditional Yoruba Days of the Week

Originally, the Yoruba calendar consisted of four-day weeks, and each day was dedicated to a particular Orisha. If you want to follow the traditional Yoruba calendar, the following days make up a week.

1. Ojo Ogun

This is the first day of the traditional Yoruba week and is dedicated to Ogun, the god of iron. On this day, you can make numerous food offerings to Ogun. His favorite food items are ekuru, iyan, and ewa. Ogon likes a balanced diet, so your food offerings should be at a balanced level.

2. Ojo Jakuta

The second day of the traditional Yoruba week, Ojo Jakuta, also known as Ojo Sanga, is dedicated to the Orisha of thunder and lightning. The best way to pay tribute to Sanga is to wear red or white clothes, which reflect the Orisha. Food offerings can include guguru, bitter kola, gbegiri soup, amala, and sacrificial ram.

3. Ojo Ose

The third day is dedicated to the worship of the Orisha Nla. On this day, you should wear white to pay tribute to the great deity and also worship Obatala, Iyaami, or Egungun. Food offerings should include beef, but snail sacrifices are also common.

4. Ojo Awo

Also known as the day of the deity, Ojo Awo is dedicated to Ifa, the Oracle. Food offerings should include beef, just like the Orisha Nla. This day can also be used to worship Orunmila, Esu, or Osun.

Yoruba Months

Like the Gregorian calendar, the Yoruba calendar divides the year into 12 months. The only difference is that the Yoruba year starts in June, whereas the Gregorian year starts in January. Each Yoruba month has been dedicated to an Orisha. There are festivals, rituals, and events that take place during each of these months. However, not every month is limited to a single festival and can hold multiple events and rituals that take place every year. Here are some of the many events that are held every year during each of the Yoruba months.

January - Ṣẹrẹ

January, or Sere, is the month dedicated to Obatala, the great Orisha who created the human body. Due to the nature of Obatala's wisdom, rituals related to this Orisha can help solve conflicts, get rid of spiritual wars, help promote peace, tranquility, and calmness, and encourage the balance of peace, good familial relationships, and healing of physical and mental illness.

Luck Ritual. This ritual can be used to bring luck and fortune into your household. For this, you need a white scarf, cocoa butter, cotton grass, white marigold seeds, husk, and plenty of blades of grass. Take each of the ingredients and grind them into a fine powder. Place a leaf on the white cloth or scarf. Place the powdered ingredients on the leaf and set your intention for the ritual. Ask Obatala to charge the magic dust with luck and fortune and leave it for eight days. After this, clean yourself with this dust, and blow it out of the house.

February - Èrèlé

February or Erele is dedicated to Olokun, the Orisha of Okun, or the ocean. He was considered the guardian of souls lost at sea, the controller of deep seas and oceans, and the patron of sailors. Olokun is considered the harbinger of health, wealth, and other material things. One of the most common ritual substances associated with Olokun is the Akh'Olokun or Olokun pots.

The ritual itself consists of a bath for purifying the souls of worshippers. A pot should be filled with fresh river water and some river leaves. The Orisha Olokun should then be asked to charge the water to purify whoever it touches. Finally, the water should be poured over your head. The pot itself needs to have imagery of a python, a ram, and a cock, which are all sacrificial animals for this particular Orisha.

March - Ẹrẹ̀nà

Erena, or the month of March, is associated with multiple Orishas and festivals. First, the annual rites of passage for men are celebrated during this month. Secondly, it is dedicated to Oduduwa, the Orisha of Earth, also known as the father of the Yoruba people, and secondly, to Osoosi, the Orisha of hunting and adventure. The annual rites of passage for men consist of a series of tests and rituals boys undergo. If they succeed in completing these tests, they will have passed the rites of passage and be considered men instead of boys.

April - Igbe

This month begins with the onset of the rainy season. It is dedicated to Ogun, the Orisha of metalworking, crafts, and engineering. He was considered to be the custodian of truth and justice. Oshun, the Orisha of fertility and pregnancies, also has a part in the month of April. Usually, the Oshun festival is the most popular event during this month. The festivities start with a lamp-lighting ceremony followed by a visit to the Arugba shrine. After that, the procession is led to the sacred grove where thousands of people get cleansed from the water. There are also brilliant pageants and parties thrown for the goddess of love and springs.

May - Ẹ̀bìbì

May has been dedicated to Egungun, which signifies the ancestors' commemoration, especially the community's founders, and is celebrated by the Egungun festival. The annual masquerade festival pays tribute to the ancestral spirits through a series of masked dances, depending on the history of the local ancestors. For instance, if your region's ancestors were famous warriors, then the Egungun festival dances should be chaotic and wild, reflecting the nature of the ancestral spirits. Exquisite Egungun costumes are designed to cover your whole body, and the ancestral spirit is considered to be concealed inside the cloth. The cloth itself acts as an offering to the spirits.

June - Òkúdù

Okudu (or June) is the month the new year begins in the Yoruba calendar. Dedicated to Shopona and Osanyin, the Orishas of disease and healing, respectively, both of these Orishas are connected together because where there's a disease, there's healing. This month also celebrates the annual rites of passage of women. And finally, dedicated to Yemoja, who is considered the mother of Orisha.

It is said that Oduduwa gave birth to Yemojaa (water) and Aganju (land) from marriage with Obatala. She then gave birth to many other Orisha and is considered the Orisha of water, fertility, and women. The Yemoja-Moremi festival is celebrated this month. Throughout the celebrations, many pageants and fertility dances take place to pay tribute to the mother goddess of Yoruba. The rites of passage for girls also occur during this time, similar to the masculine rites.

July - Agẹmọ

The month of July is dedicated to Orunmila, who is associated with divination and is considered the founder of the Ifa sciences. This is the month of mass Yoruba gatherings for festivals and rituals. Oko, the Orisha of agriculture, is also paid tribute to during July. This time is considered perfect for harvesting the new yam crop. Agemo is also dedicated to Esu-Elegba, the great communicator and messenger of Olodumare. Finally, the Orisha of energy, Sango, is also worshiped this month. The Sango festival takes place during the last week of July. The festivities pay tribute to the Alaafin of Oyo, who later became the god of thunder and lightning.

August - Ògún

The famous Osun-Osogbo festival takes place in August. This month is dedicated to Osun, the Orisha of fertility and female essence. At the same time, the month of Ogun is also dedicated to Ogun, the Orisha of metals, technology, and engineering. The fact that there are two months in the Yoruba calendar paying tribute to Ogun reflects the esteem of this Orisha in Yoruba culture. August also consists of the annual Obatala festival, where many plays and stately dances are performed to show respect for the patron god of Yoruba culture.

September - Ọwẹ́wẹ̀ or Owewe

September or Owewe is considered a month of blessings and celebrations. During this month, many new yam festivals are celebrated, and the Yoruba culture in its entirety is celebrated.

October - Ọ̀wàrà or Ọ̀wààrà

Owara translates to rain and refers to the rainy season that begins during October. This month is thus dedicated to the Orisha of rivers, Oya. He was also considered the guardian of the gateway between the physical and spiritual realms. This month is the onset of the dry season. It is also dedicated to Sigidi, the Orisha of unsettled spirits that have left the physical realm but are forbidden to enter Orun-Rere or heaven. Moreover, King's day is also celebrated during the first week of October to honor the king's birthday. A grand series of processions, feasts, and banquets are observed during these festivities.

November - Bélú

November is not considered a particularly special month. But it can still be considered spiritually enhancing. Several Yoruba rites and rituals are not associated with any particular month or day that can take place during this time.

December - Ọ̀pẹ

December marks the onset of the Hammayan season and is dedicated to Obaluaye, the Orisha of healing and disease. Festivities during this season include tributes paid to Obaluaye through sacrifices and offerings. Sacred dances and processions are also held to worship the Orisha of this month.

There are countless Yoruba rituals, festivals, and events to show your devotion to your spirituality. However, until you understand the timing of each festival and rite of passage, you cannot perform them successfully. Once you're aware of each Yoruba festival's occurrence throughout the year, you can successfully add many rituals and rites into your daily life, and better follow your culture.

Extra: Orisha Glossary

- **Aganju:** Aganju is considered the Yoruba spirit of volcanoes. He embodies the essence of fire and is considered one of the fathers of nature. This Orisha is represented by the sun and is tasked with assisting humans in reaching their destinies. He transforms the fire within into passion or empowerment.

- **Agayu:** The alternative name of Aganju Orisha.

- **Aje:** Also known as the other mothers, Aje are wise women having extraordinary powers who can make people both fear and revere them.

- **Ajé Saluga:** The Yoruba wealth god, Ajé Saluga, Aje Shaluga, or Aye Shaluga, is considered to be extremely generous. He showers his followers with riches, as he's one of the richest Orishas.

- **Babalú Ayé:** The Yoruba healer god, Babalú Ayé goes by many names, including Babalu Aye, Babaluaiye, Babaluaye, or Obaluaye. He is a hardworking Orisha who helps treat infections, epidemics, and nasty infestations.

- **Bayani:** The goddess of hats, sister of Shango, and bearer of knowledge that the ceremonial headpiece encrusted with shells provides. She is also known by Babayanmi, Banyani, Bayanni, Bayoni, and Bayonni.

- **Chango:** Also known as Shango, or Xango, the god of storms, is a popular deity in Yoruba culture. He is also considered to be the god of war. Originally, he was a famous warrior hero of the Yoruba people and ascended to be an Orisha. He is the brother of Ogun, who he doesn't get along with, and the lover of Oya.

- **Dada:** The abundance god of Yoruba people, Dada, more commonly referred to as Dada Segbo, produces organic natural goods. Thus, he is also believed to assist in the birth of children.

- **Eda:** The alternative namesake of Dada Sagbo, god of natural produce.

- **Egungun-Oya:** The goddess of divination is in charge of fortune-telling and prophecy readings. She can predict people's future, as well as their powers.

- **Eleggua:** Eleggua, Èṣù-Ẹlẹ́gbára or Elegua, is the Yoruba trickster god, also considered the guardian of the crossroads of life. Therefore, he is also the Orisha of crossroads, opportunities, and beginnings. He is also the messenger for other Orisha, particularly Olorun. He's usually associated with mischief, trickery, and mayhem.

- **Elusu:** Also commonly known as Olokun-Su, or the wife of Olokun, the Orisha of the sea. Elusu is as benevolent as she is beautiful. She represents the many creatures of the sea, especially fish. She is mostly associated with water.

- **Eshu:** Another Yoruba trickster god, Eshu or Esu, is tremendously popular and known by everyone. He's considered the god of instant messaging, communication, and opportunity and is said to direct people on the road of life at the crossroads of fortune. He is associated with trickery and mischief, fortune, and luck.

- **Hare:** Yet another trickster god associated with mischief and mayhem. His most common form is a twitchy-nosed rabbit or hare, hence the name.

- **Jakuta:** A Yoruba thunderstorm god, also known as the thrower of light. While many confuse Jakuta with Shango, they are two separate Orisha deities. Jakuta was present long before Shango was declared an Orisha. He is also associated with lightning.

- **Morimi:** A Yoruba fire goddess, Morimi is known as the goddess of bush burning. Associated mainly with fire, Morimi is said to have quite a temper, as all fire-associated Orishas do.

- **Obatalá:** The creator of the human race and the Yoruba god of purity, Obatala goes by many names, including Obàtálá, Orisha-Popo, Olufon, Orisanla, Orisala Orisha-Nla, Oshanla, and Orishala. Considered one of the high-ranking Orishas, Obatala was tasked with creating the Earth by his father, Olorun. While he's mainly associated with purity, other roles falling under his jurisdiction include fortune, childbirth, and fertility. Obatala is married to Yemaya.

- **Ochosi:** A Yoruba hunting god, Ochosi, Ocshosi, Oxósse, or Oxossi, is among the most influential and skilled Orishas. He is great at hunting his prey, no matter how elusive. He is also commonly associated with justice and has a bow and arrow to help with the task.

- **Odudua:** One of the most renowned Orishas, Odudua goes by many names, including Odudu, Odua, and Oduwa. She is the Yoruba earth goddess, with skin the darkest shade of ebony. Tales of her beauty are legendary in Yoruba mythology. She looks after children and women, promoting love and laughter among humans. She is one of the highest-ranking primordial Orishas and the sister of Olomare. Together, both siblings form an earth-sky bond. She is associated with the essence of life and is married to Obatala.

- **Odùduwà:** Oduduwa is the hero god of the Yoruba people. He is the one who showed up for the creation of the earth after his brother, Obatala, failed to complete it. As a reward, Oduduwa was given the title of the Orisha of Earth. He later went down to rule over the Yoruba people and was their first King. Oduduwa and Odudua are often confused with being the same deity but are, in fact, two different entities.

- **Ogun:** The Yoruba weaponry god, Ogun had many titles, including the Orisha of metalwork, engineering, and iron. Although he is one of the hunting Orishas, he specializes in weapon creation using iron and other metals. He is also often associated with justice and oaths.

- **Oko:** The Yoruba agriculture god, Oko is considered to be the Orisha of farming. He is the son of Yemaya and was sent to the earth to encourage the bountiful production of goods. He is thus associated with fertile farming.

- **Olodumare:** The supreme Orisha and Yoruba god, Olodumare or Olorun, is one of the primordial deities who started it all. He is considered to be the sky god of peace, justice, and the Yoruba way. He is associated with everything supreme.

- **Olokun:** Another highly popular Orisha, the Yoruba god of the sea and the husband of Elusu, Olokun is associated with the ocean, rivers, and the sea. He is quick to anger and easily agitated. He was often at odds with Obatala and other Orishas.

- **Onile:** The Orisha of metalwork, Onile is often confused for Ogun; however, she is associated with soft metalwork. So, while Ogun is associated mainly with iron and other hard metals, Onile is associated with soft metals like aluminum and blacksmithing.

- **Orunmila:** The Yoruba god of wisdom and divinity, Orunmila is also very famous in Yoruba mythology. He is one of the most useful spirits of knowledge.

- **Osanyin:** The Yoruba god of herbs, Osanyin is another popular Orisha. He's mainly associated with medicinal herbs, plants, and vegetation. In contrast to agriculture Orishas, Osanyin is connected to the herbs and medicinal purposes of plants instead of being responsible for growing them. He has knowledge of all the herbs.

- **Oshe:** A safety staff used by storm gods. This staff is associated with the thunder god Shango, who is the calmest thunder Orishas of them all.

- **Oshun:** The Yoruba goddess of love, Oshun (or Osun) is associated with love, sensuality, and creativity. She is also considered to be the protective Orisha of the river Oshun. She blesses all kinds of intimacy.

- **Oshunmare:** Known as the Yoruba rainbow spirit, Oshunmare is a serpent Orisha who is said to be a colorful serpent that makes up the rainbow.

- **Oya:** The Yoruba goddess of practically everything, Oya is a multitasking Orisha mainly tasked with the duty of protecting the River Niger. She is also associated with funerals, weather, and different diseases.

- **Shapona:** He is the scarlet-robed Orisha of smallpox and is definitely not the most popular Orisha, though he is much feared. He's mainly associated with sickness and diseases but also checks the correct observance of rituals.

- **Yansan:** The Yoruba wind goddess, Yansan, is the most mysterious Orisha among them all. Some people say that this is Oya in disguise. She is associated with the wind.

- **Yemaya:** The Yoruba goddess of Childbirth, Yemaya is a famous female Orisha who is not just powerful but also sensuous. She is associated with water, and her personality is fluid, just like water. She is also considered to be the moon goddess and is Obatala's wife. She also goes by the names Iamanjie, Yemayah, Yemanja, Yembo, Yemonja, Yemoja, and Yemowo.

Conclusion

African spirituality is based on beliefs that reflect a strong respect for the divine and the souls of the departed. Ancestral souls are often given the same amount of significance as divinities. The various traditional customs in the different beliefs create a highly diverse set of practices that evolved through history and now span across multiple continents. Several other religious systems have influenced African spiritual practices.

Yet no matter how different their cultural background may be, the traditional African beliefs of Yoruba, Santeria, Voodoo, and Hoodoo all have similar elements. One aspect all these religions have is the existence of a Supreme god, also called Olodumare or Olorun. His contribution to the creation of life on Earth makes several appearances in the respective practices, as does the existence of the Orishas, the divine souls responsible for communication between the Supreme god and people. The Supreme god's energy flows through their Orishas, which is how they carry the messages that otherwise wouldn't reach their destination.

Apart from their role as messengers, the Orishas can also help people on their spiritual journey using their Ashe. This is a unique form of energy that can fend off misfortune and subdue malicious spirits. Practitioners of various African spiritual arts may call upon it when they need protection, guidance, or help with healing. Instead of the Orishas, some African belief systems have the Loa as their divine messengers. In fact, one of the most prominent roles of Loas is guiding souls between the world and helping them move on to different lives after passing.

The Orishas are classified as white, or cool-tempered, and dark, or hot-tempered Orishas. White Orishas are known for having calming and gentle natures. They are usually contacted when one needs help with emotional trauma. Red and black Orishas have more passionate natures and can provide protection. All Orishas have their preferred Ebo (offering) and favorite colors to be used during spells, rituals, and ceremonies. The dark Orishas are particularly sensitive to these objects and often consider certain offerings taboo. Before asking for their assistance, you must be sure they will be properly pleased. Otherwise, you risk angering them.

As you may have surmised, another common factor of African religions is their spiritual nature. The unique worldview of African spirituality revolves around the soul's journey through birth, death, and rebirth. And with each reincarnation, the soul is elevated to a higher level until it becomes one with the Supreme God. One of the most common ways spirituality is practiced in these religions is by building an altar. This is a dedicated space to honor the deities, your ancestors, and your spiritual journey. While having an altar to develop your practice is unnecessary, it can be helpful for beginners who are just learning how to use their intuition. Whether making Voodoo dolls, gris-gris, mojo bags, enacting spells, or rituals, doing a cleansing ceremony, or any other African magical practice, your most important tool will be your intuition. As an extension of your spiritual self, your gut will tell you the best way to approach each practice. You can also follow the Yoruba calendar. This is a great tool for incorporating African spirituality into your day-to-day life. It teaches you how to honor each Orisha, the best time to connect with your ancestors, and much more.

Part 2: Voodoo for Beginners

Explore the World of Haitian Vodou and Louisiana Voodoo

Introduction

You're about to discover the wonderful, powerful world of Louisiana Voodoo and Haitian Vodou. This book will take you by the hand and walk you through what it means to walk this spiritual path, whether you're simply interested in the lore and spirituality or want to make it a part of your life. Choosing this book is the best thing you could have done to make that happen. It's a guidebook packed with all you need to know about the central tenets of the religion and the beliefs that drive it. Louisiana Voodoo has its roots in Haitian Vodou, and the fact that the Nigerian Yoruba culture profoundly influences them both. In this book, "Voodoo" represents both, unless there's a need to distinguish between history and anything else.

Whether you're entirely new to Vodou or Voodoo or have an impressive grasp of this spiritual path, you'll find this book is chock full of golden nuggets that will enrich what you already know. It will also help you see the religion's practices in a whole new light so that you can deeply and sincerely appreciate it. This book is in clear and plain English and has been written to avoid confusion about Voodoo's terms and concepts.

As you read this, it is essential to consider this religion's roots. Consider that it is African and that most people in the West are aware of it because those original Vodouists were taken away from their homelands by force. As a result of slavery, they were forced to abandon wonderful lives and the ones they loved. It was a terrible time to be alive and African. They were forced to travel thousands of miles to strange places, treated as though they were less than human, brutally punished, and bullied into working as enslaved people. One of the things that remained a source of comfort for the African captives in the "New World" was their religion. They turned to their gods, seeking comfort and strength in those dark and trying days.

The internet doesn't quite offer enough information about Voodoo, and much of it is inaccurate. This book has been written to fill in the blanks and correct the wrongs. You can trust that all the information you receive on these pages is far more than a simple search on the internet could yield. The book has been written with respect for the practice, so it is vital that if you're going to read this to learn about Voodoo, you must appreciate it and not disrespect or appropriate it. If you choose to walk this path, you need to understand that there's so much more to Voodoo than trying to seem interesting or searching for something to belong to. It's a way of life that should be honored in all ways, all the time. If you're ready to lead a spiritually rewarding life as a Vodouist, let's get started.

Chapter 1: Voodoo, from Haiti to Louisiana

The word *Vodou* is from the Fon culture. It represents the pantheon of gods and goddesses that the people of Haiti worship and the ideologies of the spiritual movement. You may also find this word spelled as Voodoo, Vundun, Vudu, Vodon, and so on.

Haitian Vodou and Louisiana Voodoo

Haitian Vodou is a religion practiced by the African diaspora, and it grew and developed from around 1501 to the 1900s. It resulted from the combination of West African traditional religions and Catholicism. In this religion, you'll find no single authority in charge, unlike in Catholicism, where you have the pope. Those following this path are Serviteurs, Vodouisants, or Vodouists.

Louisiana Voodoo is also called New Orleans Voodoo. This religion came about due to the combination or syncretization of the West African traditional religions, Catholicism and Haitian Vodou. Haitian Vodou and Louisiana Voodoo venerate certain intermediaries such as Papa Legba, the Grand Zombi, etc. This religion is a path that also involves working with the spirits of those who have passed on. In other words, ancestor worship and prayer are vital. Around the 19th century, some of the saints were also revered. Still, by the time of the revival in the 20th century, it was more common to revere other gods and goddesses from various African religions. Equally important is the idea of gris-gris, charms used to achieve various purposes.

So how is it that Vodou made its way from Haiti to Louisiana? Early in the 18th century, the West African Bambara and Kongo people (who had had their freedom stripped away by the colonialist enslavers) were transported to Louisiana, previously a French colony. It was there that they would combine their religion with the French Roman Catholic practices. This practice kept happening even as Louisiana was taken over by the Spanish and then bought in 1803 by the United States of America.

In Saint-Domingue, the enslaved people who had set themselves free had been actively fighting the French colonialists in Haiti. They decided to take back their land, and their revolt started on 22nd August 1791. It finally ended in 1804 when they successfully regained their independence. This revolt was known as the Haitian Revolution. Many migrants were escaping Haiti and wound up in Louisiana at the time. They continued to practice Haitian Vodou there, which led to the creation of Louisiana Voodoo. Eventually, the enslavers would create laws to regulate the practice of the tradition. While these laws didn't ban Voodoo outright, they were restrictive, discouraging black people from coming together at certain times in certain places. So, the enslaved people practiced in secret.

Voodoo somehow found its way from Mississippi to Missouri. In the 19th century, there were certain practitioners held in high regard by Vodouists, among them Doctor John and Marie Laveau, and they both drew a lot of eyes.

Early in the 20th century, there was a drop in the practice of Voodoo — at least in public. Most of the practices would continue as hoodoo. At the end of the 60s, the New Orleans tourist industry would use Voodoo concepts to draw visitors in. At the same time, the religion was reawakening, and the Vodouists of the time would draw from Cuban Santeria, Haitian Vodou, and other religions of the African diaspora.

Key Differences and Similarities between Vodou and Voodoo

Voodoo is heavily rooted in Nigeria's Yoruba culture and religion and also draws influences from Benin and Togo. For over 2,500 years, the Yorubas have lived in Africa. Yoruba traditional religion centers on the worship of Olorun, who is known as the Grand Master. There are other lesser spirits or intermediaries (at least 400 of them, some more popular than others) who were once regular humans who did the extraordinary in their lives.

Yoruba religion involves the belief that there's a connection between the living and the dead. Among its practices are animal sacrifice and prayer.

It is on account of the Spanish and French slave traders that some Yoruba people were forced out of their lands to Haiti, among other places. It was in Haiti where they would develop Vodou, combined with Catholicism, only because the Spanish and French forced it on them and discouraged them from practicing their original religion. The enslaved people were forced to combine their beliefs with Catholicism. They did this not because they wanted to but because they were trying to avoid being too heavily scrutinized by the enslavers. So on the surface, it appeared they were worshiping in the Catholic way, but in truth, they were busy venerating the spirits of their homeland. With time, the enslaved people would begin to warm up to some of the tenets of Christianity. They found similarities between that religion and theirs.

When it comes to Louisiana voodoo, there's such a thing as magic. Specifically, there's white magic called Juju, and left-handed magic, which is evil. Left-handed magic involves cursing with mojo and inflicting pain and suffering on others using voodoo dolls. Juju is about making romantic spells, good luck charms, and spells to remove hexes. Voodoo dolls can also be used for good when it comes to Juju. Gris-gris bags are also part of Louisiana voodoo. These are bags that have magical recipes made up of various ingredients. Sometimes they're called gray because they can have a combination of white and black magic. When it's for good, you can hang your gris-gris above a door or up on a wall. When it's for evil/bad, it's usually left at one's doorstep.

Vodou and Voodoo involve working with certain intermediaries to help one with daily life issues. They can connect you with the supreme being you cannot approach directly when necessary.

Voodoo in Pop Culture

The trouble with the presentation of Voodoo in pop culture is that it is wildly inaccurate and only causes stigmatization of the practice. The stereotypes are ridiculous and only cause people to be needlessly afraid. For some reason, Hollywood continues to perpetuate the myth that the Vodouist is a villain to be feared or considered crazy and unstable at worst. The wonderful path of Voodoo has become nothing more than a representation of evil, black magic, according to American culture and Hollywood. The representations of Voodoo are often not just incorrect but are rooted in racism and slavery.

Why is Hollywood so determined to paint Voodoo as evil when it's a folk religion? To answer this, we must return to the Haitian Revolution. Haiti was once called Saint Domingue and was colonized by the French, who wanted to take advantage of the sugar cane in the land so they could sell it to Europe. To do this, the French would have to use slave labor, which was terrible for the natives. Eventually, their mistreatment of the people of Haiti grew too much to bear.

The natives came together that night in August 1791 at Bois Caiman. The goal was to have a religious ceremony about staging a revolution. It was headed by Dutty Boukman, a Vodou priest held in high regard at the time. As they met, a tropical storm raged while they planned how to fight back against the French. For them, the flashing lightning and roaring thunder were a sign that their plan would work. In the days following this auspicious meeting, the natives began their revolution. They were ruthless and with good reason. They successfully decimated those who had oppressed them, specifically the crème de la crème who lived in the Northern Plain. This slave uprising led to the creation of an independent nation ruled exclusively by the black people of the land.

The United States of America, of course, had a serious problem with this uprising. They were troubled, mainly because they were a nation built on the backs of enslaved Black people. So the fact that the Haitian Revolution was a success was something they couldn't stand and was also dangerous in terms of ideology. Imagine the enslaved people they had in their possession being inspired to do something similar. What would be the fate of the white enslavers, then? President Thomas Jefferson had enslaved people, too, and he was feeling the heat from Haiti. He was very vocal and active in trying to get the new Haiti destroyed. He wouldn't trade with the new sovereign nation because he genuinely believed Haiti would become too successful to the point where the enslaved people in America would begin feeling empowered. That's the last thing enslavers want — enslaved people with confidence and ambition. This fear from the Americans is what started the propaganda against Voodoo.

Propaganda War

The concern that the Haitian Revolution would spark more revolutions in slaveholding America led to Vodou being demonized and stigmatized. The French colonists in America at the time made it their mission to hunt down and destroy whatever whiff of Voodoo there was in Louisiana, but that wasn't enough for them. They needed to rally more minds to their cause, and what better way to do this than through the media? So, using the media as puppets, they spread tall tales about how Vodou is all about ritual sacrifices and killings. They took the concept of *Zombi* and turned it into something it is not.

Originally, *Zombi* represented what it felt like to go from being a free independent African full of life and joy to being stripped of one's rights and dignity, forced into slavery, as good as a walking corpse, and nothing more. They took that idea and turned it into the "zombies" of the screen today. The first zombi and voodoo representation on the big screen was the movie *White Zombie*, released in 1932. The movie starred Bela Lugosi as Murder Legendre, who was supposed to be a white Haitian Vodou master. He used what he knew about potions and spells to turn a woman into a zombie.

Since Lugosi was well known for playing Dracula in another movie some years before, the public equated that character with this new one, and that was it. Now, in everyone's minds, all Vodouists are villains. From then on, the idea of zombies would continue to be rubbished and sensationalized. *White Zombie* also used the voodoo doll, which you can find in movies like *Pirates of the Caribbean: On Stranger Tides, The Princess and the Frog, and Eve's Bayou.*

There was also the Bizoton Affair of 1864, a very controversial matter. What happened was that eight Haitian Vodouists had to stand trial. The allegations against them were ritual sacrifice and a little girl's cannibalization. The media, naturally, was in a frenzy. The media prioritized sensationalized reporting over the truth. They made the world view Haiti as a brutal place and Vodou as an equally barbaric practice. The Bois Caiman ritual and the Haitian Revolution that led to their independence were things that were no longer celebrated but instead now sullied as demonic. So even before Hollywood began making money demonizing Voodoo, the enslavers had ideologically ruined the practice in the minds and hearts of non-Vodouists. However, there's an ideological revolution happening right now in favor of Voodoo. The damage is being undone, and with time it should be apparent to one and all that Voodoo is a powerful tool that brought much-needed revolution and freedom.

Marie Laveau and Doctor John

Marie Laveau is a very prominent character in Louisiana Voodoo. Her Voodoo skills were unparalleled, as she had studied with the great Doctor John, a well-known Voodoo doctor. She was very good at telling fortunes accurately. She made effective gris-gris bags and developed a reputation as someone you could turn to when you needed to teach someone who had wronged you a lesson. She grew to be rather wealthy, and she was respected and feared. It's said that her power was so great that she could show up in more than one place simultaneously and that if you asked for it, she could drive you crazy with her gris-gris.

Doctor John was revered as a Voodoo King of sorts in New Orleans. He was also known as Jean Bayou, Jean Grisgris, Jean Montaigne, Prince John, Jean Racine, Jean Latanie, Jean La Ficelle, Bayou John, and Vodou John. His skills with Vodou mysticism were unparalleled. The slavers noticed that he had some sort of occult hold over his coworkers. This power he had is known as the obi power. He could predict the future by looking at the cotton bales. Many colored and white people would reach out to him for his predictions and advice, which led to him becoming wealthy enough to buy his property and build his home.

Doctor John had as many as 15 wives, or so he claimed, and over 50 children. When he moved around in public, he'd do so in a fine carriage with elegant horses, just as the white men at the time did. His flamboyant display of wealth, of course, drew a lot of eyes. He tended to favor gaudy Spanish attire when riding horseback. Eventually, he'd opt for wearing a black outfit with a frilly white shirt.

Doctor John's specialty was with gris-gris bags (earning him the name Jean Grisgris) and telling fortunes. He combined these two skills with Creole medicine. With time, his reputation grew so much that he began to charge exorbitant rates. People of all races from all places would travel to see him. They'd pay anywhere from ten to twenty dollars at the time for his services, whether to make their hair grow, learn which Havana Lottery ticket was worth buying, get back something stolen, or fix family problems. He could create poltergeist phenomena by raining stones on someone's home. He would only stop the harassment when paid. Once, a certain slaver called Samuel Wilson had paid John $62 to stop a rain shower. After paying, he took the Doctor to court to get his money back. Naturally, days later, Doctor John made it rain again.

Chapter 2: Bondye and the Lwa

To start this chapter, let's examine the connection between the Voodoo Lwa and the Roman Catholic Saints. As mentioned in the previous chapter, there was a combination of Voodoo and Catholic practices to get the slavers to pay Vodouists no mind. Eventually, some Catholic ideas became truly accepted as part of Vodou. There is a lot of controversy regarding the true origins of the New Orleans and Louisiana Voodoo. Researching this information online will only get you a lot of conflicting information. One fact remains certain: Louisiana Vodou had a fair bit of African influence, and many practices continued to thrive where they were lost in other places. New Orleans was also closely overseen by the Catholic church, more so than Haiti, where it was okay to practice Vodou with no interference from Catholics.

The Lwa are grouped into families, pantheons, or nations.

By 1803, the United States had bought Louisiana, and as a result, many practitioners chose to continue the path in silence and privacy. Certain religious laws also kept the people from doing their work on Sundays when they'd have to gather in Congo Square or Place Congo. The enslaved people who wanted to be more private about their practice would worship at Lake Pontchartrain, among other places where they could better observe the true traditional practice instead of the performance-based rituals held at Place Congo.

In New Orleans, you will notice that many a traditional Voodoo altar has Catholic Saints decorating them. It was the smart play to syncretize the Lwa with the saints, but some misinformed people assume that Voodoo is a result of Catholicism. This belief is not the case, as African traditional religions are thousands of years older than Christianity.

The Great Master

Vodouists believe in Bondye, which means "Good God." He is considered the Great Master or Gran Met and is also known as Bon Dieu in French. This God is ideologically similar to the Christian God. The Vodouist knows better than to ask this God for anything directly because they know the proper channels to follow, and those channels are intermediaries known as the Lwa. The Lwa are the expressions of Bondye's power and might. Bondye shares a connection with everyone and has a bond with all living. It is standard practice for Vodouists to unite to venerate Bondye with proper ceremonies.

The thing about Bondye is that he's rather mysterious. He's the God at the very center of Voodoo and the one responsible for ensuring that life goes on as it should. Don't assume that because he's known as the "Good God," there's a "Bad God" that has equal power and can stand in his way. So this begs the question, what is good and bad in Bondye's book and the eyes of the Vodouist? The answer to that question is simply the degree of expression of Gran Met's power in our lives, and it all comes down to what we do. So, whatever feeds our health, wealth, prosperity, and joy is considered good. Anything that takes away from those things would be bad.

Bondye is beyond human comprehension, and because of this, it is important to interact with him through his Lwa rather than directly. The Lwa are spirits that you can notice as active forces in your life, causing things to play out in your favor. All Vodouists know that their focus should be on the Lwa weather than Bondye. It is the Lwa that have always possessed Vodouists. Bondye possessing a follower is something unheard of. Bondye is the Unknowable Knower, transcendent, remote, and uninvolved in earthly matters. His energy flows through the Lwa, so to seek his help, approach the Lwa instead. For the Vodouist, it is important to accept that things will always go according to Bondye's plan. This mindset is why the Haitians say, "Si Bondye vle," meaning, "If Bondye wills it."

All of humanity was created by Bondye, and he crafted one and all in his image. He then infused every living soul with the divine energy that animates the physical body. The physical body is nothing but a tool for Bondye's divine energy to function through. He made the body out of water and clay. He crafted humanity from the same elements that make up the universe around us. Just as the waters and trees of the earth and the materials we use to build homes and other buildings are from the earth, so are we from the earth. We are born from earth's sacred womb, only to die and return to the earth from which we came. It is believed in Voodoo that no one is a stranger to the world around them and that the world doesn't work against us. However, we are one with the cosmos because we're composed of the same elements.

The Voodoo Pantheon

The Lwa are grouped into families, pantheons, or nations. The nations are known as nanchons. Each one has its ethos and unique demands that have to be followed. It is said that there are seventeen nanchons, but not all of them are known by name. The Wangol and Nago nanchons have been assimilated into the Rada. The Ibo and Kongo nanchons, better known than the Wangol and Nago, are now part of the petro. Also part of the Rada nanchon now is the Ginen nanchon from Guinea. In this book, we'll be discussing the major nanchons:

- The Rada Lwa
- The Petro Lwa
- The Gede Lwa

Rada is from the word Arada, and this was an important kingdom in Dahomey when Haiti was colonized. Petro is derived from a character known as Dom Pedro, who was responsible for leading the maroon rebellion of the eighteenth century. Scholars once assumed that the difference between the Rada and Petro Lwa is that the former is good, and the latter is evil. However, this is not correct at all.

One cannot try to box in the nanchons with strict ethics. Sure, once upon a time, the Petro was linked to evil magic, while the Rada was linked to good magic. As a result, it became the standard assumption that the Petro Lwa are aggressive beings, rather violent and given to destruction, while on the other hand, the Rada is gentle and kind, but this isn't the case. The Petro can also offer good things to devotees, like their protection. Also, the Rada, while kind, can be ruthless when needed. This ruthlessness plays out when the devotees do not carry out their religious duties as they should.

The point of all this is that you cannot classify the Lwa in terms of morality. It doesn't mean that Vodouists have no sense of morals or can't tell what's good from what's bad. These people have very clear standards about what is right and wrong. Looking at it empirically through the lens of science, the Vodouist would insist that all of life, including the principles that drive it, come down to a single principle: Bondye. Bondye is the one who makes sure that there is order in the universe.

The Rada Lwa

The Rada Lwa are known as the Gentle Ones. They're not as quick to act as their Petro counterparts, but this is good because they take their time to weigh entire situations and all the players justly before they take action to restore balance. These Lwa are of a sweet disposition and tend to be rather cool-tempered. Very dependable, they're also called Lwa Rasin, which means "root Lwa." They tend to be intimately connected with devotees, and usually, their names indicate a familial connection. For instance, they may be called *Kouzen* (meaning "cousin") or Papa (meaning "father"). The Rada Lwa are from West Africa, and the rituals practiced in their honor are from Arada in Dahomey. These benevolent beings are often connected to the color white.

The Petro Lwa

The Petro (also spelled "Petwo") or Petro Lwa are also known as *dompete*. Compared to the Rada Lwa, they are rather hot-tempered and volatile. They are said to be rather aggressive. They act with force and can be quite bitter. It is always important to have these Lwa separate from the Rada Lwa, not just where their altars are placed in an *ounfo* (meaning "temple") but also by ensuring they're invoked at different times in a ceremony or ritual. Vodouists know to be careful with the Petro Lwa, who tend to be very good at making things happen, especially regarding financial affairs. The Petro Lwa favors offerings like gunpowder, hot peppers, blood, coffee, etc. The drums for these lwa during rituals tend to be very harsh and rapid. You can expect to see whips cracking, gunpowder exploding, and whistles blowing harshly during a typical Petro ritual. These lwa are connected to the color red.

The Gede Lwa

This Lwa nanchon is in charge of fertility and death. They are also known as the Ghede Lwa or Guede Lwa. Banda is the dance and drumming music that they're known for. When they possess devotees, they often cover themselves in a mix of raw rum, 21 goat peppers or scotch bonnet peppers, and clairin, a form of raw rum distilled from sugarcane in Haiti. Fet Gede is the time when they're celebrated, and it falls on 2 November, which happens to be the Festival of the Dead or All Souls' Day. The Gede offer boons to their devotees. Any good thing that hasn't been repaid by this time will be avenged once the celebration ends. The Gede are also connected with sensuality. They can act in a very irreverent manner, with dances that are reminiscent of sex. This nanchon is responsible for the transportation of dead souls. The spirit of the Gede Lwa celebrates life even when faced with death, and they're connected to the color black.

Veves

In Voodoo, practitioners have to reach out to the Lwa to ask them to ride their human bodies or possess them to help them communicate with devotees directly. The rituals involve chants, drums, dance, and specific symbols called *veves*. Just as certain drum rhythms, dances, chants, and colors are used with certain Lwa, the same applies to the veves. You use a veve in a ritual that matches the Lwa with whom you want to connect. The veves can be drawn on the ground in the sand. They can also be drawn on cornmeal or on any other substance that is in powder form.

During the ritual, the veves are erased. Devotees can also put offerings and sacrifices on the leaves. These offerings could be food, drinks, and other objects that resonate with the Lwa being summoned to the ceremony. After the veve has been traced, spray it with a libation. It would be best to put a candle in the middle of the drawing. The veve can then be activated by a ringing bell while the devotees say their prayers to the Lwa with whom they want to connect. When several entities need to be present, all their veves will be drawn and connected. It is also important to use the right powder for each deity's veve. You don't want to use brick powder when you're supposed to use coffee powder or white flour, for instance.

The veves have designs that differ from one Lwa to another and from one custom to the next. There are, however, certain elements that are shared among several veves. Please think of the veve as a homing beacon of sorts, meant to attract the Lwa you want to work with and represent their energy during a ritual. Don't be surprised if you find that a Lwa has multiple veves. Often, this is because of the differences that exist from one region to the next.

Some of the veves are simple, while others can be very complex. The horizontal line in a veve represents the secular world, while the vertical line represents the Lwa's cosmic realms. The intersection of the vertical and horizontal lines is the zero-point of contact. This zero-point is where all the devotees have to say prayer and supplication. During the part of ceremonies where the veves are traced, it's common to experience spirit possession and a phenomenon known as glossolalia, where the devotees speak in strange languages.

Spiritual possession in the context of Voodoo is not a bad thing. On the contrary, it is a sign that the Lwa being addressed is willing to participate in the activities of the devotees, and that's why the devotees don't mind experiencing it. Those possessed after tracing the veves become the connecting point between the worlds of divinity and profanity, filled with the Lwa's power.

It is important not to mistake the veves for the Palo *patipembas,* or the Quimbanda and Umbanda *pontos riscados.* Those are very different religions. It is postulated that the veves may have originated from the Kongo *cosmogram,* which shows cosmology in a flat form with shapes. Veves also have their roots in the Igboid languages of Nigeria, specifically from the Nsibidi writing system. Think of each veve as representing forces from the astral realm. When a Voodoo ceremony takes place, these forces are reproduced by drawing the veves, which, in turn, summon the Lwas to the earth to participate in the ceremony. Some Vodouists use the veve made as a painting or hang them up in their homes as art, banners, and so on. Keeping veves close invokes the presence and energy of the Lwa in their space for protection, provision, or whatever else they may ask of the Lwa.

The process of tracing the veves is seen as a reenactment of the creation of the world.

It is important to treat the veves with respect. For instance, it's a terrible idea to tattoo yourself with a veve. The cool points aren't worth it. You should also make sure you don't use these symbols mindlessly as decoration, for instance. The reason is that you might anger the Lwa into totally ignoring you when you call them for an actual issue you're dealing with. Also, the moody Petro Lwa could find it very disrespectful and insulting, and they'd be more than happy to communicate that to you in ways you don't want. You should always be intentional in your use of the veves. Make sure you know the Lwa you're trying to connect with, the proper way to draw the veve, and what it is you want them to help you with. This way, you can avoid the wrath of the Lwa.

Chapter 3: Meet the Lwa I: the Rada

In this chapter, we're going to take a look at the cool, gentle Rada Lwa. Before Haiti, Hispaniola (so named by Christopher Columbus), and before the slave ship got to Ayiti's shores on Taino Island, Haitian Vodou was already in play as Vodu. Vodu was a popular practice in West Africa in a place known as Arada, now an area in present-day Benin. The coastal Aja tribe of that kingdom took over the land of the inland tribes around them. After the conquest, Dahomey (Daome) was created. Dahomey is where all the enslaved people sent to Hispaniola came from, and this was the start of Haiti.

Voodoo mythology says the physical body is made of the substance that makes up the ocean.
https://www.pexels.com/photo/aerial-photography-of-turquoise-water-on-the-sea-4637298/

For the formerly enslaved people of Haiti, Arada was the holy land. It was holy to those from Ginen or Guinea, the land of black people across the sea in Africa. The Arada from the Yoruba, Oyo, and Fon tribes, who were lost to slavery and the people of Aja, arrived in Haiti with their spirits unbroken. These different groups came together in a melting pot, blending their religious and cultural beliefs and ways so that they could continue to thrive. Out of these tribes arose the Rada nanchon. The Lwa of this nanchon are considered older and, therefore, more honored than the other Lwa groups. Most of them are still being honored in Africa in different ways and with other names.

The Rada Lwa are more stately in their services, with more formal religious services. They are to be honored before other Lwa after saying prayers to Bondye. They're called on one at a time, starting with the Allada Lwa and ending with the Nago Lwa. The Rada is generally associated with the color white, representing the formal air with which devotees should approach them and the concept of purity.

Agwe

Agwe is powerful. This marine spirit embodies the element of water. Voodoo mythology says the physical body is made of the substance that makes up the ocean. It holds that blood is similar to the sea and the cosmos. How? All three continue to move due to a force whose origin can be traced back to Bondye.

In the same way, the sweat on your brow has the same elements as the salty sea. The Vodouist works in flow with the universe, and they flow with the sea, being nourished by it. So not surprisingly, the sea is overseen by a Lwa. His name is Agwe.

Also known as Agoue, he is powerful, but unlike the other Lwa, his power is only related to the sea. He is in charge of the water, its creatures, and all vessels that travel on its waters. All the rituals for this Lwa are done at sea. The entire community prepares for the rituals over several days, and the whole process can cost a pretty penny. Days before the ceremony begins, the devotees bring food offerings and choose a ram to sacrifice to this Lwa. Then they create a raft which they keep in the ounfo. This raft is meant to serve as a banquet table for the Lwa. The banquet table has tablecloths of white and blue, which are Agwe's colors. The tablecloths go around the table, and the people believe that Agwe's spiritual guests sit around the table. The drums are painted blue and white, and the skins are fixed to rouse the Lwa from the murky sea's depths. The ram is fed a specific diet over the next few days; then, it is bathed and ritually cleansed with certain leaves steeped in water that turns it blue. The banquet table has everything from rice and beans to champagne and wine. The ram is also tied up and placed in the center on its side.

The guests who attend Agwe's banquet include La Sirenn (his wife and Ezili's sea aspect), the Wedos, Ogou, Azaka, Damballah and Ayida, and Ezili. Flags with the veves of each of these beings are set around the table. The devotees then draw a fish or crab to represent Agwe's lieutenant, Agasou. At the head of the table, another fish is drawn to represent Agwe. The preparations up to this point take up a whole day. After a few more preparations, the devotees load up the raft and everything on it on a truck. They then take it all to the sea as they sing on their way there.

The fish is an important symbol when working with Agwe, but one must not assume it is an element taken from Christianity. It's from Fon mythology, as Agwe is said to be the same as the Fon Agbe, who was said to have become a fish after he was sent down to rule the sea by Sogbo, the ruler of the sky pantheon. Agwe himself is connected to all the cosmic Lwas. He rules over the waters along with Damballah. He is syncretized with Saint Ulrich, who is sometimes shown with a fish in his left fist. The Vodouists do not care for who Saint Ulrich was, so one must not assume that the fish represents the message of Christianity in any way. While Agwe's name is from the Fon, his mythology is Nigerian, specifically rooted in the Yoruba tradition of Western Nigeria.

Legba

Legba is known as the Keeper of the Gates. It is said that one of the very first things Bondye created was the sun, and without it, nothing could exist — not even the Lwa. So everything comes from the light of the sun, which is considered life's fire. This sun is synonymous with Legba's creative power, which is why Haitians practice lighting fires for him when there's a Vodou ceremony. Any ritual in which he's invoked has devotees referring to him as *kataroulo,* which refers to the four wheels of the sun's chariot as they make their way through the sky each day, and *cleronde,* which means "circle of light."

Legba is the very life force that leads to regeneration. He is the patron of the entire universe, acting as the go-between between Bondye and the rest of the world. Where Bondye created the world, it is Legba that nurtured and sustained it. This Lwa is androgynous, and so his veve depicts that. He is also summoned when issues about sex need to be addressed. The Yoruba people and the Fon see him as the cosmic phallus. He shows up as an older man with a pipe in his hand or mouth. He also carries a little sack containing some food hanging from his shoulder by his side. He moves with a totter, quite slowly, with the help of a cane called *baton Legba*. The cane represents man's virility, human life, and the connection from one generation to the next.

This Lwa acts as a mediator between the sacred and profane worlds. He performs the same role between devotees and the Lwa, between generations, and between both sexes. His symbol is the potomitan, which is why he is considered the gatekeeper to Vilokan, where the Lwas reside permanently in Dahomey, Africa. It's a mythical island that you can find below the sea. No living person makes it into Vilokan except those that are let in or taken there accidentally. Legna is known as the Lwa of the Crossroads and the Master of the Great Way to Vilokan. He is also responsible for the order in which the Lwas possess devotees. In his inverted petro form, he is known as Met Kafou Legba. Where Legba keeps life going, Kafou destroys it.

Loko

This Lwa is the patron saint of plants and healers. He lives in the trees. He's wedded to Ayizan, another Lwa who acts as the archetypal mambo or priestess, which makes sense since Loko is considered the first houngan or priest. They are both like the spiritual mother and father of the Voodoo priesthood and are heavily invested in the Kanzo initiation rites. Loko can be likened to the Arawak Louquo and is connected to the Ceiba pentandra and the Iroko, both sacred trees in Mesoamerica and Africa, respectively.

Loko is considered to be the authority on all things historical and esoteric. He is the keeper of religious secrets and sanctuaries, the master of discipline, and the lwa trees and herbs that speak to and let him know the secret, sacred things. It is worth stating that Loko has nothing to do with the American slang that implies being crazy. An erudite being, he doesn't care for those who practice Voodoo on their own. However, he's there to guide those who want to be formally initiated into Voodoo, and you can reach out to him when you need to be healed or feel empowered.

This Lwa is syncretized to Saint Joseph and revered on Joseph's feast day, on 19th March. His other names are Papa Loko, Papa Loco, King Loko, and Loko Atisou. He is particularly partial to men. His colors are white, yellow, gold, and sometimes a combination of red and white. The sacred creatures to him include snakes, butterflies, fighting cocks, and regular roosters. His sacred tree is the Mapou. You can offer him any white food, white rum, and herbs meant for healing.

Damballah

Damballah is a great snake that supports the earth, keeping it safe from falling into an abyss of water below it. Once upon a time, he remained beneath the earth for so long that, eventually, he had to move, and as he did so, this led to the creation of valleys and mountains. His movement also caused the sky to be filled with stars, releasing sacred waters that created streams, oceans, ponds, rivers, lakes, and so on. His movement also led to the very first rain, and the rainbow appeared. However, the rainbow wasn't ordinary. It was Aido-Hwedo, who was and still is Damballah's love. Their love radiates worldwide and shows up in humans as white liquid, specifically semen and milk.

Damballah is in charge of wisdom, wealth, and life. This primordial snake is loved because he offers fertility, wealth, health, and prosperity to all who seek him. He can also show you the location of the missing treasure. He's the reason for the rain and all moisture. Together with his rainbow love, he keeps all forces in balance. This Lwa shouldn't be bothered with trivial things, but he is quite generous, so you can reach out to him if you're in big trouble or desperate for help. Despite how ancient he is, he is quite invested in people's affairs.

This Lwa shows up in dreams. Curiously, he's not the best at communication, so you have to pay attention, as he doesn't speak any human language. He has syncretized with Moses, the law-giver, and Saint Patrick. The reason he's syncretized with Moses is that Moses had a staff he turned into a snake. Damballah likes to hang out with Ezili Freda Dahomey.

This Lwa appreciates cleanliness and hates strong smells, especially from tobacco smoke. It would be best if you never smoked near his altar or sacred spaces. He also isn't a fan of strong-smelling cleaning products and air fresheners. It's enough for his space to smell clean and fresh and for air to circulate well in the room. He likes light floral smells like orange blossom water, Pompeii Lotion, or rose. He's also called Papa Damballah or Damballah. His favorite color is white, and he loves the royal palm, bombax ceiba or silk cotton tree, bougainvillea, and other trees in general.

His special day is Thursday, and if you're going to revere him, you have to make sure that there are shallow bowls of fresh and clean water so he can curl up in them comfortably. A good offering to make is to put some white flour on a clean, white plate, then set a raw white egg right in the middle of the flour and offer that to him. He also likes milk, rice, whole raw eggs, other white foods, snakes, white fabrics, porcelain and crystal eggs, and orgeat syrup. You can also mist or rub the white eggs you offer with floral-scented water.

Ayizan

This Lwa is the Queen of the Marketplace. She is also the one who keeps many mystical secrets. As the first mambo ever, she is to be revered. You can call her Mambo Ayizan, and if you're going to make offerings to several Lwa, you should honor her first. Her name means "sacred earth." A very old spirit, she isn't one to be bothered with trivialities either. She's in charge of ensuring that the Hounsi initiation process works well. She also acts as market women's matron and ensures they succeed in their business.

Ayizan offers protection from jealousy, envy, the evil eye, and malicious intentions. She has great disdain for those who exploit others. If you feel like someone is exploiting you or you're oppressed, reach out to her, and she'll help you if you truly deserve it. You can also ask her to help you with your spiritual journey, as she has great knowledge of the spiritual world and power. You can ask her to share information with you that you can't get anywhere else or ask her to intercede on your behalf. She also has the power to eliminate evil beings, purifying and cleansing space to make it sacred.

Ayizan is also called *Aizan*. She shows up in nature, using earth mounds and palm fronds. Sometimes, she can show up as an older woman. She's represented with earthen mounds, palm branches, and palm fronds and is also syncretized to Saint Anne or Christ. You may anoint these items with oil. When shown as Christ, he is shown being baptized by his forerunner, John the Baptist. Anyone who would like to protect their place of business or home could get some palms, craft them into a cross or an X shape, and place them over their door. Then they can ask for Ayizan's blessings. Her favorite tree is the palm, while her favorite colors are silver and white. You can offer her sweet liquors, bananas, yams, plantains, dirt or sand from the market (it must be an outdoor market crossroads), yams, and white flowers.

Anaisa Pye

This Lwa is known as the queen of love. She happens to be a well-loved spirit, too. She's exquisitely beautiful, full of laughter and joy, and rather flirtatious. She is sometimes seen as the same as Eili Danto or her daughter, but to be clear, she's different from Czestochowa's Black Madonna. She's more like Saint Anne and the future Virgin Mary, who is her daughter. This Lwa may be syncretized with Saint Anne, but all Vodouists know that she's more identified with the little girl known as Little Anne. The myth is that Anaisa was Ezili's daughter, and at age three, she was sent off to convent school to be guided by very strict nuns. At age thirteen, she became quite rebellious and abandoned the convent. This story is reminiscent of Mary being at the temple at age three and then getting married at age thirteen.

Anaisa Pye is a jealous Lwa. You must be devoted to her as you would be to a jealous lover who is fiercely possessive of you, with a catch: she's dangerous. You cannot abandon this Lwa without consequences. The good thing about her is that she is rather generous and quick to respond to those who call on her. Also, she's fine with serving many devotees, but you shouldn't reach out to her unless you want to remain completely committed. She takes it personally when devotees decide to abandon their devotion to her.

You can communicate with this Lwa using perfume; she also lets you know she's around through a pleasant fragrance. You can consecrate some perfume to her and set it on her altar, and also have another bottle of the same fragrance you can wear when you want to summon her. She's fine with sharing an altar with male spirits but doesn't play nice with female ones. You should always keep her away from other spirits because the odds are she has flirted with their husbands, which can be problematic. While she prefers men, her service is to women. Any female devotee dealing with reproductive issues can go to her for help. She can also help to increase a woman's beauty, make her more desirable, and teach her to be sensual. You'll automatically be blessed with these things by remaining in her presence. The blessings will keep coming as long as your offerings to her are consistent and continuous. She's also the one to turn to for marital, romance, and home affairs. You can invoke her by grabbing a champagne flute or some other fancy glass, pouring some beer into it, and then adding seven drops of Florida Water. If you don't have Florida Water, some other perfumes will do.

Anaisa Pye's special day is July 26th. Her element is water, and she loves all colors on the spectrum, from gold to yellow. Sometimes when she's at the cemetery, she wears pink. She also does well with rose gold. Her number is 7, representing all seven days of the week on which she expects your devotion. Her altar must be beautiful, and it helps to decorate it with loads of flowers and yellow candles. You can offer her champagne grapes, miniature bananas, and other delicate fruits. You can also offer her fruits dipped in chocolate, marzipan fruits, champagne, and beer in a lovely champagne flute. You can also buy her cosmetics, scented soaps, some nice fragrances, and jewelry.

Chapter 4: Meet the Lwa II: the Petro

Now it's time to turn our attention to some of the most popular Petro Lwa. The Petro Lwa are sometimes called the Petro (or Petwo), a large group. This nanchon is not about the tomes from Ginen. They are the spirits who heard the cries of the enslaved people in Saint-Domingue, and they are the ones who are responsible for the change. While the Rada is more about the peaceful lives that the people led before slavery became a thing, the Petrol is rooted in regular Haitian life from 1492 to the present. This epoch is when pain, poverty, violence, and bloodshed reign supreme. Among these Lwa, spirits represent the Ibo people, a great warrior tribe, and the Kongo. There are also the magician spirits from Bakongo and Kikongo and the most powerful and deadly of Haiti's safe keepers. Since the Nago nanchon was crafted from Ginen, it is honored by devotees just as the Rada rituals close. Still, it has forceful energy reminiscent of war, acting as an introduction to the Petro rituals. The Petro Lwa tend to have very descriptive names that reflect their force, violence, and strength. For instance, there's Linglessou Basin Sang, which means "Linglessou Bucket of Blood," and Ezili Je Wouj, which means "Red Eyed Ezili).

Both the Rada and Petro Lwa are good aspects of what it means to be Haitian.

The Petro rituals are full of bright colors. You'll find loads of red scarves, fire, machetes waving wildly, and very angry, loud Lwa. At first, non-Vodouists assume this is all about evil spirits, especially when compared to the Rada rituals. It also doesn't help that some hot Petro spirits are nicknamed *djab*, which means devil. However, there's nothing sinister going on. Those who demonize these Lwa don't realize that there is a balance between peace and violence in Voodoo. Both the Rada and Petro Lwa are good aspects of what it means to be Haitian. On the one hand, the people had a life worth holding on to and being celebrated, while on the other hand, they had to have strength, resilience, passion, and the guts to keep that world intact. While you'll find that the Petro Lwa originates from Africa, the rites are very Haitian.

Ezili Dantor

She happens to be the black sister of Ezili Freda. She works hard and doesn't care to be accountable to anyone. She's had more than her fair share of tears and is sick of it, so now she is filled with the energy of rage, which she uses to drive herself to take the initiative. She is revered for being the spirit that spurred the Haitian Revolution. She fought with the men during the revolution and was in a relationship with Ogoun at the time. At the end of the revolution, Ogoun cut out her tongue. He did this because he didn't want her to reveal pertinent secrets to anyone. Apart from Ogoun, she has Simbi Makaya and Ti Jen petro for consorts. It is said that the only reason she has sex with the male Lwa is that she wants to have children. In truth, she'd rather have sex with women.

Ezili Dantor's entire world is Anaïs, her daughter. Some argue that this is her only child, but others say she has other children, including Jan Dantor, a son. Some say she's got exactly seven children, so they put seven dolls on her altar to honor her and her children. Ezili Dantor looks after women, focusing on mothers raising children all by themselves. You can reach out to her if you need help with child support. You could tell her you need to become financially independent or you need her to help break free from an abusive relationship.

Ezili Dantor punishes people or shows displeasure by inflicting stabbing and shooting pains on her target. Anyone who hurts a devotee of hers will begin to throw up blood without warning. She is also good at getting rapists to tie a noose around their necks and hang themselves. She takes part in mystical marriages with her devotees of all sexes. This Lwa is syncretized to Czestochowa's Black Madonna. You can venerate her along with Anaïs, her daughter, who clearly understands her mother's communication style and is articulate. She is also called Sili Danto or Eziili Danto. She loves working women, single mothers, female soldiers, children, devotees, all stroke victims, and lesbians.

Ezili Dantor shows up as a dark-skinned woman with a sturdy build. Sometimes she has scars on her face. Other times, she may be unable to say anything because of her missing tongue. In one hand, she holds a knife, and in the other, a child. She is sometimes represented with the Queen of Spades playing card, the Queen of Swords from tarot, and the La Madama statues. Her emblem is a bowl of blood, and her preferred animal is the Haitian black pig. You may get her Florida Water or Rève-d'Or so you can use it on her altar to connect with her. Her preferred days are Saturday and Tuesday, and she favors the colors blue and red. Ezili Dantor's favorite plants include the *Eugenia crenulata*, also known in Haiti as zo-devan, and the red hibiscus. Offer her honey with cayenne pepper and cinnamon, muffins, corn and pepper omelet, corn products, sword-pierced milagro of hearts, pineapples, daggers, knives, cigarettes, homebrew, Barbancourt rum, corn with gunpowder, pepper jelly, born bread, and fried pork.

Don Petro

He was the one who founded the Petro Vodou culture. Named Jean-Philippe Pedro, he was in charge of the Maroons. Maroon is from the word Cimarron, which means "wild one." This name was what the enslaved people who escaped were called. The Maroons were able to come together to create entire communities in the most remote locations possible. In these places, they could galvanize themselves into creating a movement that would challenge the colonial enslavers.

The Haitians created the Petro tradition in the year 1768. The ceremonies would occasionally get very violent, and this was what led to their infamy with the colonials, who were terrified. The Petro spirits and their devotees are driven by defiance. They refuse to be treated with condescension. They never let themselves kowtow to the patronizing nonsense of the colonialists, and they took no orders.

When Don Petro passed, he returned as a Lwa in the Petro tradition. He is considered a true ancestor of the practice and therefore is revered as such. He is well known for fighting against oppression on behalf of those who followed in his footsteps. According to the lore, he and Ezili Dantor are the Petro pantheon's father and mother. While this could be interpreted literally, it also implies that they are in charge of the spiritual tradition of the Petro. They are the answer to Loko and Ayizan of the Rada lwa.

Bossu

Some say that Bossu came from an ancient bull spirit responsible for keeping the King of Dahomey safe. Others say he has European roots, being from the bull spirits with three horns that were once common in France, specifically in pagan Gaul. The bulls represented good luck, invincibility, virility, power, victory, and fertility in this place.

Bossu represents male vigor in its most primal form. He represents masculine energy and is reminiscent of the Biblical bull named Ba'al. He is rather volatile, which is to be expected considering how much testosterone rages through him. This Lwa is considered one of the most aggressive, being more volatile than most. He also is the patron of those who want to practice evil sorcery. Devotees will invoke him when they would like to control Baka.

Bossu isn't all that bad. You can ask him to help you eliminate tough issues or stumbling blocks along your path. Both men and women reach out to him to ask for help with fertility. When men struggle with erectile dysfunction or need to have more potency, he's the one they petition. He can bless your psychic ability and keeps all his devotees safe, especially when traveling at night. He is also known as Bosou Twa Cornes and Bosou. You may decorate your altar with horns to honor him. His favorite day is Tuesday. His best colors are red and black, and for offerings, you can offer him rum, overproof rum, whiskey, or cocktails with Red Bull in them. If you want, you can offer him steak or fried beef. It helps to add some hot sauce to the food you serve him, and Tabasco is a good option since it's red.

Simbi Makaya

Simbi is also called Simbie and is the best magician ever. He is a water snake spirit in charge of magic in all its forms. He offers his protection to those who practice magic, and he teaches them as well. The lore goes that children who go missing aren't actually missing but have been borrowed by this Lwa, only to be returned to the home years after, being experts at magic like Simbi is.

Simbi can offer you magical abilities, as well as help you with clairvoyance. He is also an excellent healer and has a green thumb. One of the things he does for those in the line of healing work is to help them correctly diagnose conditions. When you want Simbi to speak with you, imagine you've got a snake wrapping itself around your body, sidling up to your ear, and whispering.

Simbi belongs to Ogou's army, being the Coast Guard. He is connected to Rada and Petro practices but is actually from the Congo. This Lwa has been assimilated into the Petro. Simbi goes wherever he wants to and can make any place home. He has patience in spades, and he can also be pretty insistent. Devotees of Simbi tend to be very interested in esoteric affairs. Also, he tends to be invoked a fair bit by secret societies. Simbi is a freshwater spirit. He rules over fountains, waterfalls, springs, wells, ponds, marshes, and even regular drinking water. He can control the flow and current of the river, as well as all other things that flow as water does, like words, tears, and carousel electricity.

Serving as the conductor of souls, this Lwa controls how spirits flow into devotees during possessions. Simbi is also in charge of the waters that keep the worlds of the living and the dead apart. Sometimes, he works as a psychopomp, leading souls where they should go, especially when those souls belong to dead occultists and shamans. He also rules over currents, crossroads, and communication, meaning he can control how energy and information are exchanged. So you can think of him as the patron of technology like the phone and the computer, allowing instant transmission. This Lwa acts as a "way opener" by helping you eliminate the obstacles keeping you from your path. He can twist and turn and find a way around all kinds of red tape and turn a stalemate into a checkmate on your behalf. You only need to ask for his help, and he's willing to offer it to you. He's also there to help when communicating is vital or problematic.

You can put a picture of a snake as wallpaper on your computer, which will keep your system safe and give it more power. Simbi is also excellent in healing, so he can offer you all he knows about medicinal herbs that apply to your situation. He knows about all diseases, whether physical, spiritual, or magical, and he can heal them. It doesn't matter if the illness resulted from demons, curses, or anything else.

Simbi is syncretized to Moses, who also showed the Egyptians a few magic tricks of his own. This Lwa favors diviners, astrologers, herbalists, occultists, and healers. His children or devotees tend to show amazing precocious occult skills and interest. They could have a caul, or they may have a head with lots of curls. The Haitians refer to locked hair as "Simbi's hair," and it's the answer to Medusa's head of snakes. Simbi is often a snake, but he is an amazing shapeshifter and magician who can surprise you anytime. He shows up as a small or medium-sized slim snake, unlike Damballah, who is huge. Simbi dwells in the water, and at other times, he likes to hang out in trees. His best metal is quicksilver (mercury), and he prefers quartz crystal.

Simbi's preferred colors are gray, white, and green, but on account of how great he is at transformation, it's best to remember that he's also open to other colors. He loves mango, elm, and calabash trees. He also loves turtles and snakes. His favorite days include every weekday (besides Wednesday) and Saturday. You can decorate his altar with divination tools, magical tools, as well as images of snakes. Being a water snake, he needs to remain moist. So you can offer him water or milk. He's partial to pond water, rainwater, or spring water. He's also okay with rum and whiskey. Sometimes, he'll want more than one beverage simultaneously.

It's important to note that not all Simbi spirits are alike regarding offerings and requirements. You'll have to experiment to determine what your Simbi wants from you. Many of them enjoy alcohol, particularly the sort that looks like water. So you could try gin, white rum, aguardiente, cachaca, Mahia, and vodka. Try giving him some Liqueur Saint-Raphael, an aperitif with quinine in it.

This Lwa is the master of many details, so he can get rather fussy. Remember that snakes don't do well with cold, so he may prefer that the drinks you serve him remain at room temperature. It's not hard to tell when he's upset with you because whatever piece of tech he's taking care of for you'll begin to act up. Other than drinks, Simbi loves shed snakeskins, ribbons, rover rocks, quartz crystals, yams, and mangoes.

Gran Bois

The Father of the Forest, Gran Bois, is a healer in charge of the forest's power and knows every secret of every plant. This Lwa has existed since the dawn of time and has great power. Some say he's from Congo, while others say he was a Taino spirit. Gran Bois is in charge of the petro and Kongo nanchons and is the initiation patron. Along with Maître Carre-four and Baron Cimitière, he makes up a trinity of magicians who are exceptional at their craft.

Gran Bois is the representation of the Tree of Life that acts as a link between the worlds of the dead and the living and the celestial worlds. He is in charge of the forest and a mystical island beneath the sea, known as Ginen. Ginen is where both ancestors and Lwa reside, and it is the world of the dead. Naturally, he would rule over this place since he has all occult knowledge about life and death. This Lwa is syncretized to Saint Sebastian, who is usually shown as bound to a tree.

Gran Bois is considered a tree man of sorts. Rather than feet, he has roots. Usually, Gran Bois is mute, and this is because this Lwa existed from the dawn of time, way before language was a thing. He takes care of all the animals in the forests, but he also has certain creatures near and dear to him — specifically red snakes and monkeys, which happen to live in the trees. His colors are red, green, and brown. His special tree is the Mapou, either the Ceiba pentandra or the Bombax ceiba.

The Mapou is a silk cotton tree used in most Voodoo rituals, and the Taino believed it was incredibly sacred. The Taino were the people who existed in present-day Haiti way before the slavers came around to destroy things. The Roman Catholic Church almost eradicated the tree in a campaign against what they deemed "superstition" in the 40s. They did their best to get rid of everything sacred to Voodoo. When making offerings to Gran Bois, it's best to let them hang from a tree branch. You can also set his offerings at the foot of a tree. Offer him cornmeal with honey drizzled over it, leaves, flowers, roots, fallen branches, and cassava bread. You can also plant more trees in Haiti or preserve the forests.

Marassa Petro

The Marassa are three in the Petro nanchon. Depending on the lineage, the Marassa is depicted as the Three Graces. These Lwa are sometimes known as the Three Ladies of Egypt.

The Marassa are usually greeted after Legba. The best days to work with them are Thursday and Saturday. The Marassa are among the more mysterious Lwas, and parents with twins are known as manman and papa marassa. The child that comes right after the twins is known as dossou marassa. The Marassa are the epitome of the sacred, the mysterious, and all blessings one can be bestowed with. These Lwa are children blessed with healing abilities, knowledge, wisdom, and incredible power. They are divine twins who know ancient mysteries.

The Marassa are rooted in Yoruba culture, where the first of the twins is known as Taiwo, which means "Go out and explore the world," and the second is known as Kehinde, meaning "The second will come after the first." It is believed that the second twin is the first. This twin sends Taiwo out to see what the world is like before coming. Taiwo is the more adventurous, exploring twin, while Kehinde is more careful and practical. When the Marassa possesses their devotees, you can expect playing, crying, and acting like there's nothing wrong going on, much like kids do.

Petro Marassa tends to be much more difficult to impress than their Rada counterparts. You can offer the Rada Marassa candles, sweets, and toys. When it comes to the Petro Marassa, you've got to give them meat. Not just any meat, but the meat from black pigs. Their colors are green and red in Petro, as opposed to white and yellow in Rada.

Simbi-Dlo

Simbi-Dlo is the title of an entire Lwa family. Simbi-Dlo is the first one of the Petro Lwa. At first, this Lwa comes off as peaceful, acting as the quietest of all the Petro Lwa. However, that's not the case. This Lwa is a Kongo spirit that loves to show up as a snake and can be found in freshwater streams in little pools. He's responsible for taking children who aren't careful and even adults to the grave before their time. If he thinks they're worthy, he'll take them somewhere they can learn specific forms of magic. This Lwa is a magician of note himself, and those possessed by him will wet themselves with water, slither on the floor, and other times spring into the air, catching people around unaware. Sometimes, one possessed by Simbi can climb trees with ease or suddenly leap from the floor to the rafters of the sacred room in the middle of a snake-like dance. Some people represent Simbi-Dlo with John the Baptist as a kid in the middle of baptizing Christ, while others will use a picture of Moses as he raised a snake. Others still use the Three Wise Men to honor all three Simbi Lwa (Dlo, Andezo, and Makaya).

Ti-Jean

Some hold that Ti-Jean is Mami Danto's husband, while others say he's her son. One thing remains certain: Ti-Jean is powerful and often called open for his magic, healing, and exorcism abilities. When he possesses his devotees, it's nothing short of a show. You can expect to see extraordinary dances and amazing displays with burning coals and fire. If anyone were skeptical of Voodoo rituals, all they'd have to do is witness Ti-Jean in the process of possessing a devotee for them to become believers. You could see the possessed devotee snacking on flaming logs like it's nothing, setting fire to their hair, and more. In one instance, it's reported that Ti-Jean filled his mouth with gasoline and set it alight as he blew fire all over someone's injured knee. This fire didn't hurt the person with the injury. After this, the Ti-Jean drank the gasoline from its container like water. Some assumed that was a stunt. One person was bold enough to ask for a sip from the bottle. He was rewarded with a night of vomiting outside the peristil (temple) where the rites were held. This Lwa is a very loud and boisterous one. When he shows up, you can expect thunderous singing and shouting as he waves kleren-soaked machetes, flares, and logs alight with fire. The thing about him, though, is that his love is fierce, and he makes sure his children are cared for. He is syncretized with John the Baptist as a child holding on to a white lamb.

Chapter 5: Meet the Lwa III: the Gede

It is inevitable that sooner or later, we will all meet our maker. We're all connected with death, even in life, in one way or another. This connection could be in the form of our ancestors, dead relatives, loved ones, etc. Eventually, we will also have to pass on. Death is natural, and it is only a doorway to more life. The Lwa recognize that there's a natural order from life to death, which is why there's a nanchon reserved only for those long-forgotten and yet unknown spirits, The Gede Lwa.

These Lwa can reveal the future, heal, offer their advice, and keep people safe.
Nationaal Museum van Wereldculturen, CC BY-SA 3.0 <https://creativecommons.org/licenses/by-sa/3.0>, via Wikimedia Commons:
https://commons.wikimedia.org/wiki/File:Collectie_Nationaal_Museum_van_Wereldculturen_AM-670-15_Madame_Lionne_Haiti.jpg

In Haiti, when someone dies, they will have a funeral, and their family will remember them. However, if that person happens to be a Vodouisant, they will have two occasions on which they will be honored. The first one is the Dessounin, which takes place shortly after the person's death, and the other is the Kase-Kanari, also known as the breaking of the pots ritual. This ritual is meant to help take the deceased's spirit out from beneath the water, or *anba dlo*. There, their soul will remain with Met Agwe for up to a year and a day. After this, the Kase-Kanari will take the soul to Ginen to be with the other ancestors.

Sometimes, a soul will go under the water only to remain unclaimed forever. Remaining unclaimed is what happened when the deceased wasn't a Vodouist, died a while back or alone, or their offspring refused to honor them traditionally. Rather than being left in the world between worlds, two Lwa take all the souls and give them a role to perform as the Gede Lwa. The Gede continue to grow as they are made up of all the dead, forgotten souls. Baron Samedi and manman Brijit (his wife) are the parents of these Lwa.

The Gede Lwa are closer to humans than the others, being very invested in our affairs since they remember what it was like to be human and miss that sometimes. They realize how important it is to live a happy life, which is why they show up as often as possible in our world. Some erroneously assume that being the Lwa of the dead makes them terrible and scary, but that's not the case. They also represent death in other ways, such as the end of a terrible situation. They represent the transformation that happens when death gives way to life. These Lwa can reveal the future, heal, offer their advice, and keep people safe.

The Gede nanchon is the only one anyone can serve, no matter how much or little they know about Haitian Vodou. You don't need Legba's permission to speak with them. These Lwa are naturally intertwined with life, making it possible for one and all to reach out to them. They're amusing too, as when they show up in the peristil, they crack jokes, steal money and food, pretend to have sex with each other and those present, and so on. However, they are very good at offering comfort and advice when needed. The Gede are often sent for at the end of a ritual, assuming they haven't just shown up uninvited, only to be sent away often. They love to gatecrash occasions, trying to take over at the end of other possessions and sing bawdy tunes. All of November is reserved for honoring these Lwa.

Every Vodouist's home has Gede, and they are invited to come to the peristil before an initiation cycle starts. This invitation is to appease them and keep them from disrupting the rest of the day's affairs, especially as these rituals are where the presence of the Gede is neither needed nor permitted. They will often be asked to stay away as politely as possible. Those who aren't Haitian are fascinated by the Gede Lwa because they're relatable since we all know death intimately. For others, they're gripped by the spiders, coffins, skulls, and purple and black combinations, which are often connected to Halloween. Other interesting things about the Gede include their very sexual way of life. They love to use vulgar words and speak with sexual innuendo. They also dance the banda, a dance that is almost like two people making love. In addition to this, they always carry a baton-shaped like a phallus.

The Gede love the attention they get. Sexual energy aside, they are harmless. The filthy words they use are only used humorously and drily. It's not like they go around making people feel bad or cursing others. They also don't have sex since they can't anymore. They only mimic it to show the connection between life and death and for laughs. They are a reminder not to care what anyone thinks and to express oneself fully. Let's take a look at some of the Gede Lwa.

Baron-yo

These are the Barons. The title of Baron or Bawon is an honorific one that is given to the more powerful Gede Lwa. It is also specifically given to Baron Samedi and Baron Simitye. Some lineages are the same, while others hold that they are different Lwa. They are the ones who lead and judge the dead — the dead in question being lost, forgotten souls, and not the ancestors who have moved on to Ginen and are blessed.

The Baron shows up in a top hat and a fine black suit. He wears dark shades to keep himself safe from light that's too bright. Sometimes one lens will be broken, representing how the Baron can see into both realms. His food tends to be spicy, more than regular humans can bear, and he smokes strong cigarettes with no filters. He loves to indulge in drinking piman. Purple and black are the colors used to represent him. Some parts of Haiti have him syncretized with Saint Gerard Majella, Saint Expedite, or Archangel Gabriel. Every image used to represent him will have crosses and skulls. The Gede Lwa represents death, but the Baron is the epitome of control and judgment over all things death-related. While he may not be directly responsible for one's death, he can order one to live or die by either issuing a command to "dig his grave" or withholding anyone from doing so. Sometimes the Baron can speak, while at other times, he lies on the floor and only speaks after his jaw has been firmly closed using cotton gauze to mimic the practice that people once used in dealing with corpses before the present embalming techniques became common.

Manman Brijit

She is the Baron's wife and is sometimes called Manman, an honorific bestowed on respectable and very older women. Some say this Lwa may be the same as Brighid, the Irish Saint, also a Celtic deity, but there's no proof that this is true. There are, however, some lineages that have a song about Manman Brijit being from England. In any case, this Lwa doesn't resemble the so-called Irish counterpart, either in looks or function. Brijit makes her home in the biggest tree in the cemetery or the largest cross. These places are also where you can find Baron if you want to serve him. She's not usually present during possessions or rituals since she's only one of very few female Gede Lwa. Some lineages see her as her person rather than honoring her along with the Baron. When this is the case, she is shown with Saint Rosalia saying prayers to a skull in a cave. She could also be shown as Saint Helena with her large cross.

Brav Gede Nibo

This Lwa is also called Brav Gede or Gede Nibo. He is known as Baron's axe-man, meaning he executes the commands given to him by the Baron. You could think of him as the Baron's consigliere if the latter were a Mafia don. Brav Gede is responsible for ensuring that the Gede army does what it should and that their affairs run smoothly. He is often depicted with Saint Gerard Majella, like most other Gede Lwa.

Gede Plumaj

This Gede Lwa has a fascinating name. Plumaj means "feathers" (think of plumage). In some lineages, he has a mask in the style of a Mardi Gras masquerade with feathers. He can wear this mask if he wants to, but he lets it sit near his altar more often than not. This Gede is like the others in that he engages in vulgar talk and does the banda, but he's unique in that he's very patient and good at teaching and divining the future.

Gede Linto

This Lwa is a 5-foot-tall miracle worker with dark skin. You'll find him wearing glasses, holding a cane with an old black hat perched on his head. He has great manners, and his disposition is so peaceful that some assume he's just a boy. One of the things he enjoys doing is teaching his devotees songs. He will offer gifts like rum, cigarettes, fire, and Florida Water. His peculiar practice is to cut some thread for each Vodouisant and put them in a mix to form needles. There are times when he will offer gold rings and chains as gifts.

Gede Linto has a soft spot for children, being very invested in their safety and well-being. He represents all the children who have been lost and neglected, including stillbirths, miscarriages, and abortions. He is also interested in caring for the ones who were abused so badly that they died. He is the youngest of the Gede Lwa, so when he possesses his devotees, he makes them act like children. Sometimes, that means he'll have them walking like babies who are only just learning to balance. He may also make the devotees cry just like babies cry for food. He's good at spotting trouble a good six months away and can show you what to do to make it through the situation or stop it from happening. When you choose to work with him or vice versa, you can expect that the solutions he offers are rapid and exactly what you need.

Baron Kriminel

This Lea is the Baron of criminals. He was the very first murderer, and his victim was Nobo. Therefore, this Baron is in charge of people who hurt others with violence – and especially murderers. Families of those who have been murdered will reach out to Baron Kriminel so he can affect revenge. When he possesses his devotees, they display a ridiculous appetite and antagonize everyone unless and until they're offered some food to eat. If the food doesn't meet their standards or it doesn't arrive on time, they'll merrily bite people close to them or their devotees until they're satisfied. This Lwa is syncretized with Saint Martin de Porres. To honor him, you should sacrifice black roosters to him on the day of the Gede feast. It is known that these roosters must be bound, soaked in very strong spirit, and then set ablaze.

Papa Gede

Papa Gede is the very first person who died. This dark and short Lwa always wears a high hat on his head. His one vice is smoking cheap cigars, and he also loves apples. He's the one who waits patiently at the crossroads to take the souls of the newly dead to the afterlife. He works with Baron Samedi.

When a child is about to die, Papa Gede is the one all Vodouists pray to. He is also known as Baron La Croix or Bawon Lakwa, which means "Baron of the Cross." He oversees the Gede rites. You can trust him to assist you with any legal issues you have or call on him when you want to see justice done. You can represent him with a cross or a coffin. His colors are purple, black, and white.

Gede Nibo

This Lwa is a psychopomp, acting as a channel between the living and the dead. He was the first person to die from violence, so he is the patron of all the souls who passed on due to violence, disasters, and accidents. He stands guard over the graves of those who passed on before they should have, especially those souls who passed on without anyone knowing exactly where their bodies are. He can possess people and make them speak for those who have passed on and are still unredeemed from under the waters.

Other Lwa

Since the Gede are made up of the forgotten dead, many of them exist. Most of them have very vulgar names. Some are familiar to certain families, but not others. For instance, there are some female Gede, such as Gedelia. Some are children, like Ti-Mazaka. There's a spider Gede named Gede Zaranyen who will send swarms of spiders as emissaries. Then, there's Gede Hounsou, a medical doctor. He offers his medical solutions in English rather than the traditional French or Kreyol, and he does so with a British accent. Gede Nouvavou will dress up like a Mexican bandit or a native of South America, with blankets and a hat. Then there is Gede Vagabond, a beggar with quite a mouth. Every Voodoo lineage has its own Gede, either a favorite or one who shows up a lot. Also, every Vodouisant has their own Gede Lwa, plus another one belonging to the entire home or family. The Gede could be from any background or country.

Gede Babaco is Papa Gede's brother. He is also a psychopomp who does the same thing Papa Gede does, connecting the living and the dead. However, he doesn't have the same power as his brother does. Gede Double is a Lwa known for offering his devotees the gift of second sight. Gede L'Orage is only ever seen when a storm is in progress. Some call him Gede L'Oraj. Gede Massaka is a helper to Gede Nibo. An androgynous Lwa, he's easy to spot because he wears a black shirt, white jacket, and white scarf, along with a poisonous gris-gris bag. Gede Ti malice is a trickster Lwa, smart yet guileful. He's a hard worker who is as greedy as he is hard-working. So it's not the easiest thing in the world to come to a fair agreement with him if you choose to work with him. Then you've got Gede Oussou, who favors dressing in a mauve jacket with a white cross embroidered at the back and a mauve headscarf. Sometimes he wears that outfit in black. The word *oussou* means "tipsy," and this is a fitting name for him because he just can't put down the white rum!

The Dangerous Ones

There are other Lwa that no one talks about in the open. You may have heard tales of them, like a magician sending one to hurt someone. The reason they're not talked about is that they're dangerous. The most experienced Vodouists will opt not to work with these beings because they know they'd be playing with fire. They're not dangerous in a cutesy way but in life-threatening ways. Mostly, these Lwa will ignore people who try to reach out to them (a good thing). However, bad things could happen if one were to be unfortunate enough to grab their attention. It's natural for them to hurt unfamiliar people who disturb their peace. It would be rather irresponsible to name these Lwas, which this book won't cover. The Vodouists who reach other to these Lwa will only do so under certain strict conditions and won't try that without the appropriate precautions and protective measures. This need for caution should be enough for you to see why these Lwa are best left alone. However, if you ever have any reason to connect with one of them, you can get an introduction. You'll also get all you need to connect with them safely, but you'd better follow all the instructions you receive in the letter. Connecting with dangerous Lwa is definitely outside the scope of this book, but let's cover the matter of connecting with the Lwa mentioned so far by going over what an altar is and how you can set one up yourself.

Chapter 6: Your Voodoo Shrine or Altar

What is the importance of keeping a Voodoo altar or shrine in one's house? Voodoo altars help balance one's home spiritually by providing a place for worship and reverence of the divine Lwa. In addition, these altars remind us that our ancestors continue to watch over us and can help us in times of distress. Altars are spaces for the living and the dead to interact with each other and for the divine and the profane to interact.

Altars are made up of several colors and elements representing different aspects of life and morality.

A Voodoo altar or shrine provides a place for people to show their religious piety and worship the Lwa. They are often placed in the living room, where everyone in the household can use them. They are often made up of several colors and elements representing different aspects of life and morality. The altars' appearance is symbolic because it is supposed to reflect how much respect one has for the honored spirits.

Having an altar at home is good because you can use it to develop a deeper, stronger connection with the Lwa and to serve them properly and regularly. At your altar, you can make offerings to the Lwa easily, speak with them about anything you like, ask them for their help and favor, and more. The question is, how do you set up your altar? No matter how you go about it, you should know that it doesn't have to be overly complicated or have intricate designs. You also don't need to clutter it with too many items. Think of your shrine or altar as a personal space that reflects your Lwa and you and the connection you share with them.

Before Setting Up Your Altar

Before you prep your altar at home, it's a good idea to get in touch with a Mambo or Houngan to help you learn which Lwa you're supposed to work with. The thing about Voodoo is that you don't get to choose which spirits you want as though you were picking a meal from a menu. The spirits are the ones who do the choosing. So you must be in service of the Lwa who are interested in working with you and want your service. So it would be best if you got in touch with a Mambo or Houngan who can give you the reading you need.

Another reason you should get the Mambo or Houngan to help you with your altar is that you can ask them any questions about the proper rites needed for honoring your Lwa. You need to know about the Lwa's correspondences and the requirements that they have of you. For instance, you could be in the service of Ezili Danto, and she may want you to have a specific knife to work with you. You may have Damballah as your Lwa, and he may want you to put some sugar on a plate and top it off with a raw egg to cause your life to be sweeter. These are things you can only learn from reading. The thing to note about Lwa correspondences is that they differ from one house to another, which is why you should ensure that you're only getting your information from a trusted source that you feel is dependable. This way, you don't feel confused about whether you're doing it right. In an ideal situation, you should be accepted by the house first and receive guidance from spiritual parents who can let you know about the Lwa attached to that house.

When choosing the space to put your home altar, you must remember that it must be baptized. Ideally, the Mambo or Houngan will help you with this. The reason the baptism is necessary is to help with attracting your Lwa to you. If you can't get a priest to help you with this, you could do the baptism yourself. Here's how:

1. First, clean the table you're using for the altar. Make sure you get rid of all grime and dust on it.

2. Mix Basil, Holy Water, and Florida Water in a clean bowl.

3. Dip a clean cloth into that mixture, and use it to wipe the surface of your altar. As you do this, you should declare aloud that you're cleansing the altar in the name of the Father, the Son, and the Holy Spirit. Declare that the only spirits allowed to gather at your altar are the ones who only want what's best for you and that any that seek to harm you'll find they cannot make their home at your altar.

4. Let the table air dry, and you can begin setting up your altar when it's done.

Setting Up Your Altar

1. When you have finished cleansing your table, cover it with a white cloth. You want the cloth to hang on the ground. If you put Gede under the table, it should hang halfway to the ground.

2. You're going to devote half of your altar to the Rada and the other half to the Petro Lwa. So, for the Rada, cover the right side of the altar with a good quality white cloth. In honor of the Petro, cover the left with an intensely red cloth.

3. Next, set a glass of clean, cool water slightly off-center on the altar, favoring the Rada side. Some Vodouists will add some drops of Florida Water to the water, while others add fresh basil instead. Before you set the glass on the altar, you should offer it to the four cardinal points by raising the glass to the East, West, North, and South.

4. Now, it's time to place the pictures representing the Lwa you'll serve on the wall behind your altar. The pictures (or chromoliths) will depend on what Lwa the Mambo or Houngan told you to serve during your reading.

5. Every Lwa has its unique items. For instance, if you're working with Ezili Freda, You will need: to ensure that she has perfume. This perfume could be Anais Anais, or Chanel no. 5. She also likes to have a mirror and chocolate. For Damballah, you'll want to have Pompeii lotion. When working with Marassas, you'll want to have toys. Make sure that they're in sets of two. All Rada Lwa will require Florida Water, Ti Jean Dantor loves a pack of cigarettes, and Ezili Danto is a fan of Magie Noir perfume. Damballah will need white flour on a white plate topped with a white egg.

6. Next, place the favorite drinks of your Lwa.

7. Next, you should place candles on the altar, ensuring that the candle colors match the Lwa you're serving correspondingly. It would be best if you also had a large white candle in the middle for Met Tet. Met Tet means "master of the head," basically the spirit that rules your life.

Normally, all spiritual activities are carried out in an ounfo, but that shouldn't stop you from having your home altar. The great thing about creating your altar is that you have no reason to spend your life's savings trying to do this. The only important thing in serving the Lwa is that you're sincere and truly want a connection with them. So, if you want to, you can work with items you find all around your home. Many new to Voodoo don't realize they already have the things they need to make their altar work.

One thing to note about your altar is that you should treat it respectfully because it is living and breathing. It has energy and life. It would be best if you kept it fed by showing up daily to serve the Lwa and ensure its energy remains active. The altar is your conduit to the divine, so you should keep it sacred and cleansed before, during, and after use.

Alternative Altar Setup

Here's another way you can set up your altar:

1. Cover your altar with white cotton or satin cloth.

2. Place the picture of the Lwa you want to work with behind the altar. You can set up just one picture or several.

3. In front of the picture, place a standing crucifix. Alternatively, you can hang one above the picture of the Lwa.

4. Set a white candle on one side of the altar to represent the Rada.

5. Set a red candle on the other side to represent the Petro.

6. Place Holy Water, Florida Water, or Rève d'Or, Pompeii, frankincense, and flowers on your altar.

7. Place a bowl of clean water on the altar.

8. Put a bell on the rattle as well. You'll ring it when you want to summon your Lwa.

9. Ritual items like taper candles, holy oils, and other tools should go beneath the altar.

10. Burn some frankincense in a censer to baptize the altar before use.

11. While the incense burns, you should say the Lord's prayer three times and the Hail Mary prayer seven times. It helps to master the words and meaning of the prayers beforehand.

12. Sprinkle Holy Water on your altar as you declare, *"I baptize you in the name of the Father, the Son, and the Holy Spirit. You are now consecrated for good Lwa only. Amen."*

Tips for Setting Up Your Altar

Regardless of where and how you set up your altar, here are some basic tips to help you:

1. Let your altar have items that are not just connected to your Lwa but also very inspirational to you. It helps to work with beautiful or intricately designed items when you can find them.

2. Place your altar in a room where you spend a lot of time. It is good to have the altar in sight at all times because it can be a great source of inspiration and motivation.

3. Use items from the plant kingdom to make your altar, as opposed to plastic or artificially manufactured materials that are not always respectful to Vodou. All the Lwa love nature, so it is natural to keep them surrounded by it. You can also use clay or painted pots for some of your offerings or as a place for things like candles or vases full of water.

4. Don't let your altar become disheveled. Every once in a while, do a cleansing ritual. Sweep the floor around your altar, and take care of things like dead flowers and candles that have burned almost completely down.

5. Have a special place on your altar to put down knives, scissors, or other sharp objects to show respect for the spirits.

A Voodoo altar is a sacred space in which one uses imagination to communicate with the spirits or deities one worships. The altar is considered a protective space for one's ancestors who watch over us. It is also an area of power that helps connect the practitioner's mind, body, and spirit. Thus Voodoo altars are meant to be treated with respect so that when working on them, you can experience what they represent, peace, power, and spirituality.

It's important to avoid eating, drinking, sex, and bad thoughts while working on the altar. If you have finished your work and are ready to clean up, you should also do so with respect. How you treat your altar says a lot about your character, so it's important to be aware of that. It's also not uncommon for Voodoo practitioners to ask for forgiveness from their ancestors for lack of respect before cleaning the altar.

An altar is set up with intention, and it's not just about a tool for helping yourself. Once an altar is set up for a specific purpose, it becomes a sacred space that helps meld together the practitioner's mind, body, and spirit. An altar can help us concentrate on achieving specific results or solving certain issues we've been facing. Depending on the practitioner's intentions, it can be used as an aid in meditation or trance work.

Frequently Asked Questions

Can I have multiple altars? The answer is yes. If you have room for multiple altars, you can have them. Some people have a general altar that the family can use in the living room, and their altar is set up somewhere private, like in the bedroom. You can also have an altar in a workshop or business. You can have altars for different purposes, something for healing work and something for help finding a mate, etc. Some Voduisants come from homes or lineages where it's okay to have the Rada, Petro, and Gede Lwa represented on the altar. Others will require separate altars for these Lwa.

What do I put on my altar? Almost anything you want. Some people like their altars very elaborate with things like handmade statues, candle holders, etc. Others prefer a minimalist look. The important thing is that the altar must have items representing the Lwa you're serving on it.

Can I create one altar for a Lwa and an ancestor together? This question is one of the most common ones that people ask. Yes, you can, but it depends on the Lwa. Some Lwa don't like being associated with your ancestors, and others won't mind. To figure it out, you need to get a reading from a trustworthy Mambo or Houngan to know the right Lwa to serve and how their connection is with your ancestors.

Can I dedicate an altar to two Lwa? It depends. Have you received information from a Mambo or a Lwa that it's okay for you to do this? If you have, you may go ahead. Also, think about the lore behind the Lwa you want to work together. For instance, it makes sense to have Manman Brijit and Baron Samedi on the same altar since they're happily married. If unsure, you should check in with a priest to determine if it's a good idea.

How often should I spiritually cleanse my Voodoo altar? The choice is up to you. Some people do it once a day, others once a week, and some only once a year. The important thing is knowing that your altar is clean before any spiritual work starts. Sometimes you may get the inclination to clean your altar when you normally wouldn't. Trust your intuition and perform the cleanse anyway.

If someone visits my home and uses my Voodoo altar while here, should I cleanse it afterward? Yes, you should. Your altar is yours. When someone uses it, you can't be certain what their intentions and energies are. Ideally, no one should use your altar without your permission, but even if they do get your permission, cleansing it before you begin your prayers and rites is always a good idea. It also demonstrates to the Lwa that you have nothing but the utmost respect for them. If you don't want to go through the trouble of cleaning it because someone else used it, let them know as they come into your home not to go near your altar.

Chapter 7: Gris-Gris and Voodoo Dolls

Gris-gris bags and voodoo dolls are some of the most popular Voodoo charms. This chapter will dive into each of them, how you can create them, and what you can use them for.

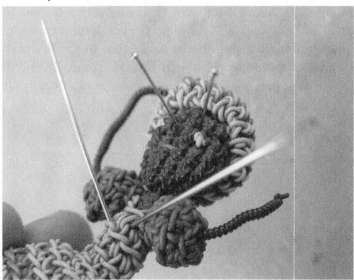

You can use voodoo dolls for healing, boosting wealth and fertility, or hexing and blessing.
*https://www.flickr.com/photos/eliogarcia/ (nick in flickr:creo que soy yo), CC BY 2.0
<https://creativecommons.org/licenses/by/2.0>, via Wikimedia Commons:
https://commons.wikimedia.org/wiki/File:Vudu.jpg*

What Are Gris Gris Bags?

Gris-gris bags are so misunderstood. Hop on the internet, and you'll find many "gris-gris bags" being sold that are anything but, as they haven't been made the way they're supposed to be. Buy one of those, and the odds are you'll get a hastily put-together mojo bag, which is a different bag of tricks altogether. Another thing about gris-gris is that it's often mispronounced. The S in *gris-gris* is silent, and it's pronounced *gree-gree*.

The term gris-gris is used to describe the religious and magical system of Voodoo that was and is still being practiced in New Orleans Voodoo. According to the New Orleans Voodoo Museum, the word is etymologically rooted in the Mande language groups, which are spoken close to the northern part of Benin, present-day Mali, and Senegal. Thanks to the transatlantic slave trade, devotees incorporated the word into the official lexicon of Louisiana Voodoo. Since it is pronounced and spelled like the French word that means "gray" and French-influenced New Orleans culture, it makes sense that many would think that gris-gris means "gray-gray." It also makes sense that one would interpret it this way since gray straddled black and white, and the gris-gris bags' ingredients have materials that Vodouists can use for black and white magic.

Gris-gris is a term that can work as a verb and a noun. Gris-gris is the practical magick of making the charm into a bag or pouch. The person who creates these bags is the gris-gris woman or man. In the end, what you get from the practitioner is a prayer, charm, or spell that you can carry around. Gris-gris is talismanic magic, and it works with the basic tenets of contagious and sympathetic magic. When it comes to sympathetic magic, the first thing that must happen is that an object has to be made in the likeness of the one the gris-gris is for, like a doll. As for contagious magic, the idea is to have something that belongs to the person the charm is for added to the charm itself. This item could be old gum, a strand of hair, fingernails, or something they've worn. It has to be a personal item of theirs, as it will connect them to the spiritual world, allowing the gris-gris to have some effect on their life.

When it comes to Louisiana tradition, you'll find a gris-gris bag for everything under the sun. You can make a gris-gris from any combination of herbs and household items you want, and you can use any words or statements that fit the situation you're using the gris-gris to address. The bag can have herbs, roots, powdered minerals, bones, sacred words, graveyard dust, seals, and more. You can use the gris-gris in powder form by throwing it in the path of the one you intend it for. You can use it as part of an amulet, in a bag, or on a doll. You can also mix the ingredients in some water to drink or take a bath with them. There was once a time when the bags also had poisons and dangerous powders. Regardless of how they are used, gris-gris bags are part of the religious and magical systems in New Orleans, steeped in African practices of the Senegambian enslaved people from the 1720s.

Brief History

Thirteen slave ships made their way to French Louisiana between 1726 and 1731. All of them were from Senegambia apart from one. The others were from Congo and Benin, along with Whydah, where the serpent practices of Louisiana Voodoo come from. Most of the major crops in 18th-century Louisiana included indigo, cotton, corn, rice, tobacco, and peas, and they were all from the Senegal valley. Most Bambara men know a lot about roots, herbs, and plants. That knowledge empowered them with the ability to make wangas, amulets, charms, and of course, poisons. All the plants that became part of Creole and Cajun recipes were well traded in Louisiana. They were part of the gris-gris magic.

Some Africans were Muslim, led by marabouts, and they thrived in Africa by making gris-gris and educating the children. Even now, you can find some people wearing gris-gris as an amulet prepped by the Senegalese marabout. Some wear them around their waists to boost fertility, and others wear them around their arms, necks, ankles, and heads, depending on what the gris-gris is meant to do. It is often housed in beautifully designed or plain leather pouches. The other ingredients are handwritten words from the Koran combined with specific numbers with powerful meanings. Before using a bag, it must be blessed with specific prayers and sanctified with holy water first. The marabout will speak certain words to achieve a specific result, charging the gris-gris with energy.

How to Make a Gris-Gris Bag

Gris-gris is a system of magic that all comes down to the intention of the maker and the purpose the magic is meant to serve. The gris-gris has always been used to help in all earthly affairs, acting as charms meant to empower us, whatever our intentions or goals we want to accomplish. So you're going to learn the basics about making a gris-gris bag, and you'll find that with the knowledge you're about to get, you can figure out how to make it work for you in any situation.

The gris-gris bag is usually a drawstring bag of about 2 inches by 3 inches. It's often made of red flannel, leather, or chamois. Among the things that can go in the bag are metal charms, bones, cowries, personal effects, carved stones, good luck tokens, crystals, coins, bones, plants, roots, and so on. You can also put sigils and seals penned with magical ink on special parchment paper. Equally important are the ink colors you use, as color can represent all kinds of meanings. Also, you're only to have an odd number of things in the gris-gris bag, and the items must always be at least three – or, at most, 13. The items aren't just thrown willy-nilly into the bag. They must be blessed and then dressed with holy water or anointing oil. You can then use some incense to smudge it, speak powerful chants, and then breathe three times on it. With this, you'll have activated the gris-gris and its magic.

The gris-gris is usually kept hidden from view regarding Louisiana Voodoo. There is a ritual meant to prepare it that must take place before an altar, and also, it's important to consecrate the gris-gris to the four classical elements of earth, fire, air, and water. Here are some guidelines to follow as you fix yourself a bag:

1. You must understand that the gris-gris is created based on the Kongo cosmogram's cardinal points or a certain Lwa.

2. The color you use matters, so you should only opt for colors that match the goal of your gris-gris.

3. The odd number rule of the gris-gris bag is important, so you must do your best to respect that.

4. The bag must be full of items that can spiritually and energetically lend themselves to your cause. In other words, you can't and shouldn't choose conflicting ingredients.

5. You have to dress the bag in some holy liquid.

6. You must be mindful of your words as you make the gris-gris because these words will empower and energize the gris-gris. Your words will have no choice but to be executed accordingly.

7. To activate the bag, you need to speak powerful words over the bag to energize it with divine energy.

8. Breathing on the gris-gris is like giving it life and permission to do what you've created it for.

How to Create Your Gris-Gris

You will need: your altar, which should have something representing each of the four elements. So, to represent the earth, you should have some dirt from a graveyard. To represent water, a bowl of water will do. You can use a candle flame and burning incense to represent fire and air. You should set these up according to the Kongo cosmogram. The cross pattern represents the crossroads. The veil splits the divine world from the earthly one at the center. This cosmology is circular, reflecting the continuous cycle of life and death and life once more. On the Kongo cosmogram, all four points are to be read counterclockwise, beginning from the south, moving on to the east, then the north, and finally the west. Here are the steps you need to take:

1. First, put some graveyard dirt at the southern tip, the start of birth, and where the ancestors dwell.

2. Now, place a candle at the eastern point to represent the transformation of a person as they grow and become a part of society.

3. Place your burning incense at the northern point to represent intellectual power.

4. Grab your bowl of water and put it at the western point. This point represents comprehension and departure.

5. Put your gris-gris right in the middle of the crossroads.

Making the Gris-Gris Charms

Now it's time to explore some examples of these charms. They're versatile, so you can use them for whatever you want. Since working with gris-gris bags is intuitive, it's a good idea to practice some of these and see how it works. Then, you can rely more and more on your intuition and what you know of minerals, herbs, and plants to craft your gris-gris. Remember, you don't have to limit your gris-gris to a bag. Some are potions or powders. You can craft them into dolls if you want. The gris-gris has to be made in the middle of the gris-gris altar, and you need to smudge the ingredients with incense. If you're going to make them into a bag, make sure to draw it shut with leather cording, hemp string, or some wax thread.

Gris-Gris Powder to Eliminate an Enemy

You will need the following:

- Blue glass (powdered)
- Dirt dauber nests
- Shed snake skin
- Cayenne pepper

Instructions:

1. To make this gris-gris, mix all the ingredients thoroughly.
2. Then, sprinkle the result wherever you know your target will have to pass.
3. If you can't get close to them, you can sprinkle the mix on a picture of your target.
4. Wrap the photo nicely in a package, and fold the paper away from you and not towards you.
5. You will need: some black thread to bind it properly.
6. Throw the package in the garbage, or even better, bury it in a graveyard.

Protection Gris-Gris

You will need the following:

- Camphor
- Piece of High John the Conqueror
- Dried toadstool top
- Hand-drawn talisman for protection
- Powdered jellyfish

Instructions:

1. Mix all the ingredients thoroughly.
2. Place all the ingredients into your red flannel bag, preferably with drawstrings.
3. Say a quick prayer of protection in your own words. If you don't want to use your own words, you can recite the 44th Psalm.
4. Place the bag on your palms, then close both hands.

5. Raise the gris-gris bag to your mouth and gently blow on it to activate it, so it begins to do what you want it to.

6. To recharge the energy of this gris-gris bag, you can soak it in some whiskey every Friday.

7. Hang this above your doorway, making it impossible for negative energy to enter your space.

8. If you like, you can let this bag hang on your neck from a cord, or you can keep it in your pocket. If you're a woman, keep the bag in your left pocket. The bag should be in the right pocket if you're a man.

Voodoo Dolls

Voodoo dolls and other puppets in magic are nothing new. You can use them for many purposes, from healing to boosting wealth and fertility to hexing and blessing. Voodoo dolls are gris-gris but in the form of a doll rather than a bag. Sometimes they represent a deity, acting as a house for the Lwa. Before making a Voodoo doll, you must sit for a moment and think about your intention. If you choose to do bad, remember that your actions will have consequences. Here's how to make a Voodoo doll that you can use for any purpose.

You will need the following:

- Two strong sticks
- Scrap fabric cut into strips of 2 inches, about 2 or 3 feet long (any color you want)
- String, waxed thread, or hemp cord
- Spanish moss
- Two buttons (for the eyes)
- Tacky glue
- Needle and thread in colors that match your fabric strips
- Seven pins of these colors: black, white, blue, yellow, green, red, and purple.

Instructions:

1. Take the two sticks and form a cross shape.
2. Use your string to tie the sticks together. Note that waxed thread or hemp cord are better options than string as they're more durable.

This construct is your doll's foundation.

3. Wrap the Spanish moss around both sticks. Begin from the middle, and work your way up to the head and around it. Move down an arm to the other, back to the center, and down to the bottom. If you can, you should work with long enough moss to help cover the sticks without breaking in the process. You want to wrap the doll up in one uninterrupted motion. It's fine if you can't do this because you broke apart the moss, but note that you may need a string to hold the broken moss in place so it doesn't fall apart. Make sure to wrap it tightly so you don't need string.

4. Wrap the strips of fabric around the moss. Expose some moss around the top (representing the hair), at the ends of both arms, and at the bottom.

5. Secure this with your tacky glue. It's okay to stitch this a bit with your needle and thread so it remains secure.

6. Now it's time for the face. Take a couple of beads and fix them to the doll with your needle and thread. Those are the eyes. Alternatively, you can glue two black-eyed peas on the doll's face.

7. Add a bead or a button to represent the mouth.

8. This step is optional, but you may want to dress your doll. You should follow your intuition on how best to dress the doll. You may work with some personal items that belong to the person the doll represents. It is best to tuck the items into the doll as you make it (rather than pin or glue it to the outside, where it can easily fall off).

9. Use some contrasting material or yarn to wrap it up wherever you prefer to accentuate it.

10. Stick all seven pins into the doll's chest. Now your doll is ready. You can charge it to do good or evil, and it will obey.

What the doll is to be used for comes down to how it was created and the material that makes it. For instance, fertility dolls have over-the-top genitals and big breasts. When you make a doll, you infuse it with your energy. If you intend to lead people into trouble and deceive them, then that's the energy the doll will have. If you're angry as you make the doll, the energies will transfer to the doll and affect your work with it accordingly. If you create a doll with a positive mindset and nothing but love, you'll find blessings for doing the right thing. Before anything else, think about your intention for making this doll, and also, as you make the doll, make sure your mind is focused on the task at hand and the goal you want to accomplish. Otherwise, you'll end up wasting your time.

Chapter 8: Getting Ready for Voodoo Rituals

In this chapter, you'll dive into what you need to prepare for Voodoo rituals. Preparing yourself mentally and physically before performing the rites and ceremonies is important. First, you have to ensure that you're in a good head space, focused, and relaxed. Your attention should be on your intention and the actions that you must perform during the ritual. When you're grounded and present, it will help further fuel your intention and bring it to fruition. When your head's all over the place, you may not even be able to draw the Lwa's attention, let alone keep it.

Meditation can help you mentally prepare for a Voodoo ritual by bringing you to the required state of mind.

https://unsplash.com/photos/ie8WW5KUx3o

It is also important to ensure that you're physically prepared for the task ahead. For one thing, you want to ensure that the environment is clean. For another, it should have the items, colors, and other things necessary to represent the Lwa you'll work with during the ritual. It is also recommended that you dress in the appropriate colors and ensure that you're nice and clean, not just physically but energetically as well. To be energetically prepared means you'll have to take a bath and possibly smudge yourself to get rid of heavy, negative energy you may have picked up along the way. Cleansing baths and spells before you begin your rituals are important and not to be skipped.

Cleansing Baths

Just as is the case with other religions, water is an essential element in the practice of Voodoo. It comes to play in all ceremonies and rituals, whether you're doing a cleansing, divination work, a baptism, or anything else. Water can take in negative energy and transmute it to positive. Cleansing baths are necessary when you're about to do a ritual or when you notice fatigue, anxiety, a sense of danger, or depression. After dealing with something traumatic, you can also use these baths to help you find peace and balance in your mind. Here's what you need to know before you take a cleansing bath:

- You'll have to enchant the water by praying to the Voodoo Lwa or the Saints with which they're syncretized.

- Before you get into the bath, you must wet your body from head to toe as you name your struggles in life aloud.

- You shouldn't spend less than 15 minutes in the bath, but don't remain there for longer than 30 minutes. While in the bath, you can meditate. Focus your attention on how there's a solution for all the things you're dealing with.

- As you release the water, envision all the struggles you're dealing with melting away. See them being washed away from your life as you exit the bath.

- You should use salt water to clean your bath each time you take a cleansing bath to eliminate any residual negative energy lingering in the water or around the area. Ideally, you should use a mix of water and sea salt, but regular salt works just fine if you don't have sea salt.

Another thing to remember is that before you have your cleansing bath, you should first wash your body with water and soap as you normally would. Make sure your soap doesn't have any herbs, particularly of the cleansing sort. When you're done with the cleansing, let your body air dry. Don't use a towel.

Voodoo Meditation Exercise

Meditation can help you mentally prepare for a Voodoo ritual by bringing you to the required state of mind. The most commonly recommended meditation technique involves focusing on your body or the altar. You can think of this as part of the preparation process. When you're engaged in a Voodoo ritual, the process will require a lot of energy from you, so it's best to prepare for it beforehand by getting into that meditative state of mind.

To begin with, make sure you're seated comfortably on the floor, your back straight, and your arms folded across yourself at about waist-knees level. The image of an altar will help you get into the right state of mind, so either shut your eyes and picture one or focus your attention on your altar. It would be best if you didn't start thinking about the ritual. Instead, think about the actual objects on your altar and whether or not they're ready for Voodoo rituals.

As you do this, try to keep your attention focused on these objects and what they represent at all times. If you get distracted and lose focus, start over again. It may take more than one attempt to get it right, but eventually, you'll be able to keep your focus and achieve a meditative state of mind. Once you're in this state of mind, do whatever you need to do before the ritual begins. Also, you can meditate on the Lwa you're planning to work with and stay open to their energy.

The reason why this is helpful is that it will help clear your head of all other thoughts. If there's something else on your mind, it will come up as part of meditation for you to address it and get rid of it. Thus, it will not disturb your trance, and you'll be able to focus better when the meditation is over. It's also highly recommended that you take some time each day, especially in the morning, to meditate. On most days, you may want to set aside about 30 minutes for this exercise. If you're starting with meditation, try to dedicate 10 or 15 minutes daily to achieve the state of mind required.

Chants

The chants used in Voodoo are very similar to those used in other religions. Hymns are sung before and during rituals. Generally, hymns are in the native language of a person or a particular person. The chants help the Lwa identify with their followers. They also help bring harmony to the entire environment so those present have peace and tranquility in their minds and bodies. Certain chants are used for certain Lwa, and if you're a follower of a particular Lwa, You will need: to pay attention to which chants they're usually associated with so that you can use them during your rituals.

The most important thing about Voodoo chanting is that it's very rhythmic. This rhythm will help dissipate the negative energy from the body. Thus, anything rhythmic will be useful in this regard. You can use singing, clapping, drums, and other instruments during chanting. Suppose a particular chant is being used for a specific Lwa. In that case, you'll have to pay attention to its meaning to properly identify with the spirit you're doing Voodoo rituals for. In this way, you can ensure harmony between your mind and the energy of that spirit.

Raising Your Vibration and Intuition

Before you conduct a voodoo ritual, you may find it helpful to raise your vibration. Here's what you need to do: Set aside time for reflection. You can do this before or after practicing the above exercises. However, make sure that the time you set aside is long enough for you to focus on yourself and your thoughts effectively. Some people prefer doing this at night because there are fewer distractions during that time of day. However, you can also do this during the day. It's up to you, as long as you can reflect on yourself.

Focus on the things that are going right in your life. Positive thinking is a common exercise used by people with a positive outlook. Some people call it gratitude journaling because they write down everything they are grateful for every night before they go to bed. Others call it journaling because they write down their thoughts and feelings every time they remember them. The point is that this exercise allows you to reflect on all the things that are going well in your life, and you can use it during the day or night while you're doing other things to help raise your vibration.

Meditation and Voodoo rituals can be powerful in bringing positive change to your life. However, you must do both for the best results. The reason is that you must have good connections with spirits before contacting them during a Voodoo ritual. These spirits are like our higher selves; when we focus on them and get to know them, our consciousness raises its vibration to their level, which helps in connecting with other spirits from higher dimensions simultaneously. This way, you can do Voodoo rituals to bring positive change to your life.

Devote a lot of time and effort to meditation and chant practice, as these tools will help you reach the higher dimensions. At this point, You will need: to connect with higher beings for success in Voodoo rituals. It would be best if you relied on your trust in the Lwa that comes to your aid. Typically, these higher beings will guide you through the rituals, and this is why you need to focus on them, their essence, and what they represent during meditation practice and chanting practice. The following is a list of activities you can do to raise your vibration and improve your intuition before a Voodoo ritual:

1. **Guided Meditation:** There are many guided meditations available online. If you search for them, you can find several that interest you. Try to listen to them every night before going to bed so that you can fall asleep more easily. You can also try guided meditation on YouTube or other websites and read books on the topic. Many people find this process beneficial because they don't have to focus on breathing exercises, making focusing easier during meditation.

2. **Chanting:** The most common chants are the ones associated with the Lwa. However, you can pick any mantra that appeals to you and chant it every night before going to bed and for ten to fifteen minutes before you begin your rituals. It's not about the words you repeat but the meaning behind them. Thus, you can choose any powerful mantra for you and use that during your chanting practice.

3. **Singing:** Singing is another form of chanting. It's beneficial to repeat the same notes because of the refrains involved in most songs. These refrains are a great way to help focus on the mantra because of their rhythm. However, try not to use songs with lyrics that you don't know because this can distract your mind and may prevent you from focusing on the meaning behind your mantra.

4. **Drumming:** Praying while drumming is a fairly common way to practice Voodoo. If you're not familiar with this, it's when you drum your hands and feet simultaneously on your drum while chanting certain words. A popular type of prayer is the sort that

starts with "Blessed be!" You can combine your rituals with prayers like these if you want to raise the vibration. Remember always to be grateful in all that you do, and remember that Voodoo rituals aren't meant to bend the will of others but to give you the power to control your fate through manifestation.

Body Cleansing Ritual

This ritual is performed to clear your body of the impurities that may have accumulated after a day's living and allow it to heal while you sleep. It's possible to cleanse every part of your body using this ritual, do it at least once a week, but you can repeat it if necessary.

You will need the following:

- A white candle
- A white bowl filled with water (preferably spring water)
- A lemon
- A small glass of plain water or bottled spring water

Instructions:

1. Start by washing your hands, feet, face, chest, and back while cleansing your spirit. Focus on the lightness that comes to you from all this washing, sending any negative feelings that may be in you away.

2. Squeeze a few drops of lemon juice on your tongue. Taste the zing of the lemon as you breathe in and out slowly to stimulate your glands and aura, raising your vibration to a higher level.

3. Get a white candle (preferably unscented) and light it. Watch the flame for a few minutes, focusing on the feeling of being centered, balanced, and grounded as it burns.

4. Stand before your altar while you say aloud, "I cleanse my body, mind, and soul." Repeat this two more times. When you repeat this, you're purifying your body of the negative emotions that may have been weighing it down.

5. Wash your hands once again.

6. Get a cup of plain or spring water and slowly drink it, focusing on purifying your body. Release any negative feelings to be cleansed.

7. Now light the candle and put it on your altar. Focus on cleansing your mind while watching the wick burn down until you feel

completely clean and clear in your mind.

Creating a Spiritual Barrier

Before you get into your ritual properly, creating a spiritual barrier is a good practice. This barrier is meant to keep you safe from any evil or unwanted influence that may want to hijack your ritual for whatever reason or cause things not to work out in your favor.

You will need the following:

- Bay leaves
- Rosemary essential oil
- Angelica essential oil
- 1 piece of mandrake root
- Almond oil (as a base)

Instructions:

1. Crush the bay leaves and the mandrake root.
2. Mix the dry ingredients with the oils.
3. Use this mixture to anoint your doorways, doorknobs, and window sills.
4. Anoint the entrance to your shrine or altar and the windows in the space.

Why Protection Is Important

Don't ever naively assume that there's no reason to protect yourself. For one thing, you need to consider that there are other Lwa that we haven't talked about who could decide to cause trouble for you simply because that's what they do. So, it would be best if you enlisted the assistance of your Lwa after performing your cleansing ritual to make sure that the eye of the evil ones doesn't see you.

Another thing to consider is that no matter how good you think you are, you've got enemies. Everyone does. Some people say they don't need to be protected because they've done no one harm, but that's not the way it works. Some people and entities don't need you to provoke them before they decide to make your life difficult, and this is why you should do protection spells not just when you're about to do a ritual but regularly.

It would be best if you also considered that you may have wronged someone. You don't need to have meant to annoy or hurt people before they feel upset. You may be completely unaware that there's a problem to begin with, but there's likely someone mad at you for something you did. Sometimes, the hate and hostility we get are deserved, and it takes some boldness and humility to admit that. Not everyone you've hurt will tell you how you made them feel, so it's better to assume that you've got enemies than to think you're blameless and stainless.

Finally, in life, bad things happen without rhyme or reason sometimes, and this is why you should know and practice protection rituals to keep you safe from the random madness that is life. Consider these spells as a form of general protection to give you extra assurance.

Signs You've Been Hexed

1. **You Find Yourself Stuck in a Rut and Unable to Move Forward:** This can be especially frustrating. Every time you feel like you're on the brink of success or finally about to make headway with a situation, something happens to ruin things for you.

2. **You Feel Drained, Sad, and Exhausted Every Day:** You may be feeling powerless or depressed, like there's no point in trying to move forward in life. This phenomenon can happen when another person is sending negative vibes your way.

3. **The Money You Make Gets Drained Easily:** It's tough to explain how it happens. You'll find that as soon as you make a little bit, all kinds of emergencies crop up, and next thing you know, you've got nothing once more.

4. **Your Friends and Family Start to Distance Themselves from You:** You may notice that people who used to talk to you all the time suddenly stop. They could stop calling you or stop coming around altogether.

5. **You Begin to Feel Increasingly Vulnerable and Afraid:** People are being rude and nasty at work or causing problems in your family. It could be anyone, a neighbor, someone at work, or even your boss.

6. **You Start Having Terrible Nightmares:** Sometimes, they can be hyper-realistic. Often, you'll dream about being chased, beaten, or killed. As if that's not enough, when you wake up from these dreams, you get the distinct sense that there's something in the

room with you.

Getting Rid of Hexes and Staying Clear of Them

1. **Reach Out to Your Lwa for Help:** You can let them know what you've been going through and ask them to help you undo what's been done to you. Ensure that you give them offerings and thank them in advance for their assistance.

2. **Ask a Trusted Mambo or Houngan for Help:** They can often see the problem and know what you need to do to fix it. If you're working with a genuine one, that would be even better because you know they're not trying to rip you off.

3. **Do Protection and Cleansing Spells Regularly:** The more often you make protection and cleansing a practice, the less likely it is that you'll have to deal with any hex being placed on you in the future. Sometimes, just bathing in salt water is enough.

4. **Pay Attention to Your Dreams:** If you're supposed to go somewhere the next day, for instance, and you have a dream about things going terribly, trust the dream. Don't go. Also, your Lwa could reach out to you through your dream to share information about someone trying to hex you or how to free yourself from a hex.

5. **Pay Attention to Your Intuition:** It doesn't matter if the person you're dealing with appears to be the reincarnation of Mother Theresa. If something feels off, trust your intuition and steer clear of them.

Chapter 9: Voodoo Herbs, Roots, Candles, and Oils

Let's Talk about Herbs and Roots

Voodoo requires knowledge of herbs, roots, and plants. You will need them to perform your rituals, whether for protection, prosperity, wealth, health, or so on. We'll take a look at popular roots and herbs in Voodoo, as well as their magical traits, so that you know how to craft your spells, gris-gris bags, Voodoo dolls, and so on. Remember that you can use many of these roots and herbs for more than one thing. It all comes down to the traits of the other ingredients you're blending them with.

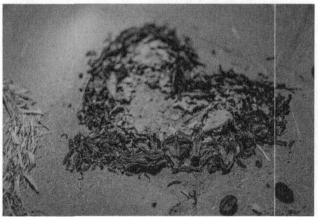

Voodoo requires knowledge of herbs, roots, and plants.
https://pixabay.com/photos/herbs-tea-art-voodoo-death-life-7358467/

Adam and Eve Root: This is a good use when you want to foster or create romantic love between a couple.

Allspice Berries: These are recommended when you want to craft charms and spells that will increase your fortune in business matters, giving you good luck. They're also recommended for relieving mental stress.

Alfalfa: This is a plant that will offer you luck in general, as well as luck in gambling. This plant is the one if you want great finances and success in your business endeavors. It will help keep poverty far from you so that you never have to deal with money issues.

Alkanet Root: This root helps in all financial affairs and business. You can use this to give you or someone else good fortune when they play games of chance.

Allspice: Use this one to give you health, gambling luck, and good luck in general.

Aloe Vera: If you want to experience the peace of mind of being perpetually protected, use this plant to help you in your work.

Amber: This plant will draw love to you if you use it for that purpose.

Anise: Excellent for protection. You can also use this to protect yourself from the evil eye, increase your gambling success, give yourself luck in all your affairs, and boost your psychic abilities.

Basil: Use basil when you want to connect with Erzulie. You should work with this plant if you want peace and happiness in your life. It will also bring you love and keep you safe.

Bay Leaves: These leaves are well known for the prosperity they can bring you. They're also excellent in protection spells. You can use them to boost your health, help you think more clearly, receive unique insight and wisdom, boost spiritual blessings and gifts, chase your enemies away, and ensure victory.

Birch: This plant has powerful protective properties.

Black Peppercorns: You can use these when you're seeking revenge. Also, use it to inflict pain and suffering on your enemies and keep people you don't want around you away.

Cactus: Excellent for jinxing — particularly the spines. You can also work with the cactus to get protection.

Catnip: If you're a woman and want to be more attractive to men, use catnip. It will surely bring you love.

Cayenne Pepper: This is useful for jinxing those who wish you evil. You can use it to send your enemies running and to cause confusion in their midst.

Cedar: if you need health, blessings, and protection, use cedar. You can also use it for cleansing purposes. This plant is packed with good power.

Chamomile: if you would like excellent luck in gambling and life in general, chamomile is the one. You can also use it to get rid of money jinxes and to protect yourself.

Cinnamon: Use this spice to help bring some fire to your relationship. It will give you protection, good fortune in all your business affairs and games of chance, and good health.

Cloves: Every Vodouist knows that cloves are excellent for use in money-drawing spells. You can also use it to attract love and friendship into your life.

Clover: Use the clover to help you get love.

Dandelion: If you want your wishes granted, use the dandelion. You can also use it to improve your psychic visions.

Devil's Shoestring: Expect good luck in general and gambling when you use this one.

Dill: Those who seek protection and love can use dill to achieve their aim. This plant will keep sickness far from you, help you win in court, bring back your sexual arousal, and destroy all love jinxes.

Dragon's Blood: If you want protection, good luck in gambling, and good luck in life, work with dragon's blood.

Eucalyptus: When you need to stop bad habits, remove evil from your life, and protect yourself from being jinxed, eucalyptus will save the day.

Fennel: This plant is great for keeping the law off your back. It will also keep you away from people with bad vibes, always troubling and meddling where they don't belong. Fennel is also good for protection.

Five-Finger Grass: This grass will bring you luck if you're a gambler. Use it when you're traveling so you can stay safe. You can also use it in general protection spells, health rituals, and spells to help you gain favors. It's equally useful in uncrossings and for money drawing.

Garlic: Use this spice to get rid of evil and protect yourself.

Ginger: Ginger also offers protection – but of the fiery sort. It helps to bring the heat back into your romantic relationships, and gamblers, for good luck, favor it. You should also know that ginger acts as an accelerator, making your spells and rituals happen much faster.

Ginger Root: Use this for luck in general and gambling.

Ginseng: This is a good root to create protection spells.

Holly: This plant will keep your home safe and bring good luck.

High John the Conqueror: Use this one to increase your financial abundance and personal power. It will bring you success, give you remarkable strength, improve your luck in games of chance and gambling, improve your health, attract love, and grant you protection.

Irish Moss: This moss is excellent for gambling, business, and all money matters.

Ivy: This plant offers you protection.

Jasmine: This flower is synonymous with love.

Job's Tears: Use this to make your wishes come true and have better gambling luck.

Juniper: Juniper is excellent for blessing, protection, cleansing, good luck in sexual affairs, love, and healing.

Lavender: Use this plant to bring you peace, protection, and love.

Lemon Balm: if you'd like better health, new love in your life, or better luck with your love life, you should make use of lemon balm.

Licorice Root: This powerful root will give you dominion and control, making it easy for you to command people to do your bidding.

Lilac: Use this flower to give you protection.

Lucky Hand Root: To get good luck in gambling and good luck, use the lucky hand root. It's also excellent for protection.

Magnolia Leaves: You can make sure your husband remains faithful and protects you with these leaves.

Mandrake Root: If you incorporate this root into a doll, you can use it to create wealth and love for yourself. Mandrake root is also good for protection and love.

Marigold: Use this flower for protection.

May Apple: You can use this to get gambling and general luck.

Mimosa: Mimosa is also good for protection.

Mint: Sometimes, spirits latch on to people. Mint is the best herb to get them to leave. You can also use it for uncrossing, repelling your enemies, protecting yourself, and boosting your psychic abilities.

Mistletoe: Use mistletoe to keep yourself safe from those who wish you harm and whatever they try to do. Some Vodouists also use it in love jinxes.

Mustard Seed: The white mustard seed, in particular, is great for bringing you general and gambling luck, keeping evil away from you, bringing love into your life, and keeping you safe.

Myrrh: Purification rituals can be supercharged with myrrh. As a bonus, you can expect to be blessed and protected.

Nutmeg: Use this for your love life, gambling luck, and general luck.

Oak: Oak can also be used for luck in general and gambling. If you're struggling with unwanted spirits, you can use them to chase them away. It's also powerful for uncrossing.

Orange Peel: Excellent for gambling and general luck.

Onion: Use this to protect yourself.

Parsley: Use this to boost fertility and love, as well as to protect yourself. Some use it when renting a home or dealing with death-related affairs.

Patchouli: You can use this for uncrossing, drawing money and love into your life, and protecting yourself.

Pine: Pine will bring you general and gambling luck.

Raspberry Leaves: If you want to ensure fidelity, raspberry leaves are your best bet.

Rose: Use the rose to bring love and luck into your life. It also has protective qualities.

Rosemary: This herb is lovely for women's empowerment. It can keep evil away from you, guard you at all times, give you good dreams, good luck in the family, and protection.

Sage: This herb is a classic used in cleansing and blessing rituals. It's also protective. Use it when you need wisdom. If you're a woman, you can use it to gain strength.

Snakeroot: For general and gambling luck, domination, health, and protection, use snakeroot. It's also excellent for improving virility. What's more, it can help you find money with ease.

Spanish Moss: This moss is good for money drawing and jinxing. Vodouists also use it to stuff Voodoo dolls.

Spearmint: Use this in your love rituals.

Star Anise: Star anise is good for keeping envious energy away from you. It will also give you good dreams and luck in life and gambling.

Thyme: If you need peace of mind, work with thyme. It will end all nightmares, too. You can also use it to boost your income and keep it safe from the evil eye.

Vanilla: Working with vanilla will greatly enhance your love-drawing rituals.

Yarrow: Not only does yarrow protect you, but it also improves your divination skills, makes you feel brave, and gives you courage.

Candles

Candles are important as they incorporate the element of fire in your rituals, and you can also imbue them with your intention to add more potency to your spells. Some Vodouists don't care much for color, opting to use white for everything since it is an option. You can do this too if you want. Besides, candle dye wasn't popular in candle making until the 19th century, which means that before then, Vodouists would work with the available candles they had, regardless of color. The meanings of the colors of each candle are universal. Still, if you find yourself inspired to use a certain color for a ritual that otherwise calls for a different one, you should trust your intuition.

According to Zora Neal Hurston in her book " Mules and Men, " these are the purposes of each candle color:

- **Red:** Victory
- **Pink:** Love and drawing success
- **Yellow:** Money
- **Green:** To chase away (and for success, too)
- **Blue:** Success, protection (and creating death)
- **White:** Peace, uncrossing, weddings
- **Lavender:** Causing triumph, causing harm
- **Brown:** Drawing people and money
- **Black:** Causing death and evil

Henri Gamache also wrote in his book, " Master Book of Candle-Burning, how to Burn Candles for Every Purpose, " that the following colors are to be used for the following purposes:

- **Red:** Love, affection, passion, vigor
- **Pink:** Attraction, romance, cleanliness
- **Orange:** Plans changing, way opening, prophetic dreams
- **Yellow:** Devotion, money (as in gold), prayer, attraction, good cheer
- **Green:** Money, business, gambling, good harvest, good job
- **Blue:** Joy, harmony, peace, kindness, healing
- **White:** Spiritual blessings, healing, purity, rest
- **Purple:** Command, control, ambition, power, mastery
- **Brown:** Neutrality, court cases
- **Black:** Dark thoughts, repulsion, freedom from evil, sorrow

Henri also talked about double-action candles with one color on top of another, matching the correspondences of each candle. Let's review those below:

- **Red and Black:** For removing love jinxes
- **Green and Black:** For removing money jinxes
- **White and Black:** For sending evil back to the sender

Another author of note, Anna Riva, wrote about the significance of colors in her book "Candle Burning Magic: A Spellbook of Rituals for Good and Evil. " Here's her take on the colors:

- **Red:** Impulsivity, love, life, energy, sex, strength, courage, health, magnetism, vitality, willpower, fiery.
- **Pink:** Femininity, diplomacy, honor, love, service, spiritual awakening, affection, leadership, unselfishness.
- **Orange:** Friendship, joy, attraction, enthusiasm, self-control, intellect, stimulation, adaptability, receptivity, organization.
- **Yellow:** Action, invoking spirits, activity, concentration, success, developing occult powers, inspiration, unity, universal love, creativity.
- **Green:** Health, healing, peace, envy, harmony, greed, money, luck, ambition, fertility, generosity, success, cooperation, abundance.

- **Blue:** Serenity, loyalty, inspiration, health, wisdom, immortality, truth, honesty, fidelity, kindness, peace, patience, devotion, sincerity, and harmony at home.

- **White:** Sincerity, truth, purity, innocence, cleansing, clairvoyance, prophecy, respect, outgoing, generosity, wholeness, spirituality, expansion.

- **Purple:** Ambition, dignity, progress, power, psychic ability, wisdom, pride, idealism, honors, protection, independence.

- **Brown:** Earthiness, balance, thrift, concentration, study, indecision, intuitive communication, telepathic power.

- **Black:** Evil, repelling black magic, shielding from the evil eye, adversity, loss, protection from evil spirits.

Oils

When it comes to oils, please be mindful about using them directly on your skin without doing a patch test. To do a test, just put a drop of the oil you're working with on your inner wrist and see how it feels over time. This way, you know if it's safe to apply. Also, most oils will require carrier oil to avoid burning or irritation. Here are carrier oils you can work with safely:

- **Grapeseed Oil:** Its shelf life is about 3 to 6 months. If it is solvent-extracted, it can keep for nine months. Please refrigerate.

- **Mustard Seed or Abyssinian Seed Oil:** Its shelf life is about 18 to 24 months.

- **Sweet Almond Oil:** Its shelf life is about 3 to 6 months when not in the fridge. When in the fridge, it can last 12 months.

- **Jojoba Oil:** Its shelf life is indefinite.

- **Olive Oil:** Its shelf life is about 12 to 18 months, as long as it's stored somewhere cool and dark.

To make your oil, get a mortar and pestle, put two ounces of the base oil in the mortar, and then add your herbs and any other oils you want. Crush gently, pour the mix into an airtight jar, then store it somewhere cool and dark. Four days later, check on the oil, paying attention to the fragrance. If you want it to be stronger, let it sit for longer. You can then strain the particles out of the oil with cheesecloth into the storage container in which you'll keep the final product. If you prefer, you can let the herb remain in the oil. If you think the fragrance isn't strong enough, simply strain the oil with a cheesecloth back into the mortar, and then add enough base oil so that you've got two ounces in the mortar once more. Then add more ingredients, crush them, and store them for three more days. Keep doing this until you have the fragrance strength you want.

To Be Safe

1. Keep essential oils out of the reach of children and pets.
2. Don't use these oils if you have health issues or are pregnant without informing your doctor first.
3. Never use essential oils undiluted directly on your skin.
4. Please don't ingest the oils.
5. Even products made with only natural ingredients can cause irritation and allergies in some people.
6. If you notice an allergic reaction, immediately flush your skin with clean, cool water and head to the hospital. The same applies if the oil is in your nose, mouth, eyes, or a cut or sore.

Oils That May Cause Skin Irritation If the Skin Is Sensitive: French Basil, Ylang Ylang, Bay Laurel, Yarrow, Benzoin, Violet, Cade, Verbena, Canagaa, Vanilla, Virginian Cedarwood, Valerian, Roman and German Chamomile, Turpentine, Citronella, Turmeric, Garlic, Tolu Balsam, Geranium, White Thyme, Ginger, Tea Tree, Hops, Styrax, Jasmine, Scotch and Long-leaf Pine, Lemon, Peru Balsam, Lemongrass, Orange, Lemon Balm (melissa), Mint, Litsea Cubeba, Mastic, Lovage.

Oils That Cause Skin Pigmentation When Exposed to Sunlight Directly: Include Verbena, Angelica Root, Orange, Bergamot (except the kind free from bergapten), Mandarin, Cumin, Lovage, Ginger, Lime (expressed), Lemon (expressed).

Avoid These If You Have High Blood Pressure: Thyme, Rosemary, Spanish Sage, Common Sage, and Hyssop.

Avoid Sweet Fennel: If you have epilepsy.

Avoid the Following If You Have Diabetes: All kinds of Sage, Angelica, Rosemary, and Hyssop.

Avoid These If You're Receiving Homeopathic Treatment: Peppermint, Eucalyptus, Camphor, and Black Pepper.

The following are the different kinds of oils you can buy or make and what they represent.

Abramelin Oil: This oil represents happiness at home, stability, sweetness, male love, male sexuality, and warmth.

You will need the following:

- 7 parts Olive oil
- 1 part Calamus essential oil
- 1 part Myrrh essential oil
- 1 part Cassia essential oil
- ½ part Cinnamon essential oil

Altar Oil: For blessing yourself, others, ritual items, the altar, and so on.

- 1 drop cedar
- 2 drops of myrrh
- 4 drops frankincense
- 2 ounces olive oil

Anointing Oil: For blessing and consecrating.

- 35 drops myrrh
- 35 drops frankincense
- 1 ounce Extra Virgin Olive Oil

Attraction Oil: Meant to draw love and money. Mix the following equally:

- Lovage herb
- Lemon flowers or grated lemon peel
- 1 lodestone (a small piece per bottle)
- 2 ounces grape seed oil (for 2 tablespoons of the mix)

Attraction Love Oil: For drawing love. Blend the following in equal amounts:

- Sandalwood oil
- Vanilla oil
- Lavender oil
- Rose fragrance (synthetic)
- Essential oil of rose Geranium

- Essential Oil of Roses (Rose Otto)

Bend-Over Oil: This oil is meant to command others, break hexes, and send evil spirits back to whoever sent them. It's also good for anointing Voodoo dolls and candles.

- Essential oil of bergamot or bergamot leaf
- Licorice root
- Calamus root

Blend with some grains of frankincense in vitamin E and almond oils

Black Arts Oil: This oil is powerful for working black magic. It is always brown. There are more than a few recipes for this oil.

You will need the following:

- Half a dropper of essential oil of black pepper
- Half a dropper of essential oil of patchouli
- A pinch of black poodle dog hair
- A pinch of valerian root
- A pinch of Spanish moss
- A pinch of black mustard seeds
- A pinch of powdered sulfur
- A pinch of mullein
- 9 black peppercorns (whole)
- Half an ounce of carrier oil (almond oil works well)

Blend all of this to get your black arts oil.

Blessing Oil: Add two tablespoons of each ingredient to 2 ounces of oil.

- 2 parts frankincense
- 1 part benzoin gum

Another Blessing Oil Recipe: You will need: to blend the ingredients below.

- Rose petals
- Rose fragrance (synthetic), or
- Essential oil of rose geranium, or
- Essential oil of roses (rose otto)

- Essential oil of benzoin
- Almond oil

Come to Me Oil: For more love and passion.

- Lemon oil
- Gardenia
- Jasmine
- Rose

Confusion Oil: To confuse someone and make it hard for them to think clearly.

- Chicory root
- Guinea pepper
- Licorice root
- Mineral oil (as the base)

Dream Potion: For clear, prophetic dreams. Anoint your forehead before bed.

- Honey
- Rosemary (1 handful)
- Red wine
- Red wine vinegar

Ezili Freda Oil: To boost personal magnetism, draw prosperity, and attract love.

- ¼ teaspoon ylang-ylang essential oil
- 1 teaspoon geranium essential oil
- ½ teaspoon lavender essential oil
- ½ teaspoon rose essential oil
- ¾ cup jojoba oil

The Essence of Van Van: This potion is a powerful one. You can use this Louisiana conjure potion to bring you power, good luck, and success. Just add 10 percent oil of lemon grass to alcohol, and you've got the essence of Van Van.

Fast Luck Oil: For sex, love, luck, and gambling success.

- Alkanet flakes
- High John the Conqueror Root
- Nutmeg
- Oil of Patchouli
- Oil of Vanilla
- Oil of Wintergreen
- Oil of Cinnamon

Blend in almond oil as the carrier. You can anoint your money with this before you spend it.

Four Thieves Vinegar

You will need the following:

- 1-ounce lemongrass
- 1-ounce peppermint
- 1-ounce sage
- 1 ounce powdered camphor
- 1-ounce wormwood
- 1 ounce1-ounce rosemary
- 1-ounce rue
- 1-ounce lavender

Gambler's Luck Oil: This is useful for all things connected to gambling. Just anoint your hands with the oil, and before you play any games, you should rub your hands together. Here's what you need:

- Three parts cinnamon
- 1 part carnation petals
- 1 part anise seed

Mix the above ingredients together, and then add the mixture to two ounces of carrier oil. In each bottle, put a little High John the Conqueror root.

Holy Anointing Oil: It is said that this recipe was from God, given directly to Moses. You can use this to anoint anyone or anything, bless people, and consecrate items. You will need: to blend equal parts of the following:

- Olive oil
- Cinnamon oil
- Calamus oil
- Cassia oil
- Myrrh oil

Holy Oil of Aspiration: In the 20th century, Aleister Crowley, a British occultist, had his brand of Abramelin oil. He called this the "Oil of Abramelin," which some circles call the "Holy Oil of Aspiration." This oil was inspired by Mathers' choice to substitute galangal for calamus in the recipe for Abramelin Oil. Here are the ingredients below:

- 7 parts olive oil
- 2 parts galangal essential oil
- 4 parts of myrrh essential oil
- 8 parts cinnamon essential oil

The way Crowley weighed the proportions of these oils is also inspired by Mathers' choices for measuring the raw ingredients. As a result, cinnamon has a powerful presence. The idea is that putting it on your skin will leave you with an intense burning sensation. This formula is unlike the original recipe in the grimoire, and you can't use it for any spell that requires anointing the head. Instead, Crowley crafted this blend to use in small quantities, on top of your head or forehead, and also to anoint magical tools to consecrate them.

Love-Drawing Oil: This oil is meant to strengthen love and bring more passion into a relationship. You will need: to blend the following:

- Rose petals
- Oil of jasmine
- Dried orange rind
- Patchouli

Blend the ingredients in some carrier oil. The patchouli brings passion, while the rose petals bring love.

Legba Oil: This is also known as Saint Anthony oil. It's the perfect oil to eliminate obstacles in your life and create the opportunities you seek. You will need: the following ingredients:

- 1 dropper of rum
- 1 pinch of sugar
- Palm kernel oil
- 3 drops of coconut oil
- 3 drops of avocado oil
- 1 pinch of coffee grounds

Blend all the ingredients in almond oil, and use them in spells and rituals to eliminate obstacles in your life.

Ogun Oil: This is also called Saint John the Baptist Holy Oil. You can use this oil to stay safe and protected from all who wish you harm. Use it to defend yourself from evil and eliminate barriers you encounter in any situation. Here's what you need:

- 2 tablespoons of rosemary leaves
- 2 tablespoons of eucalyptus leaves
- 2 ounces of olive oil
- A piece of rock salt

Mix all the ingredients. Please don't skip the rock salt because it's meant to honor Ogun and to draw his power to the oil.

Peace Oil: For peace.

- Sandalwood oil
- Lavender flowers
- Rosemary leaves
- Basil leaves

Blend this in a carrier oil.

Protection Oil: You can wear this as a perfume or use it to anoint your charms to keep you safe from negative energy and evil.

- Gardenia petals
- Patchouli leaves
- Sage oil (just a few drops)
- Frankincense resin
- Sandalwood oil (just a few drops)

Blend the leaves in equal parts and add them to two ounces of olive oil.

Chapter 10: Voodoo Spells, Rituals, and Baths

A Note on Psalms

Before we get into Voodoo spells, it is important to clarify that Voodoo work sometimes involves using chapters from the book of Psalms in the Bible. These Psalms are chosen to match the intention of the spell in question. For instance, when you need to perform an uncrossing or remove a jinx, You will need: Psalm 91. Voodoo spells are very easy to perform, and you don't need to perform a long, complicated ceremony before you can make the magic work for you. Some rituals can be long, but that doesn't always have to be the case. Also, you can allow your intuition to guide you as you do your work.

Voodoo work sometimes involves using chapters from the book of Psalms in the Bible.
https://pixabay.com/photos/bible-open-book-pages-open-bible-1846174/

A Note on Animal Sacrifices

If you're concerned about sacrificing animals, the good news is that you don't have to. There are other ways to make sacrifices without actually killing animals. In Haiti and Africa, blood sacrifice still happens, but it's not something to be judged negatively. At the end of the ritual, the community shares the meat, which means that hungry people enjoy a nice meal, strengthening the community. Blood sacrifices aren't just for show, as they're meant to add more power to the spells and other magic being worked by the Vodouist. However, the spells in this book don't require you to kill animals, so you're in the clear.

A Note on Disposal

When it comes to the materials left over from the ritual, you can take them to a crossroads and leave them in the middle, then walk away from the crossroads, making sure not to look back at what you just disposed of.

A Note on Working with Lwa and their Veves

As for which Lwa to work with, you could opt for working with your personal Lwa, as they can easily connect you with the best Lwa for the job, depending on your spell. This way, you don't have to worry about selecting the wrong Lwa only to have your spells ineffective. Some of the spells indicate which Lwa are appropriate for them, while others do not. With the latter, trust your personal Lwa to handle the details. You can have the veve of the Lwa you're working with handy when working these spells.

A Note on Herbs, Roots, Candles, and Oils

For the spells you're about to learn, refer to the previous chapter on herbs, roots, candles, and oils. Please choose any of them that would work well with your spell. All you have to do with the herbs and roots is to sprinkle them around you. Alternatively, you can burn them in fire, tap them against the forehead, or simply hold them in your hands while you work.

As for candles, choose colors that match what you're doing. Work with the information in the previous chapter. If you can't figure out which candle to use, white always works, no matter what you're doing. As for oils, you can anoint your ritual tools, hands, altar, and anything else you are intuitively led to anoint with the oils you want.

When applying oils to your body or other things, you need to consider the spell you're doing. Say you're working on a banishing spell or a spell meant to send something away from you. In that case, you should apply the oil from the inside to the outside or away from you. For instance, apply oil from the elbows down to your fingertips to anoint your forearms. If you're doing a spell that means drawing something towards you, you'll apply the oil from your fingertips to your elbows. To anoint your whole body, apply the oil from your feet up to your head for drawing and attraction spells. Apply the oil from your head to your feet for banishing or repelling spells and rituals.

A Note on Voodoo Magic

The thing about Voodoo magic is that it's not about tricks. It's about spiritual work carried out by the Mambo, Houngan, or any other Vodouist. The work is meant to make life in the physical realm better. To work Voodoo magic, You will need: tangible and non-tangible aspects. There will be prayer, for one thing. You'll have to light candles, sing or drum, use invocations, dance, and so on. It all comes down to the requirements of the spell you're working on and what your intuition guides you to do. Voodoo magic can be complicated or simple. You may complete it in minutes or keep doing it throughout your life. There are as many Voodoo magical practices as problems that need to be solved.

The philosophy behind the magic in Voodoo is that there's nothing in this world that is free. Even the great Bondye doesn't have the power to reach down and hand things to you simply because you ask or because you're a "good person." Vodouists call magic "work" because they understand that no matter what they want in life, they've got to work for it. Magic doesn't imply a lack of effort. It is a tool you use to ensure that the work you're already doing to achieve what you want is boosted. This way, you're sure to get the results you seek. You could think of life as a boat and fate or destiny as the wind that drives the boat's sails. Magic, then, would be the sailors and boat rigging. The sailors are ultimately in charge of directing the boat, helping the sails to catch the wind and the boat head in the correct direction.

You can change where the ship is heading by working with the sails. With enough effort, you can even get the vessel moving against the wind's direction. You could do this by using the oars, giving the sails a trim, or redirecting the wheel. If it's a modern boat, you can work with the motor.

In the boat, though, certain parameters limit what the boat can do. Will the boat make it to the right shore? It depends on the crew and captain, the boat's condition, and external factors beyond one's control, such as weather and wind.

In the same way, magical work may or may not be successful depending on several factors. For instance, there's the skill level of the person performing the magic and whether or not the Lwa or the Gran Met will support the work. There are times when certain kinds of magical work have to be done at different points to help you get through troubling situations. When progress isn't being made, it might be necessary to reach out to a Mambo or Houngan so they can see what the problem is through divination. With divination, a Vodouist can learn the real problem they're facing and how the Lwa can help them solve it.

Banishing Spells and Rituals

These spells are meant to remove enemies and other unwanted people, illness, unwelcome spirits, jealousy, and so on. It's best to do these spells when the moon is waning.

Enemy Banishment

1. Buy or make a Voodoo doll that will stand in the place of your intentions.
2. Write your intention on a piece of paper. For instance, you could write, *"I intend to banish all bad energies from my home. Right now, (name of person) is acting as a negative agent in my life. I call on Baron Samedi and Manman Brijit to help me eliminate this destructive force once and for all."*
3. Take what you've written and put it into the doll.
4. Take the doll out of your home, somewhere far. Dig a hole in the ground and put the doll in the hole.
5. Burn the doll as you say, *"I now declare my enemy is far away removed from me."*
6. Cover up what's left of the doll with some dust, and thank both Lwa you called on by leaving them some black coffee on the doll's grave. Walk away and don't look back at it.

Illness banishment

1. Take a handful of salt and throw it into a fire. Watch as the fire becomes blue.

2. Stare into the flames, and as you do, focus on your intention to be free of illness.

3. Keep staring into the flames as you say, *"As this illness is consumed, so does good health now resume."*

Luck Spells and Rituals

These spells are meant to help you in life in general and when you decide to gamble or play the lottery. Again, if you want to make this more powerful, you should work with herbs, roots, candles, and oils that would work well with your intentions.

Gambling Luck

You will need the following:

- A whole nutmeg
- A green ribbon

Instructions:

1. Look up the Apostle's creed prayer, and write it backward on paper.
2. Fold the paper around a nutmeg.
3. Use your green ribbon to secure the paper to the nutmeg.
4. Anoint this charm with any fast luck oil.
5. Carry this around with you wherever you go gambling.

Good Luck Spell

You will need the following:

- Hemp cord
- Money drawing incense
- Charcoal block
- Coin
- Abalone shell (a small piece)
- Miniature broom
- Cowry shell

Instructions:

1. Light a piece of charcoal and set it on a fireproof plate.

2. Pinch a bit of the money drawing incense and place that on the charcoal to burn.

3. Get the hemp cord and tie it to the broom.

4. Attach the cowry shell (for good luck), the coin (to draw wealth), and the abalone (for business and personal protection) to the broom with the cord.

5. Now, you're going to tie seven knots in the hemp cord. As you tie each knot, pay attention to what you want in life in terms of prosperity and luck.

6. Say a prayer of thanks to your Lwa for helping you with this ritual and bringing you results.

7. Hang this in your office, home, or anywhere you want to see results.

Healing Spells and Rituals

Healing Physical Aches

You will need the following:

- A piece of fluorite, or

- A piece of clear amethyst

- Good visualization abilities

Instructions:

1. Find somewhere quiet where you won't be disturbed or distracted.

2. Sit for some minutes, breathing and clearing your mind. You can shut your eyes if it helps.

3. Take the fluorite or amethyst in your hand and hold it against the ache in your body.

4. Imagine a white light pooling at your feet in your mind's eye. See this light make its way up to your head, filling your body.

5. When the light gets to your head, allow it to expand and envelope your head, covering a radius of about a foot.

6. Bring your attention back to the place with the ache and channel the light there.

7. Repeat this a few more times for ten to fifteen minutes, then end the session. You can repeat this if you're still in pain.

Voodoo Healing

You will need the following:

- A white Voodoo doll
- A piece of paper
- A pen
- Personal effects of whoever you want to heal
- Two white candles

Instructions:

1. Write the name of the person needing healing and purification on a piece of paper.
2. Attach the paper to the doll or stuff it into the doll.
3. Attach or stuff the personal effects of the target to or in the doll.
4. Anoint two white candles with anointing oil.
5. Light the candles and place one on either side of the doll.
6. Anoint the doll with anointing oil as well.
7. Say a prayer to your Lwa, asking them to facilitate the healing process. Thank them when you're done.

Love Spells and Rituals

These spells are great for pulling love toward you or another. It's best always to intend for the universe to bring you the best person for you rather than try to coerce someone to be with you against their will. Generally, Sundays and Thursdays are the best days for love spells. You can perform them during the waxing or full moon phases for the best results.

Love Attraction

Use this when you want to attract whomever you're in love with. You'll get the best results when you do this during the waxing or full moon.

You will need the following:

- A toothpick
- A favorite perfume (or essential oil)
- A pink candle

Instructions

1. Using the toothpick, engrave a heart into the pink candle.

2. Set the candle on a windowsill, making sure the heart is getting touched by moonlight.

3. Set the perfume or essential oil in front of the candle, and then pray to your Lwa to give you the love you need. Ask them to let the person you want to be attracted to you through the scent of the oil or perfume.

4. Light the candle and wait for it to burn out totally.

5. Take the oil or perfume and put a little on your body before you head out to interact with others.

Getting Back Your Ex
You will need the following:

- A piece of paper
- Some fresh basil
- Your ex's dirty left sock (any other personal item can work if you don't have this)
- A glass of water
- A red candle

Instructions:

1. Write your ex's name thrice on paper.

2. Dig a hole in the ground outside your home.

3. Put the paper into the hole, followed by their item.

4. Light your candle by noon and set it next to the hole. Let it burn.

5. Add some basil to your glass of water and set it beside the candle.

6. Put out the candle's flame by pinching it as soon as it's 1 PM.

7. Light the candle again when it's 6 PM, and then let it burn till 7 PM.

8. Cover the hole with a barrel, then knock on the barrel thrice. Each time you knock, ask your Lwa to bring your lover to you. Make sure you use your lover's name.

Money Spells and Rituals

Money Attraction

You will need the following:

- Fast luck oil
- Whole buckeye
- A dollar bill

Instructions:

1. Wrap the dollar bill around the whole buckeye.
2. Anoint this with your fast luck oil.
3. Take this around with you everywhere you go.

Money Drawing

You will need the following:

- A permanent marker
- Dollar bills

Instructions:

1. Take one dollar bill or more and write a blessing on each one with your permanent marker. You could write, *"May I always be blessed with abundant money."*
2. Take the money and go out somewhere to hide it. You should make sure that no one sees you hiding the money, and you should make sure not to drop any of the bills accidentally. This spell requires the intention to work, so you should make it look intentional.
3. Try hiding it in places like newspapers in the "Help Wanted" sections, on a pack of diapers, on a milk gallon, and so on.
4. Leave the place immediately. You should never stick around to see who may find the money.

Protection Spells

You'll find the best days for these rituals are Tuesdays and Thursdays. You should do them under the waxing or full moon. The best colors to work with are yellow, white, and red, representing, respectively, blessings, purity, and self-defense.

Spiritual Barrier

This spell is meant to keep your home free from all negative energies. You only need red brick dust. Here's how to make it:

1. Find an old red brick.
2. Pound the red brick until it becomes nothing but dust.
3. Pour the red brick dust across your entrances.

Salt and Pepper Protection

This one is excellent for keeping you safe from all evil and ensuring that you aren't affected by any evil magic being worked against you.

You will need the following:

- Salt
- Black pepper
- Water

Instructions:

1. Get a bucket of water.
2. Mix black pepper and salt in this water.
3. Use this water to scrub your home, working from the inside to the outside. Do this each morning before sunrise.

Baths

Baths are useful because they help cleanse your body and soul. It would be best to take baths because you have to eliminate the energies you pick up from people and places throughout your day, as not all these energies are good for you. Before you have these baths, you should bless the water before getting into the tub and call on your Lwa. When you get in, submerge your entire body from top to bottom, and then talk about your problems with your Lwa. Soak up the bath, trusting that it's doing its work and your Lwa is helping. Accept that when you step out of the bath, everything will be fine one way or another. Drain the bath thoroughly after, and then cleanse it with salt water.

Purification Bath

This bath is useful for crossings or other evil work. Take this bath as you recite the 51st Psalm.

You will need the following:

- Sea salt
- 1 handful of hyssop
- 1 handful of rue
- 2 white candles

Instructions:

1. Light both candles and place one on either side of your bath.
2. Bless the water.
3. Add the ingredients to the water and recite Psalm 51.
4. Say a prayer to your Lwa about what you desire.
5. Get in the bath. If you don't have a bath, the mixture should be in a bucket so you can pour it over your head.

Yellow Attraction Bath

This bath is meant to help you fix your relationships and skin problems and find your perfect love.

You will need the following:

- Honey
- A yellow candle (or an orange one)
- Yellow food coloring
- Patchouli incense (cinnamon incense also works)
- Yarrow flowers
- Parsley

Instructions

1. Light your candle and set it on the right-hand side of your bath.
2. Mix all the ingredients in your bath water after blessing it.
3. Say a prayer to your Lwa, and then get in the water or pour it all over yourself.

Protection Bath

Use this when you are overwhelmed with anxiety, paranoia, and stress. You can also just do this once a week to keep yourself safe. Use the same instructions as outlined for the previous baths.

You will need the following:

- Lavender
- Rosemary
- Sea shells
- Peace or watermelon incense
- Blue food coloring
- Sea shells
- A blue or white candle

Courage Bath

This bath is best when you feel sluggish or inexplicably tired. Please don't use this bath if you're feeling upset or angry.

You will need the following:

- Asper
- A white or red candle
- Red food coloring
- John the Conqueror or red peppers
- Helping hand incense

Love Bath

To bring love to your life, improve the love you already have, or help you be more loving towards yourself, you can use this bath.

You will need the following:

- 1 cup of yarrow
- Rose blossom cologne
- Orange blossom cologne

Health and Wealth Bath

This bath will boost your income and keep you healthy.

You will need the following:

- White sage flowers
- Green food coloring
- Comfrey
- Myrrh incense

- A brown or green candle

Overcome Negativity Bath

Use this to remove negative energies from you.

You will need the following:

- Rue
- Hyssop
- Rosemary
- Rock salt
- Consecrated water or Holy Water
- Florida Water (1 tablespoon)

Conclusion

There is much more to learn about Voodoo, and one book barely covers it. However, you've been given more than enough for you to start your journey and begin serving the Lwa. Choosing to practice Voodoo can radically transform your life for the better. However, to reap the benefits, you've got to take the things that you have learned and put them to work. You have to walk the talk to see what it means to be a Vodouist.

The beautiful thing about Voodoo is that it provides practical solutions to your everyday issues. It's good to know that you don't have to go through life alone. You have to admit it's great to know that you have the Lwa by your side, ready to come to your aid whenever you need them. Remember, though, that you should take an interest in them. Cultivate an actual relationship with them, and you'll find that relationship will be very beneficial indeed.

You shouldn't worry too much that you might get a few strange looks if you start practicing Voodoo. After all, Voodoo is a religion, and it's *your religion*. It's *your relationship* with the Lwa. Do what makes you happy, and who cares if someone doesn't like it? You are free to live your life however you please, as long as you're not hurting anyone else.

Part 3: Hoodoo for Beginners

An Essential Guide to Folk Magic and Using African American Spiritual Practice to Enhance Your Life

Introduction

What does Hoodoo mean to you? Is it a religion or is it like Voodoo but sounds friendlier? Actually, Hoodoo is a unique mix of African, American, Native American, European, and Christian beliefs that have become a recognized spiritual practice that encompasses many kinds of magic and spellwork that are designed to make your life better, more successful, and give you control over what is in your future. It is based on the belief that every single item in the universe is connected, and every human, animal, place, and atom has a connection without which the world would cease to exist.

Hoodoo teaches us how to call on these connections and become part of the consciousness of the universe. It isn't a religion and won't "punish you" if you don't get it right. Hoodoo teaches us that our intentions are the fuel that powers magic. If you believe you should have something, and your intentions are pure, then the universe will work with you to ensure you get it. Everything in the natural world has a certain power, and discovering how herbs and roots bring something extra to your magic is all part of the Hoodoo experience.

Learn the magic of nature and how to create healing baths or powerful talismans for wealth and success. Begin to believe you deserve the best the universe has to offer, and you'll start to live the life you were meant to have. Rediscover your ancestors and connect to their spirits to learn from their wisdom and love. They are your personal connection to the spiritual realm and are waiting to be your guides.

Sometimes modern life means you forget the magic of nature and how your ancestors lived. The struggles they faced and the fights they had were all for your benefit. Their blood runs through your veins and gives you that ultimate connection, so use Hoodoo to benefit from this.

Chapter 1: What Is Hoodoo?

When enslaved people were transported to America between the 17th and 19th centuries for slavery purposes, they came from all areas of Africa. When they arrived on these hostile and foreign shores, all they had to unite them was their magic. The enslavers didn't approve of their African magical practices and forced them to follow Christian principles and beliefs. As generations of enslaved Black people evolved, this practice became the belief system we now know as Hoodoo.

The media and other sources often mistake Hoodoo for other practices like Voodoo or Pagan beliefs.
https://www.pexels.com/photo/crop-woman-near-burning-candles-during-ritual-7256682/

The enslaved people needed to improve their lives and regain some sort of control, so they based their magic on the traditional ways each community brought with them and melded into Hoodoo. It's important to understand how African communities viewed magic and spiritualism. They didn't consider magic and connections to the spirits as a separate part of their lives. It was an intrinsic part of life that was as important as the air they breathed and when they combined these beliefs with other cultures like Native American and Central European beliefs, what emerged was a type of folk magic centered on botanical, zoological, and spiritual miasma which has developed into the modern practice we see today.

One of the more traditional beliefs of the original Hoodoo was the Kongo Cosmogram which gives a general overview of the African belief system of how the universe works and where we all come from. Humans have been creating cosmograms since the dawn of time to explain the origins of mankind, to show how the physical and spiritual realms are connected, and how the eternal circle of life explains man's existence on Earth.

Put simply, it is a reminder that everything and everybody in the physical world is connected. Without this connection, the universe would fail. It also explains the alignment to the spiritual world and how the energy created by the sun and moon at different times of the day/month and year affect us. Hoodoo rootwork and rituals can be timed using this information to gain more energy and become more effective.

These beliefs and the need for a commonality to bind the communities meant that Hoodoo became the glue the estranged enslaved people clung to. They developed spells and rituals to control their existence and began to fight back against their captors in the best way they could.

What Hoodoo Isn't

The media and other sources often mistake Hoodoo for other practices like Voodoo or Pagan beliefs. Voodoo is a religion, but Hoodoo is not. It is a spiritual practice that has deities and spirits who are worshiped, but there is no doctrine or religious significance. A lot of Hoodoo is based on Christian beliefs and the saints. Voodoo has dark magic, and although there are some Hoodoo spells to get revenge and cast curses or hexes, it isn't as dangerous as Voodoo. In Voodoo, a specific set of deities and spirits are called upon for dark magic, and it is a religion with dedicated rules and beliefs. Hoodoo is more liquid and incorporates multiple beliefs and skills.

Pagan and Wiccan beliefs have a mantra that no one will come to harm with their workings and magic, but Hoodoo has no limits regarding its magic. You can find spells and rituals to break up couples or make your boss follow your commands, but they are never meant to bring real harm to anybody, just to make their lives less comfortable.

In some parts of the US, magic performed by communities who live in the mountains is also referred to as Hoodoo because of charms, spells, and amulets. These mostly white communities have similar beliefs that all elements of nature and mankind are connected but is that Hoodoo? Some practices from the southeastern US states have been given the moniker Hill folks Hoodoo, but comparisons should be avoided if you want to get the original effect of the African-based practice.

Modern Hoodoo

By the early 1900s, Hoodoo had evolved and incorporated European and Kabalistic beliefs along with Native American and African practices, and Hoodoo root workers and conjurors were well respected in their chosen communities. They acted as doctors, magicians, and priests to those who lived there and often acted as "wise men/women."

Some practitioners took to the road with their herbal tonics, oils, and bath products. They would be a regular sight in small towns and cities peddling their magical wares. Between 1910 and 1940, many African Americans emigrated from the south to escape racism and seek employment in the more industrial north of America. This led to many receiving more formal education, which led to them abandoning their ancestral beliefs in favor of more modern faiths and structured religions.

In the mid-1990s, a Hoodoo revival began that led to the status we know today. Why should you embrace Hoodoo? Why not? Some beliefs they hold are life-changing and help you gain a more balanced view of the connection between the physical and the spiritual worlds.

Hoodoo Beliefs

- **The existence of divine providence:** Hoodoo doesn't restrict its practices to just one deity and doesn't limit who you can call on for help. Some acknowledged connections include the Buddha Hotei for prosperity and Santo Muerte for help finding a lover. Hoodoo practitioners turn to Jesus to seek protection, especially in the nighttime.

- **Life after death:** Living alongside the Divine power are the souls of those who once lived on Earth. Most rootworkers and conjurors work with ancestors and the spirits of the dead to make their magic work. When you die, you don't cease to exist. You simply ascend to a higher realm where you are dedicated to assisting the living. Ancestors and the spirits of the dead regularly commune with the divine on our behalf.

- **Divination:** Hoodoo work is often based on what will happen in the future. These events are told to us by the ancestors using divination tools like bones and paying cards. This allows humans to change the course of their futures to shift probabilities and create a more successful outcome.

- **Retributive justice:** Unlike other spiritual practices that teach us to "do no harm" whatever the circumstances, Hoodoo works on the principle from Biblical times that states "an eye for an eye," which allows the person who has been wronged to retaliate. However, the retribution must fit the crime, or there will be recriminations.

- **Intention:** Hoodoo teaches us that intentions are the keys to life. Even if you use a hexing powder, it will only affect someone who deserves the curse. Anyone else who encounters the powder will be unaffected. Curses and wishes only work when a higher being approves them. Pure intentions are the fuel of Hoodoo magic.

In summary, Hoodoo originated in America brought by enslaved Africans who had been stripped of their belongings, identities, and religion. They had been ripped from their homelands and subjected to cruelty and degradation that many of us cannot even imagine. Working together to keep their traditional beliefs and practices alive, they combined their arts with the Christian religion they were forced to adopt and developed the magical practice called Hoodoo.

Your Hoodoo experience will be unique to you. Because it is based on your energy, intentions, and connections to the universe, everybody will react differently to the spells and rituals they perform. That is the beauty of Hoodoo. It is whatever you need it to be, and provided you have clear intentions and come from a good place, you'll be heard. You will succeed, and you will become part of the Hoodoo community.

Chapter 2: Hoodoo Deities and Spirits

Hoodoo is the most eclectic form of magic today, and when the enslaved people that formed the practice came together from all the different areas of the African continent, they had to find a way to communicate. They spoke different languages and followed different religions, but they were ultimately under the control of American enslavers who only allowed them to practice Catholicism. Due to this mishmash of their original African roots and Christianity, Hoodoo evolved into a magic practice that embraced many deities and spirits from a multitude of cultures.

St Joseph of Cupertino.
https://commons.wikimedia.org/wiki/File:SaintJosephCupertino.jpg

The practice has been evolving and growing for over four hundred years and has embraced religions and deities from across the globe. Today people who practice Hoodoo focus on the Christian – Jewish roots combined with the traditional African spirits known as the Lao to escape the traditional confines of modern Christianity. They recognize that in the past, they were maligned by white supremacy by the church and stripped of their self-esteem when their traditional beliefs and communication methods were deemed as evil and devil worshipping.

The enslavers of the day were determined to drive any African traditions and beliefs underground, but the slaves knew they needed that connection with their ancestors and their magic connection to nature. The spells and rituals they used were conjured to help them take a measure of control over their lives and improve their lot as enslaved people. They also used their belief in God to make them feel stronger and identify his presence in all of nature.

What Is a Conjurer?

Understanding how Hoodoo works starts with the conjurer. They represented the knowledge and wisdom of the earth and nature and how to connect the physical world with the spiritual realm by using natural substances like herbs and roots combined with magical practices to connect to deities and spirits. As the African beliefs assimilated into the Christian religious base, Germanic and European influences were added to them. The US was a mixing pot of cultures, and, as a result, Hoodoo became a melded tradition of conjure that exists today.

Conjure has two main streams: the practice and wisdom passed down by conjure-orientated families who rely on their ancestors for advice and power. The second stream relies on more formal education sources. These conjurers use religious and scientific texts from other religions to learn and improve their magic practices. Conjure doctors would seek out respected grimoires and other religious texts about the occult to incorporate them into their own Hoodoo traditions.

It is believed that if anybody showed a natural gift for these beliefs, they would be taught by their peers how to become a conjurer. They would be taught traditional and more contemporary ways to connect with the spirits and their ancestors to commune with them and learn from their wisdom. Herbs and plants were known to have certain powers, and conjurers would work with them along with natural elements to control the flow of energies and improve the situations of the people that consulted them.

Today we can use the same principles to tap into the power of nature and change our lives. It isn't dangerous or even disrespectful to the church. Hoodoo isn't religious. It is simply magical and focuses on connecting to the natural world for effective results and the power to manifest results.

The Importance of God and the Saints in Hoodoo

Hoodoo is not a religion but is intrinsically entwined with Christianity, especially Protestant Christianity. Conjurers would use a practice called "Pleading the Blood" to add the power of the resurrection of Jesus to their spells. The power of life over death and the resurrection of Jesus brought the ultimate power of Christ that could be applied to any spell by using the phrase "I plead the blood of Jesus..." to power their work.

Hoodoo believes that the Bible is the ultimate spell/magic book and that Moses was the most acclaimed conjurer of all time. They don't believe in the Christian "You will obey or be damned" variety of the religion. Most Christians read the Bible and try to live by the commandments, while Hoodoo practitioners embrace the biblical God and his son, Jesus, the Holy Trinity, and the prophets and saints. They believe that Christianity gives them the power to fight demons, raise the dead, repel poisoners and be impervious to the devil. If you read the Bible as it was meant to be read, you'll realize that Hoodoo practices are much truer to the text than traditional Christian practices.

The Bible and Christianity were used for generations to justify slavery and the atrocities carried out by white enslavers in the past, but if you study the work of conjurors, you'll find they are closer to the true beliefs of Christianity than regular churchgoers. Hoodoo folk believe they have a connection to God and that he calls them to do his work on Earth, while most churchgoers believe the opposite and are content to worship past glories and have zero spiritual connections.

Working with the saints merely involves choosing the Christian saint who represents the power you need to fuel your root work. Most people know the more celebrated saints, but there are hundreds, if not thousands, of saints you can call upon to connect to you. There are Coptic saints, Russian, Irish, Jesuit, venerable, and blessed saints to choose from, so do your research and start connecting to the higher energies they bring.

Here are a few suggestions for some lesser-known saints who had incredible powers

1. **St Joseph of Cupertino, a.k.a. the flying saint.** This levitating saint didn't just fly in front of a couple of people once. He regularly flew into the sky in front of large groups of people, and once, he even levitated during an audience with the pope. It was reported that even mentioning God or one of the saints would send this maverick saint into the air. His constant flying soon became a problem, and the church labeled him a disruptive influence and locked him in a cell for the rest of his life.

2. **St. Catherine of Alexandria** was the ultimate conversion machine. Born a princess in Egypt in the 3rd century, she was well-educated and practiced paganism until she reached her teens. She claimed to have been visited by the Virgin Mary, who told Catherine that she was married to Christ in a spiritual union and that she should embrace the Christian faith. Catherine was so affected by the vision that she converted immediately. The Emperor of Rome at the time held an audience with her when she tried to persuade him to stop persecuting Christians, and despite his best efforts, she managed to convert some members of his court. The emperor was furious and imprisoned her, but she continued to convert the prisoners. He then tried to persuade her to stop by proposing marriage to her. When she refused, he sentenced her to death by the spiked wheel, but when the instrument shattered, he ordered her to be beheaded instead. She was finally executed with an ax.

3. **St. Vincent Ferrer** was raising the dead. Vincent was a theologian praised for his missionary work, but his most spectacular feat was bringing someone back from the dead. He was attending a procession leading a man to his death for his part in a crime that Vincent knew was unjust, and the man was innocent. He tried to plead with the officials responsible for the execution, but his pleas fell on deaf ears. At the same time, a corpse was being carried through the streets on a stretcher, and Vincent asked the corpse, "Is this man guilty?" the corpse sat up and answered, "No, he is not," before he lay back down on the stretcher. Vincent asked the dead man if he required a reward for his intervention, and the man replied, "No, for I am assured of salvation" before he promptly died again.

High John the Conqueror

Another powerful influence in Hoodoo culture is High John, a mighty tall man transported across the sea from Africa to serve as an enslaved person. He was a clever wily man who loved to avoid work and trick his master with his intelligence. If he had a shovel in the field, it would break, if he went to the shed, it would burn down, but his real skills were getting one over on his "Massa."

When John's master would be ready to whip him, John would turn around and work earnestly, exceeding any other worker in the field, and his master would calm his temper and let him live another day. He was also a master fisherman, and his master accompanied him to the fishing hole to help improve his skills. John admired the walking stick his master was carrying and said, "That's the finest three-ended stick I have ever seen," to which the master replied, "John, this stick has only two ends, and I bet you a chicken that you can't prove otherwise."

John replied, "No, it has three ends, this end is the handle, and the silver pointy end is the second one." He then took the walking stick to the swimming hole and threw it in. "See, Massa, that's the third end of your stick." His master realized he had been outwitted and paid John his chicken.

Another popular story revolved around John being tasked to prepare the turkey ready for Christmas. His master told him that whatever he did to the turkey, he would do to John. If John cut the turkey's head off, his head would be removed, and if he plucked the bird, the master would probably skin John alive.

On Christmas morning, the family was waiting for their turkey to arrive and expecting a good laugh at poor John's fate. He arrived with the turkey following behind him, attached to a red string. John approached the porch and greeted his master. He then picked the turkey up, turned it around, and kissed it on the butt. The master turned purple because he was so annoyed, and as he blustered and his eyes bulged, John turned around slowly, raised his butt slightly, and said, "Take your time; I got all day, folks!"

Enslaved people had very little to laugh about, and you can imagine them huddled in groups telling the tales of High John and his antics before belly-laughing at the foolish master and how John had tricked him.

Connect to Your Ancestors

Most spiritual and magic workers know the importance of connections with the past and how generations living before us can influence their work. Your ancestors determine your DNA. They lived their lives at different times, yet when you express emotions, you are connecting to their spirits. They lived through hard times so you could benefit from their toil, and they learned lessons so they could pass on their knowledge.

Modern religions have steered us away from ancestral ties, which means we sometimes forget where we come from. The blood that runs through your veins is a direct result of your ancestors, and the worship of their power remains part of a cultural pattern in various areas of the world like India, Asia, China, and among the Native Indians. Let's take time to celebrate these connections and remember our roots.

Different Ways to Connect to Your Ancestors

Genealogy

You can use multiple resources to trace your family tree, and even though it may seem daunting, it can be tremendous fun. There are multiple archives online and advice on how to start tracing your roots back to your ancestors. The first couple of generations, including your parents and grandparents, can prove to be an effective way to bring your family closer and discover what they lived through and how their childhoods differed from yours.

DNA Analysis

This relatively new technology allows you to delve back in time and discover your ancestors' origins. You could find ties to the Vikings, Celts, or even medieval ancestors. You just don't know what you'll discover and the advantages it will give you in your magic.

Scrapbooking

Once you have details of your ancestors and their occupations and places where they lived, you can start to build a comprehensive scrapbook of your findings. Create a sacred book that can be designated to their memories, and make a page for each of your ancestors. Use the tree of life design to create a spiritual family tree and enter anything relevant and interesting to strengthen your connection.

Create a Section on Your Altar for Your Ancestors

We will cover this in the chapter dedicated to altar and shrine creation later in the book.

Invite Them into Your Dreams

Ask them to come, and your ancestors will visit you in your dreams. They may be relatives you already know about, but they could be ancestors that haven't yet been discovered. Ask pertinent questions, and you will get the answers you need. They will then be with you in spirit whenever you need them and will bring strength and wisdom to your Hoodoo work and other sections of your life. Remember to keep a notebook by your bedside table to record your dreams as part of your normal routine.

Pray to Your Ancestors

Regardless of your religious beliefs, the power of prayer cannot be overlooked. Prayer is another way to show respect and connect to your higher beings and energies. You don't have to kneel or bow your head. You must just be respectful and sincere. Talk to them as if they were in the room with you and listen to every word you say. Do it in your head or speak out loud, depending on what makes you feel more comfortable and enjoy the experience. They are just as overjoyed to hear your voice as you should be to form these connections.

Recreate Crafts They Would Have Enjoyed

Ancient skills have been forgotten, and the only place you see modern people making their own fires and hunting food is on the television in survival programs. Learning how to do these elemental skills will make you more adept at survival and keeps the connection to your more distant ancestors alive. You can still follow your more recent ancestors' skills by taking up crochet or knitting if it was something your grandmother did. Was your grandfather a skilled hunter or fisherman? Take up the hobby they loved doing and feel those connections strengthen. Ask family members if they have original tools from your heritage that you can use. A pair of knitting needles or a fishing rod that is unfused with their energy will help your connection become more personal.

Foods and Drinks

Celebrate your heritage at the dinner table by recreating dishes that originate from your ancestral ties. Is your family Irish? Soda bread is so simple to make, and Irish stew is a fabulous family meal you can share with a table full of people. Serve a side of colcannon with tasty potatoes and spring onions accompanied by a pint of Guinness and toast your Celtic relatives. Are your family from the West Indies? Make spicy curries and soul food to celebrate their heritage. Food and drink are the staples of life, and forming connections can be exciting as well as being a new experience for your taste buds.

Rituals and Meditation

Some people are skilled at creating rituals to connect to their ancestors, but sometimes beginners need more detailed instructions. Follow the ritual below to connect to your ancestors and safely cross the veil between this world and theirs.

What You Need

- Four white candles
- One red tea light
- Five holders for your candles
- Olive oil to dress your candles
- Protective herbs to keep you safe (basil, cumin, or clover will work but choose your own depending on your preferences)
- An herb with links to your ancestor's homeland (get creative here and research the herbs that are popular in Italy, for instance, or Eastern Germany)
- A dish for rolling. You can also use a cutting board as a candle rolling area
- Red ribbon or string
- Lighter or matches
- Incense to bring strength to your work (dragons blood works well)
- Incense to commemorate your ancestor's homeland
- Divination tools for your ancestors to speak through, cards or dice, bones or runes, whatever tools you are familiar with

Choose a time when the veil between the two worlds is at its flimsiest, like dusk or midnight. Choose a lunar phase incorporating the Dark of the Full moon to bring strength to your work.

Prepare the area for your ritual by cleansing it with sage or another method of smudging or sweeping. Now take a bath to make sure you are free from negative energies. Take all your supplies into the center of the room and decide where your sacred circle will be. Set the four white candles in the corners to indicate the four points of the circle, north, east, south, and west. Make sure you have plenty of room to work in and gather the remaining supplies in your work area.

Cast the Circle

1. Position yourself at the northern point of the area and take the lighter in your hand. Imagine yourself in a vast cave filled with white light reflecting off walls filled with crystals.

2. Call upon the element of the north, which is the earth, by raising your arms and saying, "I call on you to nourish me and protect me from all evil on this magical night." Light the white candle of the north.

3. Now turn to the west of the circle and ask for the element of water to assist you before you light the candle.

4. Repeat the exercise in the following two corners invoking the elements of fire and air before lighting the candles to complete your circle.

5. Now state, "The circle is now cast, and let no spirit or energy enter this sacred space without my direct invitation."

Your circle is now cast and ready for your ritual. If you have a preferred method of casting a circle, ignore the instructions above and use your method instead.

Call Your Ancestors

1. Put the oil and chosen herbs on your anointing dish or board and roll the red candle in the liquid.

2. As you roll the candle, imagine your ancestors watching over you and how they look. Remember the struggles they endured in their lifetimes and the joys they felt when they succeeded. Imagine how they feel connecting to you at that moment as you dress your candle.

3. Place the candle in the holder and light your intensifying incense.

4. Raise the energy in the circle by doing your favorite activity. Dance, chant, or pray to increase the energy and positivity in the circle, and take as long as you like.

5. Once you feel the levels are at their optimum, light the red candle.

6. Take the red string or yarn, weave it through your fingers, hold your hands to your heart, and say the following words: "*I call upon*

my ancestors to join me in this world. I lead the way with this symbolic light and ask those who have gone before me to protect me in this dimension. Bring your strength and wisdom to my world, and I invite only the ancestors that have my best wishes in their hearts. I thank them for the blood, sweat, and tears they shed for me to allow me to enjoy my life on this earth."

7. Ensure the string or yarn is secure and not a fire hazard by tying it securely around your wrist.

8. Light the offertory incense and say, *"May my offering of scented smoke bring you joy and cement our relationship. I give you this offering to celebrate the protection and love you bring to my world. So it shall be."*

9. Now sit and speak to the relatives you have summoned. You may wish to use your divination tools to assist the conversation or use your psychic abilities to hear them. Listen to what they are saying and let the session last for as long as the candle takes to burn down.

10. Once the ritual has ended, thank the ancestors for their input and the messages they have sent you.

11. Close the circle by snuffing out the candles, releasing the elements in turn, and thanking them for their assistance.

Once the ritual is complete, it's time to ground yourself and recover from the excess energy you created. A simple meal of bread and cheese with a soothing cup of tea will help, or you can meditate to regain your equilibrium. Moving on will take a couple of hours, and this is normal, so don't worry. Once your energy levels have been restored to normal, you can sleep and recover.

The ritual remains will include the incense ashes and the candles' wax. Take a red bag, place these remains in the bag, and tie it with the red string. Hang it on your door for protection, or carry it with you so you can feel their protection throughout the day. Use the bag to center yourself if you require further communication with your relatives.

Remember that you have formed a contract with your ancestors, and this should be celebrated with regular offerings. Leave a glass of wine on your shrine or even a simple cup of coffee every week. Place an item of food or a small bunch of flowers. Your offerings should reflect their personality and what they enjoyed on Earth before they passed.

Loa Spirits

A more traditional form of spirit in Hoodoo centers upon the Loa spirits, an original form of spirit from the Voodoo tradition that Hoodoo has adapted to bring benevolence and love to the magic. They are connected to the voodoo dolls and headless chickens in the movies, but the Loa are important spirits that you can choose to work with or ignore.

They are the Hoodoo version of guardian angels who guard the realms of the dead, and while figures like Papa Legba or Baron Samedi may seem dangerous and frightening, some Hoodoo practitioners will call on them when they need added power to fight their enemies. This is not something beginners should try, and even advanced Hoodoo rootworkers would stay away from the Loa. They are mentioned here purely as a source of reference and a matter of interest. They inspired the Hoodoo's use of poppets and mojo bags for added magic.

Chapter 3: Ingredients and Materials You Need

Original Hoodoo practitioners had little to choose from to form their spells and potions. They were enslaved and didn't have access to materials apart from what was in their environment. As enslaved people, they would be responsible for food preparation and would often have a full run of the kitchen. This explains why a lot of their spells and magic are based on the power of herbs and roots. As the enslaved people converged in the US, they brought their knowledge of magical herbs and roots with them and worked together to make their Hoodoo magic stronger and more effective.

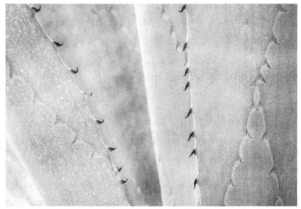

Used for protection and security, aloe vera plants would often be planted at the doorways of the home to keep evil spirits away.
https://www.pexels.com/photo/close-up-photography-of-aloe-vera-plant-1578501/

Magical Hoodoo Herbs and Roots

Adam and Eve Root, also known as the putty root or Aplectrum

This root was used to promote relationships and help couples form stronger bonds. It was a popular ingredient in potions to cure sexual problems and promote fertility and sexual energy. The root originated from an orchid found in eastern parts of the US and Canada, and the leaves are pinstripe with dark green stripes. The male part of the plant was carried by the man, while the woman carried the female part to ensure they would stay together and remain faithful. A new love was also attracted to practitioners who carried the Adam and Eve root in their mojo bags.

Unfortunately, the plant is now labeled as endangered, and products purported to contain the root will probably have a substitute ingredient. Make sure any products you buy have sourced their ingredients ethically.

Allspice Berries

Original Hoodoo workers used these to bring good luck and prosperity. Gamblers would take allspice berries when they played games of chance or needed luck in business matters. Today the allspice berries are known for relieving psychological stress and anxiety. Allspice is also known as Jamaican pepper, myrtle, and pimento and can be found in all good spice shops. If you want to prepare your own, pick the berries of the Pimenta tree and dry them in the sun.

Alfalfa

Also called lucerne, this plant is cultivated for foraging, used as food for livestock and cattle, and made into hay for the winter. It has recently emerged as a superfood because it is packed with vitamins and is effective in boosting your immune system. Hoodoo uses rootwork for general good luck, money spells, and overall prosperity. Keep it in your purse or in a money box to attract money to you and your family.

Alkanet Root

This herb from the borage family was used to dye clothes red and was a common part of Hoodoo work. It attracts money and increases good luck.

Aloe Vera

Used for protection and security, aloe vera plants would often be planted at the doorways of the home to keep evil spirits away. Today the plant is widely available and provides a decorative plant for the home.

Angelica Root

Also known as the Holy Ghost or Archangel root, this herb is a form of wild celery that has impressive health benefits. It is a staple ingredient in Hoodoo workings and should be included in potions to help women find strength and peace. It also breaks jinxes and is a powerful guardian for the user. Carry this in your mojo bag to ward off evil spirits and attract luck and prosperity.

Anise

Also called aniseed, this potent plant is a powerful protection ingredient that keeps evil spirits at bay and helps the rootworker to enhance their psychic abilities. Some Hoodoo spells include anise to connect with the spirits.

Basil

Widely used in the kitchen in Hoodoo, this common herb brings love and happiness to a household and is representative of peace and harmony. It is associated with the Haitian goddess Erzulie and the Hindu god Vishnu.

Bay Leaves

A common ingredient, bay leaves are incredibly powerful in Hoodoo spells. They bring protection, security, and clarity of mind to spells. They also ward off evil spirits and banish enemies, ensuring victory in conflicts. Use them in potions for increased health and spirituality and to increase personal insight.

Black Peppercorns

Whole black peppercorns were added to spells to enable revenge for the spell caster and to cause pain and sorrow to their enemies. Use them to guard your home against unwanted visitors and evil spirits.

Buckeye Nuts

In the UK, these nuts are called conkers and are used in childhood games, but when used in the US, they are a potent ingredient in Hoodoo practices. They bring power and luck and increase sexual potency for users.

Cactus

Use the spines to jinx your enemies or as protection from evil and attacks.

Catnip

A plant from the mint family, which has a pungent smell that attracts cats, is also a powerful way to attract women. Men should carry it in their pockets to attract the fairer sex and increase their sexual potency.

Cayenne Pepper

This popular ingredient in spicy Cajun dishes is also used to create chaos in your enemies' households and drive away your enemies.

Chamomile

A fragrant herb popular in teas, chamomile is a general good luck ingredient and will help you calm your household and remove any financial jinxes.

Clover

A popular plant in folklore from diverse cultures, this is a commonly used ingredient for good luck and prosperity. It is also used to promote love and fidelity in relationships. Its leaves are thought to represent the holy trinity, and three leaves are more sacred than four.

Coconut

Use the whole coconut to represent the whole head and the mind. You can work with the coconut to dominate the target's thoughts and experiences to reward or punish them depending on your intentions.

Dandelion

This common weed is a potent ingredient for granting wishes and increasing psychic visions.

Devil's Dung

This aromatic and pungent dried latex originates from the roots of the rhizome root and is used to repel illness and evil. Also known as asafetida, it is named after the Latin term "foetidus" which literally means stinky. Use it to protect your home and family from evil and cast curses on those who would harm you. Wear gloves while you work, as the smell will linger for days on your bare skin.

Devils' Shoestring

This member of the pea family will often appear on the dining table and is a powerful herb in most witchcraft. The long stringy stems are thought to be effective in tripping the devil and keeping him away from your house. Carry the roots when gambling, and luck will follow you.

Dill

Another popular herb found in most kitchens, dill is added to spells and potions to break love curses and lift any jinxes placed on the practitioner. It brings luck in legal matters and reinforces sexual feelings and attraction.

Dragon's Blood

A natural plant resin that originates from the sedum plant dragon's blood is used in spells for protection and general good luck. Use in potions to bring prosperity and luck when gambling.

Fennel

Wild fennel is a hardy plant that is delicious in recipes, but in Hoodoo, it represents a barrier against legal issues and keeps away meddlers who want to know your business. Use it in spells to protect your home from troublesome spirits.

Five Finger Grass

Also known as cinquefoil, this plant looks like a human hand with its five segmented leaves. It is used to draw money and wealth and improve career prospects. Carry it with you when you travel to keep you and your money safe from harm. Five-finger grass is also a powerful plant for uncrossing curses and hexes.

Garlic

Popular in vampire lore, garlic is the ultimate protection ingredient.

Ginger

A fiery spicy ingredient in food, it also brings heat to Hoodoo spells. Use it to inflame passions and bring luck to gamblers.

Ginseng

Traditionally used in sex potions, Hoodoo practitioners used ginseng to protect themselves and their loved ones.

High John the Conqueror

One of the staple ingredients in any Hoodoo household, the root is obtained from the plant Ipomoea purga and is used for prosperity, luck, and the strength to conquer your enemies. See chapter 2 for more details about John and his origins.

Holly

The popular leafy green plant protects the home by placing it at the doorway and in windows.

Ivy

Another popular and fast-growing plant you should use is ivy to keep your home safe.

Jasmine

Use this pleasantly scented herb to bring love and joy to your potions and spells.

Job's Tears

A tall growing grass crop, the roots and the seeds are both used in Hoodoo root work. They represent the wishes of the worker and ensure they come true. The seeds should be carried when gambling to bring success and good luck.

Juniper

The lush green leaves and roots of this tree bring love and luck to your work, and the berries are used to create teas and baths to increase sexual attraction.

Lemon Balm

Use in baths and potions to cleanse the body and soul while dispelling any bad luck regarding your relationships. It draws in new love and attracts healthy connections.

Lettuce

Any kind of lettuce will do. Use the leaves to draw money towards you. The fresh leaves on the darker types of lettuce work best.

Licorice Root

Used to command the will of others and make them bend to your will. Use it to dominate and control your enemies.

Lucky Hand Root

This root is from a wild orchid named the salep and is a highly regarded ingredient in magical terms. It gives extraordinarily strong protection and luck, especially in gambling.

Magnolia Leaves

The leaves from the flowering magnolia should be used to control husbands with wandering eyes. Keep them faithful and focused on their wives with this ingredient.

Mandrake Root

Originally from the nightshade family of plants, this root has regained notoriety due to its use in popular Harry Potter stories. Carve the root into a doll form to inspire love and passion, or carry it in its original form to bring prosperity.

Mimosa

You may know it as a tasty cocktail, but in magic, the mimosa genus contains over five hundred species of plants. The leaves of the common mimosa tree are used for protection in spells and potions.

Mint

Common wild mint brings fresh and cooling energy to your spells. It can calm arguments and bring peace to your home. Use it to create barriers your enemies cannot cross and keep yourself safe. Carry it with you to increase your psychic abilities.

Mistletoe

A common parasite in the natural world, mistletoe is used to ward off all forms of evil. Hang it in your thresholds to protect yourself from evil and keep your home safe.

Mustard Seed

Use this common ingredient to improve male sexual energy and restore luck, especially in business.

Nutmeg

Another common kitchen ingredient, you can use nutmeg to attract love and bring good luck.

Orris Root

Also known as the Queen Elizabeth root, it is originally sourced from the rootstock of the iris flower. It tastes like raspberry and is used to flavor tinctures and potions. In Hoodoo, it is used to attract men to women and is also used by men to control their enemies.

Onion

The common onion is often used for protection, and its pungent odor both cleanses and repels evil.

Parsley

The common herb found in most kitchens has specific powers in Hoodoo. Use it when negotiating housing issues like rental or negotiating contracts to ensure success. Parsley is used to celebrate the passing of relatives and loved ones and to increase fertility.

Patchouli

A strong-smelling oil patchouli is used to draw love and money to the wearer and uncross any hexes placed on them.

Raspberry Leaves

Use it to create fidelity in your relationship and bring good luck to you both.

Rose

This fragrant flower is used to bring luck and love to your household.

Rosemary

Especially powerful for spells cast for and by women. It brings good dreams and keeps them safe and empowered. Use rosemary to bring strength and femininity to your work.

Rue

A sprig of this evergreen bush worn under your clothes will ward off evil and make you impervious to the evil eye.

Sage

A protective and potent herb for cleansing your home and bringing blessings to your door. It is especially powerful for female users and attracts wisdom and knowledge to the user.

Spanish Moss

This moss is often found growing on trees in subtropical climates, but it can be bought from good herbal outlets. Use dried Spanish moss to stuff your poppets or dolls used in your Hoodoo practices. It can be used to jinx and curse others or draw money to your spells.

Thyme

Add thyme to your spells to stop bad dreams and bring peace of mind. It also has strong financial benefits.

Violet

Use the violet's flowers and roots when dealing with innocence and chastity. It brings pure and innocent power to your spells and can be used in potions or in baths.

Willow

The magnificent willow tree is a powerful part of Hoodoo magic; the leaves are used for protection and health. Use it to attract love and passion.

Witch Grass

Also known as devil's grass, this common ingredient is used to break up lovers and cast spells on your enemies. When dried, it can be used to stuff dolls and poppets.

Yarrow

Also known as old man's pepper and the devil's nettle, yarrow is a perennial herb that is found in the wild. It is used for courage and to make the user brave in times of conflict. It is also used for divination purposes.

Tools for Conjure

Just like the herbs and plants they used, Hoodoo workers were restricted by their lack of possessions and had to make do with their everyday tools. This means that conjuring tools are often multipurpose items found in the house or nature. No fancy implements or exotic items need to be cleansed at certain times of the day or kept sacred. Hoodoo is all about everyday folk using everyday items to create magic.

Today, Hoodoo tools can be more ornate and purchased from dedicated sites and stores, but keeping your magic real should involve using tools that resemble the original Hoodoo practitioners used.

Below are some ordinary items that can be used for magic – and an explanation of how they can provide multiple uses, keeping it simple and inexpensive to practice the craft.

Screwdriver

Every household should have a screwdriver, and, in magic, these handy tools are perfect for writing on your wax candles and carving symbols on pliable materials. Use it to make holes to insert oils and herbs into your candles to make them more potent and magical.

Wine Glasses

Flat-based glasses can obviously be used to hold wine, but they can also be used to cover open flames when they are burning down to form seals.

Aluminum Cans

Perhaps the most versatile items in your home. Wash them out and use them to hold candles, melt the wax to form your own candle, or deposit burning pieces of paper with spells and petitions on them so they can burn safely. Use the cans to keep your herbs and roots in, and engrave the lids with a list of what they contain. Use tuna cans for more shallow burning needs or substitute with metal ashtrays instead.

Laces and Ribbons from Old Clothes or Shoes

Use these to perform cord magic and add color and texture to your spells.

Saucers

Because of the curved shape of the common saucer, you can place pieces of paper with your spells under the saucer and then burn a candle on the surface. They are sturdy enough for pillar candles to sit on and are handy to store.

Coin Purses

Later in this book, we will cover the art of making mojo bags, but if you haven't had time to make one, then a coin purse will do for now.

Cork Coasters

These handy objects are the perfect size for use as talismans, and you can easily burn magical symbols on the cork for an effective appearance.

Cutting Board

Because they are designed for mixing ingredients and working with food, they are perfect as candle boards. Use a cutting board to spread herbs and powders into a mixture in which you can roll your oil-anointed candles to ensure a smooth and complete coverage.

Children's Dolls

If you enjoy the idea of a poppet or a Hoodoo doll but don't have the time to make your own, any action figure or child's doll will work. Choose one for housing your spirits or to represent an individual.

Board Game Tokens

The tokens used in Monopoly and Cluedo are great for representing your needs and desires in mojo bags. The shoe represents travel, the money sack is financial strength, and the rope is a binding tool. Search for other tokens in more abstract places to make your collection quirky and magical. Tokens from arcades are also a decorative way to improve your magic tool arsenal and depict all forms of magical images. Look out for them on Internet auction sites and in antique shops.

Candles

One of the staple parts of your tool collection, you should have candles of varying colors and sizes so you can adapt them to your needs. Candles are everywhere, and there is no need to splash too much cash when buying your candles, especially when you are a beginner.

Divining Items

Some Hoodoo practitioners have a psychic connection with the spirits and use traditional divination methods to connect to them and foresee the future. Most readings are from items thrown by the user onto a clean white cloth and interpreted by traditional methods to predict the future. These items can be as diverse as dried bones. Chicken bones are perfect when dried or use stones or crystals.

Playing cards are another cheap and effortless way to practice divination, and an ordinary pack can be used for beginners. When you decide that cards are your preferred method of connecting with the spirits, you can progress onto specially designed Hoodoo cards that are both decorative and more dedicated to the magical world.

Dice are popular divination tools and can be read simply using instructions. They also represent a connection to the olden ways as they were often made from bones, so if the thought of handling actual bones repels you, try to find a set of dice made from bone instead.

Paper for writing petitions to the spirits

Brown grocery sacks are hardy and handy for writing your petitions, but the paper you choose isn't that important. What you write on it is the key to conjuring the response you require.

Some practitioners have adapted tools from other practices, but the original Hoodoo rootworkers didn't have that luxury. Keep costs low and be creative with your spiritual toolbox.

Dust and Dirt in Hoodoo

You will have noticed that there are no bowls or mixing implements here; they will be covered in the chapter about your Hoodoo altar. Also, many spells and traditional Hoodoo practices used dirt, more specifically graveyard dirt, which is now considered inappropriate and, in most cases, illegal. The thought of somebody entering a graveyard and taking the soil from a grave doesn't sit well in today's society, so it's probably best if you don't use it.

Alternative sources come from burning coffee grounds, patchouli leaves, sage, or other flammable sources that can be burned safely. Another alternative is to burn any plants from your garden that have withered and died to represent the connection to the dead, but as most Hoodoo practices are concentrated on connecting to your ancestors, this may seem redundant. However, if you believe that the spirits of the dead plant are just as powerful as human spirits, this gives you a safe way to connect to the afterlife. As with all your magic work, the choice is yours.

You may still want to practice the original art by using dust or dirt from crossroads. This represents turning a corner and is used in spells where a decision needs to be made, or a change in circumstances is required. Collect dirt from a place that is a recognized crossroad or a place that represents your personal space, depending on the spells you are conducting. There are no fixed rules, as crossroads mean different things to different people.

Keeping a Checklist of Your Tools and Ingredients

Who said that witches and root workers couldn't be organized? Just like you have a shopping list for your kitchen, it can be helpful to keep a checklist for your Hoodoo work. Keep a list of your favorite herbs and ingredients somewhere you can check them regularly and refill any of your ingredients that are getting low.

Chapter 4: Getting Ready for Hoodoo

How do you prepare for a job interview? What do you do before a big date? What rituals do you follow in the morning to ensure you face the day at your best? You prepare using certain routines, take extra care over your appearance, and take care of any items you need to use to make these experiences better and more successful. So why are you wondering what to do before starting your Hoodoo practice? Inexperience in beginners sometimes mean they forget the basic rules of life regarding Hoodoo. They are so committed to getting to the fun stuff that they forget that the prep is just as important as the process, if not more.

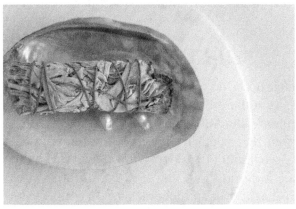

Cleansing with smoke helps you breathe in the healing smoke and let go of the negativity and excess anxiety.
https://www.pexels.com/photo/a-burning-sage-on-a-shell-with-pearls-6766465/

First, let's answer some FAQs about cleansing and why it's so important

1. **Why is spiritual cleansing so important?**

Negative energy will accumulate in your energy field during normal life. You are regularly subject to stress, anger, fear, and other negative forces and absorb negativity from other people in your space. Removing this energy will clear your spiritual aura and allow positivity to flow to you. Your sacred space is also subject to these negative forces; some spirits and divine beings will be more likely to visit clean and positive spaces. After all, who wants to visit somewhere filled with negativity and spiritual debris?

2. **Why should we clean our sacred spaces even if nobody has been there?**

If your sacred space is in your home or your garden, it will be affected by your visitors, even if they are nearby and not in the actual space. All the traffic that flows through your home and the energies they carry will invade your space even through airborne means. Remember that you also carry your own negative forces into the space and deposit them whenever possible. It isn't worth the risk of muddying your energies with negativity just to avoid a cleansing beforehand.

3. **What rituals should I use?**

As with all cleansing rituals, you tend to follow a set pattern and use materials that suit your needs. Spiritual cleansing is just the same. We will consider some effective cleansing methods that you can try and choose the ones that feel right for you. In time the methods you use will become so natural that you won't even think about them, and they will come naturally.

Self-Cleansing Rituals

- **Bathing**. A classic relaxing bath in water infused with salts, herbs, roots, or other ingredients will help you relax physically and metaphorically. Add crystals and play soothing music to help you sink into the water and let go of all that negativity. If you don't have a bathtub, consider bathing in a natural water source. Taking a dip in the ocean or a cool flowing stream will cleanse and recharge your spirit and leave you connected to nature.

- **Smudging**. Cleansing with smoke helps you breathe in the healing smoke and let go of the negativity and excess anxiety. Use classic sage to cleanse yourself, or choose from the multiple cleansing herbs that will do the job just as well. Try rosemary, rose, lavender, or citrus leaves to mix it up a bit. Mix your herbs and light them safely to smudge your aura, and move the smudging stick from your head to your toes in a sweeping motion to clear your body and mind.

- **Crystal cleansing.** Crystals provide a powerful way to draw negative energy from you. Use selenite or black tourmaline to remove the energy from your personal space by passing them over your body to absorb the destructive energy forces.

- **Fire cleansing.** Older forms of Hoodoo used the element fire to cleanse people who had been possessed and filled with the spirit of another, but today we can use the same principle to cleanse our bodies and minds. Jumping over a bonfire was a ritual that has been consigned to history because of safety issues, but you can still represent the element with an unlit candle. Choose a white candle and then roll it over your body to absorb the harmful energy by lighting it once the ritual has been fulfilled.

- **Magical sprays.** Spraying yourself with liquid infused with magical properties is a great alternative to bathing. If you don't have time for a shower or bath, then use a cleansing spray to bring positivity to your body and feel refreshed and ready to work your magic.

- **Detox.** Using healing teas and other detox liquids will cleanse you from within and help you feel refreshed and hydrated.

- **Egg cleansing.** If you love thinking outside the box, try this nifty way to cleanse using nature's products. Take an egg in its shell and roll it over your body. Make sure you cover the entire body and even roll it over your face and head. Now crack the egg in a bowl of water and see what it tells you. If the yolk is dull or the white is cloudy, it is a clear sign that you have transferred your negative energies into the egg.

- **Cleanse your energy directly.** Use ancient methods like Reiki or yoga to boost your positivity and banish the residual energy lurking there. We will examine meditations you can also use later in this chapter.

Cleansing Rituals for Your Home

- **Smoke cleansing.** Smudging for the home is just as effective as it is for the body. Use traditional herbs and rid your sacred space of negative energy. Make sure you are safe and have methods for always dowsing the fire and smoke. Remember to open the windows to allow the harmful energies to escape and clear the smoke. You want clean and positive energy, not a smoky room, so you can begin your Hoodoo workings.

- **Blessing the space.** Use infused liquids and dip a branch of your favorite tree to bless your space. Sprinkle the liquid from the branch and say a few words of blessing to strengthen the process.

- **Floor washes and sweeps.** Just like regular cleaning, this type of cleansing begins with the basics and cleans the surface of your space from negativity. Use a sweeping brush made from natural twigs to add intent to your process, and wash the floor with specially infused cleansers. Another way to freshen the area is to spread dried herbs around your floor – and then sweep them up. The energy they leave behind will stay with you until it's time to cleanse again.

- **Spritz the room.** Just like you used a spray to cleanse yourself, you can use a spray to concentrate your cleanse in certain parts of the space. Spritz your shrine or altar to give it a deep cleanse or spray around the doorway and windows to create strong barriers.

- **Diffusers.** Modern Hoodoo practitioners know that they can benefit from more modern methods of cleansing, and diffusers offer a balanced and safe method for getting the essence of their favorite herbs into the atmosphere. Essential oils are a fun and inexpensive way to bring the power of lemongrass, lavender, ylang-ylang, and all your favorite essences to your space.

- **Cleanse with light.** The sun's healing rays are a natural and effective way to clean your area. Don't sit in the dark; get those curtains open and let the power of solar energy flood your space. Open the windows and let all that stale and negative energy go. The sun will soon have those low-level entities heading for the hills.

- **Cleanse with sound.** Use bells and gongs to drive out negative energy. If you don't have any instruments, walk through your home from the front door to the back, clapping your hands, especially near the walls. Create a loop of energy in your home that you can fill with positivity by using sound and noise to create barriers.

- **Cleanse with salt.** Use Himalayan salt for a deep and pure cleanse. Sprinkle the salt at the doorway and on the sills of any windows. If you aren't a fan of the messy salt method, use a Himalayan salt lamp to bring the same energy.

As a routine, you should perform some form of self-cleanse at least once a week but especially after discord or arguments. If you feel a heavy atmosphere in your home, cleansing will help to lift spirits and create a calmer atmosphere.

How to Recognize If You Need a Cleanse

1. When you feel deep emotions without any explanation. Your mood swings from gleeful to deeply upset without any outside influences, and you feel affected by the smallest incidents.

2. Certain people make you feel drained or exhausted. You can't face them and actively avoid being in their company.

3. You need to shield yourself from the outside world. Feeling reluctant to leave the house and mix with other people is a clear sign that your energy levels are depleted. It isn't normal to isolate yourself and avoid company.

4. Your anxiety levels are on full alert. You constantly feel that you are in danger or that something is about to happen that won't be good for you.

5. You feel like somebody else's energy has invaded your mind or body. Do you feel haunted by someone else in your space or mind despite them not being there physically?

6. You are dogged by feelings of doom or negativity and see the worst in everything you see or feel. Evil seems like a part of your world, and you can't shake those feelings off.

7. Picking up other people's illnesses and health issues. If you begin to feel symptoms of illnesses you *don't have* but someone close to you *does have*, you are experiencing a transfer of energy from them, and you need a cleanse.

8. Other people's emotions and relationship issues infringe on your own emotions. If a friend of yours has a damaging breakup yet you feel the effects that aren't healthy and want to be of assistance to them, you need to cleanse your energy so you can be there for them.

9. Whenever you can't let go of arguments or conflicts, you are held back by your emotions and the energy they have created. Cleansing your energy will help you let go of past issues and resolve them by drawing a line in the sand.

10. When you feel something is off, but you don't know why.

Meditation Routines to Raise Your Vibrations

These simple meditation routines are designed to help with varying issues and target why you feel uncoordinated. Choose the one that speaks to you, and you will benefit from their tailored instructions.

Self-Forgiveness

For complete peace of mind, the first person you need to forgive is yourself. If you are holding on to negativity, you'll be unable to forgive others. Self-forgiveness is a precious gift you can give yourself. It brings peace to your spirit, transforms your life, and is helpful to those who come into your social circle.

For all your meditation, you need to find a space where you feel safe, calm, and able to express yourself without fear of being disturbed. Seat yourself on the floor and close your eyes before you focus on your intentions for five minutes. See your breath enter and leave your body and draw strength from it. Now picture yourself in your mind.

Think of what you have done to yourself to cause pain. Sometimes it can be helpful to imagine yourself in the third person and refer to yourself by your name. When you have a thought about the alternative, you and the harm they have caused throw the thought away as if it is a physical item.

What were the weaknesses that caused the alternative you to act like that? Was it a lack of self-awareness or emotional influences that made them act that way? Understand what fueled their behavior and why they did what they did. As your awareness grows, it will help you understand that, as humans, we are all flawed and that sometimes we expect too much. Tell yourself you forgive them and have let go of the pain they caused you. Tell them you forgive them, you understand why they acted as they did, and that you'll be more understanding and show more self-love in the future.

Relax for ten minutes and refocus on your breathing. Feel your emotions and spirit return to normal, and open your eyes. You should feel lighter and forgiven with a renewed understanding of your character and spirit.

The self-forgiveness meditation script can be adapted to work if you need to forgive others for the pain that they have caused you. Simply imagine their faces instead of your own and address the issues they have caused you. The process is cathartic, and you control the energy you bring to the experience. You can safely express your anger and frustration before letting it go forever.

A Healing Meditation Exercise

This exercise takes around seven minutes, including a minute at the end of the exercise, to relax and return to normal.

1. Sit or lie down in a comfortable place in a relaxing position.
2. Make your body completely still and relaxed.
3. Feel your muscles and limbs expand and grow longer as your body relaxes and softens.
4. Notice any additional sensations that are happening in your mind and body.
5. Ask yourself why you are feeling the things you are and how they make you react emotionally.
6. Listen to your body and the messages it is sending you.
7. Slow your breathing and let your focus rest on the air as it enters and leaves your lungs.
8. Close your mouth completely and breathe through your nose, taking notice of any changes to the messages this triggers.
9. Feel your abdomen rise and fall, and be aware of any sounds you make as you inhale and exhale.
10. Permit your body to declutter.
11. Name your breaths and breathe in love.
12. Breathe out tension.
13. Breathe in peace.
14. Breathe out anger.
15. Breathe in harmony.

16. Breathe out conflict.

17. Breathe in healing.

18. Breathe out illness.

19. Let your breath become deeper before you repeat the last exercise of inhaling and exhaling.

20. With the final breath, let out all self-judgment and criticism.

21. Breathe in love and joy.

22. Let your mind travel from the top of your head to the tips of your toes and heal your body.

23. Allow your body to share the energy equally and begin to heal.

24. Feel the here and now as you return to your conscious state.

25. Feel the silence for a minute before returning to your conscious life.

Inner Peace Meditation

Change your posture for this meditation to experience energy flow with your body shape. Sit in a comfortable place with your feet firmly on the floor approximately a foot in front of you. Let your knees relax and keep your ankles firm. Roll your shoulders to relax your posture, and then lower your chin to lengthen your neck.

Close your eyes and focus on your breaths. Take mindful breaths for a count of twenty and focus on the path the air takes. How are you feeling? What are your emotions and energy levels? Do you feel inner peace? Is there still turmoil? If you still feel unbalanced, repeat the breathing exercise. Is your body warm or cold? Relax and feel every sensation you can feel.

As you feel the peace descending, thank the spirits for their help and open your eyes slowly. Now begin to regain your normal senses and return to the waking world.

Harmony Meditation

Sit in a comfortable position where your back is supported, and you feel peaceful. Close your eyes and take a deep, meaningful breath.

Imagine a candle flickering brightly in your mind and allowing the flame's warmth to flow through your body, warming your aura. Let the warmth fill your soul and heart, and feel the glow reach your skin.

Keep your focus on the candle flame for as long as it feels comfortable, and bring your breath back to your focus. Remember to keep the glow of the candle in your heart as your eyes flicker open and you rejoin the world.

As you go about your daily routine, take the time to stop and reconnect with your inner candle to experience the harmony it holds for you.

When to Perform Cleansings

When should you cleanse your space? Every week, every month, or just when you feel the need? Here are some basic tips to help you craft your cleansing routine and make sure it works for you:

- **When there is a waning moon, cleanse your space.** When there is a new moon, cleanse your space. The natural energy will automatically cleanse your aura, but it needs to infiltrate your space, cleanse in the moonlight, and take advantage of the natural rays whenever you can.

- **Following illness, death, or serious misfortune in your home.** Has someone passed away or contracted a serious illness? Cleansing is essential to keep yourself immune, and you should cleanse both yourself and your space. If you perform rituals and spells to deal with the grief or to help the illness wane, you'll get better results with a positive space and attitude.

- **Always clear your space if you are collaborating with new spirits or deities.** You don't want residual energy sources to interfere with your connection, so cleanse yourself and your space, so you provide a blank canvas for their energy to impact upon.

- **After collaborating with new spirits and deities,** it's time for another cleanse. You don't want to bring any unfamiliar energies to your regular spirits, or they may rebel and start to pull away. The spirits need to know you respect them, and if you turn up with an aura or space soiled with unfamiliar energy, they may take offense.

- **Whenever visitors have left or if someone new moves into the home,** it will affect the spiritual balance of your space. Cleanse and restore the equilibrium before you start any rootwork or spells.

Chapter 5: Create a Hoodoo Shrine

What is a shrine? The definition says it is a place marked by its association with a sacred deity or relic and is a construction or building that people can visit to mark that respect. In Hoodoo, we recognize that deities and spirits are important, but worship can occur anywhere and at any time. It is an ongoing process, so your shrine has a different meaning in Hoodoo and can be whatever you like.

Your shrine could be constructed outdoors to improve your nature connection and show your respect for the powers of the natural world.
https://unsplash.com/photos/MnKWt1W1GDg

A shrine makes your work more resolute and focused; you can have as many as you like. Some practitioners have portable shrines they take with them when they travel, and others have dedicated shrines in their homes. A sacred space is a haven for you to return to where you know what is there and has a special place in your heart. Your shrine could be constructed outdoors to improve your nature connection and show your respect for the powers of the natural world. In this chapter, we will examine many forms of shrines, and you can then choose the one or more that suits your work.

A Portable Shrine

Keep it simple and choose a design that suits your style. You can be as decorative as you like and cover your shrine in stickers, symbols, and other decorative touches, or you can keep it neutral and inconspicuous to the outside world. If you are less keen to share your Hoodoo leanings with the world, the neutral option is best, but if you want to benefit from a dedicated shrine, the decorated item will suit you better.

Use the ideas below as a springboard for your own projects and a chance to get creative with your craft.

What You Need

- A box can be wooden, plastic, or any material you choose. An unfinished wooden box is more adaptable
- Sandpaper
- Cloths for cleaning
- Items relating to Hoodoo
- Small candles and holders
- Shells for offerings
- Small incense burner
- Craft items to decorate your box
- A protective spray to cover the finished product
- Paint or foil to cover your box
- Creative additions
- Woodburning tool for decoration
- Stickers and decals

Choose the symbols that relate to Hoodoo from the following

- **The triskelion,** or the triple whirl, is a symbol of magic and brings change to the interlocked energies in its form. It symbolizes spiritual, energetic, and material force and uses the power of the trio.

- **The pentagram** is the five-pointed star encased in a circle that represents the power of the four elements combined with the element of the spirit. The top point represents the strength of the deity and the divine, while the circle that surrounds the star is the ultimate barrier to unwanted energy and spirits. If you are creating the pentagram yourself, always draw it with a single stroke.

- **The spiral** is a universal symbol for all earthly needs. When it is drawn rotating to the right, it represents the power to summon material needs, while the spiraling left symbol deals with energies beyond the earthly planes and is also effective in dealing with illnesses and diseases.

- **The crossroads symbol** is representative of change and a need for new directions. It is used to help the user choose a path to walk and improve their life.

- **The Star of David** is a hexagram with the compound of two equilateral triangles and was used as the seal of Solomon in the Bible. In Hoodoo workings, it is a powerful protection symbol that can be used to keep out negative energies and spirits.

Hoodoo Items for Your Portable Shrine

- Curios like a coin, lodestones, or animal bones
- Incense for luck or love
- Powders you may use
- Lucky oil
- A rabbit's foot for luck
- John the Conqueror root

Decorate Your Box

Paint or varnish your box ready for your decoration and then use your imagination to make the box a part of your personality and something you'll enjoy for years. Make sure you create a solid seal or locking device, as your loose items will be stored inside. Use ribbons or stoppers to ensure your box's lid forms an L-shaped surface for your work when you are away from home.

Think about where and when you will use your shine and how to utilize your limited space. Your portable shrine should be available to go at a second's notice, so make sure it is easy to stash away in your home and can be reached easily when you need to go.

Ancestors Shrine

Our ancestors hold a sacred place in Hoodoo beliefs, and a shrine dedicated to them makes your work more intense and fueled by their influence. A shrine to your ancestors can be constructed anywhere in the home where visitors can admire and respect it. Asian and Eastern cultures believe that shrines to the dead should be part of the entrance space in their homes, so they are one of the first things visitors see.

Use pictures of your relatives and items they once owned to decorate a small table covered with a rich gold cloth. Place candles and incense sticks at the side of their portrait pictures and light them whenever you send a request to the spirits. Add an offering bowl so you can gift them with tokens of your respect and love. Clear a space for your additional offerings, like a glass of wine or a piece of homemade bread. A bowl of their favorite sweets or a piece of cake is symbolic of your love and will feed their energies and yours. Place a bowl on your shrine that represents their lineage and the connection that they have to you. Add a small amount of cool water, a drop of your favorite scent, some of your bodily fluid – a tear or a small drop of sweat. Now dedicate the shrine to the spirits by saying a small prayer and sprinkling the liquid across the shrine.

Whenever you replace the water or other elements of the shrine, remember to name any ancestors that you are aware of and acknowledge the ones you cannot name due to a lack of knowledge. Offer your gifts to your ancestors and the spirits that reside with them so they will band together and become part of your spiritual team.

A Living Shrine Dedicated to Nature

Suppose you have a spacious garden or a space. In that case, you can construct a living shrine to nature and benefit from the energies created by performing your rituals and spells outside. Use natural materials to create a sacred place to perform your spells; stone and wood are readily available and extremely durable. Use plants to decorate your shrine and create a tranquil place – yet one filled with living energy.

If possible, incorporate a water feature in your shrine so you'll benefit from the natural force of running water. Represent the four elements on your shrine in the most natural forms you can find. A wind chime represents air, water features for water, plants represent the earth and candles for the element fire. Remember that your shrine will change as the seasons progress, and you can replace items that appear as the year progresses.

A More Traditional Shrine for Your Home

Concentrating on a space in your home where you can practice and perform your spells is an intensely personal experience and depend on several factors. The size of your home, the area you have to work with, and how secret you want your shrine to be are just a few.

The most important part of your decision is how permanent your shrine will be. If you must move it every time you finish your work, this will affect how elaborate your shrine can be. A better alternative for you could be a series of portable shrines that you can use whenever you like. The instructions below are more dedicated to those of you that have the space for a permanent shrine and how to use the space to create a sacred place for your Hoodoo work.

Choose Your Space

Ideally, the surface of your shrine should be level with your waist or higher. You don't want prying hands and eyes to have access to your sacred space, and you want to avoid family pets disturbing your items. Try a regular table in your chosen space to see if it works for you before you start constructing your ornate shrine.

Create the Shrine

You should build your shrine from scratch if you are good with your hands. Create a solid and decorative structure that has multiple levels to place your special items and dedicated offerings to the spirits and nature.

If you want a simpler multi-level shrine, a coffee table or TV stand works well and sits well in most spaces. Another alternative shrine space is a cupboard mounted on the wall. The shelves work well for multi-functional offerings, and the doors mean you can shut the shrine away until you are ready to use it once more. The key thing to consider is that whatever your chosen shrine was in a former life, it has now become redundant. You can't use a coffee table as a shrine one day and as a table the next. Your shrine should be sacred and not multi-functional. Once you have blessed it and dedicated it to your Hoodoo work, it should stay in shrine mode from that moment.

Decorate Your Shrine

Choose a cloth to cover the surface and place a representative object of each of the four elements in the corners. A feather from a bird represents air, a stone represents the earth, a seashell represents water, and a candle represents fire.

Add bowls for your offerings. Ideally, they should be made from natural substances and differ in size to hold varying offerings you may place there. Add a cup and glass for liquid offerings and a coaster or plate for holding heated elements.

Add symbolic shapes to your shrine and pictures of the deities you follow. A cross or a star of Bethlehem represents Christ, and you can include religious icons if your faith is strong. Your shrine is a celebratory way to connect to the spirits, and how you decorate it is a strong statement to the spirit world that you believe in. What you believe is the power that makes you a magical being and gives you the strength to operate as such.

Add Light to Your Shrine

It should be a wondrous place filled with positivity and hope. Lights bring that energy. Use candles, lamps, and reflective surfaces to light the darkness and illuminate your soul. Some candles have special wicks that crackle as they burn to add the element of sound to your work. Use additional light sources around the rest of the room to make the shrine bathed in light whenever you use it.

Engage the Senses

Your shrine should be interactive. Including all your senses will make your work more comprehensive and powerful. Bells are a perfect way to bring sound to your work, and you should find decorative bells with differing tones to bring music to your shrine. You could have a CD player or another form of music source so you can record pertinent music for your work or record your mantras to play as you work.

Incense and perfumes will enhance your shrine and bring your sense of smell to life. Incense brings energy and intention, and it smells great so use it whenever you can.

You can represent the sense of touch with tactile objects for your shrine, like prayer beads and other pleasantly shaped objects. Include a decorative cushion for seated activities or a soft and welcoming wrap to wear around your shoulders. A rug to stand on will help you become grounded and leave your excess energies behind when you finish your work.

Key Things to Consider about Your Shrine

- Your home shrine is a sacred space and should be treated as such. Tell your family and friends that it is your space, and they shouldn't invade it. Don't use the space for functional uses. You will only diminish the space and make it less sacred. The objects on your shrine are blessed, and moving them will only make them mundane and lose their power.

- Replace fresh items regularly. If you have a bowl of water or fresh flowers on your shrine, you should never let them decay and rot. Fresh energy comes from living sources, while any sign of neglect will affect your work and bring negativity.

- Make sure your shrine is in a safe space away from drafts and chilly air. You should treat the shrine as a living object of your faith and ensure it is comfortable and able to breathe.

- Cleanse the area regularly with normal cleaning routines as well as spiritual ones. Smudge the area with sage and use blessed water to sprinkle on it. Dust and dirt will only bring negativity to your space, so clean it thoroughly and with care as if it was a temple.

Your shrine is your sacred space and should be the crucial point of your magical life. Use the space to create magic but also to regenerate your energies. Visit it whenever you need to be reminded of your connection to the spirits and the joy and love they bring to your life.

You can have multiple shrines in your life to represent varying events. You could have a small shrine to mark the passing of your favorite pet that marks where they are buried. Shrines will often be built for the ashes of a loved one to rest upon and for the people who miss them to connect to their spirits. You may prefer a mental shrine to your Hoodoo beliefs, a mind palace filled with your wildest dreams and expectations. A mind palace doesn't cost a penny and can be taken with you wherever you go. You can store information, images, and other relevant information to make you a better magician and conjuror. Fill your mind place with the knowledge of your ancestors and add to their wisdom with quotes and inspiration from more traditional sources from the origins of Hoodoo.

Create a Mind Palace as a Shrine

1. Choose a place to feature in your mind palace. This can be a place already known to you or a completely unique environment. It could be your home or a place you felt safe as a child.

2. Note the distinctive features. What do you see that makes you comfortable and instinctively marks the place where you are? It can be furniture or scenery. It could be a smell or familiar scent that identifies the spot you are in. Every piece of your mind palace will contain relevance so make sure you take the time to note them all and the significance they hold.

3. Remember the details by writing them down and committing them to memory.

4. When you revisit your mind palace, always enter the environment from the same direction, so the place looks the same.

5. Fill your mind palace with the tools of your craft, and remember that the magic you create will be just as relevant as your physical work. You have a place you can experiment with your Hoodoo, and no one will disturb you.

A mind palace is normally a place you can go to improve your memory, but if you don't have the luxury of building a regular shrine to your beliefs, it provides you with a sacred space you can escape to. Hoodoo and magic are all about embracing ideas and building on them. This psychological exercise could become the most important part of your landscape and give you a chance to grow and expand your spiritual being.

Another way to create a shrine without physical space is to use online resources to create your place of peace. An online shrine can be another extension of your imagination with boundless access to amazing resources. You can create a place of wonder with just a couple of clicks of your mouse. Online shrines travel with you and are just a tap of a button away. You can create online icons and elaborately write your petitions to make your shrine a tribute to your imagination and skills. You don't have to be a tech wizard to create online magic. You just need access to a PC or a similar smart device and the Internet.

FAQS about Shrines

Can I have more than one shrine?

Of course, you can. The limit on how many you have is for you to decide. If you travel down the mind palace shrine option, you can create as many as you like, as the possibilities are endless. You can create a shrine to the African people who lived and breathed Hoodoo or a shrine to the people who join you on your quest in the modern world. Your shrines can be physical, mental, and even online.

Can a shrine be dedicated to both spirits and ancestors?

Yes. You have a spiritual team dedicated to you and who work together to bring magic and love to your life. Your ancestors are just a part of that team and if you want to include them and the spirits within your shrine, just do it. Remember to name them when you give thanks, and they will be satisfied with your efforts.

Can a shrine be dedicated to more than one ancestor?

Again yes, if you had a shrine for every ancestor, your home would be filled with them. Your ancestors are your life's blood, and they understand that they have all contributed to your life.

Should I include relatives in my shrine?

As nouns, the difference between ancestors and relatives is that ancestors are from your direct bloodline, while relatives are someone connected by marriage or blood ties. Does this make them less significant? Surely the person your grandfather married had an equal part to play in creating the person you call your father. It's your call. Ancestors, forefathers, and progenitors are all significant, but all relatives have played a part in the amazing person you are today.

Chapter 6: Hoodoo Candles and Bottles

Candles and bottles are an intrinsic part of Hoodoo magic. They were always readily available in slave households, so using them in their spells and rituals made sense. Candles didn't just bring light and warmth to the home. They provided an inexpensive magical tool for use by all ages. Today we can all use candles to create magic and learn the correct way to use these simple items to create impressive results.

Candles and bottles are an intrinsic part of Hoodoo magic.
https://www.pexels.com/photo/red-pillar-candle-with-black-background-6129843/

Candle Colors

Just like choosing the color of your mojo bags, the color of the candles you use influences your work from the very start. They set your intention and work with the other elements you choose to create a strong bond with the spirits and ensure success. The meaning of the colors in candle magic is slightly different from the mojo bags, so it is worth reexamining them and what they signify.

- **Black:** The occult and dark magic, removal of negativity and binding with the night. The womb and feminine power, especially in relationships.

- **White:** Angelic connections, purity, freedom of spirit, transformation, and rebirth.

- **Red:** Courage and strength in combat, anger, fire, lust, and sex. Red also represents the passion for relationships and your career.

- **Orange:** Control in legal matters, opportunities, harvesting, and also power over your enemies.

- **Blue:** Communication and mental clarity. The healing power of water and dreams.

- **Purple:** Spiritual awakening, magic, intuitive powers, wisdom, and knowledge.

- **Yellow:** The color of the sun, joy, love, and peace. Creativity and inspiration it is the color of success.

- **Green:** Abundance and wealth. Green is the color of the earth and fertility and represents money and love.

- **Pink:** Self-confidence and love, friendships and relationships, emotional healing, and harmony.

- **Brown:** Animal connections, grounding, and focusing on your emotions. Recovering lost items and security.

Types of Candles and What They Represent

- **Tealights** are small colorful candles that are sometimes scented and often come in packs with multiple color options. They don't burn for long and are found in most dollar stores and discount outlets. Use these for your first few spells to ensure that candle magic is right for you before investing in more elaborate options.

- **Birthday candles** are another cheap and cheerful option; these are taller than tea lights and can be used as a quick-burning substitute for regular candles.

- **Tapers** are long thin candles you probably saw in your grandmother's home; their shape makes them perfect for altar work and for sealing your bottles with wax.

- **Novenas** are for working with selected religious figures. They are decorated with pictures of saints or other leading religious figures. Specialist stores have extended novenas to include more varied deities and spirits, and if you want to work with specific deities, they can commission candles just for you.

- **The 7-knob candle** is part of African American folklore and is designed for extended spells that take place over the seven days of the week. Light each knob daily and let them burn until the week has ended and the spell is complete.

- **Pillar candles** come in a range of sizes and burn for hours. They are perfect for lighting your shrine and honoring your ancestors.

- **Figure candles** are more specialized and represent whatever they are modeled on. There are figure candles featuring male and female forms and a couple's candle for spells regarding relationships. Animal candles help you connect with animal spirit guides and familiars.

- **Floating candles** are especially effective when used in conjunction with other water elements. They also work well when working with fire elements as they create spiritual polarity.

Candles need to be charged to work in spells and rituals, which involves dressing the candle and then charging it with your energy. Dressing a candle is a skill you'll learn as your experience grows, but here are a few simple tips to start with:

1. Use a knife or a pin to carve your intentions into the candle. Use short, powerful words to indicate what you want from the magic, and your requests will be heard more clearly.

2. Anoint the candle in oil, choose an oil representing your intentions and coat the candle in your chosen oil.

3. Coat the candle with herbs and powders to make it more effective. Lay the herbs and powders on a wooden board and gently roll the anointed candle until it is covered.

4. Load your candle by carving a small portion out of the top of the candle and loading oil or herbs to create a concentrated section.

5. Scatter herbs, oil, crystal, and talismans around the base of the candle to intensify your intentions.

Safety Tips for Candle Work

- Never leave the candle unattended
- Don't overload your candles. Just a pinch of herbs and plant matter will make sure you don't pose a fire risk.

Charging Your Candle

When you are beginning to understand Hoodoo, you'll encounter the term "charging" a lot. What does it mean? Simply put, you transmit your energy into the tools and items you work with. The charge comes from the electricity supply when you charge your electrical devices. In Hoodoo, *you are the power source.* Your visualization powers, and your sheer will, coupled with desire, will charge your items with a power that makes electricity seem lame.

Cast a Basic Candle Spell

So now that you have the basics, it's up to you to create a signature style that works for you. Most rituals and spells follow the pattern listed below:

1. Choose the type and color of your candle.
2. Add the oils and herbs to the board, ready for charging.
3. Use a sharp tool to carve your intentions and sigils into the candle.
4. Start to visualize your intentions and how they will manifest.
5. Anoint the candle.
6. Dress the candle.
7. Light it and let the candle burn down naturally. This is recommended for beginners, so they don't snuff out the candle prematurely and halt the spell.
8. Dispose of the remnants.

How to Dispose of Candle Remnants

This all depends on your intentions. If you cast a spell to draw something to you, then bag the remnants and keep them close, in your wardrobe or under your bed. If the spell was a banishing spell, then dispose of the elements in a natural source like running water or fire. If you can't do that, then throw them in the trash on the other side of town. The further away, the better.

Ceromancy

The fine art of candle reading is one of the world's oldest forms of divination, and learning to read what the candles are telling you will add to your psychic skills and improve your understanding of the spiritual world.

Reading the flame is the natural way to practice ceromancy and is a simple way to begin using this particular art. When you light the candle, the initial smoke that is created is the first sign of ceromancy. If the smoke is white, it means your answers will come immediately, and black smoke means they will come, but there will be obstacles. If the flame doesn't smoke, it can mean the matter is now irrelevant and has been dealt with. The strength of your flame also indicates the strength of your success. A robust bright flame bodes well, while a weak and low flame shows opposition to your petition.

Stare at the flame for a more in-depth reading from your candle. If the center of the flame is a blazing red color, it means you'll get a resolution for your needs, while a dimmer light indicates you must work for your results. Suppose the candle's wick is forming a bulb shape. In that case, it indicates that a third party is working against you, and you need to remove their negative energy.

If your candle's flame is spitting, popping, and behaving erratically, it strongly signifies that you have forces working against you. Listen to your instincts and if you feel the flame is growing uncomfortably, then extinguish the flame; if you gain a feeling of security from the conflict, sit back and enjoy the light show.

Burning candles for love follows a different set of rules. If you burn a single candle and a secondary flame rises from the ashes or the wax remnants, it means you have a rival. If you want to discover your relationship status with ceromancy, then burn two candles side by side; one represents you and the other your partner. Suppose one candle burns away significantly quicker than the other. In that case, it signifies an imbalance in the relationship and suggests that it won't last or needs serious attention.

Wax Readings and What They Mean

Reading the wax left by a burning candle is an art similar to reading tea leaves. The shapes and images created by the wax indicate what the candle is trying to tell you. However, how the candle burns is also a significant way to obtain information. If the candle burns down on one significant side, your issues haven't been resolved. Try the process again with a different candle if you get the same result something or someone is standing in your way.

As the candle burns, you will notice tears forming in the wax. If they melt away naturally, the omens are good for your spell, but if they harden on the side of the candle, you are experiencing bad luck, and your spell will be ineffective. The sides of the candle represent different areas of your life; the front is the material world and represents your health, prosperity, and your home. The back of the candle represents the spiritual and emotional world and will indicate how your energies are in this realm. The right side is the future, and the left side is the past.

The shapes formed by the wax as it solidifies are called "persistent" images, which indicate how the spell has worked. If spells for love are cast, and the persistent image resembles a heart, this is a good sign. If you are burning a money spell and the image resembles a coin or a bill, it looks good for your spell.

Enclosed candles are a powerful part of Hoodoo rituals when a candle is placed in a bell jar and left to burn. The residue left on the glass provides further clues, and the color of the soot created by the candle is also significant. If soot appears at the top half of your candle, you have successfully resolved any obstacles. If the soot is at the bottom of the candle, you still have unfinished business. White soot anywhere in the jar is a positive sign from the spirits that all is well.

Wax on Water Divination

To answer your questions clearly, you should use candles to get clear indications from the spirit.

What you need

- Scrying bowl: This is a bowl to store your water and use it to cast your wax. Natural materials are best, like glass, ceramic, or wood but avoid using plastic or metal containers.

- Fresh water.

- Candle/s and lighter, white candles work, but colored candles cast more focused intentions.

- Pencil and paper to write the answers down.

- Oil.

Choose a calm space to place your bowl and sit next to it. Fill the bowl with water and take a few minutes to compose your mind. If you use oil to anoint the candle, take three drops of the same oil and put it in the water. This will charge your water and make your intentions stronger. Write your question or your petition on the paper and set it to one side. Take time to reiterate your question in your mind before you start the ritual.

Light the candle and hold it vertically over the water until a good amount of wax has formed. Now tilt the candle and set the tip an inch above the water. Let the molten wax flow into the water, and continue to ask your question. Be patient and let the wax form a nice pool rather than random drips. Don't interfere or move the bowl or the candle but let the wax and water blend naturally.

The wax will naturally move and form shapes, and you can observe the interactions between the two elements. Once you feel the process has reached a natural end, snuff out the candle and observe what the wax tells you. At this point, it is important to understand that there are no right and wrong ways to interpret wax readings. They will speak to you and form images to answer your questions because they are controlled by natural forces working with you.

Have fun with your readings; remember, the wax is there for you, and you'll see what you need to see.

Bottle Magic

Perhaps the most popular form of Hoodoo bottle magic is the bottle tree. Bottle trees originated back in West Africa in the 9th century and traveled to the US with the communities of people brought to these shores from West Africa during the slavery era. The Hoodoo belief uses bottle trees to keep marauding spirits and nocturnal entities from entering the home and creating havoc. The idea is that the bottles will be too interesting and shiny for the spirits to ignore, and they will be tricked into entering the bottle to check it out. They then become trapped in the bottle so the householder can cork the bottle and get rid of them. The sunlight will destroy nocturnal spirits but if you aren't sure, cast the bottle into the water to ensure they are destroyed completely. As all Hoodoo practitioners know, evil spirits hate sunlight and water.

Bottle trees are also used to commemorate the dead and honor the ancestors. The traditional blue bottles represent the color of heaven, where the ancestors reside. Use a basic bottle tree and adorn it with shiny, eye-catching vessels and household items. Add cups, bowls, knives, forks, and different colored bottles to make your tree beautiful and impressive.

Bottle Spells

You can use many different bottle spells, but here are a few that are more specific and will give you an idea of how to use bottle magic in your Hoodoo work.

The Boss Fix Bottle Spell
What You Need

- One white candle approx. 4" long
- Candle holder in the shape of a star
- Blessed High John oil
- Herb mix including sage, parsley, garlic, and anise
- A sheet of paper and a pen
- A small jar of honey
- An empty bottle

Take the parchment paper and list everything you dislike about your boss and co-workers. Place it in the bottle. Add the honey, oil, and herb to the candle by dressing it. Burn the candle down as you ask the spirits for their help to make things better at work. Add the honey to the bottle, and when the candle has burned down, add the wax and ashes to the honey. Seal the bottle and place it in a dark space. The requests you have made will soon be met.

A Business Spell Bottle or Jar
What You Need

- White sand
- Mint leaves
- Rose petals
- Cardamom pods
- Crystalized ginger
- Paper and pen

Write your intentions on the paper. "I ask the spirits for their assistance in making my business thrive. I will work hard and bring my positivity, and I ask that they do the same. Thank you."

Add the paper and the other items except for the sand to the bottle and then fill it with the sand. Bless the bottle with your intentions and place it on your shrine.

Spell Jars

Spell jars are another way to cast your intentions and create protective and powerful spells that last. When you use jars, they give you a choice of size, meaning they can come with you when you travel or remain in the home to bring their magic.

Jar spells are generally based on strong intentions and corresponding ingredients. These include the following

- Personal items like fingernails, photos, hair, or a piece of paper with their name on it.

- Written intentions on a piece of paper asking for the spirits to come to your assistance and what you require from the magic.

- Liquids to fill the jar, including vinegar for banishing, urine for breaking a curse, honey and nectar for compulsion, and tinctures that contain your intentions.

- Solids like rusty nails or broken glass to break a curse. Cat hair and dog hair break a couple up, so they fight like "cats and dogs," but beware, the spell can backfire. Money-related spells should involve coins or banknotes, while love spells use ribbons or glitter to represent the joy of love.

Crystals and Herbs for Specific Intentions

Feel free to add this list to your ingredient section to intensify your knowledge and source of reference:

- **Intent banishing** uses obsidian, black tourmaline, quartz, and jet as crystals and clove dragons' blood and garlic as herbs.

- **For binding spells,** combine jet with knotweed and hazel or spiderwort when available.

- **For improved communication,** use turquoise and tiger eye crystals with mint or orris root.

- **Curse breaking** uses onyx, selenite, and clear quartz with salt, sage, and rue.

- **Fertility** spells use agate, emeralds, peridot, and ivy.

- **Health** spells use agate, jade, and sunstone with galangal root, rosemary, sage, and thyme.

- **Knowledge** spells involve fluorite and nutmeg, and rosemary.

- **Love** spells require amber, rose quartz, and emerald combined with Adam and Eve root, rose, laurel clove, and lavender.

- **Money** spells use gold, malachite, and moss with ginger, citrus vervain, and patchouli.

- **Peace** spells use blue agate, silver, and amazonite with lavender, violet, and sage.

- **Productivity** spells are fueled by gold, ruby, and hematite with allspice and vanilla.

- **Protection** spells use amber, sandalwood, malachite, and citrine combined with salt, angelica, and mugwort.

- **Psychic connections** use jet, malachite, silver, and turquoise with yarrow as acacia.

- **Relationships** involve pearl and agate with sapphire and turquoise and agate with pansy and rose.

Sealing Your Jar

Once you have chosen your ingredients, add them to your jar and cast a mantra to seal your intentions. It doesn't have to be fancy. Your words are the power behind the spell. Try something like this "I call on the power of the elements to help me find love. I ask for the magic energy of the rose and the goddesses to bring me true passion and help me find my soulmate. Thank you for your consideration and energy."

Now use a candle to seal your jar. You can use ribbons and other methods, but candles are spectacular and add intent to your jar. Place a correctly colored candle on the lid of your jar and let it burn down completely so the wax covers the lid and effectively seals it. You can burn additional candles to recharge your jar spell later or multiple candles in the first instance.

Chapter 7: How to Make Mojo Bags

A mojo bag is a must-have accessory in Hoodoo circles. They are colorful small bags filled with things that keep you safe, keep you connected to your roots, and give you a sense of connection to the spiritual world. Your mojo bag is a personal piece of kit and should never be handled by anybody else just in case their energy interferes with the intention you invest in your bag.

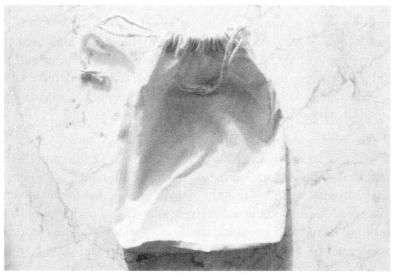

A mojo bag is a must-have accessory in Hoodoo circles.
https://www.pexels.com/photo/white-textile-bag-with-drawstrings-placed-on-marble-table-3850465/

You can create mojo bags for all your needs by customizing the ingredients and the colors you use. A bag for love will help you set your intention to find a new partner, while a money-based mojo bag will attract wealth and prosperity. Choose each element of your bag to make them into powerful, easy-to-make bags of magic that can be carried on your person or left on your shrine to recharge when they aren't needed.

Choose the Color of Your Bags

Why is color so important? We know that vibrations fuel the universe and life, and colors are an elevated expression of these vibrations. Hoodoo uses the power of colors in candle work, potions, spells, and all forms of magic, so mojo bags are directly affected by the color of the cloth chosen.

White

A white mojo bag is the ultimate part of your magic tools and ingredients, as it can be used when other colors aren't available. It is the color of purity and protection and has associations with the Moon and the zodiac sign Cancer. It brings light to dark spaces and imbues the holder with spirituality, peace of mind, and soul. White is especially protective of the young and represents their elemental purity and innocence. It neutralizes negativity, ill feelings, brings healing energies to your magic, and repairs both physical and psychic wounds.

Yellow

The color of the sun, the bringer of life, and the warmth of the universe. It is a happy color that represents the color of wheat and its importance in our daily life. Its golden hue also brings energy and love to you, and it improves vigor and energy for those who are depleted and run down. Yellow bags help creative people find inspiration and flourish in their fields. It symbolizes knowledge and happiness.

Orange

The color of Buddhism, orange, symbolizes health and helps the holder fight depression and sadness. It is a gentler form of energy than red, but it stimulates you without the violent energy that forms the color of fire. Orange is soothing yet invigorating and is the balancing point between the blood life of red and the mind intellect of yellow. Use an orange cloth to promote success and power alongside friendship and positive events in your life. It brings success without any casualties and helps you overcome your inhibitions and social conditioning. It is the color of the setting sun and reminds us to connect to nature and reap the rewards.

Red

The color of love, red, is also the most powerful color for a mojo bag. The ingredients you add will set the intentions so that the outer bag could hold some explosive surprises. You need to be careful when using red bags, they can burn anyone who isn't prepared for their energy, and they can become destructive in the wrong hands. Use red to attract sexual energy and passion and to express your self-belief to the spiritual world. It can be therapeutic for people who have lost their inner strength, but if they are anxious or nervous, it can be too much for them to handle, and they should choose yellow or orange instead.

Pink

Often referred to as a female color, pink is actually quite powerful for both sexes. It is a calming color that attracts friendship and genuine affection. It can solve disputes and strengthen relationships, especially for shy people who are less likely to form relationships naturally. A pink mojo bag will give you the confidence to express yourself without worrying about what other people think.

Purple

The color of regality, this deep shade is associated with the Moon and is a symbol of spirituality and morals. It attracts spirit guides, helps you connect to your enigmatic side, and intensifies your psychic powers. Use a purple bag to protect yourself from psychic attacks and negative energy. As the true color of energy, it will help you find peace and increase your powers of devotion. Keep items you use in rituals in purple bags to keep them strong and intensified with positivity.

Green

The color of the planet Venus, this verdant shade is associated with Mother Earth and nature and gives you the strength of rebirth and creation. It is especially effective for money-based bags and brings prosperity and growth to the objects inside and the wearer. Green inspires creativity and growth and protects the holder from envy and jealousy. Green mojo bags are linked to the earth, the natural cycle of seasons, and the power of the harvest. It is a strong standalone color of a mojo bag and should never be mixed with a red bag; the balance of both colors would be disrupted and lead to miscommunication and possibly misplaced and dangerous magic effects.

Black

The color of funerals and death, black, is probably the most misunderstood color of the spectrum. It is associated with Saturn and brings protective energy that is both powerful and nourishing. It provides a shield from evil and a primordial unity that gives the holder strength to join the universe and benefit from its energy.

Blue

The color of Jupiter, blue, is the symbol of inner peace and meditative energy. It brings calm, healing energy to you and helps when you need to quit your domestic situation and stop the noise. Use it to create reconciliations and restore love and harmony to your life. Blue works well with other colors and can be used as a catalyst for other energetic forces.

Brown

The color of the earth – don't be fooled into thinking this drab hue is lacking in power when used for mojo bags. It is a staple color of nature and provides security and tenacity, which is just as magnificent as the trunk of a mighty oak tree. Brown is safe and will keep you protected from legal matters and injustices while solving your material issues.

What Materials Should You Use for Your Bags?

The choice is yours. The most practical bags are cotton or a polyester mix to provide a cheap yet durable source of the material. You can use recycled cloth to make your bags. In this way, you are connecting to your past and telling nature you recognize the power of recycling. Some bags will be especially dear to your heart, and you can mark that fact by using rich and expensive materials like velvet and silk. You must treasure these materials and only use them for your highly prized mojo bags.

The instructions below show you how to make a simple mojo bag that you can fill with your magic items to give them the power to work. Use this template for your bags to ensure they are durable and will withstand the refueling that is a natural process of owning a mojo bag.

How to Make a Basic Bag

1. Cut a square of your chosen material.
2. Form a pouch that is big enough to hold your chosen items.
3. Stitch the sides with strong yarn.
4. Fold over the edges to form a place to thread a drawstring.
5. Add the string to close the bag once you have your items inside.

You can also take a rectangular piece of material and simply draw the edges together while your items are already in the center. Take a piece of string and secure the edges of the bag with it. These bags are less fiddly to make and aren't meant to be opened at any time. The items in them should be chosen to stay there for a long time and shouldn't be fresh or prone to degrading.

Items You Can Include in Your Bags

Most basic bags have at least three items and never more than thirteen. The number of items you include should always be odd, and an even number will bring you bad luck or render the bag ineffective. The items you include can be as simple as the following:

- A personal item or a representation of yourself like a fingernail, a lock of your hair, or blood.
- A petition to the spirits that states what you require if you want a specific outcome.
- Herbs or minerals that show your intention.
- A talisman or coin.
- Trinkets from nature, like a seashell or twig from a tree.
- Jewelry.
- Keys.
- Dirt or soil from your favorite place.

Every item you place in your bag should be chosen carefully and have a specific purpose. Don't mix your intentions; focus on what you want to achieve with each mojo bag, and avoid muddying your spiritual intentions.

Here are some common items you can choose and what they represent:

- The Ace of Spades playing card – for good luck in gambling matters.
- An arrowhead for love and security.
- Black hair from a cat to break up relationships and bring prosperity from gambling.
- Black hair from a dog to create trouble for your enemies and break up their relationships.
- Black salt for protection and cleansing.

- Brick dust for good luck in business and financial matters.
- Copper coins for luck and prosperity.
- Lucky charms like a horseshoe.
- Business card for improved business luck or better communication
- A picture of your intended mate to ensure love is part of your relationship.
- Seashells represent your connection to nature.
- Lodestones for love.
- Crystals for fixed intentions.
- Earth from your garden for healing.
- Herbs and roots.

Of course, the list is endless. Providing you feel a connection to an item, it can be added to your mojo bag. Now that you have the contents of your bag, it's time to bless them before you seal the bag for good.

Light a candle in a color that represents your intent. For example, a mojo bag for luck would be blessed with a green candle. Now give your bag a name that represents its intent. For luck, you may call it Chance or Shiva, which represents the power of luck.

Now add your items while reciting the following,

"May you bring me a light in the dark,

May you give me the luck and fulfillment my life desires,

Stay by my side (add name) and be my sweet companion,

I feel safe in your company, and I trust my vision will be enhanced,

Luck be with me, and luck is my fate. "

Now Feed Your Bag

Just like a living object, the bag needs to be nurtured. The most common options are oils that have been blessed or water that has been charged by the moon or sun. Some Hoodoo workers use whisky, while others use Florida water. Once again, the choice is yours. Using bodily fluids is an option but be careful who you share your choices with.

Breathe Life into Your Bag

Hold the bag in the palm of your hand and give out three short breaths to give it life and connect it to your inner psyche.

Charge Your Bag

Keep the bag next to your skin for seven whole days to charge it with your intentions. Keep it in your underwear or a pocket beneath your clothes. When you sleep, keep it in your nightwear or in the pillowcase you sleep on. The only time it isn't with you should be when you are showering or in the bath. Your bag should be with you whenever you leave the house.

Charging your bag is an ongoing process; you should feed it monthly and charge it whenever possible. It should be as normal as picking up your house keys whenever you leave your home, and if you leave your bag behind, you should feel naked and like something is missing.

Your mojo bag is a living, breathing extension of your spirit and needs to be kept healthy. Some people believe they should always be accessible, while others think they should be sealed forever. Again, the choice is yours.

Ideas for Your Initial Mojo Bags

As beginners, it can be intimidating to make your first mojo bag. Will I get it right, and will it be effective for me? These are questions that most inexperienced Hoodoo workers will ask. The first thing to realize is that you can't cause any harm with your bags; the worst thing that can happen is that they don't work because they have mixed energies and send out the wrong message to the spirits. You should see results almost immediately by keeping it simple with your first bags.

These examples will give you an idea of how to use simple ingredients to create a powerful mojo bag:

Financial Mojo Bag: Used to attract wealth, prosperity, and money to your life

Choose a green cloth to fashion your bag and gold or black string to fasten it. Select some herbs to add to your bag; bay leaves, thyme, and laurel all work well. Add something that represents your intentions. If you want fast cash, then show your hand by adding a banknote or a coin to your ingredients. Now write your intention on a piece of paper, an amount you need, or a specific way you want your wealth to improve and add that to the pile.

These three items are a perfect way to power a money bag, but you can add your own representations depending on your feel for the bag. Once you have sealed the bag, feed it with smoke from incense or essential oil to activate your bag before you say a prayer or a mantra to bless it. Name your bag with a suitable word. Rich works if you want a powerful name or something more subtle like Penny or Will.

Keep the bag with you for at least seven days, and then use it whenever needed to improve your financial status. Imagine money flowing toward you whenever you feel the need, and your wishes will come true very soon.

Love Mojo Bag

Are you looking for new love, or do you want to get your ex back? Are you ready for love to be part of your life and want to give yourself more chances with a powerful mojo bag to hurry along the process?

Choose a red or pink cloth depending on the strength of the passion you want to attract. If you want to meet someone and gradually fall in love, then pink will work for you, but if you want a grand passion that lights up your life and makes your toes curl, then red is the cloth for you.

Add herbs that symbolize your desires. Cardamom seeds or rose petals will bring love, while lovage roots and myrtle are a powerful attraction for passion. Add a love token like a carved heart or a picture of the object of your desire. If you don't have specific intentions, then write a petition for love on a piece of red paper instead. Crystals that are red or pink are another strong ingredient and can be added but don't forget to keep the number of your items to odd numbers.

Charge the bag with rose essential oil or smudge it with incense before you say a short prayer or mantra over your bag. Carry it with you to charge it, and then keep it close whenever you are looking for love.

Mojo bags are for every part of your life, and you can never have too many. Keep them close to you whenever you need them by wearing them against your skin. If you find your bag isn't working as well as it used to, then dispose of it and replace it with a new one. Be respectful when you dispose of your bag, and make sure the old ingredients are thanked for their use and then buried or burned ceremoniously. All your magical ingredients should be respected and honored even when they have lost their power; they have served you well and deserve recognition.

Chapter 8: The Magic Practices of Rootwork

Rootwork is a form of Hoodoo that concentrates on the fact that every being and object in the universe has a soul and corresponding energies. Successful rootworkers know how to tap into the energies and use them to bring magic and power to their work. The magical tools in Hoodoo simply allow rootworkers to access the natural powers and spiritual intent. They are a medium for blessings and transformations and are part of the process, not the results.

Amulets and charms provide portable vibrations that can be carried or worn by the rootworker.
https://www.pexels.com/photo/nazar-amulets-on-tree-branches-near-stony-formations-in-cappadocia-6243268/

Some cultures and religions believe the same things that Hoodoo followers believe and have named the phenomenon animism. That is the belief that all objects' places and creatures have a distinct essence. The term originated from the Latin word anima, which means "breath of life." Animism teaches us that there are no barriers between the material and spiritual world that cannot be crossed. Hoodoo teaches us the times of the day and year when the veil is at its thinnest and how to use "root" objects to facilitate the connection.

Some people mistake the term "rootworker" as meaning they only work with natural plants and roots. In Hoodoo, the root is the physical home of the spirit and is a sacred place that gives shelter to those spirits that reside there.

How Root Workers Use Items to Symbolize the Powers of the Spirits

1. **Amulets and charms.** These provide portable vibrations that can be carried or worn by the rootworker. They can be ordinary items like keys, coins, and herb bundles that cease to function in their original form. Instead, they become soaked in energy dedicated to creating a specific goal. They become part of a magical process and can be utilized as needed to create a movement in the magical spell. If they are dedicated to soaking up bad energy once the spell has been completed, they are cast out to get rid of the negative energy.

2. **Cashing in on nature's bounty.** Using natural objects is a key part of rootwork, and original practitioners would use the bones of family pets to help with the grieving process and use the residual spirit of the animal to bring good fortune. That wouldn't be as practical today, but you can use the bones of your chicken dinner to recreate the authentic workings of those first rootworkers. If bones aren't your thing, then focus on the natural items all around you and use them instead. Brick dust from red bricks is a powerful protection element; lodestones draw luck, and pyrite attracts good luck. Use nuts, stones, minerals, and herbs in your rootwork to benefit from their powers and spirit.

3. **Poppets** are often mistaken for Voodoo dolls but are much less malignant. They are doll babies that are used to represent individuals or animals in spells. They are generally stuffed with

items that belong to the person they represent and additional healing and loving herbs. A Hoodoo doctor baptizes some dolls to name them, while others are kept on altars and shrines. Poppets made for pets will often accompany them to their grave to watch over their spirit and keep them safe.

4. **Personal property.** Using belonging from individuals gives spells an unprecedented level of power. Hair clippings, tears, nails, and bodily fluids are all used in rootwork, while other less personal items include clothing and jewelry. They link the person to the rootworker and direct the magic to the source without any risk of distractions.

5. **Bottles and jars.** In regular kitchens, we know that items in sealed bottles and jars last longer than their shelf life. The same applies to Hoodoo bottles and jars that contain magic. The more durable the container, the longer the spell lasts.

Do Rootworkers Prefer Certain Locations?

Just like the items they work with, the location of their spellwork can be just as effective in their magic. A kitchen is a sacred place at the heart of the home, while their altar and shrine are sacred for different reasons. Crossroads are natural places to perform rituals where two roads meet, or a place where a stream separates into two forks is naturally powerful. Any geographical place that forms a T, X, or Y symbolizes change and is the best place to perform rituals and spells for transformations.

In the past, rootworkers would also gather at gravesides and perform rituals. They would take dirt from the grave and use it in their work. Today we don't see the graveyard as an accepted place for magic. You can visit the graves of your loved ones and ask for advice but limit your work to providing gifts of flowers or stuffed animals to symbolize your love. You don't want to be accused of performing any sort of craft in the graveyard, as that could cause problems.

How to Keep Your Rootwork Pure and Free from Negativity

Cleansing is once more part of your work. It cannot be stated enough that keeping your energy, tools, and roots clean is the most important part of your work. Use these essential washes to clean your home, tools, and feet to ensure your work is pure and successful.

Hoodoo Perfumes and Colognes

Some spiritual practitioners have always made their washes and colognes from scratch, but most Hoodoo workers today buy perfumes from trusted sources. They understand that commercial products are often more powerful since the manufacturers have access to fresher and more available magical ingredients. Some rootworkers will use commercial washes and add their preferred herbs and ingredients for added potency. A little like buying your pizza from the deli and then adding your own toppings to make it even tastier.

- Florida water is considered all-around altar water used to cleanse and protect locations and bring peaceful blessings.
- Hoyt's cologne is used for luck, especially among the gambling communities, and is also a powerful reconciliation scent.
- Kananga water is used in spells to connect to ancestors and in spells for sexual union and increased passion.
- Rose cologne is a gentle-smelling liquid that attracts love and romance, but it can be enhanced with lovage and spikenard to create a more potent cologne.
- Jockey club perfume is especially effective in bringing good luck and improving prosperity.

Washes and Waters for Cleansing

These spiritual supplies are also available for purchase rather than using your homemade potions. They are blessed with herbal and mineral salts imbued with essential oils and concentrated soaps. Some waters are based on a single ingredient, like Rose Water, Orange Water, and Willow water. They allow rootworkers to add their own ingredients and create more potent products.

Spiritual bathing is one of the most traditional rituals in the world. It involves water mixed with Epsom salts and other salt products along with herbs and minerals to provide a cleansing agent for use in the home and personal use. They can remove jinxes and crossed conditions and also draw love and money to practitioners. Rootworkers will also create bath mixtures and sacred soaps for clients and add ingredients that match their needs and desires.

How to Make an Amulet for Your Rootwork

Charms and amulets are perfect for taking your magic on the road. Here are some basic steps to choosing roots that form the perfect amulet for your needs.

Step One: Choose an object that suits the intent you want to set

Your items should be small and durable, especially if they are worn on the body. They should be non-toxic and resistant to wear and tear. Don't forget that your clothing can become a talisman when you bind magic intent in your favorite scarf or tie. Get creative and use your imagination.

Step Two: Cleanse your object

Again, the cleansing ritual should suit the object. Smoke smudging or soapy water will clean most objects and keep them from spiritual infestation.

Step Three: Charge your object

Natural sunlight or moonlight is the easiest way to charge your talismans; just leave them in the beams or rays for a couple of hours. The sun has more masculine associations, while the moon is more feminine. As they charge, add extra energy by chanting or reciting a prayer over them to increase potency.

Step Four: Choose the best time to charge your talisman

We have already covered the ties of the day to set certain intentions, so use those instructions to make your talisman extra powerful.

Once you have created the talisman or charm, wear it on your person or gift it to whoever you made it for. When you gift a root of energy, make sure to explain the power it contains so the wearer will know exactly when to wear it. If the talisman is for a child, sew it into their clothes, or if it is for a pet, put it where they sleep.

Chapter 9: Hoodoo Spells to Enhance Your Life

In this chapter, we will explore how to create spells that will improve your life and give you control over your emotions and energies and the energies surrounding you. Lots of pagan and Wiccan teachings will tell you different methods to do the same thing, but with Hoodoo, you have the resources to gain knowledge and skills from bona fide conjurers and discover their methods so you can improve your own. Earlier in the book, we explored the role of a conjuror and how they would help ordinary folk to benefit from their magic.

When you purchase a spell kit, and the results are favorable, you'll have added to your spiritual repertoire and added knowledge.
https://www.pexels.com/photo/a-person-holding-a-candle-10448633/

Imagine the scene where a fire is burning in a clearing far away from the plantation home, and a group of men, women, and children are seated near the fire with a look of expectancy on their faces. They may be carrying offerings like food or drink, and one by one, they approach a man or woman seated away from the fire. This is a consultation with a conjuror, and they would be given potions, powders, or instructions on how to resolve their issues and enhance their meager lives.

This type of magic was a step up from normal Hoodoo spells, which could be created in the kitchen, and they gave the enslaved people an enhanced feeling of hope that things could get better. They could expect revenge if someone had caused them pain or wronged them. If someone caught their eye, they would be given potions to make them more attractive to the object of their desire.

Today we don't have to consult conjurors and Hoodoo masters to take control of our own lives, but as beginners, it can be handy to have expert help. When you start to practice Hoodoo, the list of ingredients and their corresponding powers can be overwhelming, and using readymade supplies will make your magic easier to access. They provide a source of lucky mojo objects, oils for your baths, and other specific supplies that are safe to use and will expand your knowledge of exactly what Hoodoo can do if you have the knowledge.

The Lucky Mojo Curio Co is an online domain that employs proficient conjurors and skilled Hoodoo rootworkers to produce ready-made products for your use. They provide spell kits with all the ingredients you need and detailed instructions that are perfect for beginners who haven't yet built an herb collection or don't have the other tools a conjuror would have. Their spell kits are a way to test your power of magic without spending a lot of money. When you purchase a spell kit, and the results are favorable, you'll have added to your spiritual repertoire and added knowledge.

The powders and oils they include are pre-blessed and save you the worry of wondering if all your ingredients are effective. You are guaranteed to receive a spell that will work for you providing you use them correctly.

Try these basic spell kits

A Blessing spell kit for less than $60. Use to bless new homes, strengthen new ventures, and heal emotional wounds

- One white crucifix candle
- Blessing bath crystals
- Blessing incense
- Blessing sachets for good luck and love
- Chinese wash
- Lucky mojo bag fixed with oil and containing a dove charm and relevant herbs
- Full instructions for use

A Commanding spell kit costing less than $80 and is used to gain command over others in business, love, and relationships

- Nine yellow candles
- Command bath crystals
- Incense powders
- Sachet powders
- Command Mojo bag sealed with commanding oil and containing relevant herbs and charms
- Full instructions for use

Other spells include a come-to-me spell kit, cast-off evil, a court case spell kit, a crossing spell kit, and a fast luck spell kit.

Depending on your budget and needs, many different Hoodoo resources are available. Check that they are reputable and have good reviews before you make any purchases. Using spell kits isn't cheating or taking the easy route. It simply ensures you enjoy the process before you commit and spend money on your supplies.

Easy Hoodoo Spells for Beginners That Are Simple but Effective

Casting your own spells is a satisfying experience. When you see results, the feeling of power can be overwhelming. Try these simple spells for real results, and start your Hoodoo work with a bang.

The Love Spell for Someone with a Love for Desserts

If your man is losing interest or you want to get closer to a friend and take the next step, make this dessert for them, and make them fall head over heels in love with you.

What You Need

- Hairbrush
- Your favorite scent
- Salt
- Apple pie made with nutmeg and cloves
- Love oil, use rose essential oil or make your own with olive oil and sage or your favored herb

First, brush your hair with the hairbrush with the added love oil, and when you get the chance, brush his hair with the same brush. This improves your connection and plants the seeds of love in his mind.

Next, wash an item of clothing of his along with your bedsheets. As you wash them, chant the following, "*Love me (add name) and feel the soft texture of my sheets as we make love*" seven times over the water as you wash. Dry the sheets and then spray them with your favorite scent as you make the bed. Repeat the same chant another seven times before you fold down the sheets and visualize the two of you beneath the sheets later.

Bake the apple pie or reheat the store-bought one and sprinkle the hot pie with a few drops of your bathwater to get him addicted to you. The cloves will help you command him, and the nutmeg will inspire love.

Ask him to remove his shoes before you serve him the pie and put salt in the shoes to keep him safe from other women's wiles and tricks.

Finally, add some of your sexual fluids to your lipstick. Then, if you do kiss, it will drive him crazy with lust and bind him to you forever.

Honey Jar Spells

Honey is one of the most common ingredients in Hoodoo spells because it is the epitome of sweetness and attracts the people you want in your life, and because it is so sticky, it keeps them there. Honey has strong connections with the goddess of love, Aphrodite, and other prominent love deities. A jar of honey is the perfect way to bind your intentions and keep the herbs that power your spell fresh and potent.

Try this binding honey jar to keep someone you love close to you

What You Need

- A jar of honey
- Pen and paper
- Herbs

- Love oil
- Red candle
- Lighter

Take the paper and write the name of the person you wish to bind across the page. Turn the paper ninety degrees and write your name. Repeat the process until you have a multilayered representation of your two names. Now create a circle of words representing your love around the names without lifting the pen from the paper. Write "I love you, stay with me" or your own phrase to create a binding circle of love.

Add your chosen herbs to the paper and add any personal fluids or items from the two of you. These can be fingernails, hair, or fluids from your body. The choice is yours. Now anoint the paper with the love oil and add to the honey jar.

Charge your jar with additional items and herbs to create a powerful environment for your petition. Add cinnamon for lust, saffron for passion, and cardamom for loyalty. Lodestones and rose petals will make your honey even more potent.

As you close and seal the jar, repeat the phrase, *"Bless this honey that is sweet to me (add the name of your desired partner). I ask that you also show your love and share the sweet love we both can be."* Repeat three times and then seal the jar by burning the red candle on the lid of the jar.

Banishing Powder for Protection

Keeping your home and your family safe is one of the most important spells you can cast. Creating this powder will help you banish evil spirits and keep negativity from your energies.

What You Need

- Dried lemon peel
- Osha root
- Dried garlic
- Salt

Take equal parts of all the ingredients and grind them with a pestle and mortar while reciting your favorite Bible passage or mantra for protection. *"Bring your powerful protection to my life and keep us safe from all harm."*

Hoodoo Happiness Spell

When you need some joy in your life, try this simple spell to bring happiness and love

What You Need

- Three orange or yellow candles
- Cedar oil
- A couple of pinches of rosemary
- A pinch of marjoram

Anoint all the candles with your oil, and then dress the candle with your herbs. Place them in holders on your shrine or altar and stare at the flames as you repeat this mantra,

"Bring joy and love to me and mine,

Banish anger and stress, let go of strife,

I am happy, and I am free

I won't stand for negativity."

Hold your hands over the flames and feel the warmth they give off without burning your hands. Visualize the happiness and love that is about to come into your life as the candles burn away naturally. Take the remnants of the candles, place them in a yellow cloth bag with more rosemary and marjoram, and place the bag beneath your bed.

New Beginnings Spell

This spell is perfect for New Year's resolutions or whenever you need to eliminate negative elements of your life. It helps you to move on and escape any negative energies. This spell is for moving on from parts of your life rather than a specific person.

What You Need

- Two sprigs of rosemary
- A dried stick of wood around the size of your ring finger
- Black yarn
- White yarn
- Heatproof pot
- Large spoon
- White candle

- Black candle

Use the black yarn to tie one piece of rosemary to the stick and the white yarn to tie the remaining sprig to the opposite end. Lay this down and place a black candle to the left and a white candle to the right. Light the black candle and state to the room what you intend to leave behind. Now light the white candle and state to the room what you hope to attract to your life to fill the gap.

Lift the stick so the black yarn is above the black candle and the white yarn is over the white candle. Don't let the stick catch fire. Hold it high enough to avoid the flames. Now, snap the stick in half and cast it into the awaiting pot. Hold your hands over the flames and repeat the intentions you stated in the first part of the spell. Bring the pot between the two candles and bang it sharply three times with the spoon to release the energy from the stick.

You have now made the break, so let the candles burn down naturally, and add the wax to the broken stick and twine. Take the remnants to a place that is far from your home and dispose of them safely, preferably in running water or fire.

Money Spell

When casting money spells, the key thing to remember is that they will not reward greed. They are only effective in times of need and when your intentions are genuine. Ask for wealth and prosperity by all means, but it may not result in cold hard cash. After all, a happy life isn't necessarily based on your monetary worth.

Pay a Bill Spell

This is an example of how your Hoodoo magic can be used to pay a specific bill in times of hardship.

What You Need

- Green candle
- Cinnamon oil
- The incense that compliments the oil
- Paper and pen

Take the pen and create a representation of the bill you need to pay. *You will be burning it, so don't use the original!* Use words and images to create a strong and detailed idea of the bill. Making your own drawing will create personal energy rather than just using a photocopy of the original.

Anoint and dress the candle with your chosen oil and light your incense. Place the folded paper under the candle holder and repeat the following,

"As the candle burns away,

The light of the spirits lights my day,

They bring the cash that I need

So I can pay this bill at speed."

Concentrate on the bill and how it will feel to get it paid while the candle burns for ten minutes. Snuff out the candle and leave the area. Return the next day and repeat the process. Do the same until the candle has only one day left to burn. Take the paper and burn it in the remaining flame of the candle. Any unexpected money that comes your way must be put toward paying this bill. If you don't, the spirits will get angry and make sure you don't benefit from their help again.

Fertility Spell

If a young couple is struggling to become pregnant and all the health options have been followed, Hoodoo can bring that extra fertility boost to their lives and give Mother Nature a helping hand.

This spell is used at harvest time to bring a good crop to the fields, but it is also a powerful fertility spell.

What You Need

- Patchouli oil
- Sandalwood incense
- To dried pinecones
- Five grains of wheat
- Green candle
- Paper and a green pen
- Cooking pot

Take the paper and write the name of the child you want to conceive in green. Don't worry if you don't have a name in your mind. This is just a symbol of the child you hope will come to you. Anoint the candle with the oil and light the incense. Add the wheat and pinecones to the paper in the cooking pot. Light the paper with your candle as you imagine your child and what they will mean to you. Once the flames have died down, let the remnants cool before burying them in your yard or another personal space.

The Buried Egg Spell
What You Need

- An egg
- Whole vanilla pod
- Green marker
- Plant pot and soil

Take the egg and decorate it to represent your child. Use symbols and a name to create the representation of your desire. Take the pot and soil and bury the egg beneath the soil. Place the pot in your sacred space and water it every night while you say a mantra over the pot.

"Sacred egg grow and flourish,
Let the earth be your womb,
Bring that power to my body
And let my child be born."

Ensure the pot is drained properly, and concentrate all your intentions with your nightly watering.

These are just a few spells to bring abundance and love to your life. It would be impossible to list them all, but it does give you some ideas for your early work. Remember, your intentions are the fuel that powers your spells, so keep them at the forefront of your mind and always be true to yourself.

Chapter 10: Living a Hoodoo Lifestyle

Once you have experienced the joy and wonder that Hoodoo can bring to your life, some people believe the next step is to live a daily routine to incorporate their new powers into their regular life. This doesn't mean you become a witch doctor or abandon your regular job and social life to concentrate on your magic. It just means you use the things you are learning to enhance your life and make your own decisions. You are on the path to gaining control of your destiny, and you will use all your Hoodoo knowledge to live your best life.

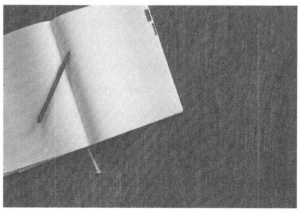

Create a journal for your thoughts and use it to get creative and list your wildest dreams.
https://www.pexels.com/photo/white-notebook-and-pen-606539/

Did you know that the spoken word is responsible for around 8% of communication? The most significant way to communicate with the universe and the spirits is to use every method of stating your intentions by living a life filled with purpose. Raise your energy and vibrations to fill your life with positivity, and then begin to receive the rewards.

State Your Intentions in Written Form

We have already established that the only way to get what you want is to ask for it clearly and to choose ingredients for your work that signal your needs. Create a journal for your thoughts and use it to get creative and list your wildest dreams. A journal can be uplifting, and you should fill it with images, words, and mantras that will state your intentions and remind you daily what you want, need, and deserve.

Tips for Keeping a Journal

So, you have your brand-new journal and your set of pens, and you are faced with that spotless first page. What do you do for your first journaling experience? Even avid journal keepers can be intimidated by a new project and get those page jitters. Don't be overwhelmed; follow these tips, and get journaling.

1. Make your first page a statement about yourself. Add a picture and some details about yourself. Writing about yourself will get your creative juices flowing and settle those nerves. Write what you know, and that first page will soon be filled with glorious details and information.

2. Create a prompt list for your day. The journal is for recording your feelings and your thoughts, but what should you be recording? Prompt lists help you start to use journaling regularly and get you into the habit of recording your thoughts.

    Here are some prompts you could use:
    - List ten things that take you to your happy place.
    - What are the three things you can't live without?
    - What three habits do you have this year that you don't want to carry into next year?
    - Write about the best experience you had last year and how you felt.
    - Now do the same for the worst experience from last year.
    - Divide yourself into three sections, your body, mind, and soul. What does it feel like to be that part of you, and how

can you make each part feel better?

- Who are you? In ten words, describe yourself and then ask your most trusted friend to do the same and compare how similar or different the lists are.

- List all the areas of your life you want to change and how starting with finances and health and then dealing with your emotional needs.

- What sort of class would you like to take, just for fun and not to improve your career?

You get the idea. Having a chat with yourself can be so revealing, and when you have the powers of Hoodoo on your side, you feel like you can actually make these changes.

Become More Mindful

Stop thinking that mindfulness is just for hippy-dippy people and start to understand exactly what mindfulness involves. Exercises to increase your mindfulness help you reach a heightened state of awareness and increased happiness. You will feel less stressed and more aware of the benefits of your surroundings. When you are mindful, you'll start to appreciate the grass that grows beneath your feet and the sky that contains the sun and the moon.

Just doing a couple of mindfulness exercises will help you raise your vibrations and become more in tune with the world. Incorporate these into your life, and you'll immediately begin to feel the benefits of your change of pace.

Create a Morning Routine
Shower

Having a routine when you wake avoids that feeling of despair some of us feel when we first wake. You know what to do and when. Start the day with a mindful shower and feel the water hitting you and the warmth it brings. Feel the texture of the soapy bubbles or creamy lather from your shower gel, and watch how it travels down your body. Finish the experience with a blast of icy water to reawaken your senses and close your pores. That tingling sensation sets you up for the day.

Have a Drink and a Light Breakfast

Start your day with a boost of energy with an energy-packed breakfast. We will cover foods and what they bring to you later. Choose a drink that peps you up, like tasty herbal tea or a cup of coffee, decaffeinated possibly. These simple ingredients will keep you alert until your next meal, so make sure they contain the energy you need.

Move That Body

Stretch your muscles to avoid any cramping before you leave the house. Bending and touching your toes limbs you up, but if you can manage more strenuous exercises, go for it. A couple of star jumps and press-ups are easy to do in any environment. If you feel like you need to take in some fresh air, go for a run or a power walk around the block. Whenever possible, ditch your car and walk to work or the shops to keep your environment cleaner and improve your fitness. You will function better in all areas of your life, including your magic.

Use Your Waiting Time Effectively

How much of your life is spent waiting for other people or for something to happen? What is your normal mental state when waiting? Frustration? Anger? Boredom? Chances are you don't use this time constructively because chances are if you try and get something done, it will be interrupted by the event you are waiting for. Next time you hang on for a zoom call or are in line in the coffee shop waiting for your drink, change how you use this time.

Use your full range of senses to notice your surroundings more. What can you hear? Coffee cups clinking and general chatter or the hum of the air conditioning would normally be ignored. When you are waiting for a call, notice the surroundings you are in and become engaged with the environment. You will soon start to enjoy waiting and see it as a positive action rather than getting frustrated and fretful.

Connect to the Earth Mindfully

This practice will help you in your grounding following Hoodoo work, so improving your technique will make sure you keep your energy fields balanced and in tune with the earth. Whenever you can connect with nature by closing your eyes and noticing the breeze on your face and the warmth of the sun as it hits your skin. Walk barefoot on the grass and feel the energy of the earth flow through your body and energize your spirit. Whenever you can connect to natural elements, swim in the sea, climb a hill or mountain and have a campfire in the great outdoors.

Mindful Eating

We will look more carefully at the foods we eat and what they bring later, but have you ever considered how you eat as well as what you eat?

Do you appreciate your food, or do you just eat and forget? Why do you eat? Are you genuinely hungry, or could it be boredom? When you change the way you eat, you change your attitude toward food and learn to recognize genuine hunger rather than other responses that trigger you to eat.

1. **Mindful beverages.** When you drink something, take the time to notice every taste in the liquid. Is there a hint of lemon in your tea, or is it infused with mint? Is your coffee freshly ground or instant? What is the difference, and how does it affect your tastebuds? Do you drink too much coffee, and are your taste buds incapable of distinguishing quality? Cut down the amount you have and improve the quality instead.

2. **Mindful eating.** When you consume food, do you appreciate every mouthful or shovel your food down simply to fuel your body? Take the time to appreciate the texture of your food and how it feels on your tongue. Is it crunchy, or is it soft and squishy? How does your food smell? Bring it up to your nose and appreciate the aromas you experience before you eat it and during the meal. What emotional triggers do you feel when you eat? How do you feel during the meal, and how do you feel after it is finished?

3. **Listen to your food.** Using all your senses is part of life, but when you concentrate on the food, you can block out all other sensual triggers. Listen to the bubbles in your carbonated drink and enjoy the sound. Does your food make a sound on the plate? What are the sounds that surround the table? If you are in a restaurant, can you hear the sounds of the kitchen or listen to the other guests?

Mindfulness is an art that can be practiced anywhere and by anyone. It takes practice but is a part of life that cannot be ignored. You may be wondering what mindfulness and Hoodoo have in common, and the answer is simple. Once you understand the basics of mindfulness, you'll see the connection. We constantly strive for a heightened spiritual connection, and mindfulness is all about strengthening that energy. Imagine visiting a celebrated art gallery packed to the brim with artworks from the greatest artists that ever lived, and all you are looking at is the floor. Raise your eyes and appreciate the wonders of the natural world, and you'll soon feel the connection.

Mojo Bags

You already know the power of your mojo bag and what the different colored bags mean. How many times do you take one with you as you leave home for the day? If you leave them behind, they will charge themselves on your altar or shrine, but they won't serve your needs in the regular world. Your bags should be a part of your normal dressing routine. Try sewing an internal pocket on some of your favorite items of clothing to make a place for your bag. This way, you can keep it close to your skin and avoid it falling out and creating interest you may not want.

Your mojo bag is the ultimate accessory to carry with you and bring magic to your life. Picking it up should come as naturally as taking your house keys and your phone. You should feel like it is a natural extension of your personality and always carry one with you.

Food and Drink

Now for the tasty stuff. Hoodoo practitioners should follow a healthy diet to keep their spirit and body strong and ready for their workings. Stamina and clarity of thought help you get the best results and improve your magic powers.

Traditional Hoodoo Food

One of the best ways you can honor the memory of the original Hoodoo workers is to make their food and revel in the taste and traditions of the African American culture. Soul food is a generic term that covers some of the classic dishes that have been passed down through the generations to become the dishes we know today.

Nobody is suggesting that you completely change your diet to soul food. That would be unsustainable and possibly unhealthy, but having soul food on special occasions will help you connect to your roots and recognize how the dishes signify the struggle they faced for survival. Enslavers gave their enslaved people the bare minimum of ingredients, and their rations were low in nutrition and often inferior. The masters failed to recognize that if they fed their enslaved people better quality food, they would thrive and become more productive. Today we consider soul food a source of comfort and decadence when, in reality, it originated from the creativity it took to turn basic ingredients into tasty and sustainable food.

Rice

Few people know that before the slave trade era, rice wasn't generally available in the US. The traders who imported enslaved people from Africa would often take crops native to Africa aboard the ships the enslaved people occupied. They used the crops to keep the occupants alive, and on arrival in the US, they planted the crops on plantations and became part of US food over time.

The two cultures came together to create fabulous one-pot recipes like Jollof and jambalaya that are popular today and give a snapshot into the early cuisine of African American folks.

Jambalaya

Try this Creole version for a hearty dish that is simple to make and delicious

Ingredients

- 1 lb. boneless chicken thighs diced and sliced
- 6oz spicy sausage
- 1 lb. medium-sized shrimp, cleaned and deveined
- I packet of long-grain rice
- Two cloves of garlic
- One can of tomatoes
- Two cups of chicken stock
- Two tbsp. tomato puree
- One white onion
- Two green onions
- Two bell peppers
- Himalayan salt
- Black pepper
- One tsp oregano
- One tbsp. olive oil

Instructions:

1. In a large saucepan, heat the oil, add the chicken peppers, onions, and seasoning, and cook for five minutes until the chicken is browned.

2. Add the spicy sausage, the garlic, and the tomato puree, and cook until it smells amazing.

3. Now add the chicken stock, tinned tomatoes, and rice to the pot.

4. Lower the heat on the stove, place a tight lid on the pot, and let it simmer for twenty minutes.

5. When the rice is tender, add the shrimp and cook for three to five minutes until they turn pink.

6. Add the green onions for crunch and serve immediately.

BBQ Pork

As you would expect, the cuts of pork given to slaves weren't the best, and they had to mask the poor flavor of the meat with sauces using their African cooking knowledge to make spectacular combinations that flavored and moistened the pork.

Try these sauces to coat your pork

Black BBQ sauce

Ingredients

- ¼ cup chopped onion
- ½ cup of distilled white vinegar
- ¼ cup soy sauce or Worcester sauce
- 2 tbsp. brown sugar
- 2 tsp lemon juice
- ¼ teaspoon black pepper
- ¼ tsp Tabasco sauce
- A pinch of coarse salt
- 2 tsp olive oil

Instructions:

1. In a solid base pan, heat the oil and add the onions, and fry until they have softened.

2. Add the rest of the ingredients and simmer for fifteen minutes with the lid off.

3. Wait until the sauce has thickened, and take it off the heat.

4. Serve warm or cold as an accompaniment, or baste your meat in the sauce for four hours before cooking.

What do you notice about the sauce that makes it stand out from other BBQ sauces? No tomatoes. Vinegar was a key part of early African American cooking as it was cheap and effective at tenderizing meat and made the sauce tangy rather than sweet.

Greens

Collard greens and boiled leafy green dishes are a staple part of soul food, and the liquid left behind after boiling the vegetables was added to any leftover fat from the pork, seasoned, and named "potlikker." The slaves would then bake cornbread and use it to soak up the juices as a filling snack.

Chitlins

Commonly referred to as chitterlings, these tasty dishes are based on the intestines of the domestic pig or cows filled with whatever was lying around in the kitchen stuffed into the pot and boiled or fried. They have a distinctly meaty flavor and aren't for the faint-hearted. If you do want to try the dish, ask your butcher to clean and prepare the pig's intestines for safety reasons. If you don't clean them properly, you can cause serious illnesses that will last for weeks.

However, professionally prepared chitlins can be easily sourced. Once you have them, the rest of the dish is all about what you have to hand. Add the chitlins to a large cooking pot and add garlic, apple, vinegar, pepper, salt, and any other ingredient you think will make the dish tasty. Boil for two hours to ensure the chitterlings are cooked, and let the mixture rest before pouring it through a colander.

Take the cooked chitlins and dry them with a clean cloth. Make a batter from flour and water with seasoning. Heat oil in a frying pan and coat the chitlins in batter before frying until they are golden and crisp. Place them on kitchen paper to drain before you season and eat them. Enjoy your soul food.

Sweet Potato Pie

Sweet potatoes are a traditional ingredient in soul food and are delicious as a side dish or cooked in this tasty pie.

Ingredients

- 1 9" uncooked pie shell
- Three medium sweet potatoes
- Two eggs
- ½ cup full-fat milk

- 600g unsalted butter
- One ¼ cup of white sugar
- One tbsp flour
- One tbsp. lemon juice
- One tbsp. nutmeg

Instructions:

1. Boil the unpeeled sweet potatoes in water until you can pierce the skin with a fork; around twenty minutes should work.
2. Let them cool before peeling and mashing the flesh.
3. Add the butter, sugar, flour, milk, eggs, and nutmeg, and mix well.
4. Add the mixture to the uncooked shell and place in preheated oven for thirty minutes.

Foods That Will Improve Your Spiritual Balance and Raise Your Vibrations

Your overall diet should be focused on providing you with the best ingredients possible to make your body work and boost your mind and spirit.

Incorporate these foods into your diet to make a significant difference to your health and your spirituality:

Fatty Fish

Fatty and oily fish are packed with essential oils that stimulate your brain and contribute to the fluidity of your brain's membrane. They contain essential omega-3 acids that combat depression and boost the development of hormones that lift your mood. Eat a portion of salmon or tuna twice a week to make sure you get the correct amount of these nutrients in your diet.

Dark Chocolate

Chocolate may not seem viable for your diet, but it is filled with mind-boosting components that release substances that boost your mood and raise your psychological response to eating it. Regular chocolate has elevated sugar and fat levels, so choose a darker option to benefit from the flavonoids and lower sugar levels. A small square every three days should provide you with the benefits and avoid the calories.

Fermented Foods

If you have taken a close look at the dairy section in your local store, chances are you have spotted fermented products like kimchi and kefir among the more regular yogurt options. Fermenting allows the growth of natural bacteria that functions in your gut to increase serotonin levels and improve your mood, raise your sex drive, and lessen stress levels. Try foods that are rich in probiotics and improve your gut function significantly.

Bananas

These tropical fruits may seem ordinary at first, but they are a healthy source of fiber known as prebiotics. This fiber works in your gut to slowly release sugar into your bloodstream to avoid mood swings and depression. They are packed with vitamin B6, which releases dopamine and serotonin, the most effective feel-good transmitters. One large banana every week will keep your blood sugar levels healthy and your mood stable.

Oats

Whole grains are a major source of fiber and are packed with iron. Just one cup of raw oats has 81g of iron which is 20% of your daily needs. These healthy doses of iron help combat sluggishness and raise energy levels.

Fruit and Vegetables

A diet filled with fresh ingredients is obviously better for you than processed ingredients, but it isn't always achievable. You can stick to seasonal ingredients in your food choices to make sure you get fresh ingredients all year round, but frozen fruit and veg can be just as nutritious if cooked correctly. Choose fruit high in antioxidants, like berries, to boost your energy levels, and fight disease.

Keep yourself hydrated and choose fresh ingredients whenever you can; organic and wild options are also better for you but can prove more expensive. You know the value of a good diet and how it helps you function at an optimum level, so budget for a better diet, and you'll soon see the difference.

Timing Is Everything in Hoodoo Rituals

Knowing when to perform rituals is an art that is part of your learned knowledge. A lot of your work is based on instinctively knowing what works for you, but the "good and bad" hours are part of your research.

Timing will help you bring the intention to your work and make your rituals and spells more effective.

The time of day you cast your spells or perform your ritual adds certain strengths to your work, so it is worth familiarizing yourself with these correspondences.

Sunrise is all about power

Casting spells at sunrise helps you shine light onto darkness and is perfect for new beginnings and new love. Rituals for healing and friendship should be performed at sunrise – and any spells that include financial and career matters. Working in the sunrise will enhance your spiritual connections as you bathe in the first light of the day.

Noon magic is all about amplification

Noon is the balanced hour of the day and the perfect time to banish unhealthy habits and dispel toxicity from your life. It amplifies your intent and ensures the negativity you seek to get rid of is gone as the noon hour passes. Spells for drawing success and love will be strengthened if you start your ritual before noon and finish it at the end.

Sunset spells and rituals are all about saying goodbye

When you are ready to release old aspects of your life, the best time to do so is at sunset. Intentions should include banishments, healing from toxicity, peace, and rest. If you want to bury any remnants from your banishing spells, it is wise to bury them in the west so the sun will set on them every day and ensure the intentions remain in the ground.

Midnight is the time for energy spells and rituals

It is the wakening hour for the spiritual world, and as the clock hands move toward midnight, it is the time for growing intentions, and as it passes the midnight hour, it is time for releasing them. Banishing spells should begin before midnight and finish just after.

Witching hour

Folklore states that the hour between 3 am and 4 am is the Devil's hour and a time for paranormal activity. If you do find yourself awake at the witching hour, cast a circle of protection, take some divination tools, and throw them down just to see what happens. Who knows, you may have a message sent to you through the veil that separates the physical and spiritual world when it is at its thinnest.

The Days of the Week and How They Affect Your Spells and Rituals

Sunday magic

Best for prosperity and strength, vitality, healing, and financial victories.

Monday magic

Best for love, healing, psychic connections, and friendship. Perform shadow and spirit work to enhance your dreams and emotional balance.

Tuesday magic

Best for legal matters, protection, courage, and confidence. Rituals should be performed for power and passion and to reverse any spells that have been cast against you.

Wednesday magic

Best for communication, divination, clarity of thought, spiritual enlightenment, wisdom, and knowledge.

Thursday magic

Best for good luck, especially in legal and business matters, fiscal growth, career moves, health, and political matters.

Friday magic

Best for love and passion. Also, a powerful day for all female magic like fertility and household matters, beauty, and love.

Saturday's magic

Best for self-improvement and transformation. Use Saturday to perform rituals for liberation and banishing unpleasant habits.

Taking Hoodoo Baths

No matter what the day of the week or the work you have done, you'll always benefit from a bath to set your intentions and heal any parts of your energy or physical self that your magic work may have drained. Try these specialized baths to energize and relax you at the same time.

These recipes are for baths that will solve any issues and bring positivity to your spirit.

Purification Bath

If you feel weighed down by some emotional or physical matters, this bath will release any negative energy and release your anxiety. This bath will also ease any flu or cold symptoms.

- Three cups of evaporated milk
- 3 tbsp. anise
- Sprinkling of rue
- A bowl of sea salt
- Two white candles
- Coconut incense

Instructions:

1. Draw a hot bath and add the milk, anise, and rue. Swirl the water until it forms a milky bath.
2. Light the two white candles and place them at the head of the bath before you lie in it.
3. Now take the bowl of salt and wash yourself from your head to your feet with a gentle exfoliating motion.
4. Once you have finished, let yourself relax in the water until you feel relaxed and cleansed.
5. When you leave the bath, dab yourself dry with a clean towel.

The Yellow Bath for Attraction

Do you need to get your relationship in order or attract a new love? Try this attraction bath if you need to attract any form of passion, love, or friendship. It is also good for skin ailments like dry skin or psoriasis.

- Yellow food coloring
- Yarrow flowers
- Parsley
- Citrine crystals
- Lemon incense
- Yellow and white candle
- Honey-based body scrub

Instructions:

1. Draw the bath with the yarrow and parsley and add the food coloring.
2. Light the candles and place the crystal at the head of the bathtub.
3. Gently wash yourself with the body scrub until your skin tingles.

4. If you have a person in mind you want to attract, try visualizing them or saying their name aloud.

5. You can use natural honey to wash but be warned. It will get sticky.

Spiritual Bath for Complete Refreshment and Clarification

Sometimes you just need a thorough clear-out, both mentally and physically. This bath will refresh your body and soul.

- One cup rainwater
- Coconut water
- Rice water
- Dried milk powder
- Egg white
- Three white candles

Instructions:

1. Draw your bath as usual and add all the ingredients except the candles.
2. Place the candles at the head of the bath and light them.
3. Soak yourself for twenty minutes and submerge your head in the bath at least twice.
4. Relax and feel the stress and worry flow out of you and into the ether.

Money Bath

Try this bath whenever you need to improve your financial status or attract fast cash. It is also effective in promoting good luck in business and gambling.

- Red clover
- Rose petals
- Calendula
- Chamomile
- Three green candles
- A jade crystal

Instructions:

1. Add all the ingredients to a hot bath except the candles and jade.

2. Place the candles at the head of the bath and put the crystal at the foot of the middle candle.

3. Sit in the bath and relax while you visualize your new future filled with wealth and prosperity.

Of course, these are just a few ideas for your Hoodoo baths. Take a look at the ingredients chapter to inspire you with ingredients to set your intention. Remember that some ingredients may cause skin irritation, and you should only use items that are safe in the water.

Conclusion

Now you have the knowledge, the instructions, and hopefully the passion for your new life as a Hoodoo practitioner. Are you excited? You should be. This was the first step in a whole new universe filled with everything you need to make your life become filled with your every desire. Hoodoo is a community of people who love to share their stories and experiences, and as you become more immersed in the magic, you'll become a willing member of this community. Sharing skills and new discoveries will become second nature to you, and the joy you get from your work will grow with your experience.

Good luck on your journey, and congratulations, you are now Hoodoo-ready!

Part 4: Orishas

Explore Orisha Deities, Yoruba, Voodoo, Santeria, the Ifa Divination System, and Ancient African Spiritual Practices

Introduction

There are an estimated 4,000 or more distinct religions worldwide today. It would be next to impossible for a single person to be familiar with every single one. Most people have at least heard of the major religions like Christianity, Islam, Judaism, Hinduism, and Buddhism. However, many other religions are just as old - if not older - than the main five. A few of these include the Yoruba religion, Voodoo, and Santería.

When you start exploring new religions, it's important to remember that simply learning their history or how they work doesn't mean you're betraying your current religion. Investigating a religion besides the one you practice doesn't even have to mean that you're seeking to convert to a new one. Understanding other people's religious and cultural practices is a great way to encourage empathy and cooperation between different groups of people.

If everyone took the time to explore different religions, there might be far less violence and war associated with them. Ignorance breeds hate and hate breeds conflict. The Yoruba religion, Voodoo, and Santería are some of the most misunderstood religions on the planet, particularly due to their cultural associations. Many films, television shows, comics, books, and video games appropriate aspects of these religions, then utilize them in ways that give them a negative reputation. The only way for this to change is to delve into the truth behind them.

Taking the time to explore these religions can be very rewarding. There are interesting myths, complex figures, and deep history for you to discover. You'll learn about the different beliefs held by practitioners. Still, you may also find many more similarities to your current religion than you would have anticipated. With many religions springing from a shared source, it's no surprise these religions could have some very familiar aspects. All you have to do is read on to find out more.

The main goal of anyone who picks up a book like this is to obtain knowledge. You wouldn't have chosen to open this guide if you weren't interested in learning more about the subject. That's a great sign that you aren't prone to judging a book by its cover – if you'll excuse the too-on-the-nose idiom. If you embark on this with an open mind, you'll be rewarded for your curiosity by discovering a fascinating history and belief system rooted in fascinating myths and engaging practices. By the time you reach the end of this guide, you'll be enriched and gratified that you chose to go on this journey.

Chapter 1: Understanding African Spiritual Practices

Belief in the Orishas originated in West Africa between 500 and 300 BCE. The primary religion that established these practices was that of the Yoruba people. After the advent of the transatlantic slave trade, the beliefs and religious practices of the Yoruba people found their way to places like the Americas and Caribbean, where certain aspects of the Yoruba religion were incorporated into other African diaspora religions, such as Voodoo and Santería.

Yoruba slaves shared their religion with other Africans transported to the Americas and the Caribbean.
https://www.pexels.com/photo/close-up-shot-of-a-person-holding-a-bible-7219814

Since many of the stories, rituals, and other religious practices involving the Orishas were passed down orally, many variations exist, sometimes even within the same ethnic groups. This can make it difficult to find definitive versions of these aspects of the Orishas and their related religions, but most share some commonalities. Understanding the similarities and differences between the major African diaspora religions can help you sort through your beliefs, determining the specific practices you'd like to follow.

The Religion of the Yoruba (Ifa)

The religion of the Yoruba people, also known as Ifa, has a major presence in Southwestern Nigeria. This includes the states of Ekiti, Kwara, Lagos, Ogun, Ondo, Osun, Oyo, and parts of Benin, Kogi, and Togo. Because its origins date back so far, the religion was deeply ingrained in the culture of the Yoruba people, which resulted in their beliefs and practices, which migrated to the New World during the slave trade.

Yoruba enslaved people shared their religion with other Africans transported to the Americas and the Caribbean. They eventually intermingled with other religions to create new variations, like Voodoo, Santería, Umbanda, Haitian Vodou, Trinidad Orisha, and Candomblé. And, in some cases, aspects of Christianity, especially Catholicism, during the 16th-18th centuries.

Olodumare

Olodumare and his other aspects of Olorun and Olofi are a key part of the African diaspora religions. He is believed to be the creator of the universe and the source of all energy. The practices of Ifa, and to a lesser extent, Voodoo and Santería, focus on Olodumare as the ultimate source of knowledge and power. Everything eventually connects to him, even if done indirectly, so a person's actions and venerations are carried out in his name.

Aṣẹ

Aṣẹ is the energy or life force imbued within all living and nonliving things, comprising both the spiritual power and the power to initiate actions and events in the physical world. Anything that occurs is due to aṣẹ, including prayers, songs, conversations, and curses. Since it is possessed by everything, from human beings to water, stone, animals, ancestors, and even other gods in the Yoruba pantheon, it's an extremely important aspect of the Yoruba belief system. This is the energy granted by Olodumare and the power wielded by his Olorun aspect, using aṣẹ to rule the heavens. There is also an association with the sun, which allows all life to exist.

Orún

Orún is the invisible realm on a higher plane than the physical world. This is where Olodumare dwells and from where the Orishas originally came. Every living being starts life in Orún before being sent to Earth to enter its physical form. It is similar to the Christianity concept of Heaven, Valhalla, and Fólkvangr from Norse mythology and the Greek and Roman afterlife known as Elysium or the Elysian Fields. Orún is presided over by the aspect of Olodumare known as Olorun.

Ayé

Ayé is the name used by the Yoruba people for Earth or the physical world, where humans live and die, as well as all the plants and animals that exist as part of the natural ecosystem. Aṣẹ permeates all of Ayé, and the Orishas can travel there from Orún at will. Olodumare brought it into being through his will, assisted by the primordial Orishas. Everything that happens in Ayé is overseen by the aspect of Olodumare, known as Olofi.

Ori

Practitioners of Ifa maintain that every human being's head contains their essence, spirit, or soul, which is known as their ori. Before the ori is sent to Earth to inhabit a human body, it's brought before Olodumare, who bestows upon it the core traits, characteristics, and personality it will possess. At this point, the ori is connected with its personal Orisha, who will help influence and guide them throughout their lives. Most importantly, the ori resides within a person's head, meaning that the Yoruba people place significant importance on this part of the body.

Iponri

The iponri is considered a higher state of consciousness, essentially the ultimate goal for people to reach. It is also believed to be a counterpart to the ori that resides in Orún. When people can fully discern their destiny, they will attain an open connection to their iponri, which will grant them access to the wisdom and knowledge of the Orishas. When a person dies, their ori will be reunited with their iponri, allowing them to become an egun in the afterlife. Some Ifa practitioners believe that a person can be reincarnated within their bloodline, in which case the ori and iponri will split once more.

Ebo

Ebo is the concept of ritualistic sacrifice to the Orishas. It is only ever done in a religious context, most commonly during the practice of divination associated with Ifa. A practitioner will do ebo to appease the divine beings whose power and guidance are being called upon for assistance. This sign of respect proves you are devoted to maintaining the harmonious balance between the Earth and heavens and that your desire to glean wisdom from the Orishas is in service to discovering your appointed destiny. Taking the time to find the proper sacrifice for the Orisha you wish to commune with shows that you are a true believer, willing to learn about the Orishas and apply that knowledge in practice.

Animals are often the chosen sacrifice for the ebo rituals. This is because the Orishas can gain benefits from many different parts of the animal. The blood and vital organs contain the essence of life within it, the Aṣẹ, nourishing the Orishas' own energy. The meat offers sustenance, allowing the Orishas to maintain their physical strength. The head, in particular, is of significant value since that is where their untapped divine power resides, having been bestowed upon them by Olodumare at birth. While animals do not have the same degree of power as humans, all living things are touched by the Supreme Being and therefore possess a portion of his essence.

When inanimate objects are used for the ebo rituals, they must strongly associate with their particular Orisha. These items generally reflect the symbols or favorite foods of the Orisha. The objects associated with the Orisha possess an energy that can be absorbed and turned into the essential power needed to sustain them. During the ritual, the participants empower their sacrificial items through prayer, and the Orisha can then channel the energy created into themselves. This can be equally as strong as animal sacrifices but takes more time and practice to get right.

Yoruba Creation Myth

According to the Yoruba religion, the universe was created in its entirety by Olodumare. However, as the Orishas toured the universe in search of inhabitable planets, they deemed the Earth to be too wet for anyone to live there. After some time had passed, the Orisha known as Obatala returned to Earth, where he decided to alter the planet so that it would become a place for mortal beings to dwell. He created landforms using a mollusk containing a special type of soil, winged beasts, and a material similar to cloth. Obatala dumped the soil into the water, and the winged beasts spread it out across the world, creating the Earth's crust. As their wings beat against the newly-released earth, it caused the soil to spread unevenly in some places, forming mountains, hills, and valleys.

At the same time, Olodumare collected gasses and cosmic matter from the farthest reaches of space, bringing them together into an orb-like celestial body. Using his powers, he caused this orb to erupt into a massive fireball and set it in place near the Earth. This was the sun, and its light and heat could now dry the lands, allowing them to set and become solid ground. It also provided a way to see clearly during the period when a part of the planet was facing the sun. Olodumare also created the moon as a gift to the Orisha known as Yemọja, considered the mother of all Orishas. The moon would reflect the sun's light upon the part of the Earth that was facing away from the sun, granting a small measure of silvery glow to prevent the lands from engulfing by total darkness.

With the land now firmly set within the seas, Obatala climbed to higher ground, giving the name Ile-Ife to the location where he had chosen to settle. The earth became fertile, and flora flourished across the land. Trees, bushes, flowers, and grass shot up through the soil, reaching upward to the sun and absorbing its life-giving essence. Obatala determined that the world could sustain mortal life, so he started constructing figurines from the mud and clay within the earth. The sun's light baked these figurines as if in a kiln, and Olodumare released the breath of life into them, imbuing each with the gift of consciousness. Because of this, Ile-Ife is known to the Yoruba as Ife Oodaye, which means the *cradle of existence.*

Yoruba, Islam, and Christianity

During the 14th century, trade between the Yoruba people and a nomadic caste of Soninke merchants from the Mali Empire, known as the Wangara, resulted in the introduction of Islam to the Yoruba culture. Islam gained a strong foothold amongst the Yoruba people, with many mosques built throughout the 17th, 18th and 19th centuries. By the time they were captured and sent to the Americas as enslaved people, many Yoruba people had either converted to Islam or practiced a pluralistic form of religion that included Islamic and local Ifa customs.

Christianity and ideas from western civilization were brought to the Yoruba people in the 19th century. Missionaries from Europe arrived alongside traders who had come to establish commercial relationships with the locals. They spread Christianity to the Yoruba people, often using the tactic of syncretism to equate the stories and members of the Yoruba pantheon with their Christian counterparts. They identified Olodumare and his aspect of Olorun as the Abrahamic God, while Yemoja was interpreted as the Virgin Mary. French and British colonizers saw the most success in converting the Yoruba people, with the French pushing Roman Catholicism and the British pushing Protestantism.

These foreign religions intermingled with the Yoruba religion, creating new forms of worship and further dividing the various sects of Ifa that were already quite different in their rituals and practices. Like the mosques, churches were erected to serve as places of worship, even though the traditional Yoruba religion did not have any such centralized gathering place for shared prayers and ceremonies. In the 1970s, a religion known as Nigerian Chrislam was founded by the Yoruba people who lived in southwestern Nigeria. It sought to merge the common aspects of both Islam and Christianity into a single form. They also maintained some parts of the traditional African diaspora religions, but most of the Yoruba people in the region remain Muslims, with a significant Christian minority.

Yoruba Beliefs and Mainstream Culture

For any Star Wars fans, the beliefs of the Yoruba about Olodumare may sound very familiar. The concept of "The Force" in Star Wars took inspiration from several religions worldwide, including the African diaspora religions. Just as with Olodumare, the Force provides energy to all living things, and when someone dies, their energy is returned to the Force. There is also the fact that the Force has both good and evil aspects, manifested through the light and dark sides. The Force is responsible for creating the universe and determining the fate of everyone and everything. It's also often viewed as a distant entity that won't directly intervene in events taking place in the physical universe but still works through practitioners of the Force religions (i.e., the Jedi and the Sith) to carry out its will.

The beliefs of the Yoruba have also influenced popular music. Musicians such as Bobby Benson, Cardinal Rex, Ebenezer Obey, and Segun Bucknor pioneered the genre of highlife, while others created genres like jùjú, apala, fuji, and waka. These types of music drew inspiration from the Yoruba and other African diaspora religions, using imagery and folklore taken directly from them. The music of these genres often heavily features drums as the driving force behind their songs, giving them a strong rhythmic quality that encourages dancing and clapping along as the music is played.

Voodoo

Voodoo isn't a single religion but is the label used to describe a group of African diaspora religions that includes West African Vodun, Candomblé Jejé, Haitian Vodou, Dominican Vudú, Cuban Vodú, Hoodoo, and Louisiana Voodoo. They have roots in African ethnic groups like the Aja, Ewe, and Fon, who were among those transported to the Americas and Caribbean, spreading their beliefs through these regions. As their belief systems developed and were shared with other pockets of enslaved people during the 16th-18th centuries, Voodoo became a widespread religion practiced in many areas, although the specific practices varied from place to place. Because of this, there is no central authority over the religions, similar to the case with the Yoruba religion.

Priestesses

Many Voodoo sects have a hereditary matriarchal lineage of priestesses known as the Queen Mother. The role of Queen Mother is generally passed down from mother to daughter. It will always be given to the firstborn female in a family collective. In the absence of a direct descendant of the current Queen Mother, if she does not have any daughters of her own, the priestess role will be passed to a close blood relative or, in rare cases, a woman who has married into the family.

The Queen Mother has the right to lead her community's religious ceremonies, like marriages, funerals, and baptisms. In the past, when the men of the community would go off to war, the Queen Mother was responsible for maintaining the village and gathering the women for prayers and rituals to ensure that the men would return home safely. They are also responsible for the organization and upkeep of the local market, which is a key focal point of each village since it serves as a gathering place for the clan members.

In addition to the Queen Mother, there are high priestesses, regular priestesses, and an oracle. Even if the role is passed down to the first-born daughter, the oracle would be the one to choose which of the priestesses of their community would be raised to the position of high priestess, as well as ordaining the new Queen Mother. When the oracle calls a woman of the community to become a priestess, they cannot refuse the responsibility. The oracle ensures that each family collective has a proper priestess lineage, and those roles will usually remain with the blood relatives. Only members of the community are permitted to worship with them. Outsiders are restricted to worshiping only the standard Voodoo pantheon and not any of the ancestral spirits that the community holds in high regard.

Ancestor Worship

A major component of Voodoo is ancestor worship. The religion holds that the spirits of the dead exist alongside the living and that priestesses in every family can communicate with them. When a community member dies, a ritual is held to assist their spirit in joining the rest of their ancestors in the spirit realm, which can be felt but not seen by the living within the community. These ancestral spirits often guide their descendants, offering advice and blessings through the priestesses, who serve as a conduit between the living and the dead. When living family members face a significant challenge or must make a major decision, they will often consult their own priestesses to ask for advice from their ancestors and have great respect for whatever wisdom is passed on to them.

Voodoo and Christianity

Due to the cosmological system of many sects of Voodoo, the similarities to Christian doctrine allowed the two religions to be syncretized, especially regarding the Voodoo pantheon deities that serve as counterparts to the Christian angels and saints. As Christianity became more prominent, there were attempts to supplant the deities and spirits worshiped by Voodoo practitioners with their Christian counterparts. This was met with mixed success. Some sects adopted these angels and saints into their religious system, while others rejected them outright. Some Voodoo sects began using certain rituals from the Christian liturgy, like marriages, funerals, and baptisms. Still, they put their own spin on the ceremonies to better identify with their personal beliefs.

Loa

Some sects of the Voodoo religion, particularly Haitian Vodou and Louisiana Voodoo, worship a group of spirits known as Loa. They serve as intermediaries between human beings and a Divine Creator deity called Bondyé. Communication is usually achieved through divination or the Loa sending dreams to people. In turn, humans make offerings or sacrifices to the Loa, especially animals like chickens, hogs, or cattle. After performing the sacrifice, despite the stigma generally attached to the idea of animal sacrifice, the meat of the animal is shared and consumed with the family.,

Thousands of Loa exist, with more than 200 being named. Every Loa has its own personality and distinguishing characteristics that set them apart from one another, as well as particular colors and objects associated with them. They are divided into two nanchons, which means nations or families. These are the Petwo and the Rada. The Petwo is related to "hot" characteristics, such as brashness and volatility, while the Rada encompasses the "cool" traits, like having an even temper and serenity. Many of the Loa have counterparts in Roman Catholic saints, sharing similar symbols and traits.

Santería

Santería can be roughly translated as "the way of the saints." It is an Afro-Caribbean religion that is specifically rooted in Cuba, having developed during the 19th century. It was originally formed by the syncretism of the Yoruba religion, Roman Catholicism, and a branch of Spiritualism known as Spiritism. Like the other African diaspora religions, Santería has no centralized authority, so there is significant diversity between those who practice it. Practitioners are called "creyentes," which means "believers."

The cosmology of Santería is similar to Ifa and Voodoo and is considered a polytheistic religion. While they believe in Olodumare as the Divine Creator, they view him as even more distant and inaccessible than in the other African diaspora religions, focusing their worship on the Orishas, whom they also refer to as santos (saints). The Orishas of Santería are held in high regard. Still, they are not considered entirely benevolent, having both good and evil traits and possessing the capability to help or hurt human beings. They are complex deities, having a rich combination of different emotions, virtues, and vices that result in a pantheon of very interesting figures.

Humans and Orishas

Creyentes believe that humanity and Orishas have an interdependent relationship with one another. Humans make offerings and prayers to Orishas in order to appease them, and in return, the deities will intercede in the affairs of mortals on behalf of those beseeching them for aid. Many Santería practitioners believe every person is born with an innate connection to a specific Orisha, and whether this connection is cultivated or not through worship and veneration, it will influence the individual's thoughts and personality. The Orisha is said to be a person's "father" or "mother," depending on their gender, making a chosen human their "child."

The creyentes believe that Orishas can communicate directly with their "children" through music, dance, dreams, divination, and prayer. Many practitioners of Santería perform rituals, have ceremonies, and make offerings to their personal Orisha to ask for divine blessings and assistance. It's common for creyentes to see signs, omens, or messages from the Orishas in everyday tasks and events, which they interpret so that they can determine what course of action to take.

Birth, Death, Destiny, and Ancestor Worship

The Santería belief system calls their ori the "eledá." They preach that eledá is received before a person's birth, during which time they are given their destiny, or "destino." However, it is not a predetermined fate, but more like a path they will follow to lead them through their life, which can be strayed from during the person's journey on Earth. For this reason, their destiny is also known as "camino," which means road.

When a creyentes dies, they become an ancestor, which allows the ori to continue existing in spirit form. These ancestor spirits are called egun, espíritus, or muertos. Ancestor worship is an important aspect of Santería, and creyentes maintain that the egun should be treated with great respect, reverence, and courtesy. It is believed that all humans can learn how to see and speak to the dead, allowing them to confer with the egun. Their opinions and counsel are often sought during special ceremonies where the creyentes honor their ancestors. These ceremonies usually involve a ritual where the living will leave seven glasses of water as an offering to the egun.

While most of the egun an individual communicates with are hereditary ancestors, they can also be past members of the same congregation. Most creyentes have what is known as a cuadro espiritual, or a spiritual portrait. This means they have a collection of egun protecting them, which can be in numbers as high as 25. The egun who are part of a cuadro espiritual are called protectores, or protectors. They don't just serve as guides but also provide physical aid when someone finds themselves in potentially dangerous or threatening situations, keeping them safe and leading them out of harm's way.

The protectors are considered benevolent eguns, but a person can also have malevolent eguns or a combination of good and bad eguns attached to them. There is also a distinction between evolved and unevolved egun. The evolved ones can guide and protect a creyente, while the unevolved ones are unwise and lack the skill to be helpful, instead causing chaos. A person can help an unevolved egun to become evolved through prayer, offerings, and sacrifice. Once an egun has evolved, they can provide additional guidance and protection for the individual to whom they are attached.

Categories of the Egun

In Santería, the egun are categorized based on their relationship to an individual. These egun include:

- **Egun Baba/Egun Lya:** These are the egun of a person's immediate family, such as their parents or siblings.
- **Egun Idile:** These are the egun of blood relatives and hereditary ancestors.
- **Egun iIu:** These are the egun of the founders of the person's town, community, or clan.
- **Egun Eleko:** These are the egun who are friends a person met in a past life.
- **Abiku:** These are the egun of children who died during childbirth or shortly after.
- **Egun Enia Sasa:** These are the egun who were famous or accomplished people in life, such as great priests and priestesses.
- **Oso:** These are the egun of indigenous warlords and medicine men or women.
- **Egun Gun Olufe:** These are the egun who were Babalawos or the high priests of the Ifa oracles.
- **Eleye/Aja:** These are the egun of witches.
- **Ebora:** These are the egun that represents fire and lava.
- **Egun Igi:** These are the egun who inhabit sacred trees.

Egun is also divided into different categories based on cultural stereotypes, each offering its unique characteristics, abilities, benefits, dangers, and colors associated with them. These categories include:

- **Africanos y Congos (Africans and Congo):** These are egun that originated from the kings, queens, and those of royal heritage in Africa but became enslaved people in the Americas. They aid in defending against enemies that use the occult to cause harm.

Offerings: Tobacco, cigars, rum, coffee, okra, corn meal, okra

Colors: Black, brown, purple, orange

- **Orientales (Asians):** These are egun originating from Asian countries, including China, Japan, Korea, and India. They bring luck with money and love, helping with financial issues and improving businesses.

Offerings: Incense, citrus fruits

Colors: Red, pink

- **Haitianos (Haitian):** These are egun that originated in Haiti. They encourage hospitality, friendliness, and respect for one's family and elders.

Offerings: Beef and pumpkin soup, sweet potato pudding, cocoa, bitter oranges

Colors: Blue, red, orange

- **Indios (Native Americans):** These are egun that aid in judicial matters, spiritual warfare, patience, and seeking wisdom and knowledge.

Offerings: Black coffee, corn meal, tobacco

Colors: Yellow, blue

- **Arabes (Arabs):** These are egun who help with knowledge of magical forces, particularly the djinn.

Offerings: Flatbread, garlic, garbanzo beans, oil

Colors: Black, green

- **Gitanos y Gitanas (Gypsies):** These egun provide assistance with fortune telling, divination, palmistry, passion, and romance.

Offerings: Tarot cards, cigarettes, crystals, Aguardiente liquor

Colors: Red, black

- **Santos (Saints):** These are the egun of saints, usually of the Roman Catholic variety. Each saint has its own attributes and protections, such as Saint Christopher, who protects against sudden death, or Saint Jude, who is the patron saint of lost causes.

Offerings: Religious iconography and items associated with a particular saint.

Colors: Each saint has its own colors associated with them.

- **Angeles (Guardian Angels):** These are the egun of guardian angels. Like saints, there are many different guardian angels with their own characteristics, such as Gabriel, who protects messengers and members of the military, and Nuriel, who protects against hailstorms.

Offerings: Guardian angels do not require offerings.

Colors: Every color of the spectrum is connected to angels, as they are transcendent.

- **Médicas / Curandera / Santiguadores (Doctors / Healers /Faith Healers):** These are egun who aid in medical matters of all kinds, medicine, herbalism, faith healing, encouraging recovery, and finding a cure for illnesses.

Offerings: Herbal teas, candles, religious paraphernalia

Colors: Yellow, white

- **Heroes y Liders (Heroes and Leaders):** These are the egun who aid in wars and battles, both literal and figurative.

Offerings: Alcohol, cigars, weapons

Colors: White

- **Chamanes, Yerbateros, Brujos y Trabajadores Espirituales (Shaman, Herbalists, Witches, and Spiritualists):** These are egun who help with matters of herbalism, magic, visions, omens, and healing.

Offerings: Black unsweetened coffee, liquor, cigars

Colors: Brown, green

- **Escalvos (Slaves):** These are the egun of dead slaves, and they aid with patience, hard work, and overcoming obstacles.

Offerings: Okra, coffee, cigars, corn meal

Colors: Purple, white

- **Infantiles (Babies):** These are the egun of babies who died during childbirth or infancy. They often manifest as tricksters, playing pranks and jokes on humans. However, they can also be very protective of those to whom they are connected.

Offerings: Toys, sweets, candy, coins

Colors: Orange, yellow

- **Ánima Benditas y Anima Solas (Blessed and Lost Souls):** These are the egun of those whose spirits are bound for heaven or purgatory. They will aid in any endeavors during the period where they remain bound to the Earth, so long as you pray to them and give them light to find you.

Offerings: Holy water, ice cubes, drinks, liquor

Colors: Red, black

- **Libertadores (Liberators):** These are the egun who help with gaining freedom, court trials, studying, and learning.

Offerings: Cigars, brandy

Colors: Yellow, white

- **Vagabundos y Bohemios (Wanderers and Bohemians):** These are the egun who assist artists, writers, and musicians. They can provide inspiration for painting, drawing, poetry, novels, short stories, letters, singing, songwriting, and playing instruments.

Offerings: Crackers, toast, bread

Colors: Green, brown

- **Elementales (Elementals):** These are the egun associated with the four elements (fire, earth, air, water), cardinal directions (north, south, east, west), and four winds (Boreas, Notus, Eurus, Zephyrus).

Offerings: Anything related to a specific element or cardinal direction.

Colors: Red (fire and north), white (air and south), blue (water), brown (earth), black (west), yellow (east)

- **Piratas y Marineros (Pirates and Mariners):** These are egun who bring courage, fearlessness, strength of will, and overcoming adversity.

Offerings: Cigars, sugarcane, rum

Colors: White, black, red

Connection with Roman Catholicism

Santería has a very strong connection to Roman Catholicism. The concepts of angels and saints greatly influenced the egun, and there are even categories of egun reserved for these beings. Many prayers, rituals, and ceremonies mimic those used by the Catholic Church. The hierarchy of priests and priestesses is similar to that of the Catholic priesthood. This is because the primary practitioners of Santería lived in Cuba. During the 15th-18th centuries, many Spanish colonists on the island brought their strong Roman Catholic faith with them. Even after control of Cuba was turned over to the British in the 19th century, a strong Spanish presence remained there that influenced the practitioners of Santería as it developed.

Frequently Asked Questions (FAQs)

Q: Can anyone practice Ifa (Yoruba religion), Voodoo, or Santería?

A: Yes, anyone can practice Ifa, Voodoo, or Santería. However, it's important to make sure that you take it seriously and educate yourself on the history, traditions, and rituals associated with your chosen religion.

Q: Do I need to be initiated into Ifa, Voodoo, or Santería before officially practicing it?

A: This depends on exactly how you intend to practice these religions. For Ifa, initiation is usually reserved for people who seek to become priests or priestesses or if you want to have a spiritual connection to the Orishas. The specific rituals used for the initiation process are kept secret. To undergo one that the core practitioners recognize, you would need to go to Nigeria, where Ifa originated.

Voodoo is much more relaxed when it comes to initiation and can be conducted by manbos or oungans, who are the priestesses and priests of this religion. They will wash your head to cleanse it for the spirits believed to reside there, followed by a period of seclusion. The final step is when the manbos or oungans teach you more about Voodoo so that you'll be knowledgeable in the important aspects of practicing their religion.

Santería requires a relatively in-depth process for initiation. The primary ritual takes seven days, but there is also a two-day preparation period. A priestess known as a misa espiritual will perform a ceremony to gain the blessing of the egun. The egun is allowed to take possession of the initiate, establishing a connection between them. A series of offerings and sacrifices are made to the Orishas, and the initiate removes their clothes so they can be purified in the river waters. The seven-day initiation ritual involves different tests and actions each day. If it's successful, the initiate will accompany a priest or priestess to a Roman Catholic church so they can light a candle, signifying the end of the process.

Q: Can I practice a hybrid version of these religions, taking bits and pieces from each in order to create my own?

A: Technically, you can practice any version of these religions that you want as long as you only intend to do it privately. There's no reason you can't pick whatever aspects of Ifa, Voodoo, and Santería you desire to create your own variation of these African diaspora religions. However, you may run into trouble if you attempt to establish your own religion publicly, as there are practices associated with each that are regarded as unique to them and them alone. This doesn't mean it's illegal or impossible to accomplish. Still, you should be aware that you'll likely receive a significant amount of pushback and resistance from the practitioners of each religion you've drawn from.

Q: Is it disrespectful for white people to practice Ifa, Voodoo, or Santería?

A: If you are a white person of European descent interested in practicing any of these religions, the best option is to find someone who is a current practitioner and ask their opinion on the matter. You could always practice privately and not tell anyone about it, which would be harmless. Still, if you want to join others in worshiping the Orishas and participating in the religion's ceremonies, you'll have to acknowledge publicly that you are also a practitioner.

Historically, all these religions and their many different iterations are rooted in pre-colonial Africans' practices and the Christian and Islamic colonizers who arrived between the 16th-18th centuries. The modern versions of Ifa, Voodoo, and Santería were developed by enslaved Africans and their descendants, including those who were born free but continued to suffer from the bigotry and systemic racism that resulted in the aftermath of the end of slavery.

Much of the various religions' practices and beliefs contain aspects of cultural reactions to this reality, and the fact that white people (primarily of European descent) perpetrated disgusting abuses against those of African heritage cannot be ignored. The unfortunate reality is that race is inextricably linked to the development of these religions, and many would find it disrespectful for a white person to appropriate the practices traditionally carried out by those of African heritage. European colonization robbed them of so much over many centuries, so plenty of people would see a white person practicing Ifa, Voodoo, or Santería as yet another instance of white colonizers trying to take something that doesn't belong to them.

Ultimately, if you are white, it is your choice whether you want to practice any of these religions. While nobody can stop you from doing so, it would be wise and respectful to consider the historical implications before you commit to anything. The best option would always be to actually speak to those in your community who are current practitioners; consider their opinion. They would be the ones you are most likely to encounter during your religious endeavors. Only they can tell you if they would be comfortable with you joining in with their worship.

Chapter 2: Orishas and Ifa Basics

The Orishas are a key component of all African diaspora religions, including the Yoruba religion of Ifa. Ifa, in particular, has an extensive belief system, maintaining that the Orishas number "400+1", which is their way of saying there is actually an unknowable amount of them. There is a pantheon that includes the most important of the Orishas, but this isn't even close to the complete scope of how many exist. They are involved in the divination system used by Ifa practitioners, Voodoo, and Santería religions known as Ifa.

There are certain Orishas who are shared across every belief system, and these are usually thought of as the chief beings of the Orishas.

The Orishas

Orishas are supernatural beings considered divine spirits or deities, as well as conduits through which the Supreme Being of Olodumare can communicate with humanity. Many African diaspora religions that believe in the Orishas have their own version of the traditional pantheon. There are certain Orishas who are shared across every belief system, and these are usually thought of as the chief beings of the Orishas.

Within the pantheon itself, they are divided into two groups: the gbigbona, the "hot" Orishas, and the tutu, the "cool" ones. The gbigbona are considered strong, emphatic, fearless, and easily upset. At the same time, the tutu is seen as gentle, tranquil, agreeable, and benign. Each of the Orishas has its own symbols, colors, foods, and items associated with them. Still, usually, the gbigbona use red and black as their colors, while the tutu uses white.

Categories of Orishas

The Orishas can also be categorized by those who were present at the time of creation, those who were brought into existence later, and who personified natural forces. Some of the Orishas began as mortal beings and eventually earned a place amongst the gods through deification. Others are personifications of natural phenomena, such as the elements of fire, earth, air, and water. The idea of "good and evil" is not as clearly delineated in the African diaspora religions as it is in a religion like Christianity. While there are associations between the Orishas and angels or saints, none can be considered wholly good or wholly evil. They may tend to lean one way or another, but there are positive and negative qualities about each Orisha.

The Core Pantheon

The most important of the Orishas make up the core of the pantheon. We will discuss them in more depth later, but so you can familiarize yourself with the basics, here is a brief rundown of the core pantheon:

- **Orunmila:** A conduit between Olodumare, the Orishas, and humanity.
- **Obatala:** The Sky Father and the creator of humanity.
- **Ogun:** A warrior and metalworker.

- **Shango:** A royal ancestor of the Yoruba and a mortal raised to the status of an Orisha.

- **Yemoja:** A major water spirit and mother of every Orisha.

- **Eshu:** A primordial deity and the Orishas' chief enforcer.

- **Oshun:** A river deity and a former mortal-turned-Orisha.

- **Oya:** The Orisha of death and rebirth.

- **Iya Nla:** A primordial Orisha and the source of all creation.

- **Otin:** A legendary warrior and protector of the Otin River.

- **Oshosi:** The Orisha of animals and nature.

- **Osanyin:** The Orisha of healers and herbalists.

- **Babalu-Aye:** A spirit of the Earth.

- **Ori:** The personification of the essence of life.

- **Oshumare:** The Orisha of rainbows.

- **Nana Buluku:** The mother of the sun, moon, and stars.

- **Oduduwa:** A former divine king of the Yoruba and founder of the holy city of Ile-Ife.

- **Olokun:** The Orisha of water.

The Extended Pantheon

The rest of the pantheon is made up of many Orishas - far too many to include them all here. This list contains the most popular members of the extended pantheon:

- **Logun Ede:** They are unique amongst the Orishas in that they have both masculine and feminine characteristics, presenting as male for half the year and female for the other half. During their time as a male, they dwell in the forests; when they are female, they live in freshwater lakes or rivers.

- **Aganju:** An Orisha that was once mortal and was either Shango's father or brother. Like Shango, he spent time ruling the Oyo Empire. In contrast to Shango (associated with lightning and thunder), Aganju has a connection to **fire.**

- **Egungun:** They are the patron of the blessed dead. There is a festival in his honor known as Odun Egungun, where celebrants dress up in ornate costumes and masks, masquerading as the

Orishas or egun to pay tribute to their ancestors and the revered dead. Part of this festival involves the concept of "layering," in which participants will have multiple layers to their costumes, each representing different Orishas or egun, allowing them to quickly change throughout their performances.

- **Yewa:** She is the patron of the Yewa River in Nigeria. In some variations of Ifa, she is a protector of fishermen, crabbers, loggers, and sand miners. There is a strong association between Yewa and the blue crab, a popular food caught in the river.

- **Ajaka:** He ruled over the Oyo Empire during two non-consecutive periods. During his first reign, Ajaka was considered weak because he gave his warriors more freedom than was traditionally allowed, and they overthrew him. After Shango's death, he was recalled to the throne, and his second reign saw him rule like his predecessor. By his death, he was so beloved that he underwent the same type of deification into an Orisha as Shango.

- **Olumo:** He is the patron of the city of Abeokuta, Ogun State, Nigeria. There is a natural fortress near Abeokuta known as Olumo Rock, and this was used during inter-tribal warfare in the 19th century. Associated with earth and stone, it is believed by the people of Abeokuta that he continues to protect their lands to this day.

- **Iroko:** They are the personification of the Iroko trees that grow on the western coast of tropical Africa. The Iroko is a hardwood tree that can live for nearly 500 years and is believed to possess healing properties. The Orisha Iroko protects these trees, and his power is invoked when using them for healing purposes. However, it is said that if anyone catches a glimpse of the Orisha while looking at an Iroko tree, they will die soon after. When cutting an Iroko down, it is customary to offer a prayer to the spirit within to appease the destruction of a tree under its charge.

- **Ayangalu:** He is the patron of drummers. As a mortal, he was believed to have been the first drummer. When he died, he underwent deification into an Orisha. He is believed to be a muse to musicians, particularly drummers, inspiring them in their creative endeavors. As drumming became more popular in the 20th century with the rise of popular music and recording artists,

Ayangalu's importance grew among the drumming community.

- **Ibeji:** They are a gender-fluid Orisha, being the patron of twins. In Yoruba culture, twins have a magical connotation. They are considered under the protection of not just Ibeji but also Shango. Because twins are believed to have a spiritual connection to one another, if one should die, it is viewed as an omen of bad fortune. To offset this, the parents will have a babalawo carve a representation of the deceased twin, and they will care for it as if it were a living person. The living twin's connection is transferred to the carving, which the spirit of the dead twin inhabits, retaining the magical power granted to them.

- **Oko:** He is the patron of hunters and farmers. Oko provides protection against sorcery and is a key component of the annual harvest festival that celebrates the new crop of white African yams. Although he is a close friend of Shango, he married Shango's second wife, Oya, and Yemoja. It is believed that bees are the personal messengers of Oko, bringing his correspondences to his fellow Orishas.

- **Moremi:** She was a legendary queen of the Yoruba people and a folk hero who aided in freeing the kingdom of Ile-Ife from that of Ugbo. Moremi married Oranmiyan, who was the son of Oduduwa. Her strength and courage were displayed when she allowed herself to be captured by the Ugbo in exchange for the lives of her people. Because of her great beauty, the Ugbo king decided to marry her and make her his queen, which allowed her to discover their secrets, which she brought back to her own people after a daring escape. This helped the Yoruba defeat the Ugbo Kingdom and earned her a place in the pantheon of the Orishas after her death.

- **Oronsen:** She is the patron of the Owo, a local government area in Ondo State, Nigeria, which traces its origins back to Ile-Ife, founded by the sons of Oduduwa. Oronsen began her political life when she met King Rerengejen of Owo while he was on a hunting expedition. He was so taken by her beauty that he immediately made her a part of his harem. Later, she revealed to him that she was actually an Orisha but that she was happy as his wife, only asking that he and his other wives never break her three unbreakable taboos. While the king was out hunting, his other wives broke all three taboos out of jealousy, causing Oronsen to flee. Before departing the mortal world, she told her husband that if he held a festival of remembrance in her honor, she would forever watch over Owo.

- **Oba:** She is the patron of the River Oba. Oba was the first wife of Shango but was tricked by his second wife, Oshun, into severing her own ear and attempting to feed it to her husband. When Shango realized what had occurred, he sent her into exile. As a result, where the River Oba meets the River Osun is plagued with turbulent rapids. Oba protected the people of Iwo while in exile, and this caused them to deify her as an Orisha.

- **Ara:** An Orisha who is the personification of thunder, but his role in the pantheon is usually overshadowed by Shango. Ara is venerated in localized pockets of Nigeria, but worship of him has never been as widespread as his fellow Orishas. It's believed that Ara had been part of the common pantheon across all Yoruba peoples, but he was supplanted once Shango died and was deified as an Orisha himself.

- **Orò:** He is the patron of justice and bullroarers (ritual musical instrumentalists). An annual patriarchal festival is held in his honor, which only the male descendants of native parents are permitted to attend. All females and foreigners must remain indoors for the duration of the festival, as it's held to be a sacrilege for them to look upon Orò. A special Orò festival is often called part of the mourning period when a monarch dies.

- **Erinle:** He is an Orisha of hunting, farming, and herbalism. Erinle was originally a mortal being – famed for his skill as a hunter and for protecting the town of Ilobu from invasions by the Fulani. A local tradition maintains that he went out hunting one day and ended up sinking into the earth outside of Ilobu, becoming the Erinle River. He was deified and is now worshiped throughout the lands of the Yoruba as an Orisha.

- **Oranyan:** He was the heir to the throne of Ile-Ife while his grandfather Oduduwa was still alive. Upon Oduduwa's death and deification as an Orisha, Oranyan became king. He is credited as the founder of Oyo-Ile, which later expanded into the Oyo Empire. His son (by his wife, Erinmwide of Egor) eventually became known as Eweka I, the God King of Benin. Their descendants continue to rule over the kingdom today. When Oranyan died, he followed his grandfather into the pantheon of the Orisha.

The Ajogun

The Ajogun is the personification of evil spirits and malevolent forces that beset humanity and the Orishas. They are said to number 200+1. Like the Orishas, this just means their true numbers are unknown. However, it is well-established that eight warlords lead them, each personifying a specific negative concept, which includes:

- **Ikú:** The Ajogun of Death. Ikú is generally considered the chief of the eight warlords, wielding a massive spear whose shaft is carved from an elephant's spine and a head made of blackened iron. He wears a necklace whose beads are the skulls of his victims and is usually accompanied by an African wild dog named Ahwinahwi.

- **Àrùn:** The Ajogun of Disease. Most depictions of Àrùn are of a crooked, elderly shaman carrying a night adder as a staff member. The earth beneath his feet becomes ash, and any vegetation dies at his touch. When healthy animals suddenly expire, and their corpse rots unusually quickly, it is believed that Àrùn is lurking nearby.

- **Òfò:** The Ajogun of Loss. The air around Òfò is heavy, making it difficult to breathe, and the weather turns dark and stormy upon his arrival. Depression is viewed as the product of Òfò's intervention, clutching a person's heart upon losing a loved one and refusing to let go.

- **Ẹgbà:** Togun of Paralysis. The phenomenon of sleep paralysis is said to be Ẹgbà's doing, and many who suffer from it report seeing a dark, malevolent figure out of the corner of their eyes when struck by it. Many believe that he can seep into the dreams of mortals, causing terrifying nightmares.

- **Ọràn:** The Ajogun of Trouble and Problems. Ọràn is a shapeshifter, able to mimic any form. He often shapeshifts into people when they are away from home to wreak havoc on their lives and relationships, disappearing before his victim returns.

- **Èpè:** The Ajogun of Curses. Èpè is often depicted as a thin man in tattered clothing who carries a gnarled walking stick with an eye set within its head. The eye is said to be able to move on its own accord, and anyone whose gaze falls upon it will be cursed.

- **Èwọn:** The Ajogun of Imprisonment. Èwọn delights in torturing the victims he imprisons, making them suffer horrifically without allowing them to die. His fingers are hot pokers he can jab into his victims' flesh, and he keeps a red-necked buzzard named Ilozumba that pecks at their eyes.

- **Èṣe:** The Ajogun of Affliction. Èṣe wields a double-sided axe, with one side representing physical afflictions and the other representing mental afflictions. His arms and legs are different lengths, giving him a noticeable limp. He drags his axe behind him as he shuffles around. When he descends upon his victims' home, his arrival is heralded by the rattling of the finger bone necklace he wears.

The Ifa Divination System

Among the African diaspora religions, there is a strong belief that the power of the Orishas dwells within all humans, specifically in their heads. This merging of the mortal and the divine within the essence of human beings, where consciousness and spirit reside, means that everyone has the potential to tap into the supernatural power of the Orishas. Having the power of the Orishas connected to a person's essence is important for the Ifa divination system since it is by exploiting this connection that divination of any kind is possible.

What Is the Ifa Divination System?

The Ifa divination system is a practice among the Yoruba people that uses mathematical formulas and an extensive collection of religious writings. The massive corpus is known as the Odu Ifa. It contains 256 different parts (or odus) subdivided into individual verses called ese. Each odu comprises around 800 eses, and they have their own divination signature. This signature is determined by a babalawo, which employs a divination chain and sacred palm nuts to discern it.

As one of the oldest indigenous religious practices in the world, Ifa has been around for around 8,000 years. It was first developed by the progenitors of the Yoruba people in West Africa, specifically in a place known as the Cradle of Civilization. Some sources even claim that Ifa has influenced all global religions. By the 8th century, the Yoruba people had established Ifa as their predominant religion centered around Ile-Ife.

Yoruba People and Ifa

Ifa has been an important part of Yoruba culture since its inception. Religion and mythology play a significant role in the daily life of the Yoruba people, especially the Orishas, egun, and Ifa divination systems. Many of their major cities were founded by historical figures who were later deified, joining the pantheon of the Orishas. Since they maintain that Olodumare and the Orishas were responsible for creating everything within the physical world, they honor these deities in every part of their life. Prayers, rituals, and religious ceremonies are often centered around the worship of the Orishas.

Yoruba mythology asserts that after King Oduduwa died, his children spread out across the land, with many of them founding their own kingdoms. These kingdoms followed the same religious practices as the people from Ile-Ife. When the Yoruba settlers came into conflict with the aborigines who already occupied the land, wars broke out between the two peoples. Even Ile-Ife was threatened until Moremi's arrival. She liberated Ile-Ife, saving the city and preserving its culture. This allowed Ifa to flourish.

Creation of Ifa

The founding of Ifa was considered to have occurred when the first oracle, Orunmila, was given a vision from the Orishas that laid out the fundamental principles of Ifa. The first place of worship was established in Ile-Ife, which came to be known as a holy city. Orunmila then took on his first students, Aseda and Akoda, teaching them the principles of Ifa and ordaining them as high priests, or babalawos. When Orunmila died, the babalawos chose a new oracle, and Ifa's founder was deified as an Orisha, becoming the patron of all future Ifa oracles.

There are also two lesser-known origin stories for Ifa. The first claims that a man from Nupe named Setiu came to an already-founded Ile-Ife and introduced Ifa to the people there. Not much information is available about how he came up with the principles of the religious system, but it can be assumed that, like Orunmila, they came to him in a vision or dream. The second story says that Ifa was the product of Arugba, who was the mother of Onigbogi, the eighth Alaafin (emperor) of Oyo. Arugba initiated a student, Alado of Ato, giving him the right to initiate others into

Ifa. It was then Alado, who ordained the high priests of Oyo, and Ifa spread from there to Ile-Ife.

In all versions of the foundation of Ifa, Orunmila was eventually involved in the religion, codifying the principles of Ifa and passing the belief system down through oral tradition. He incorporated tales told to him by the various priests and priestesses who practiced Ifa, creating an extensive collection of myths, folklore, and knowledge that became the core of the religion. This material was later written down and turned into the corpus known as the Odu Ifa.

Sixteen Main Rules of Ifa

1. There is only one Supreme Being.
2. There is no supreme evil being.
3. Other than the day you were born and the day you'll die, nothing in your life cannot be foretold and, if necessary, changed.
4. You are granted the right to happiness, success, and fulfillment the moment you are born.
5. Your goal in life is to learn and grow as a person.
6. Your essence is preserved through your blood relatives.
7. Your home is in Heaven; Earth is just a marketplace. You are in constant transition between the two.
8. You are a physical part of the universe in a literal sense, not a figurative one.
9. You must never cause deliberate harm to another person.
10. You must never cause deliberate harm to the environment you inhabit.
11. Your physical and spiritual aspects must work in unison.
12. Your path is set before you when you are born, even if you cannot see it. Your goal in life is to remain on that path, and divination can give you a road map to do so.
13. The spirits of your ancestors exist and must be honored accordingly.
14. When you sacrifice for the greater good, success is guaranteed.
15. The power of the Orishas lives inside you.
16. You have nothing to fear in your life.

Chapter 3: Olodumare, the Creator of Ifa and the World

The core of the Yoruba religion is the belief in Olodumare, also known as Olorun, and Olofi, who is viewed as the creator of the universe and the source of all energy. His name comes from the Yoruba phrase, "O ní odù mà rè," which means "he who possesses the source of creation will never be empty." Regardless of which name he is called in each of the different varieties of the African diaspora religions, Olodumare is the chief deity, the creator of the universe, and the one responsible for all life in existence.

Olodumare is considered the head of the pantheon of the Orishas.
Omoeko Media, CC BY-SA 4.0 <https://creativecommons.org/licenses/by-sa/4.0>, via Wikimedia Commons: https://commons.wikimedia.org/wiki/File:Orishas_in_Abeokuta.jpg

The Aspects of Olodumare

While Olodumare is the Supreme Being and Divine Creator, his other two aspects are just as important to the African diaspora religions. These aspects include:

Olorun

Olorun is the aspect of Olodumare, the ruler of the heavens. He is considered the head of the pantheon of the Orishas. However, he doesn't take an active role in dictating the actions of his underlings. Most of the Orishas are free to do whatever they want - within reason, of course. Olorun's actions are usually constrained to delegating tasks to the Orishas and ensuring they can carry out their duties. Any situation that forces Olorun to intervene must be extreme enough that doing nothing would result in serious negative consequences for the entire world.

When Olodumare first created the universe, Olorun assigned the job of crafting the Earth to Obatala. Unfortunately, Obatala could not complete such a difficult task, forcing Olodumare to do it himself. In the end, Obatala created mortal shells to serve as bodies for human beings, and Olodumare gave life to them. Olorun then declared that the Orishas should use their powers to aid humanity and help them seek out their predetermined fates.

The influence of the African diaspora religions can be seen through the figure of Olorun in author J.R.R. Tolkien's Lord of the Rings mythology. Tolkien was a devout Roman Catholic, but he looked to other religions for inspiration. The character of Gandalf was originally an Orisha-like spirit known as a Maia. His name in the heaven-esque land of Valinor was Olorin, just one letter from Olorun. Like how Olodumare breathed life into the inert vessels of humanity, Olorin enters an uninhabited mortal body, taking on the guise of the wizard Gandalf.

Olofi

Olofi is the aspect of Olodumare, who is the ruler of Earth and serves as a conduit between Earth and the heavens. He is responsible for the manner in which the hierarchy of power is ordered, as well as for preventing any cataclysmic events from destroying the mortal world. When important messages need to be conveyed to the Orishas, egun, or humans, it is Olofi who communicates with them. It is also Olofi who confers the personalities, traits, and destinies to the essence of human beings and sends them into their mortal bodies. Although Olodumare does not communicate with humans very often, in the rare cases that he does, Olofi will be the one who speaks to them. Of the three aspects of Olodumare, Olofi is considered the weakest, yet his responsibilities may be some of the most important.

Similarities to the Abrahamic God

Olodumare, as the Supreme Being of the Yoruba cosmological pantheon, can be roughly equated with the Abrahamic God of the Judeo-Christian and Islamic religions. He is the creator of all things, including the tier of higher beings directly beneath him, similar to how the Abrahamic God created the ranks of angels. While Olodumare didn't form the physical bodies of mortals, he was the one who breathed life into them. One major difference between the two is that the Yoruba don't dedicate any places of worship to Olodumare or have a hierarchy of ordained religious leaders, like priests, rabbis, or ministers.

There are three aspects to Olodumare, similar to the Trinity in Christianity, which holds that God is made up of the Father, Son, and Holy Spirit. Olodumare is the primary aspect, the Divine Creator of all things and the source of all energy that encompasses every form of life. This means humans, animals, plants, and even inanimate objects are believed to possess energy bestowed by the Divine Creator. When anything dies, that energy returns to Olodumare and becomes one with him. As far as the other two aspects go, Olorun is seen as the ruler of the heavens, and Olofi is the conduit between the heavens and earth, called Orún and Ayé, respectively.

Powers of Olodumare

Olodumare is omnipotent, omniscient, transcendent, and considered good and evil. Many practitioners believe that Olodumare's aloofness when it comes to humanity should prevent any direct worship, instead honoring the Supreme Being through the Orishas. However, some do worship Olodumare directly, which has caused controversy within the religion. Opinions on the matter are somewhat divided, and since there is no centralized authority to determine which practice is correct, it's left up to each individual to choose how they prefer to worship their god. The one common trait between the two viewpoints is that no shrines or sacrifices should be made to him.

Olodumare as the Supreme Being

Another part of Olodumare is the belief that all knowledge, virtue, and morality are given to humanity by him when a person is born. Àyànmọ́, or destiny and fate, is an integral part of life for everyone and everything. You receive your Àyànmọ́ at birth, alongside the other traits bestowed by Olodumare, and when you die, you'll rejoin him through your spiritual energy. While Olodumare will not take direct action in matters occurring in Ayé (Earth or the physical world), he does influence events indirectly since he is the one who provides the power and knowledge that every human possesses. The Orishas were also created by the Supreme Being to carry out his will amongst humanity, aiding or impeding the course of actions taken by people throughout their lives.

Connection to the Ifa Divination System

Since Olodumare is responsible for laying the fate upon all mortals, he is closely tied to the Ifa divination system. One of the system's primary goals is to determine which path a person should follow to reach their destiny. It is believed that before birth, when a person's essence goes before Olodumare, they receive their personality, traits, and destiny. However, the journey from the heavens to their mortal body causes them to forget these things, so they need to rediscover them throughout their life.

The Ifa divination system is a way for someone to learn the attributes and fate set by Olodumare to get themselves on the right path to reach that destiny. Suppose a person strays too far from their predetermined path. In that case, it may become impossible for them to reach their destiny, resulting in a life filled with hardship and suffering. It is imperative to avoid losing track of the path bestowed by Olodumare, and the Ifa divination system can help ensure this doesn't happen.

Olodumare in Voodoo and Santería

Olodumare's importance to the Yoruba people is well-documented, but he also plays a significant role in Voodoo, Santería, and other African diaspora religions. However, the way these other religions view him is slightly different from how he is viewed in Ifa. In some cases, the differences are more academic, as how he operates is essentially the same. Still, in other cases, some key differences set their version of Olodumare apart from that of the Yoruba people.

Olodumare in Voodoo

In many sects of Voodoo, Olodumare is the god of divination and destiny, responsible for bestowing a fate upon all living things. Olorun is considered the Supreme Being but is believed to be formless universal energy, lacking any anthropomorphic characteristics. Practitioners of Voodoo assert that Obalata was successful in creating the Earth, in addition to human beings.

Some sects of Voodoo, such as Haitian Vodou, call the Supreme Being and One True God by the name Bondyé, but he is functionally equivalent to Olodumare. Bondyé is believed to be responsible for creating the universe and everything within it and assigning his will to all living things. However, like Olodumare, Bondyé does not interfere in mortal affairs. Instead of praying directly to him or the Orishas for aid, practitioners deal with the Loa.

Olodumare in Santería

In Santería, the three aspects of Olodumare are viewed more like the Christian idea of the Holy Trinity than the god of other African diaspora religions. Olodumare is the Father, Olofi is the Son, and Olorun is the Holy Spirit. Olodumare created the universe and is considered the Supreme Being, like in Ifa. He is omniscient and omnipotent but does not have contact with those beneath him in the cosmology of Santería. Instead, he leaves it to his other aspects to take care of their day-to-day responsibilities.

Olofi deals directly with humanity, holding dominion over the Earth, and is analogous to Jesus. Santería practitioners believe that Olofi has more contact with mortals than in Ifa or Voodoo, either speaking directly to humans or connecting with them through the Orishas. The Orishas keep watch over individual human beings, and they report back to Olofi, who uses his power to keep the world in harmony. Just as Olofi is like Jesus, the Orishas are like guardian angels or saints, particularly the Orishas who were once human and deified after their death.

Olorun's domain is the sky, or more specifically, the sun. Practitioners of Santería believe that the sun is actually the physical form of Olorun, and the vital heat and light emitted from it are his powers nourishing all life on Earth. In this way, he is like the Holy Spirit in that the energy from the sun surrounds and penetrates human beings, filling them with the essence of life from the gods. This allows the Orishas to make a direct connection to them, particularly to their consciousness, with most practitioners believing the power of the Orishas dwells within their heads.

The Trials of Olodumare

One of the lesser-known rituals of Ifa involves a rite of passage known as the Trials of Olodumare. The Yoruba send a group of boys who reach the age of majority out into the wilds for three days, where they are given basic survival tools and must prove they can make a shelter, fire, and forage for food or catch small game. While out in the wilds, it is expected that the boys will make a connection with their Orishas, giving them a glimpse of the path set for them by Olodumare. The lucky few may even see something that can clue them into their ultimate destiny. Often, this trial can help to detect who among the youths is amenable to becoming a priest within Ifa.

Chapter 4: The Cool-Tempered Orishas

The cool-tempered Orishas, also known as the tutu Orishas, are characterized by their calm, gentle, or patient natures. These are associated with the color white, and they are considered to be more helpful than harmful.

The cool-tempered Orishas are characterized by their calm, gentle, or patient natures.
Burkhard Mücke, CC BY-SA 4.0 <https://creativecommons.org/licenses/by-sa/4.0>, via Wikimedia Commons: https://commons.wikimedia.org/wiki/File:Museo_de_Orishas_01.jpg

Orunmila

Orunmila is the Orisha of knowledge, wisdom, and divination, particularly the Ifa divination system. He is also considered the patron of the Ifa oracle. His name is often invoked during rituals involving the priests and priestesses practicing Ifa divination, and they believe that there is a duality to life - females exist because of the male essence. In contrast, males exist because of the female essence.

It is said that Orunmila was a witness to creation and fate and was considered second to the creator, coming after Olodumare himself. He has knowledge of all mortal and divine matters, and his wisdom is unfailing. It is believed that he was one of the primordial Orishas, having been made directly by Olodumare, as opposed to a human who underwent deification. As a result, he holds a special place in the pantheon, considered to be a part of the core Orishas.

After the creation of the Earth and humanity, Orunmila spent some time walking among the human race as a prophet, spreading knowledge about the will of the Orishas and teaching mortals about the greatness of Olodumare. In this way, he can be seen as similar to the prophets of Islam, Judaism, or Christianity. There are also parallels between Orunmila and Jesus, especially in the sects of Christianity that view Jesus as a divine being in mortal form.

Many stories and tales from the Odu Ifa are collected from Orunmila's time as a human. He is integral to the Ifa divination system because the system's goal is for humans to discern the path of destiny bestowed by Olodumare, and Orunmila helps facilitate the communication between the Orishas and humanity. He is often seen as one of the easiest of the Orishas to reach through prayer and divination, making him a popular focus of divination.

There is some controversy concerning Orunmila involving the gender of those initiated into Ifa. Many sources claim that only males are allowed to be initiated, but there are numerous traditions in which females are eligible for induction. The priesthood dedicated to Orunmila uses the title Awo, which is gender-neutral, for their priests and priestesses, which is seen as a validation that Orunmila has no preference for the gender of those initiated into his priesthood.

As the patron of the Ifa oracles, Orunmila communicates with them to give them visions and wisdom through divination. There is a close relationship between those within the Ifa divination system and the

Orishas, but none is as important as that with Orunmila. Other Orishas offer a variety of benefits to humanity, some directly and some indirectly. However, only Orunmila offers the direct benefit of aiding in deciphering the clues to figure out the correct path humans need to reach their chosen destiny.

- **Symbols:** Hand of Orunmila, divination circle
- **Colors:** Green, yellow
- **Food:** Nuts, yams, sweet bread
- **Ebo Sacrifice:** Rats, mudfish, fried snails
- **Number:** 2
- **Day:** Tuesday (Day 2), October 4th (Feast of St. Francis of Assisi)

How to Greet Orunmila

"Spirit of Destiny, I am greeting you. Wisdom of Nature, I am greeting you. Father of our people, I am greeting you. The light of knowledge precedes my appeasement. I ask that you relieve me of my obligation. May it be so."

Loa Equivalent in Voodoo

In some Voodoo traditions, Orunmila can be seen as the equivalent of Papa Legba. Like Orunmila, Papa Legba is an intermediary between humans and higher beings. In Papa Legba's case, it is humanity and the Loa, while Orunmila connects humanity and the Orishas or Olodumare. This aspect of communication is key to both deities, and Papa Legba is even said to speak every language in existence. Both possess great knowledge and wisdom and adopt the appearance of an old man whose physical frailty belies a vast wealth of inner power.

Catholic Saint Association in Santería

In Santería, Orunmila is associated with Saint Francis of Assisi. In the Catholic canon, St. Francis of Assisi modeled his life on that of Jesus Christ, striving to live every moment as Christ would. He held great reverence for all of God's creations, especially animals and the environment. As a believer in the power of prayer and a desire for peace on Earth, he attempted to end the devastating Fifth Crusade by traveling to Egypt to convert sultan al-Kamil to Christianity. His wisdom of both the mortal and divine worlds was considered unrivaled during his lifetime, and he was declared a saint in 1228, only two years after his death.

Obatala

Obatala, the Orisha of the sky, is considered the defender of the disabled and the weak and a guardian of purity. He was the Orisha who created the bodies used by human beings. While it was Olodumare who breathed life into them, without the existence of these physical vessels, there would be nowhere for the essences of mortals to go. He is married to Yemoja (his main wife), but it's said that he has a harem of 200+1 consorts, which means he may have many more than 200. The favorite of his consorts is named Yemowo.

According to one myth, Obatala was authorized by Olodumare to create the lands within the waters and beneath the sky. Still, he was unable to complete this task. Instead, Olodumare was forced to step in and finish the creation of the lands himself. However, other variations credit Obatala with creating the lands in addition to the bodies of all humans. In all versions of the myth, he is among the first of the Orishas and, therefore, one of the core members of the pantheon.

A key feature of Obatala is his association with the color white. He wears all white, and almost all his symbols, items, and ebo offerings are white in part or full. His favored staff is known as Opaxoro, which was fashioned from the vines of the atori shrub. This small tree stands about six feet high and has medicinal value. Although it is not naturally white, the staff has been dyed to match Obatala's preferred color.

- **Symbols:** Opaxoro (atori vine wooden staff), white crown, dove
- **Colors:** White
- **Food:** Milk, white rice, white bread, shredded coconut, eggs
- **Ebo Sacrifice:** White hens, snakes, snails
- **Number:** 8
- **Day:** Monday (Day 1), September 24th (Feast of Our Lady of Mercy)

How to Greet Obatala

"Hail Obatala, may the sacrifice I offer unto the heavens be accepted."

Loa Equivalent in Voodoo

In Voodoo traditions, Obatala is a Loa under his own name. He is also known as the King in White. All his followers similarly dress in white vestments to honor their chosen Loa. As in the Yoruba religion, he is the

Sky Father and responsible for creating human bodies. However, one peculiarity about the Loa version of Obatala is his strong connection to snails. It is said to be his favorite food, and he is often depicted as either holding or eating edible snails.

Catholic Saint Association in Santería

In Santería, Obatala is associated with Our Lady of Mercy, an aspect of the Virgin Mary. His choice of white garments is seen as a reflection of his purity, similar to the traditional depictions in Christianity of the Virgin Mary. He embodies the symbolic light of consciousness and is even sometimes syncretized with Jesus Christ.

Yemoja

Yemoja is venerated as the Mother of All Water and the Divine Earth Mother, as well as being the patron of rivers, lakes, and oceans. She is the mother of all the Orishas, having a strong connotation with the Virgin Mary from Christianity. In addition, she is a protector of women and a cleanser of sorrows, bringing comfort to all those who she considers her children.

As a primordial Orisha, during the shaping of the world, Yemoja was said to have descended to the Earth on a rope along with sixteen fellow Orishas created by Olodumare. She assisted Obatala in making the bodies for human beings and is considered his first and main spouse. Unlike some of the other Orishas, she is able to interpret the entirety of the Odu Ifa, allowing an alternative method of accessing the Odu by throwing cowrie shells instead of sacred palm nuts.

Yemoja is commonly depicted as a mermaid who dwells within the waters of West Africa, South America, or the Caribbean. She is heavily associated with rivers, oceans, and lakes, and worship of her occurs near springs, creeks, streams, or any local wells or run-offs. In Nigeria, she is considered the protector of the Ogun River, which the Yoruba believe is her primary domain. Some African diaspora religions view her as a patron of fishermen and shipwreck survivors and a spirit of wealth.

In her role as a protector of women, especially pregnant women, Yemoja presents as more matronly, highlighting her aspects as the Divine Earth Mother. She is comparable to the archetype of the Earth Mother in other religions, including Durga and Parvati from Hinduism, Gaia and Hecate from Greek mythology, the Queen Mother of the West from Chinese mythology, Terra from Roman mythology, Isis from Egyptian mythology, the Morrígan in Celtic mythology, and the Virgin Mary in Christianity.

- **Symbols:** Mermaid, sea stones, shells
- **Colors:** White, light blue, crystal
- **Food:** Obi, bitter kola nut, lelé, onion, white corn, rice
- **Ebo Sacrifice:** Perfume, jewelry, blue flowers or white roses, duck or fish dishes
- **Number:** 7
- **Day:** Sunday (Day 7), September 7th, February 2nd, Summer Solstice

How to Greet Yemoja

"Greetings to the Mother of All Water and the Divine Earth Mother. I ask you for a peaceful life and a prosperous future."

Loa Equivalent in Voodoo

In some Voodoo traditions, Yemoja can be roughly equated with La Sirène and Erzulie Dantor. La Sirène (or Mami Wata) is a water spirit who can be both helpful and harmful to those who live or work around the rivers and oceans. As her name would suggest, she is considered to be similar to the Sirens of Greek mythology, appearing as a beautiful, ethereal woman, luring sailors to their doom. However, those who are faithful in their worship of her can be blessed with great fortune and riches.

Erzulie Dantor is the aspect of Erzulie, who is the protector of women and children and the righter of wrongs. Erzulie, in general, is associated with the elemental forces, particularly water, where she is often said to reside. She embodies the feminine energy of Papa Legba, looking after pregnant women and encouraging fertility. In addition, she is depicted as being incredibly wealthy, similar to how Yemoja is shown in other African diaspora religions. Erzulie Dantor also has a connection to the Virgin Mary, although, unlike Yemoja, she is also said to be a virgin.

Catholic Saint Association in Santería

In Santería, Yemoja is associated with the Virgin Mary, particularly in her roles as Our Lady of Navigators, Our Lady of the Conception, and Our Lady, Star of the Sea. She possesses the traits often ascribed to the Virgin Mary, such as being a mother figure to the followers of her religion and a divine spirit who protects those under her charge. While Yemoja herself is not a virgin, she is often considered to be a scion of purity and goodness, with a strong connection to the untainted waters that cover much of the Earth's surface.

Nana Buluku

Nana Buluku is the Orisha who is believed to have taken part in creation, giving birth to the sun and the moon. Prior to this, she was the Great Mother but retired once she had finished birthing the sun and moon, allowing other Orishas to take her place. Most depictions of Nana Buluku show her as an old woman or an elderly crone. When combined with Yemoja and Iya Nla, they make up the trinity of the Triple Goddess, which includes aspects of a female deity that includes the Maiden, the Mother, and the Crone.

Her children are the sun, named Lisa, and the moon, named Mawu. However, some versions of the myth also claim that she birthed every star in the night sky. She is a primordial Orisha, having been present at the creation of the universe, and assisted in the shaping of the Earth. Most African diaspora religions hold her in high regard, and she is an important member of the Orisha pantheon.

Prior to birthing the sun, moon, and stars, Nana Buluku held the position of the Great Mother but retired to become more of a background figure once her children were born. Orishas, like Yemoja, took on aspects of her original role, but none filled it completely. The combined form of her children, known as Mawu-Lisa, was given the responsibility of overseeing those who reside on Earth.

Some myths claim that while Nana Buluku was able to create perfect deities, Mawu-Lisa could only make imperfect ones. This is why there is both good and evil in the world. Nana Buluku's children were pure beings who embodied goodness, but their inability to maintain that purity in their own creations led to a negative outcome for the world. However, practitioners of the African diaspora religions still worship both Nana Buluku and Mawu-Lisa as revered figures.

- **Symbols:** Sun, moon, stars, hook-shaped broom, triangle, mud
- **Colors:** Blue, purple, white
- **Food:** Coconut, coffee beans, rum
- **Ebo Sacrifice:** Clay vase, blue or purple handkerchief,
- **Number:** 7

- **Day:** Sunday (Day 7), September 27th (Feast of Our Lady, Star of the Sea)

How to Greet Nana Buluku

"I greet you, Nana Buluku, Mother of the Sun, Moon, and Stars. I request your protection and love. Nourish me with the light of your children."

Loa Equivalent in Voodoo

In some Voodoo traditions, Nana Buluku is worshiped as both a male and female, so she is equated with Papa Legba and Granne Erzulie. While Legba is traditionally a male Loa, he has a connection to Nana Buluku in that he represents the sun and daylight. He is considered the origin of life, similar to how Nana Buluku has helped to give life to other Orisha, and the light of her children nourishes life on Earth. Granne Erzulie is the wise and grandmotherly aspect of Erzulie. She represents the moon, and like Nana Buluku, her feminine, motherly energy offers protection to her children.

Catholic Saint Association in Santería

In Santería, Nana Buluku is considered part of the same Orisha as Yemoja, with the pair being different manifestations or aspects of their version of Yemoja. Therefore, Nana Buluku is also associated with the Virgin Mary, possessing similar traits to both the mother of Jesus and Yemoja. The Nana Buluku aspect of Yemoja is where her motherly traits are emphasized, particularly in regard to her relationship with the other Orishas.

Iya Nla

Iya Nla is a primordial Orisha who is believed to have been the source of power behind all creation. In this capacity, she can be considered a counterpart to Olodumare, either his mother or mate. The energy needed to initiate the creation of the universe came from Iya Nla, and for this reason, she has been called the Mother of All Things or the Great Mother.

- **Symbols:** Wellspring, tree of life
- **Colors:** Gold, white
- **Food:** Nuts, beans, and fruits such as pomegranates or berries
- **Ebo Sacrifice:** Items from nature (flowers, herbs, tree bark, etc.), small game

- **Number:** 1
- **Day:** Monday (Day 1), September 1st-October 4th (Season of Creation)

How to Greet Iya Nla

"Mother of All Things, I greet you. Great Mother Iya Nla, I greet you. To the wellspring of life and the source of all creation, I ask for your blessing and protection."

Loa Equivalent in Voodoo

In Voodoo traditions, Damballa is the equivalent of Iya Nla. Damballa, like Iya Nla, is considered the source of all life in the universe, being second only to Bondyé in importance within their cosmology. He is extremely old, unable to speak, and resorts to whistling or hissing as a means of communication. Damballa is most often depicted as a massive serpent, and he aided in the creation of the Earth through the shedding of his skin.

Catholic Saint Association in Santería

In Santería, Iya Nla is associated with St. Francis of Assisi, whose feast day on October 4th marks the end of the Season of Creation. He is also the patron saint of animals and the environment, and his realm is in the same location as that of Iya Nla, who is responsible for the creation of all such things. The Season of Creation is an important time within Santería and the Catholic Church, as it is the period when practitioners honor God and everything He created in His great wisdom and power. Similarly, Iya Nla is venerated for her role as the source of creation.

Osanyin

Osanyin is the patron of herbalists. Sometimes, he is depicted as having one arm, one leg, and one eye, but other likenesses show him with his limbs and eyes intact. He believes all healing herbs found in nature have been created by him, and herbalists beseech his aid when attempting to heal injuries or illnesses. He uses a leaf as a wand and a knife, representing nature's helpful and harmful aspects.

In one myth, Osanyin is said to have gone to war with Orunmila, seeking to unseat his fellow Orisha's position of power within the pantheon. To combat the threat of Osanyin, Orunmila called down a devastating lightning storm on Shango's palace, where Osanyin happened to be at the time. The attack killed Shango, who was later deified and joined the ranks of the Orishas and left Osanyin permanently maimed. This was how Osanyin lost an arm, leg, and eye.

- **Symbols:** Leaf, tree, bird
- **Colors:** Green, yellow, brown
- **Food:** Corn meal, gin
- **Ebo Sacrifice:** 16 herbs (any used in healing), 16 beads (green and yellow), 16 birds
- **Number:** 16
- **Day:** Wednesday (Day 3), March 19th (Feast of St. Joseph), September 29th (Feast of St. Raphael the Archangel)

How to Greet Osanyin

"Osanyin, curer of ills and healer of pain, I greet you warmly."

Loa Equivalent in Voodoo

In some Voodoo traditions, the equivalent of Osanyin is Loco, who is similarly a healer who uses plants and herbs in his endeavors. Loco was one of the first Loa to be considered a priest and is very important to the initiation rites of the priesthood. He is married to a fellow Loa named Ayizan, who is his counterpart with the Voodoo priestesses.

Catholic Saint Association in Santería

In Santería, Osanyin is syncretized with St. Joseph and St. Raphael the Archangel. St. Joseph is the adoptive father of Jesus and the husband of the Virgin Mary. He is the patron saint of the sick and the dying, often being prayed to for aid when someone is very ill. Because of this, his name has been used by several major medical centers. St. Raphael is the patron saint of healing and healers, holding a role akin to Osanyin within the canon of the Catholic Church.

Oshumare

Oshumare is the patron of the rainbow. He is associated with wealth, prosperity, and permanence. Some tales state that when a person sees a rainbow and offers a prayer to the Orisha, they will soon enjoy good fortune in whatever endeavors they currently engage in. There is also a connection between the beliefs concerning Osumare and the mythical concept of a pot of gold at the end of a rainbow.

The snake-like visage of Oshumare reflects the appearance of a rainbow, which arcs through the sky in the same shape one might see the body of a snake make as it slithers across the earth. The Yoruba believe rainbows are part of Oshumare moving across the sky. In fact, their word for rainbow is "oshumare," solidifying its connection to the aptly-named Orisha.

- **Symbols:** Rainbow, snake
- **Colors:** All the colors of the rainbow
- **Food:** Pineapples, coconuts, mangos, bananas
- **Ebo Sacrifice:** Snakes, rainbow-colored ceramic items
- **Number:** 4
- **Day:** Thursday (Day 4), March 17th (Feast of St. Patrick)

How to Greet Oshumare

"I greet you, Oshumare, the serpent of the sky and master of rainbows. I ask for fortune and prosperity from you, Oshumare."

Loa Equivalent in Voodoo

In Voodoo traditions, Ayida-Weddo is the equivalent of Oshumare. She is the Loa of fertility, wind, fire, water, rainbows, and snakes. Those last two aspects line up with Oshumare's domain. She is often depicted as a snake with rainbow scales, believed to aid the other Loa by holding up the heavens. In some versions of their cosmology, she actually possesses two genders; the male part of her is red, while the female part is blue.

Catholic Saint Association in Santería

In Santería, Oshumare is associated with St. Patrick. In Catholic canon, St. Patrick has a strong connection to snakes and rainbows, although he is famous for driving all the snakes out of Ireland. The Catholic Church usually views snakes and serpents as harmful or evil, such as the serpent in the Garden of Eden who tricked Eve into eating the fruit from the Tree of Knowledge of Good and Evil. However, Oshumare is generally seen as a positive figure in Santería, bringing color and light to the world.

Otin

Otin is the patron of the Otin River. During her mortal life, she traveled from her home, the village of Otan, to help protect the people in the town of Inisa when it was attacked by its neighbors. She led the defenders in battle and fought on the front lines, wielding her spear to devastating effect. After her death, she underwent deification and became venerated as the protector of the river that bears her name.

- **Symbols:** Spear, river
- **Colors:** Blue, orange
- **Food:** Kola nuts, baked beans
- **Ebo Sacrifice:** Butter catfish, denticle herring, or other fish caught in the Otin River
- **Number:** 11
- **Day:** Friday (Day 5), May 30th (Feast of St. Joan of Arc)

How to Greet Otin

"Great warrior Otin! Honored protector of the Otin River! I greet you."

Loa Equivalent in Voodoo

In some Voodoo traditions, the equivalent of Otin is Pie. Like Otin, Pie is considered a warrior and a protector of rivers and lakes, although, in Pie's case, he is not limited to a single river. Pie is believed to dwell in the depths of the waters he protects, occasionally causing the rivers to flood. If someone tries to cause mischief near his domain, they risk running afoul of the waters' noble guardian.

Catholic Saint Association in Santería

In Santería, Otin is associated with St. Joan of Arc. It's not difficult to see why considering that both Otin and Joan of Arc are famous for coming to the aid of beleaguered people and rallying them against an army of invaders. They both possess the spirit of a warrior and an iron will. Both were deified after their respective deaths, with Otin joining the pantheon of the Orishas and Joan of Arc being raised to the status of a saint.

Ori

Ori is the Orisha of destiny and consciousness. It is the personification of the metaphysical concepts of the essence within the head of every human being. This includes their consciousness and the destiny bestowed upon them at the time of their birth. When a person achieves balance within themselves, it is believed that they can consult Ori to gain greater self-awareness and a deeper understanding of their fate.

- **Symbols:** Nkrabea
- **Colors:** Red, yellow

- **Food:** Fried rice, ekuru, goat meat
- **Ebo Sacrifice:** Water blessed by a babalawos and offered in a basin
- **Number:** 42
- **Day:** Monday (Day 1), February 13th (Feast of St. Agabus)

How to Greet Ori

"Ori, I greet you. Guide me in discovering my destiny and the path I must walk to reach it."

Loa Equivalent in Voodoo

In some Voodoo traditions, Papa Legba is the equivalent of Ori. Papa Legba is the Loa of destiny and facilitates communication between humanity and the gods. It's believed that if he is satisfied with a practitioner's offerings, he will grant their wishes and allow them to tap into the universe's fundamental forces. He was there at the beginning, has witnessed every human receive their destiny, and will remain until the end of all things.

Catholic Saint Association in Santería

In Santería, Ori is associated with St. Agabus, the patron saint of prophets. The concepts of fate and destiny in Catholicism are not congruent with that of the African diaspora religions. It is a part of Catholic theology, but there is a complicated history with the push and pull of free will versus predestination. Some Catholics view fate as how all living beings will eventually return to God in Heaven. Others believe a predetermined destiny is set for all people by God, but this destiny can change through free will. As far as St. Agabus is concerned, his role as a prophet who could foretell the future is in line with the idea that communing with Ori can offer insight into one's path ahead.

Oshosi

Oshosi is the Orisha of contemplation, art lovers, beauty, and meals. He is associated with animals, forests, hunting, and wealth and is often depicted as wielding a bow and arrow. His huntsman aspect involves wisdom, craftiness, astuteness, and lightness while encouraging positivity and good energy. Despite being a hunter by trade, Oshosi does not kill for sport. He only hunts out of necessity and is conscious of the spirits of the animals slain by his hand.

- **Symbols:** Bow and arrow
- **Colors:** Blue, green
- **Food:** Black beans, roasted cowpeas, yams, axoxô
- **Ebo Sacrifice:** Goat, guinea fowl, cooked pig
- **Numbers:** 3, 4, 7
- **Day:** Thursday (Day 4), January 20th (Feast of St. Sebastian), June 6th (Feast of St. Norbert of Xanten), November 3rd (Feast of St. Hubert)

How to Greet Oshosi

"I greet you, great Oshosi, warrior of righteousness and the unfailing arrow. I ask you, blessed hunter, to walk beside me today and always. May you protect me, bring me luck, and see that my aim is as true as yours."

Loa Equivalent in Voodoo

In some Voodoo traditions, Oshosi is equated with the Loa that goes by the same name. Most of his characteristics are consistent with those of Orisha. He is the Loa of hunting and animals, always with his bow in hand and a quiver filled with arrows strapped to his back. It is believed that Oshosi never needs more than one shot to kill his prey.

Catholic Saint Association in Santería

In Santería, Oshosi is associated with St. Sebastian, St. Norbert of Xanten, and St. Hubert. St. Sebastian is the patron saint of archers, while St. Hubert is the patron saint of hunters, and St. Norbert embodies the aspects of Oshosi that promotes contemplation, art appreciation, and affection for all things beautiful.

Oshun

Oshun is the Orisha of prosperity, love, and fertility. She is also associated with femininity, beauty, sensuality, and divinity. Her importance within the pantheon was raised when she married Shango, becoming his second wife. She is associated with divinity, beauty, and femininity. The Osun River and the Osun State in Nigeria were both named in her honor. She is heavily involved in the practice of divination and the concept of destiny.

- **Symbols:** Mint, gold, rooster
- **Colors:** Yellow, gold, white, coral
- **Food:** Ofe akwu, pepper soup. beef stew

- **Ebo Sacrifice:** Honey, sunflowers, mint leaf, folha-de-dez-réis
- **Number:** 5
- **Day:** Friday (Day 5), September 8th (Feast of the Nativity of the Blessed Virgin Mary)

How to Greet Oshun

"We praise our mother. Oshun, I greet you."

Loa Equivalent in Voodoo

In some Voodoo traditions, Oshun is equated with Erzulie Freda. This is the aspect of Erzulie, who is flirty and vain, connected to Oshun through Orisha's youthful tendency to peer at herself in the mirror. Erzulie, in general, is a Loa of beauty, femininity, and water, all traits that Oshun also possesses. Just as Oshun can be both frivolous and protective, Erzulie has different sides of herself that represent the various characteristics of both young, energetic, and somewhat inexperienced women and older, wiser women.

Catholic Saint Association in Santería

In Santería, Oshun is associated with Our Lady of Charity, a title for the Virgin Mary in many Catholic countries, including Cuba. She is known for her generosity, offering protection and prosperity to those in need. Our Lady of Charity's feast day is celebrated on the day reserved for the birth of the Virgin Mary when these aspects of Our Lady of Charity are said to be shared by all.

Olokun

Olokun is the Orisha of all bodies of water and the patron of the sea. They influence health, vitality, and financial prosperity within devotees. Their gender changes between male, female, and androgynous. Cultures along the coasts of Western Africa worship Olokun as male, but those in the hinterlands depict them as female. In Santería, Olokun is shown to be androgynous. The Yoruba people traditionally maintain that they were the first wife of Oduduwa as a human, and this incarnation is credited with creating the Atlantic Ocean after a conflict with the emperor's other wives. In other traditions, Olokun became furious with humans and attempted to drown them all, only stopping when Obatala chained Olokun in the depths of the oceans, imprisoning them there for eternity.

- **Symbols:** Mermaid/merman, coral crown, any sea life
- **Colors:** Aquamarine, coral, blue

- **Food:** Yams, molasses, grains, melons
- **Ebo Sacrifice:** Cowrie shells, seashells, fish, ducks
- **Number:** 7, 9
- **Day:** Sunday (Day 7), April 30th (Feast of St. Adjutor)

How to Greet Olokun

"I greet you, Olokun, Spirit of the Ocean. Please grant me an abundance so that I may become wealthy and prosperous. I declare that the Spirit of the Ocean is greater than any of the chiefs of the land."

Loa Equivalent in Voodoo

In Voodoo traditions, Agwé is the equivalent of Olokun. Agwé is the Loa of the seas, ruling over the ocean depths and everything contained within it. In their various aspects, Agwé is a friend to sailors, mariners, pirates, and swimmers, helping them find their way when they become lost – while also capable of vengeance against the land dwellers, pulling them to the bottom of their watery domain.

Catholic Saint Association in Santería

In Santería, Oshun is associated with St. Adjutor, the patron saint of boaters, swimmers, and victims of drowning. St. Adjutor was captured during the First Crusade, and according to tradition, a host of angels descended from Heaven to set him free. He earned his patron status after he calmed a tempestuous whirlpool while sailing home by tossing the chains from his captivity and Holy Water into it, then making the sign of the cross.

Chapter 5: The Hot-Tempered Orishas

The hot-tempered Orishas, also known as the gbigbona Orishas, are characterized by their brash, easily angered, or impatient natures. These are associated with the colors red and black, and they can have a tendency towards zealousness, trickery, or vengeance.

The hot-tempered Orishas are characterized by their brash, easily angered, or impatient natures.
Omocko Media, CC BY-SA 4.0 <https://creativecommons.org/licenses/by-sa/4.0>, via Wikimedia Commons: https://commons.wikimedia.org/wiki/File:Orishas_in_Oba%27s_palace,_Abeokuta.jpg

Eshu

Eshu is the messenger of the Orishas, as well as the patron of law enforcement and justice. He is associated with crossroads, transformation, and doorways. In addition, he can be a trickster, embodying the contradictory nature of the gbigbona Orishas, as he is both a guardian who protects and a conniver who swindles knowledge out of others. Eshu seeks a balance between extremes - good and bad, justice and injustice, joy and sorrow.

- **Symbols:** Scale, sealed scroll, chains, lion
- **Colors:** Red, black, dark blue
- **Food:** Rice, corn, fish
- **Ebo Sacrifice:** Palm oil, rum, cigars, candy, coconuts, chicken
- **Number:** 3
- **Day:** Wednesday (Day 3), June 13th (Feast of St. Anthony of Padua)

How to Greet Eshu

"I stand at a crossroads and greet you, mighty Eshu. I welcome your spirit and energy, keeping my scales in balance."

Loa Equivalent in Voodoo

In some Voodoo traditions, Eshu is equated with Marassa Jumeaux and Kalfu. Marassa Jumeaux is a pair of *twins* – yet is associated with the number *three*. They embody justice, truth, love, and the nature of contradictions. Kalfu is the Loa of the crossroads and, like some aspects of Eshu, causes misfortune and destruction.

Catholic Saint Association in Santería

In Santería, Eshu is associated with St. Anthony of Padua. He is the patron saint of lost souls, lost people, lost items, poverty, miracles, the disabled, the sick, and the oppressed. St. Anthony of Padua represents the more benevolent aspects of Eshu, especially the part of the Orisha who spreads justice and makes right what goes wrong in the world.

Babalu-Aye

Babalu-Aye is a spirit of the Earth that is closely associated with healing and infectious diseases. Although he encourages the recovery of those with serious illnesses, especially people who are close to death, some believe that he actually brings diseases upon humanity. This duality manifests in the way his powers seem to be expressed. He can heat up the body, causing fever to burn off the disease ailing a person, but running such a high fever can also potentially kill them.

- **Symbols:** Sun, healer's staff
- **Colors:** Brown, yellow, purple
- **Food:** Roasted corn, black beans, rum
- **Ebo Sacrifice:** Burlap, black-eyed peas, corn, beans, tobacco, rum
- **Number:** 17
- **Day:** Saturday (Day 6), December 17th (Feast of St. Lazarus)

How to Greet Babalu-Aye

"Babalu-Aye, I greet you. Take from me this sickness and cure me of my diseases."

Loa Equivalent in Voodoo

In some Voodoo traditions, Baron Samedi is the equivalent of Babalu-Aye. Although Baron Samedi is the Loa of death and is often considered evil, his powers are also invoked when someone is near death and desperate for healing. His name "Samedi" also translates to "Saturday," the day usually connected to Babalu-Aye.

Catholic Saint Association in Santería

In Santería, Babalu-Aye is associated with St. Lazarus, the patron saint of lepers, the diseased, the infirm, and the hopeless. There are actually two St. Lazaruses in the Catholic canon, but both have a connection to those who are sick, dying, or diseased. Just as St. Lazarus of Bethany was raised from the dead by Jesus, Babalu-Aye can cure people who are on the brink of death. Like St. Lazarus, honored by the Hospitaller Order of St. Lazarus of Jerusalem, who was said to have suffered from leprosy, Babalu-Aye is often depicted as being in a similar condition.

Shango

Shango is the Orisha of thunder and lightning. Other forces related to him include fire, war, virility, and foundations. He is famous for his double-bladed axe called Oṣè, and he is considered a direct ancestor of the Yoruba people, as he was the third Alaafin, or emperor, of the Oyo Empire.

- **Symbols:** Lightning bolt, brass crown
- **Colors:** Red, white
- **Food:** Amalá (okra stew with shrimp and palm oil)
- **Ebo Sacrifice:** Thunderstones, red cloth with white squares, Shango god necklaces (red and white beads in alternating groups of 4 or 6)
- **Number:** 4, 6
- **Day:** Friday (Day 5), December 4th (Feast of St. Barbara), September 30th (Feast of St. Jerome)

How to Greet Shango

"The spirit of thunder and lightning, I greet you. The great ancestor of the Yoruba people, I greet you. The mighty Alaafin of the Oyo Empire, I greet you."

Loa Equivalent in Voodoo

In some Voodoo traditions, Shango is equated with Sobo, the Loa of thunder. Both are considered great warriors who control the power of thunder and lightning. Sobo is also said to hurl mighty polished stones down to the Earth, which can be collected after waiting a year and a day. Like Shango, Sobo is strongly connected to these thunderstones, which are considered sacred objects in the African diaspora religions.

Catholic Saint Association in Santería

In Santería, Shango is associated with St. Barbara and St. Jerome. St. Barbara is the patron saint of lightning, artillerymen, and anyone who works with explosives, which gives her a strong connection to the same element as Shango. St. Jerome is the patron saint of those who rediscover and catalog knowledge from the past, linking him with Shango's aspect of foundations.

Ogun

Ogun is the Orisha of metallurgy and warriors. The traits associated with him include healing, transformation, and strength. Some myths claim that it was Ogun who allowed the other Orishas to enter the Earth by clearing a path with his metal axe and faithful canine companion. Other stories assert that he has tried to seize power from the other Orishas, including Obatala and Oduduwa, but was ultimately thwarted and sent into exile.

- **Symbols:** Iron, blacksmithing tools, anvils, dog, palm frond
- **Colors:** Black, green
- **Food:** Meat, palm wine, kola nuts
- **Ebo Sacrifice:** Iron nails, plantains, pomegranates, red meat, cigars, rum
- **Number:** 3, 7
- **Day:** Wednesday (Day 3), November 23rd (St. Clement's Day)

How to Greet Ogun

"By the hammer and the anvil, I greet you, Ogun. Forge my will as you forge iron."

Loa Equivalent in Voodoo

In Voodoo traditions, Ogun is considered a Loa named Ogoun. His role as a blacksmith was phased out, and his attributes as a great warrior were emphasized instead. In recent times, he has even become a symbol of political reform and crafty leadership, with his name and image being invoked by numerous politicians in their attempts to gain power within the government.

Catholic Saint Association in Santería

In Santería, Ogun is associated with St. Clement, the patron saint of blacksmiths and metalworkers. St. Clement is said to have been the first to get iron by refining raw ore and the first to shod a horse. In other parts of Christendom, veneration of St. Clement has died out, but it remains alive in the Caribbean and parts of rural England.

Oya

Oya is the Orisha of winds and violent storms. She also has a connection to lightning, transformation, death, and rebirth. In addition, she is a protector of the dead, the third wife of Shango, and the patron of the River Niger. As a warrior, Oya is said to be peerless, able to defeat all who challenge her. She keeps the spirits of the dead safe as they make their journey to the afterlife and watches over the cemeteries and tombs where their bodies are interred.

- **Symbols:** Copper crown, lightning bolt, fly whisk
- **Colors:** Purple, burgundy, red
- **Food:** Àkàrà

- **Ebo Sacrifice:** Copper sword, machete, red palm oil
- **Number:** 9
- **Day:** Thursday (Day 4), August 14th and 15th (Feast of Our Lady of Candelaria)

How to Greet Oya

"The storms of injustice rage, and the power of Oya quells. I greet you, great warrior."

Loa Equivalent in Voodoo

In some Voodoo traditions, Oya is equated with Bade, the Loa of wind. Bade is the inseparable companion of Sobo, and just as Oya is usually depicted as a revered wife of Shango, who is equated with Sobo. Bade can also control storms, using their power to strike out at his enemies, just like Oya.

Catholic Saint Association in Santería

In Santería, Oya is associated with Our Lady of Candelaria. Our Lady of Candelaria is a Black Madonna from the Canary Islands whose statue was said to have been discovered along the coast of Spain in 1392. She had a child in one hand and carried a green candle in the other, which is how she earned her name.

Oduduwa

Oduduwa was originally a divine king, ruling from the holy city of Ile-Ife. In addition, he was the progenitor of many Yoruba royal dynasties, resulting in many rulers being able to trace their lineage back to him. He is often venerated as a great hero, leader, and warrior, a father of the Yoruba people, and given the praise name "Olofin Adimula Oodua." After his death, he was deified, becoming an aspect of the Orisha with whom he shared a name. This primordial version of Oduduwa was linked to Obatala as one of the first Orishas created by Olodumare and usurped Obatala's mission to create the waters of Earth. There is also evidence that the primordial Oduduwa may have been a female counterpart to Obatala.

- **Symbols:** Sacred Oba's crown, birds
- **Colors:** Gold, white
- **Food:** Yams, bean cakes, plantains
- **Ebo Sacrifice:** Bird feathers, birds, melons, pineapples
- **Number:** 7

- **Day:** Sunday (Day 7)

How to Greet Oduduwa

"Oduduwa, I greet you as the ancestor of the Yoruba people. Olofin Adimula Oodua, I greet you as the king of Ile-Ife. I raise my hands to the heavens as you were raised to divinity."

Loa Equivalent in Voodoo

In some Voodoo traditions, Rezan is the equivalent of Oduduwa. Rezan is the Loa of kings, protecting their throne and safeguarding the position of their bloodline so that they will continue to rule in the days to come. Some believe that Rezan can manifest as a giant, creating earthquakes with every step, his footprints like great craters that are left to become lakes.

Catholic Saint Association in Santería

In Santería, Oduduwa is associated with St. Edmund the Martyr, who is the patron saint of kings. St. Edmund was once the King of East Anglia but was killed by the Danes, who proceeded to conquer his territory. Besides his role as the patron saint of kings, St. Edmund is akin to Oduduwa in that they both were ancient rulers who were raised up after death to become divine.

Chapter 6: The Orisha Shrine

Creating a shrine to the Orishas can be a good way to connect with them when offering prayers or sacrifices during the ebo ritual. However, unlike in some other religions, having a shrine isn't a requirement for worship. There was a long period in African history where the Yoruba religion wasn't nationally recognized, forcing adherents to keep their shrines hidden and practice in secret. It was only in the 1990s that Orisha worship was finally allowed legally, and there are still many practitioners for whom it is a point of pride that they have maintained an Orisha shrine since before their faith was recognized by the government.

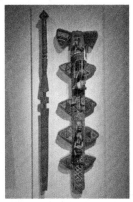

Creating a shrine to the Orishas can be a good way to connect with them when offering prayers or sacrifices during the ebo ritual.

Should I Make an Orisha Shrine?

Deciding whether or not to make an Orisha shrine is a personal choice you'll have to make for yourself. Some believe it's unnecessary, while others feel it's highly recommended to use a shrine when worshiping the Orishas. As there's no central authority to dictate how you practice Orisha worship, you can't really be wrong, regardless of your choice. However, there are pros and cons to building and using an Orisha shrine.

Pros

Stronger Connection: Having a shrine can create a stronger bond between you and the Orishas, as the continuous prayers and rituals in the same location bathe it in spiritual energy. This will, in turn, make your offerings more potent at a shrine than elsewhere.

Structured Worship: Using a shrine can offer more structure to your communion with the Orishas. There will be a specific location where all your prayers and ebo rituals will take place, so you'll always know where you'll need to be when venerating the Orishas.

Religious Pride: Having a shrine can help show your pride in your religion. Building and maintaining a shrine takes money and effort, so successfully keeping it can prove your devotion to the Orishas.

Less Preparation: After establishing your basic shrine, you won't have to keep creating a space to worship your Orishas whenever you want to pray or make offerings. Some items can be reused, so you can get several sessions with them before they require replacements.

Cons

Limited Opportunities: If you construct a shrine to worship the Orishas, you may limit your opportunities to make offerings that will be readily accepted elsewhere. The shrine creates a connection between you and the Orishas, but that means they might not accept any prayers or offerings made away from the shrine.

Expensive: Depending on how many Orishas you want to worship at your shrine, you could end up spending a lot of money setting them up. Most items won't simply be lying around your home, so you'll have to purchase them specifically for this purpose. On top of that, you'll need to constantly buy items or animals to sacrifice, which can start to add up if you frequently perform the edo ritual.

Time Consuming: Besides the amount of time it takes to set up a shrine, you also have to continuously cleanse and maintain it. Failure to do so can result in negative consequences, the least of which is the Orishas no longer accepting your prayers and offerings from a tainted shrine.

Negative Energy: If you don't properly cleanse and maintain your shrine, you're opening yourself up to negative energy corrupting your essence and inviting the more malevolent Orishas into your life. Even worse, you may become susceptible to the influence of the Ajoguns.

Making Your Own Orisha Shrine

Every Orisha shrine will be a little different, as each has its own variations when creating one. However, there are some common steps you should take and traits between them all:

1. Find an appropriate location to construct your shrine. This should be somewhere easily accessed and in a place where it won't get dirty or destroyed. You can choose a spot in your house, such as a study or extra bedroom, or an outdoor area where it won't be affected by the elements, like inside a shed or on a covered patio.

2. Create an altar using some sort of raised platform, such as a table, dais, box, etc. Place it in the area you've chosen for your shrine, ideally against a wall or another large solid object like a dresser or an armoire. If possible, choose something to serve as your altar that isn't too high, as you want to be able to access it while kneeling.

3. Cover the altar with a cloth or similar material in a color associated with your chosen Orishas. This cloth should be clean and mostly plain, with only basic decorations such as a checkered pattern. Having a cloth that's too ornate will distract from the process and make it harder to connect with your Orishas.

4. Place an offering vessel atop the altar. This can be a shallow basin, bowl, plate, etc. Wood, ceramic, clay, or non-alloy metals are all acceptable choices for your vessel. If possible, pick a vessel made with a material connected to the Orisha you are venerating at your shrine.

5. Add a candle or candles in color connected to your Orishas. Although there are shops that sell candles branded for a specific Orisha, using a basic single or double-colored candle is usually a better choice. Make sure you have something to hold your candle in place, preferably made from a non-alloy metal.

Some of the more popular Orishas to worship will have their own inclusions. These include:

Obatala

- Use a white piece of cloth, such as cotton, to cover your altar
- Place down a white candle
- Add a metal crown, sopera, and dove-handled bell
- Include a statue or other icon depicting Obatala
- Use white foods or animals as offerings during the ebo ritual. Do not ever include alcohol of any kind, as this will offend Obatala greatly.

Shango

- Use a red piece of cloth with white squares to cover your altar
- Place down a red or red and white candle
- Add a red and gold crown, thunderstones, and a double-bladed axe or swords
- Include a statue or other icon depicting Shango
- Use amalá, hot and spicy foods, or foods that are red as offerings during the ebo ritual

Yemoja

- Use a blue piece of cloth to cover your altar
- Place down a blue candle
- Add a blue and silver crown, sea shells, pearls, fans, and depictions of sea life such as dolphins, fish, or mermaids
- Include a statue or icon depicting Yemoja and blue flowers like irises
- Use perfume, silver jewelry, seafood, coffee, or white wine as offerings during the ebo ritual

Oya

- Use a purple or burgundy piece of cloth to cover your altar
- Place down a purple candle
- Add a copper crown, copper jewelry, shea butter, and a representation of a lightning bolt
- Include a statue or icon depicting Oya and a bowl of water to represent a river
- Use chocolate, purple grapes, beets, eggplants, or red wine as offerings during the ebo ritual

Oshosi

- Use a blue or green piece of cloth to cover your altar
- Place down a blue or green candle
- Add an ofá (bow) and arrows, animal pelts, deer antlers, ram horns, turtle shells, or anything else obtained from hunting
- Include a statue or icon depicting Oshosi wielding a bow and arrow
- Use small game or large game meat, bird feathers, or fruit as offerings during the ebo ritual

Ogun

- Use a red, green, or blue piece of cloth to cover your altar
- Place down a red, green, or blue candle
- Add an iron crown, blacksmith tools, and other iron objects
- Include a statue or icon depicting Ogun hammering on an anvil
- Use iron nails, red meat, pomegranates, plantains, rum, or cigars as offerings during the ebo ritual

Maintaining and Cleansing Your Orisha Shrine

Maintaining and cleansing your Orisha shrine isn't a labor-intensive process, but you do need to take the time to perform these tasks every so often to keep it from becoming dirty or corrupted. Set aside a spot in your schedule at least once a week to maintain your shrine and once every two or three months to cleanse it.

Shrine Maintenance

Maintaining your shrine involves cleaning up any dirt or debris from ritual items or offerings and washing your altar cloth. During shrine maintenance, any objects that remain on your altar all the time need to be carefully removed and placed somewhere safe while you clean your altar.

1. You first need to pick up any detritus in your vessel or on the altar itself. Any food or animal offerings will naturally leave a bit of something behind, so cleaning that up is important to maintaining your shrine. Wash out your vessel with soap and water, and clean any wax off your candle holders.

2. Next, remove everything from atop your altar so you can wash the cloth covering it. The cloth can be cleaned either by hand or in a washing machine. This will eliminate any dirt or stains accumulated during your weekly prayers and rituals. Just be sure not to damage it in the process.

3. While your altar is cleared off, take the opportunity to check and make sure it doesn't require any cleaning or repairs. If it does, wash it with an appropriate cleaning solution and fix whatever is broken. Once that is taken care of, and your cloth is clean and dry, place that cloth back onto your altar.

4. Finally, return the vessel and objects being stored back to the top of your altar. Any items that must be replaced, such as your candles, can be swapped immediately or later when you have acquired fresh supplies.

Performing a Cleansing

Cleansing your altar is necessary to prevent a buildup of negative or corrupted energy. There are a variety of methods you can use to do this, but the following are the most common ones:

Smudging

Smudging involves using herbs or incense to ward off negative energy and malevolent spirits. To perform this type of cleansing, you'll need the following:

- A bundle of herbs or incense
- A fireproof vessel or incense holder

- A clean rag

Once you have these materials, follow these steps:

1. Clear everything off of your altar and place the items somewhere safe.

2. Use the rag on your altar by wiping it around counterclockwise.

3. While using the rag, visualize the negative energy surrounding your shrine and verbalize your intentions to cleanse it.

4. Light your herb bundle or incense, then blow the smoke around your altar. The smoke will serve as a countering agent to any negative energy or malevolent forces in the vicinity.

5. Place the fireproof vessel or incense holder down on your altar and breathe in the smoke, allowing it to cleanse your own spirit.

6. You can leave your herb bundle or incense burning atop your altar for additional cleansing.

7. When you have finished, dispose of the herb bundle or incense and replace all the items that you removed from your altar at the beginning of the process.

Floral Spray or Holy Water Spritz

For this method, you'll need the following:

- A spray bottle of floral-scented water or holy water

- To perform this cleansing, follow these steps:

1. Place the spray bottle on your altar and recite a prayer, ask for a blessing, or state your intentions out loud.

2. Pick up the spray bottle and spritz the water over both your altar and all the items atop it. Offer a prayer to your chosen Orishas while you do this.

3. Wait fifteen minutes before spraying your altar again. During this time, you can meditate or recite a cleansing prayer.

4. When you have sprayed your altar five times (this should take about an hour), ask your Orishas to bless your shrine. This blessing should be enhanced by the energy from the floral-scented or holy water mist.

Quickie Methods

- Use a feather wand or sacred fan to blow away any negative energy that has built up around your shrine.

- Use a besom to sweep away corruption or evil spirits.

- Place ritual stones, crystals, or a vessel filled with salt atop your altar to absorb the negative energy in the area.

- Get an essential oils diffuser to fill your shrine with positive energy and ward off malevolent spirits.

- Spray perfume or essential oils around your shrine to eliminate negative forces.

- Offer a cleansing prayer or ask for a blessing to remove some negative energy or protect you against evil spirits.

FAQs

Q: Can I worship more than one Orisha using my altar?

A: You can use the same altar to worship multiple Orishas, but you must do so one at a time. Do not try to combine ritual items or offerings for different Orisha on your altar. You should remove all the items associated with one Orisha, perform a cleansing, and then set up the items for the next Orisha you want to worship.

Q: Can I have more than one altar at a time?

A: Yes, you can. There is no rule that you must only worship a single Orisha or have one altar at any given time. This can cut back on setup and preparation time since you won't have to swap everything out from your altar whenever you want to worship a different Orisha. However, it also means you'll have to perform additional maintenance and cleansings for each extra altar you create.

Q: Can I use the same altar to worship both the Orishas and the egun?

A: Yes, you can use the same altar for the Orishas and the egun, but just like with worshiping more than one Orisha, you must dedicate your altar to only one at a time.

Q: What should I do if I forget to cleanse my shrine for too long?

A: If it's been four or more months since you last cleansed your shrine, you'll need to perform an ebo ritual in another location in order to ask the Orishas to cleanse the negative energy and remove any malevolent spirits that might have taken root in your shrine. Perform the ritual within the general area of your shrine's location, but be sure to remain at least 30 feet away to avoid contamination by the forces corrupting your shrine.

Q: Is it okay to replace any items during a ritual if I don't have the ones listed?

A: Generally, it's fine to swap out some of the items or offerings, so long as whatever you've chosen to use has a connection in some way to the Orisha you are venerating. Don't try to use anything associated with other Orishas, as that will be seen as an insult and can have negative consequences.

Chapter 7: Getting Ready to Practice Ifa

Before you can begin to practice Ifa, you need to prepare yourself mentally and acquire the necessary tools for the rituals. Some considerations should be made before actually delving into the Ifa divination system. Trying to start before you're ready can have dire consequences, not just for yourself and your spiritual health but for those around you as well. This is why proper preparations are vital for anyone seeking to get into Ifa.

Ifa divination bowl.

Making Preparations

When you're making preparations for practicing Ifa, keep these tips in mind:

Don't Rush

When you start a new journey and discover a new world of ideas, it's easy to become a bit overeager. You may want to get to the meat and potatoes of Ifa as soon as possible, but do your best to curb your excitement. Enthusiasm isn't a bad thing, but temper it with a rational mind. Remember that there's no need to rush into things. Ifa isn't going anywhere. You can take as much time as necessary to prepare yourself for future trials.

Seek Support

Suppose you know anyone who is a current practitioner of Ifa. In that case, they can be an invaluable source of information and a pillar of support. Someone who has been practicing Ifa for a long time is going to have plenty of experience with what you'll be going through. They can help guide you along your path and give you a more personal, dialogue-driven roadmap of what you can expect. Having the support of an Ifa practitioner when you have any questions that arise during the process will make things go much smoother as you enter into the world of the Ifa divination system.

Shelve Your Ego

Having a strong ego can help you get results in other areas of your life, but when it comes to religious traditions and communing with the spirits of the universe, it will only be a hindrance. It would be a mistake to begin practicing Ifa if your reason for doing so is because you think it can help you get power or wealth. The Orishas may choose to grant you these things, but only if they believe you are worthy of such favors. You aren't their equal. Whatever offerings or sacrifices you make need to be sincere, and you should absolutely not try to make demands of them. If you prove your devotion, then in time, they may decide to give you what you ask.

If you allow your ego to interfere with practicing Ifa, you could find yourself becoming a victim of the less-benevolent Orishas or even the Ajogun. They've been dealing with humans for longer than you can imagine, and they've seen every trick in the book. You can't outwit them or overpower them with your will. Should they recognize an out-of-control ego in you, they may target that weakness and manipulate you by making you think you're working the system to your benefit, but in the end, you'll lose everything. It doesn't matter if you're a pauper or a prince; any Earthly status pales compared to the grandeur of the Orishas.

Clear Your Mind

Meditation can be a great tool to help you prepare for practicing Ifa. Your essence and ori dwell within your mind, giving the Orishas access to everything. Maintaining a calm and focused mind will make your rituals and trials less complicated, as you won't have to worry about battling yourself in the process. A clear mind is free from doubt, greed, and negativity. Encourage positive energy within you that you can carry over into your efforts with Ifa divination.

Offer a Prayer to Orunmila

Orunmila is the Orisha who can give you the most help when reading and interpreting the Odu Ifa. Offering a prayer to him may secure his aid when it comes time to practice Ifa divination. One such prayer you can recite is as follows:

"Spirit of Destiny, the first word, the last word, and the rebounding force, we call you by your names of power: Orunmila, Orúnla, Eleri Ipen, and Agbonniregun. This power is reborn to protect us from the forces of destruction and death. The power of transformation lies with you, Spirit of Destiny. Nobody is a stranger that walks beside us down the road of mystery. We praise the healing powers of the forest derived from the invisible realm of Orún, granted to us by the Spirit of Destiny. We praise the sixteen sacred principles of Olodumare, the Creator. I call upon Orunmila, the Witness to Creation, second only to the Creator himself. My path to salvation is through you, the Spirit of Destiny."

Ifa Divination Tools

To perform the Ifa divination ritual, you'll need five tools: the Opele Ifa, the Opon Ifa, the Ikin Ifa, the Iroke Ifa, and the Irukere. Each one serves an essential purpose during the ritual, so you must be sure that you have collected them all before you begin. You should know what they are, their role in the ritual, and how they are used before undertaking the divination process.

Opele Ifa

The Opele Ifa is known as the "divining chain." It's made by taking four or five nuts from an opele tree, cutting them in half, and securing them on a length of chain, string, or rope. You'll end up with eight or ten opele nut halves, which should be attached at an equal distance from one another, beginning at the two ends of the chain. However, the middle of the chain remains bare, as this is where you'll hold it. When the opele nuts are cut in half, each one has a concave and convex side. The concave side represents the number 1, while the convex side stands for 0. Similar to the binary code language used by computer programmers. In fact, there is evidence that binary code was inspired by the two-symbol system from Ifa via the diffusion of the Yoruba religion through the Islamic world and Geomancy.

Opele Ifa's Purpose

The primary function of the Opele Ifa is to open a line of communication between you and the Orishas - specifically Orunmila. Using the two-symbol system, you'll be able to interpret the readings you get from the Odu Ifa. To determine the answers to the questions asked by Ifa practitioners, an Opele Ifa needs to be used, or else the results of any divination ritual cannot be deemed accurate.

Using the Opele Ifa

Using your Opele Ifa begins by asking a question or requesting advice from the Orishas. You then swing the chain, holding it by the middle portion without any of the attached opele nuts. After you have finished with whatever you are asking, you'll allow the chain to fall to the ground, with one half of the chain remaining near you and the other farther away. How the opele nuts land will determine the answer. Each one will either have a concave or convex side facing up; by reading the associated numbers, you can interpret the answer through a corresponding portion of the Odu Ifa.

Opon Ifa

The Opon Ifa is the sacred tray of divination used as part of the Ifa divination system. A traditional Opon Ifa is made from wood carved into a rectangle or disc shape. Some Opon Ifas combine both shapes, using a rectangle for the outer portion and a circle within it. While they can be plain, unadorned trays, many Yoruba woodworkers carve decorative designs around the edges, usually depicting symbols of the Orishas, religious iconography, or personal imagery. This ornamentation can assist with Ifa divination, as representations of things closely associated with Ifa or the Orishas will function as a method of strengthening your spiritual communion.

Despite the many variations from one individual's Opon Ifa to the others, one characteristic is shared by all, the face of Eshu. This is because Eshu is the Orisha who facilitates communication between divine beings and humans. Ifa practitioners always want Eshu present during their divination rituals so he can keep that line of communication open during the process. An Opon Ifa that lacks the image of Eshu will be ineffective, making it little more than a fancy wooden dish.

Opon Ifa's Purpose

The purpose of an Opon Ifa is to mark any signs from the Odu Ifa during the divination ritual. It allows the practitioner to keep track of the information acquired while invoking the power of the Orishas, which in turn allows for better clarity and guidance. When a question is asked, and the Odu Ifa is used to seek out an answer, an Opon Ifa is integral to the process.

Iyerosun Powder

Iyerosun powder is a substance used by Ifa practitioners to help them mark the Odu Ifa. It comes from the iyosun tree, which is alternatively known as the "irosun tree" or the "tree of life." The substance's name is a combination of "iyosun" and "lye," which means powder, making the literal translation "powder of the iyosun tree." The powder itself is derived from termite dust found around iyosun trees. Ifa practitioners scatter the iyerosun powder over the surface of the Opon Ifa until it is completely covered by the substance. Prior to using it, the powder should be blessed by a babalawo, making it acceptable for use in the Ifa divination ritual. Iyerosun powder holds such an important position in Ifa that the ritual cannot proceed without it.

Using the Opon Ifa

Before you begin the ritual, set the Opon Ifa down on the ground wherever you choose to perform the divination. A straw mat or similar protective item can be placed in front of the Opon Ifa, providing you with a more comfortable surface than the hard earth or floor. Sit or kneel on the mat, positioning yourself to face east. This is because the east is considered the direction where the realm of Olodumare resides. If there are any windows or doors nearby, open them to ensure unrestricted access between you and the Orishas.

Once in position, spread iyerosun powder onto the Opon Ifa, covering the surface evenly. The powder should also be level, so smooth out any bumps or divots before proceeding. You shouldn't be able to see any part of the Opon Ifa through the powder when you begin, as scratching markings into it is how you document your discoveries. Improperly spreading the iyerosun powder can hurt your ability to get accurate readings from the Odu Ifa.

After beginning the divination ritual, you'll use the Opon Ifa in conjunction with the Ikin Ifa to commune with the Orishas through the Odu Ifa. As you ask questions of the Orishas, the answers will be channeled through you and reveal themselves in the way you mark up the powder within the Opon Ifa. The information you learn from the ritual can offer you a glimpse through the veil to the other side of the spirit realm, where you can divine the secrets to help set you or someone you are aiding on the right path in life.

Ikin Ifa

The Ikin Ifa is a set of 16 kola nuts or cowrie shells used in conjunction with the Opon Ifa during the divination ritual. This has a similar method to the Opele Ifa in that the nuts have a concave and convex side, and the shells have a flat and rounded side. The concave and flat sides indicate the number 1, while the convex and rounded sides stand for 0. Using the Ikin Ifa for divination is known as "Dafa." You can use both the Opele Ifa and the Ikin Ifa during the same ritual. Still, many people choose only one or the other for a given divination session.

Ikin Ifa's Purpose

The purpose of the Ikin Ifa is to uncover the secrets of the world and the ori. This is like the Opele Ifa, but the Ikin Ifa has more elements, meaning you can get a more in-depth answer. Sessions using the Ikin Ifa take longer to complete, so if you choose to use it, be sure to set aside enough time in your schedule. Whenever you can't devote the time and energy to using the Ikin Ifa, it's best to only use the Opele Ifa instead. Remember that whatever information you derive from the divination process with the Opele Ifa will be less detailed and accurate than those using the Ikin Ifa.

Using the Ikin Ifa

To use the Ikin Ifa, you "cast" or "throw" the nuts or shells in a manner not unlike throwing dice. By noting the results of which pieces show the sides for 1 and which show 0, you can interpret it through the Odu Ifa. You'll mark the results in the Opon Ifa to keep track of the positions the pieces display when they are cast. The 16 pieces of the Ikin Ifa can be said to correspond to the 16 *major* chapters of the Odu Ifa. There are 256 chapters total, with the 240 other chapters considered *minor.*

Iroke Ifa

The Iroke Ifa is a long tool vaguely shaped like an elephant tusk, thicker at the base and coming to a point near the top. They are typically made out of carved wood, and the base is given the design of a human or animal that is important to the owner. Popular icons for the Iroke Ifa include representations of the Orishas, a penitent man kneeling, or the birds associated with Oduduwa.

Purpose and Using the Iroke Ifa

The Iroke Ifa is meant to be used prior to the divination ritual to get the Orishas' attention, letting them know that you seek to ask a question of them. It's used by tapping the pointed end against the Opon Ifa. Practitioners of Ifa believe that the Orishas can hear this noise wherever they are, signaling to them that someone seeks their wisdom or advice. So long as the rest of your preparation for the ritual and the tools being used have been properly carried out, this should ensure a successful divination session.

Irukere

The Irukere is a tool made from the tail of a horse or a cow, joined together at the base by a handle. The handles can be either short or long, reaching up to 24 inches, and are usually made from wood. While the handle can remain unadorned, it is often wrapped with leather, beads, or natural fabric. The colors used may be coordinated with the personal Orisha of the owner – or those associated with Orunmila. A loop can be added at the bottom of the handle to allow the tool to be hung up on a peg or hook.

Purpose and Using the Irukere

The purpose of the Irukere is to ward off evil spirits, malevolent forces, and negative energy while carrying out the divination ritual. You do this by hanging it near a window, doorway, or other entrance if you're inside. If you are performing your ritual outdoors, you can hang it from a tree or other tall structure. Still, if there is nothing nearby that is suitable, you can draw a large "X" on the ground and place it in the middle. The "X" represents the crossroads between the heavens and Earth, which both the good and the bad forces use to reach your ritual site.

Blessing and Cleansing Your Tools

Before you begin performing the Ifa divination ritual, blessing your tools is a good idea. Start by offering a prayer to Olodumare and the Orishas, with particular attention paid to Eshu and Orunmila. Eshu is the Divine Messenger, so his power is necessary to ensure that your words can reach the Orishas. Orunmila is the Spirit of Wisdom, so it is his knowledge that will aid you in deciphering the results of your divination session and interpreting them through the Odu Ifa. At this point, use the Iroke Ifa to tap on the edge of your Opon Ifa. This will get the attention of the Orishas, so they will hear your prayers.

A typical prayer to Eshu is:

"I invoke the power of Eshu, the Divine Messenger. Please allow my voice to carry unto Orún and into the ears of the great Orishas. Eshu, help me with my request for knowledge from those with wisdom far beyond myself. Help me seek advice from those who can guide my hand and set my path toward my destiny. I thank you, Divine Messenger, for granting me your aid."

A common prayer to Orunmila is:

"I invoke the power of Orunmila, the Spirit of Wisdom. In all things, you have great knowledge, and in all things, you offer sound advice. I wish to light the torch to see the path ahead, and it is only through your wisdom that I can kindle the flame of understanding. Give me your guidance and lead me to my destiny. I thank you, Spirit of Wisdom, for granting me your aid."

When you are blessing your tools, you can use a candle or a stick of incense to assist you. Move it in a counter-clockwise motion, as this signifies unlocking the energy within the tools, opening them up for the ritual itself. Allowing spiritual energy to flow through your tools is the only way to ensure the accuracy of your readings, as there will not be anything obstructing the Orishas from reaching forth to guide your hand as you use your tools and the Odu Ifa. This is why it's helpful to use an Irukere, since the unrestricted flow of energy can attract evil forces, and you don't want them to infiltrate your ritual space.

After performing the divination ritual, you can similarly cleanse your tools as you blessed them. Offer your prayers and beseech the Orishas to purify the energy amassed from performing the ritual. The spiritual energy that builds up can become dangerous and cause negative repercussions to you if they aren't cleansed properly. The longer you go without a cleansing, the higher the likelihood that an evil force can redirect the energy in ways to cause harm to you or others. Be sure to use your candle or stick of incense and make a clockwise motion, as this blocks the flow of energy and prevents anything from corrupting your tools.

Chapter 8: How to Cast and Read the Ikin Ifa

When it comes to casting the Ikin Ifa and reading the results, someone new to the process may become confused. Fortunately, once you understand the fundamentals of how it works, you'll see that the basics aren't all that difficult. While it can take years for someone to master the skill of accurately interpreting the results against the Odu Ifa, you'll at least be able to comprehend the methods used for doing so, allowing you to start practicing independently.

When it comes to casting the Ikin Ifa and reading the results, someone new to the process may become confused.

How to Cast the Ikin Ifa

To cast the Ikin Ifa, start by lining the pieces up on the ground in front of you. They should all be set with the convex side of the kola nuts or the rounded side of the cowrie shells facing upward. Make four vertical lines intersect with four horizontal lines, giving you a shape that resembles a square with a grid pattern. Next, pick up the pieces and hold them by cupping your hands together. Shake your hands to jostle the pieces, ensuring that when you cast them, it will only be the will of the Orishas that decide which direction they face once they are thrown.

When you are satisfied that the pieces of the Ikin Ifa have been shaken enough, cast them by opening your hands, so your palms are facing the ground. The pieces should drop down in front of you, making them easy to locate and read. You don't want to throw them in the way you would a bunch of dice, as if the pieces end up too far from one another, they will lose their effectiveness as a divination tool. The energy conjured by casting them requires the pieces to be nearby, and letting them become separated can allow other forces to manipulate your results.

You mustn't attempt to touch or move any of the pieces. If you do, the Orishas will view it as you attempt to overrule their authority. It would be the same as loudly boasting that you are wiser or more powerful than the gods. The entire point of the ritual is to ask for help from the Orishas, so offending them will only cause the opposite to occur. Should you accidentally touch or move any of the pieces once they've been cast, recite a quick prayer begging for forgiveness, then end the ritual right then and there. Close off the energy of your tools and gather them up. You'll need to wait at least a week before attempting the ritual again.

Assuming your casting is successful, you should have the 16 pieces of the Ikin Ifa facing either up or down, representing the 1's and 0's.

The next step is to record the results of your casting by using the Opon Ifa. You can draw markings of "1" and "0" into the powder covering your Opon Ifa, or you can use hash marks, with one hash mark being the same as "1," and two hash marks together representing the "0." Make the markings in two vertical rows of four, the same as you laid them out prior to the ritual. As it is unlikely that the pieces will have fallen in this exact pattern, when recording the results, start by finding the piece farthest away from you and place its marking at the top of the left row. After that, record the rest by using that first piece to orient your marks on the Opon Ifa.

Once you have recorded the results of your casting, you'll be ready to read and interpret the results. Remember not to touch the pieces of the Ikin Ifa until after you have placed the marks on the Opon Ifa. As soon as you have finished this, it will be safe to collect the pieces, as the Orishas have done their part. Their power and their will decide how the pieces lay after being cast. They have granted you their wisdom or guidance - whether you understand what they say is entirely up to you.

How to Read the Ikin Ifa

The time has come to read the results of your casting. If you've successfully made your markings in the correct positions, the matter of reading them is very simple. You just need to match the pattern you've created to the corresponding odu or chapter from the Odu Ifa. There are 16 major odus and 240 minor odus. Each major odu has a group of minor odus associated with them. To have a proper reading, you need your first 8 pieces to correspond to one of the major odus. If that isn't the case, you'll have to recast the pieces again, following the same procedure as you would if you accidentally touched or moved the pieces. However, instead of asking for forgiveness from the Orishas for touching or moving the pieces, you'll ask for forgiveness for being unable to interpret their wisdom and guidance.

If your casting has resulted in markings that correspond to one of the 16 major odus, the second of the 8 markings will determine which minor odu from the collection of the major odu you'll interpret. The major odus have an order of seniority, with the highest major odu being Ogbe and the lowest being Ofun. Each major odu has 15 minor odus within them, resulting in 16 total when including the major odu itself. They all have a specific name and meanings associated with them, which you can recognize by the patterns assigned to them in the Odu Ifa.

The full list of markings assigned to each major odu in the Odu Ifa is as follows:

Meji (Major Odus)

1. Ogbe

I	I
I	I
I	I
I	I

2. Oyeku

II	II
II	II
II	II
II	II

3. Iwori

II	II
I	I
I	I
II	II

4. Odi

I	I
II	II
II	II
I	I

5. Irosun

I	I
I	I
II	II
II	II

6. Owonrin

II	II
II	II
I	I
I	I

7. Obara

I	I
II	II
II	II
II	II

8. Okanran

II	II
II	II
II	II
I	I

9. Ogunda

I	I
I	I
I	I
II	II

10. Osa

II	II
I	I
I	I
I	I

11. Ika

II	II
I	I
II	II
II	II

12. Oturupon

II	II
II	II
I	I
II	II

13. Otura

I	I
II	II
I	I
I	I

14. Irete

I	I
I	I
II	II
I	I

15. Ose

I	I
II	II
I	I
II	II

16. Ofun

II	II
I	I
II	II
I	I

Basic Meanings of the Major Odus

Although there is much more to each major odu than their basic meaning and tenets, becoming familiar with them can help you quickly interpret what type of answer you have received from the Orishas. This list is as follows:

1. **Ogbe:** Guidance
2. **Oyeku:** Cycle of death
3. **Iwori:** Learning
4. **Odi:** Birth and rebirth
5. **Irosun:** Ancestors and family
6. **Owonrin:** Chaos
7. **Obara:** Inner strength
8. **Okanran:** Exploration and discovery
9. **Ogunda:** Creation
10. **Osa:** Transformation
11. **Ika:** Power
12. **Oturupon:** Survival
13. **Otura:** Destiny
14. **Irete:** Determination
15. **Ose:** Fertility and abundance
16. **Ofun:** Protection

Examples and Exercises

After determining which of the major odus you have cast with the Ikin Ifa, you can begin to interpret them using the basic tenets of each one. For example, if you asked a question of the Orisha about how to handle a problem, and you ended up with markings that showed the major odu of Irosun, you might take that to mean that you should seek out help from a member of your family. However, it could also mean looking to your ancestors for aid. This is the part of Ifa divination that takes gaining experience and honing your skills to ensure an accurate reading.

As a way to practice your reading skills, start by only asking very simple questions during a ritual. The less complicated your request is, the easier it will be to interpret it properly. Basic questions can be anything from your life with a limited number of possible answers, so avoid asking something esoteric or abstract, such as "What is my destiny?" or "Who is my soulmate?"

If you're having trouble coming up with basic questions to ask during your rituals, you can try some of these:

- Should I attend the upcoming social function with my friends?

- Did my sibling take my favorite shirt without asking and get a mustard stain on it?

- Am I going to win the spelling bee?

- Where is the retainer I lost back in second grade?

- Who should I ask to attend the black and white film festival this weekend?

- Will I pitch a no-hitter during the upcoming baseball season?

- Can I still get into Yale if I start taking my studies more seriously?

Chapter 9: Odu Ifa 1-8. From Ogbe to Okanran

The first 8 Meji, or major odus, include Ogbe, Oyeku, Iwori, Odi, Irosun, Owonrin, Obara, and Okanran. They are listed in order of seniority, from the highest to lowest. The minor odus within are a combination of the major odu in question and the other 15 Meji.

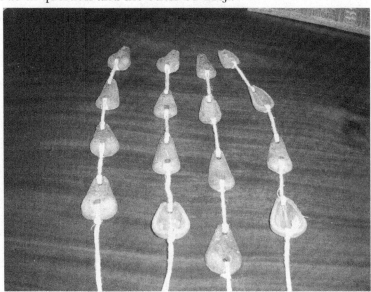

The first 8 Meji, or major odus, include Ogbe, Oyeku, Iwori, Odi, Irosun, Owonrin, Obara, and Okanran.
https://commons.wikimedia.org/wiki/File:Opele_Ifa_Orossi.JPG

Ogbe - The Lightbringer

Ogbe is the manifestation of the purest light in all of Orún. It helps to guide us down our path as we move closer to fulfilling our destiny. When you feel like you are fumbling around in the dark, it provides the assistance you need to find your way. Ogbe illuminates the road ahead so we can see where we are going.

Minor Odus

The minor odus associated with Ogbe include:

1. **Ogbe Oyeku:** Guiding the cycle of death.
2. **Ogbe Iwori:** Leading down the path of knowledge.
3. **Ogbe Odi:** Understanding birth and rebirth.
4. **Ogbe Irosun:** Helping to connect with ancestors and kin.
5. **Ogbe Owonrin:** Finding the way through chaos.
6. **Ogbe Obara:** Bringing forth inner strength.
7. **Ogbe Okanran:** Guidance to new places.
8. **Ogbe Ogunda:** Inventing a new creation.
9. **Ogbe Osa:** Leading the way through a transformation.
10. **Ogbe Ika:** Showing the path to power.
11. **Ogbe Oturupon:** Finding a cure.
12. **Ogbe Otura:** Guidance toward destiny.
13. **Ogbe Irete:** Illuminating a goal.
14. **Ogbe Ose:** Helping to achieve prosperity.
15. **Ogbe Ofun:** Showing a path to protection.

Oyeku - The Cycle of Death

Oyeku represents the cycle of life and death. However, it can also mean the end of any cycle that exists in life, such as the end of a relationship or the end of adolescence before becoming an adult. Oyeku is responsible for the end of a cycle but also the promise it will begin anew.

Minor Odus

The minor odus associated with Oyeku include:

1. **Oyeku Ogbe:** End of the cycle of searching for answers.
2. **Oyeku Iwori:** Transitioning from one level of learning to the next.

3. **Oyeku Odi:** Final rebirth as a whole being in Orún.

4. **Oyeku Irosun:** Extinction of one bloodline as another takes its place.

5. **Oyeku Owonrin:** End of the universe.

6. **Oyeku Obara:** Failure and perseverance.

7. **Oyeku Okanran:** End of one search as another begins.

8. **Oyeku Ogunda:** Ceasing production of new creations.

9. **Oyeku Osa:** Final metamorphosis.

10. **Oyeku Ika:** Toppling of a regime as a new one replaces it.

11. **Oyeku Oturupon:** Succumbing to an illness.

12. **Oyeku Otura:** Reaching one's destiny.

13. **Oyeku Irete:** Giving up on a goal or dream.

14. **Oyeku Ose:** Losing prosperity and good fortune.

15. **Oyeku Ofun:** No longer having protection.

Iwori - The Oracle

Iwori is the symbol of higher consciousness. It involves elevating our minds to better understand the world around us and the forces beyond our control. There are so many things that a mortal cannot know, but at least some of these secrets can be unlocked through divination. Iwori represents the transition from ignorance to wisdom.

Minor Odus

The minor odus associated with Iwori include:

1. **Iwori Ogbe:** Learning about the path to destiny.

2. **Iwori Oyeku:** Uncovering the cycle of death.

3. **Iwori Odi:** Wisdom from childbirth.

4. **Iwori Irosun:** Finding out about one's roots and heritage.

5. **Iwori Owonrin:** Understanding chaos.

6. **Iwori Obara:** Finding an inner strength

7. **Iwori Okanran:** Knowledge gained from discovering new cultures.

8. **Iwori Ogunda:** Learning a new trade.

9. **Iwori Osa:** Gaining wisdom from a transformation.

10. **Iwori Ika:** Finding the path to power.

11. **Iwori Oturupon:** Understanding how to fight disease.

12. **Iwori Otura:** Uncovering one's destiny.

13. **Iwori Irete:** Knowledge acquired after reaching a goal.

14. **Iwori Ose:** Learning how to grow food.

15. **Iwori Ofun:** Mentorship by a guardian.

Odi - The Womb

Odi is the word used by the Yoruba people for a female's womb, as well as the process of childbirth. It expresses that we are all born and reborn through physical reincarnation within our bloodline or being reborn in Orún when our ori is reunited with our iponri. Odi expresses this concept in both positive and negative ways, as becoming too attached to something can make us try to cling to things we should let go of.

Minor Odus

The minor odus associated with Odi include:

1. **Odi Ogbe:** Being set upon a new path.

2. **Odi Oyeku:** Rebirth after death.

3. **Odi Iwori:** Triggering an interest in learning something new.

4. **Odi Irosun:** Birth of a new family member.

5. **Odi Owonrin:** Igniting chaos.

6. **Odi Obara:** Developing willpower.

7. **Odi Okanran:** Start a new journey.

8. **Odi Ogunda:** Beginning of a new project.

9. **Odi Osa:** First stage of a transformation.

10. **Odi Ika:** Initiation of a quest for power.

11. **Odi Oturupon:** Regaining one's health.

12. **Odi Otura:** Receiving a new destiny.

13. **Odi Irete:** Becoming determined to finish a task.

14. **Odi Ose:** A sudden influx of wealth.

15. **Odi Ofun:** Protecting someone like one was protected in the past.

Irosun - The Elder Tree

Irosun is the name of the tree from which the Iyerosun powder used in the Ifa divination system is derived. Just as a tree has many branches that stem from it, every person can trace their ancestry back to a single progenitor. Irosun carries the connotation of a family tree, showing a connection to our bloodline, involving our ancestors or our living kin.

Minor Odus

The minor odus associated with Irosun include:

1. **Irosun Ogbe:** Seeking guidance from a family member.
2. **Irosun Oyeku:** The death of a loved one.
3. **Irosun Iwori:** Learning a family secret.
4. **Irosun Odi:** Rebirth of a dead family member as a new baby.
5. **Irosun Owonrin:** A toxic family dynamic.
6. **Irosun Obara:** Strength of the family unit.
7. **Irosun Okanran:** Finding a long-lost relative.
8. **Irosun Ogunda:** Building a home.
9. **Irosun Osa:** Transition into married life.
10. **Irosun Ika:** Becoming a matriarch or patriarch.
11. **Irosun Oturupon:** Supporting an ill family member.
12. **Irosun Otura:** Destiny of the bloodline.
13. **Irosun Irete:** Pushing through a family tragedy.
14. **Irosun Ose:** Creating a large family.
15. **Irosun Ofun:** Protecting one's children.

Owonrin - The Chaotic One

Owonrin represents the chaos that reigns throughout the universe on a micro and macro level. Think of the chaos involving the atoms that make up every bit of matter and how they can move and change seemingly at random. Also, consider the stars burning brightly in every corner of the cosmos and how they become supernovas when they die, obliterating everything nearby. Owonrin is the unexpected chaos that can be introduced into our lives at any moment.

Minor Odus

The minor odus associated with Owonrin include:

1. **Owonrin Ogbe:** Becoming lost in the dark.
2. **Owonrin Oyeku:** An untimely death.
3. **Owonrin Iwori:** Inability to understand a subject.
4. **Owonrin Odi:** Randomness of which seed is planted in the womb.
5. **Owonrin Irosun:** Interfamilial conflict.

6. **Owonrin Obara:** Becoming too self-reliant.

7. **Owonrin Okanran:** Getting lost in a new place.

8. **Owonrin Ogunda:** Unintended defects in creation.

9. **Owonrin Osa:** Inability to control change.

10. **Owonrin Ika:** The chaos of a dictator's regime.

11. **Owonrin Oturupon:** Unforeseen progression of the disease.

12. **Owonrin Otura:** Random assignment of destiny.

13. **Owonrin Irete:** Obstacles appearing to thwart achieving a goal.

14. **Owonrin Ose:** The nature of good luck and bad luck.

15. **Owonrin Ofun:** Fighting an enemy from all sides.

Obara - The Sleeping Giant

Obara is the strength and willpower that resides in all of us. It may not always be obvious, but once roused, that strength can overcome obstacles that might have otherwise seemed impossible. Obara shows that the inner strength we possess should never be underestimated.

Minor Odus

The minor odus associated with Obara include:

1. **Obara Ogbe:** Strength to follow the path.

2. **Obara Oyeku:** Moving on after a loved one's death.

3. **Obara Iwori:** Discipline when studying.

4. **Obara Odi:** Surviving childbirth.

5. **Obara Irosun:** Strength inherited from ancestors.

6. **Obara Owonrin:** Fighting inner turmoil.

7. **Obara Okanran:** Surviving the untamed wilds.

8. **Obara Ogunda:** Molding clay into a sculpture.

9. **Obara Osa:** Ability to affect change.

10. **Obara Ika:** Making tough decisions as a leader.

11. **Obara Oturupon:** Bearing pain from an injury.

12. **Obara Otura:** Following through on one's destiny.

13. **Obara Irete:** Strength to persevere against the odds.

14. **Obara Ose:** Not allowing wealth to change oneself.

15. **Obara Ofun:** Holding the shield against an onslaught.

Okanran - The Explorer

Okanran represents the traits associated with exploration and discovery. This can mean curiosity, adventurousness, or trailblazing. When the time comes in our lives to seek out a new direction or embrace new possibilities, Okanran is the odu that best expresses these concepts.

Minor Odus

The minor odus associated with Okanran include:

1. **Okanran Ogbe:** Discovery of a new path.
2. **Okanran Oyeku:** Seeking the afterlife.
3. **Okanran Iwori:** Confirming a theory as fact.
4. **Okanran Odi:** Finding out about a past life.
5. **Okanran Irosun:** Discovering one's heritage.
6. **Okanran Owonrin:** Traveling across dangerous seas.
7. **Okanran Obara:** Finding the willpower one didn't know they had.
8. **Okanran Ogunda:** Innovating an existing design.
9. **Okanran Osa:** Exploring a change within oneself.
10. **Okanran Ika:** Uncovering a hidden power.
11. **Okanran Oturupon:** Seeking out a new treatment for a disease.
12. **Okanran Otura:** Discovering the meaning of one's destiny.
13. **Okanran Irete:** Succeeding in an unconventional manner.
14. **Okanran Ose:** Finding a lost treasure.
15. **Okanran Ofun:** Seeking out a warrior for protection.

Chapter 10: Odu Ifa 9-16. From Ogunda to Ofun

The second 8 Meji, or major odus, include Ogunda, Osa, Ika, Oturupon, Otura, Irete, Ose, and Ofun. As with the previous 8 Meji, these are listed in order of seniority from highest to lowest.

The second 8 Meji, or major odus, include Ogunda, Osa, Ika, Oturupon, Otura, Irete, Ose, and Ofun.

Ogunda - The Crafter

Ogunda is a word is derived from Ogun, the Orisha best known as a metalworker and craftsman. It tells us that things in our life need to be made or remade. This doesn't necessarily have to be something physical; it can be a relationship, our confidence, or our career. Ogunda is the drive we have to build something or improve ourselves.

Minor Odus

The minor odus associated with Ogunda include:

1. **Ogunda Ogbe:** Paving the way for others to follow.
2. **Ogunda Oyeku:** Forging a deadly weapon.
3. **Ogunda Iwori:** Inventing a new subject.
4. **Ogunda Odi:** Raising a child you gave birth to.
5. **Ogunda Irosun:** Establishing a bloodline.
6. **Ogunda Owonrin:** Inability to control the fires of a forge.
7. **Ogunda Obara:** Hammering out the imperfections in a blade.
8. **Ogunda Okanran:** Building a ship to explore the world.
9. **Ogunda Osa:** A cocoon around an inchworm as it becomes a butterfly.
10. **Ogunda Ika:** Creating a platform for political power.
11. **Ogunda Oturupon:** Developing a medicine.
12. **Ogunda Otura:** Making one's own destiny.
13. **Ogunda Irete:** Seeing a project through to the end.
14. **Ogunda Ose:** Planting crops and harvesting the bounty.
15. **Ogunda Ofun:** Constructing defenses.

Osa - The Spirit of Transformation

Osa is similar to Owonrin in that it represents change. However, Osa is a change that is expected rather than stemming from chaos. As we transform from a baby to a teenager, then an adult to a senior citizen, change follows us the entire time. Osa means either embracing that change or trying to flee from it.

Minor Odus

The minor odus associated with Osa include:

1. **Osa Ogbe:** Turning down a different path.
2. **Osa Oyeku:** Leaving the physical body and becoming a spiritual being.
3. **Osa Iwori:** Going from student to teacher.
4. **Osa Odi:** Growing up and developing as a person.
5. **Osa Irosun:** A change within the family dynamic.
6. **Osa Owonrin:** Losing control.
7. **Osa Obara:** A weakling becoming strong.
8. **Osa Okanran:** Transition of a new settlement to a booming metropolis.
9. **Osa Ogunda:** Raw materials being forged into useful items.
10. **Osa Ika:** Starting at the bottom and climbing the proverbial ladder.
11. **Osa Oturupon:** Progression of disease from bad to worse.
12. **Osa Otura:** Being transformed upon reaching one's destiny.
13. **Osa Irete:** Becoming altered by the experience of reaching a goal.
14. **Osa Ose:** A single seed becoming a tree bearing plenty of fruit.
15. **Osa Ofun:** Transforming into a protector.

Ika - The Conqueror

Ika is all about amassing power of any kind. This can be spiritual power, political power, high social status, or physical strength. This can be positive or negative, depending on how you go about gaining power. If it's at the expense of others, it will be negative; if it's about personal responsibility, then it will be positive.

Minor Odus

The minor odus associated with Ika include:

1. **Ika Ogbe:** Following a road map to power.
2. **Ika Oyeku:** Staving off death.
3. **Ika Iwori:** Using knowledge to one's advantage.
4. **Ika Odi:** Initiation into the priesthood.
5. **Ika Irosun:** Utilizing the influence of one's family.
6. **Ika Owonrin:** Uncontrollable destructive power of fire.

7. **Ika Obara:** Imposing one's will onto others.

8. **Ika Okanran:** Plundering virgin lands for resources.

9. **Ika Ogunda:** Power of industrialization.

10. **Ika Osa:** Gaining dominance by transforming oneself.

11. **Ika Oturupon:** Using modern medicine to fight disease.

12. **Ika Otura:** Free will versus destiny.

13. **Ika Irete:** Reaching a position of leadership.

14. **Ika Ose:** Power of money.

15. **Ika Ofun:** Using offensive tactics to defend oneself.

Oturupon - The Survivor

Oturupon represents diseases, injuries, and other ailments. Everybody will experience something that causes them sickness or pain during their life. Still, Oturupon can also represent the power to fight these illnesses and heal our bodies. It symbolizes survival and doing everything you can to regain your health.

Minor Odus

The minor odus associated with Oturupon include:

1. **Oturupon Ogbe:** Following the path to recovery.

2. **Oturupon Oyeku:** Coming back from the brink of death.

3. **Oturupon Iwori:** Learning a lesson from a harrowing experience.

4. **Oturupon Odi:** A baby born with defects.

5. **Oturupon Irosun:** Reconciling feuding family members.

6. **Oturupon Owonrin:** Getting through an unexplained illness.

7. **Oturupon Obara:** Healing through mind over matter.

8. **Oturupon Okanran:** Having a rare disease.

9. **Oturupon Ogunda:** Being maimed by a weapon and surviving.

10. **Oturupon Osa:** Treating an evolving disease.

11. **Oturupon Ika:** Corrupting influence of power on the mind and body.

12. **Oturupon Otura:** Prognosis of how long one has left to live.

13. **Oturupon Irete:** Refusing to succumb to an illness.

14. **Oturupon Ose:** Cause of a famine.

15. **Oturupon Ofun:** Preempting an injury by wearing armor.

Otura - The Embrace

Otura is about comfort and aligning our conscious minds with our divine spirits. It comes from the destiny set out before us in the beginning, which follows us throughout our lives and informs every decision and every action we take. Otura can also be considered the merging of the mundane and the divine, showing us a vision of our true purpose on Earth.

Minor Odus

The minor odus associated with Otura include:

1. **Otura Ogbe:** Final destination of a long road.
2. **Otura Oyeku:** Reaching the afterlife.
3. **Otura Iwori:** Becoming an expert in a particular field.
4. **Otura Odi:** Assignment of the ori and iponri.
5. **Otura Irosun:** Egun returning to help a descendant.
6. **Otura Owonrin:** Chaos being ordered.
7. **Otura Obara:** Newfound confidence.
8. **Otura Okanran:** Colonization of unexplored lands.
9. **Otura Ogunda:** Final product of a craftsman.
10. **Otura Osa:** The end result of a transformation.
11. **Otura Ika:** All tyrants are destined to fall.
12. **Otura Oturupon:** Tragic fate of the sick and weary.
13. **Otura Irete:** Finally achieving a long-held dream.
14. **Otura Ose:** Mandate of humanity to multiply.
15. **Otura Ofun:** Successfully defending one's land from invasion.

Irete - The Determined One

Irete is the manifestation of our determination. When someone decides they want to achieve a goal and uses every ounce of will to reach it, they are expressing the concept of Irete. It pushes us to our limits and then urges us to go even further. Irete means striving to succeed, no matter what forces are against us.

Minor Odus

The minor odus associated with Irete include:

1. **Irete Ogbe:** Steadfastness in continuing on down the path.
2. **Irete Oyeku:** Setting a new goal.

3. **Irete Iwori:** Determination to understand a topic.

4. **Irete Odi:** Will to become a better person.

5. **Irete Irosun:** Fighting on behalf of a loved one.

6. **Irete Owonrin:** Wading through the chaos.

7. **Irete Obara:** Pushing the limits of one's inner strength.

8. **Irete Okanran:** Desire to explore further than anyone before.

9. **Irete Ogunda:** Refusing to quit until a project is finished.

10. **Irete Osa:** Ability for self-reflection and self-improvement.

11. **Irete Ika:** Drive to become the best.

12. **Irete Oturupon:** Working through the pain to get better.

13. **Irete Otura:** Refusal of failure to meet one's destiny.

14. **Irete Ose:** Need to amass wealth.

15. **Irete Ofun:** A vigilant defender.

Ose - The Wellspring of Prosperity

Ose symbolizes fertility and abundance. It is associated with freshwater, which has long been the lifeblood of civilizations worldwide. Before the implementation of widespread irrigation, any group of people who tried to settle somewhere without easy access to a freshwater source either failed or struggled greatly to survive. Ose encourages prosperity in all its forms.

Minor Odus

The minor odus associated with Ose include:

1. **Ose Ogbe:** Having many paths available to follow.

2. **Ose Oyeku:** Inheriting a fortune from a dead relative.

3. **Ose Iwori:** Learning to become a jack-of-all-trades.

4. **Ose Odi:** Having many children.

5. **Ose Irosun:** Being able to call upon many egun.

6. **Ose Owonrin:** Prevalence of chaos.

7. **Ose Obara:** Succeeding based on will alone.

8. **Ose Okanran:** Profiting from a rich new land one has discovered.

9. **Ose Ogunda:** High productivity and large output.

10. **Ose Osa:** Going from poor to wealthy.

11. **Ose Ika:** Acquiring a massive following.

12. **Ose Oturupon:** Curing a disease that became an epidemic.

13. **Ose Otura:** Possessing numerous destinies.

14. **Ose Irete:** Having a wide variety of goals.

15. **Ose Ofun:** Being protected by many guardians.

Ofun - The Guardian

Ofun translates to the "Spirit of White," representing the aura of protection that those who have been blessed receive. It serves as an answer to our prayers and a miracle that aids us in our time of need. In essence, Ofun is a guardian angel.

Minor Odus

The minor odus associated with Ofun include:

1. **Ofun Ogbe:** Safeguarding the path for those lighting the way.

2. **Ofun Oyeku:** Protecting the natural order of things.

3. **Ofun Iwori:** Keeping a village safe so the children can focus on their studies.

4. **Ofun Odi:** Maternal instincts.

5. **Ofun Irosun:** Defending the honor of one's bloodline.

6. **Ofun Owonrin:** Holding something together so it doesn't become chaotic.

7. **Ofun Obara:** Protecting one's ego.

8. **Ofun Okanran:** Watching over those who seek out new adventures.

9. **Ofun Ogunda:** Preserving ancient artwork.

10. **Ofun Osa:** Guarding those vulnerable during a transformation.

11. **Ofun Ika:** Protecting one's position of power.

12. **Ofun Oturupon:** Shielding an injury to prevent it from becoming worse.

13. **Ofun Otura:** Safeguarding the right one has to fulfill their destiny.

14. **Ofun Irete:** Protection of one's goals from those trying to derail them.

15. **Ofun Ose:** Defending one's possessions and assets from theft.

Extra: Glossary of Terms

Ifa: The religion of the Yoruba people from Western Nigeria.

Voodoo: An umbrella term used to describe the many variations of the religions practiced by people from the Caribbean and the Americas.

Santería: A religion developed by the descendants of the Yoruba people who lived in Cuba during the 19th century. It is a combination of Ifa, Catholicism, and Spiritism.

Olodumare: The Supreme Being and Divine Creator of the universe.

Olorun: The aspect of Olodumare that oversees everything that happens in the heavens.

Olofi: The aspect of Olodumare that oversees everything that happens on Earth.

Orishas: The divine beings worshiped by the Yoruba people and the African diaspora religions. They are similar to angels or saints from Catholicism. The Orishas are often syncretized with angels or saints in Santería.

Loas: They are higher spirits worshiped by the Voodoo religions. The Loas are more personally involved in the affairs of humanity than the Orishas. Still, each Loa is equated to a specific Orisha in many cases.

Ajogun: Evil spirits associated with the Ifa belief system who serve as counterparts or foils for the Orishas.

Egun: The spirits of the ancestors venerated by the Yoruba people and other African diaspora religions.

Aṣẹ: The energy that permeates all living and nonliving things. This energy can be used for spiritual purposes and is a key component of the religious beliefs of Ifa.

Orún: The heavens or invisible spiritual realm where Olodumare, the Orishas, the egun, and the iponri reside.

Ayé: The name used by the Yoruba people for the physical world and planet Earth.

Ori: The essence or soul of living beings, especially humans. The ori is said to reside in the heads of mortal beings.

Iponri: The divine consciousness or destiny human beings seek to achieve through the Ifa divination ritual.

Ebo: The sacrificial ritual where an offering is made to appease and gain the favor of the Orishas.

Odu Ifa: The collection of knowledge compiled by Ifa priests and priestesses that can be used to help discern a person's destiny through a divination ritual.

Odu: The individual chapters found within the Odu Ifa. There are 256 in total - 6 major odus and 240 minor ones.

Opele Ifa: A divine chain used as part of the Ifa divination ritual.

Ikin Ifa: Kola nuts or cowrie shells that are an essential part of the Ifa divination system, being cast and interpreted as a way to read the Odu Ifa.

Opon Ifa: A sacred tray used during the Ifa divination ritual.

Iroke Ifa: A tool used prior to the divination ritual to tap the edge of the Opon Ifa to get the Orishas' attention.

Irukere: A brush-like tool used during the divination ritual to ward off evil spirits or negative energy.

Dafa: The specific ritual that utilizes the Ikin Ifa in the Ifa divination system.

Ile-Ife: A holy city of the Yoruba people in Western Nigeria that serves as a center of religious reverence.

Conclusion

The religion of the Yoruba people and the African diaspora religions like Voodoo and Santería have a very deep yet somewhat mysterious history. Hopefully, having shone the light on them, you can understand why their practitioners are so vigilant about guarding their secrets. The last thing they want to see is their sacred rituals and beliefs becoming perverted by those who don't have the same love and care for these religions. However, suppose you treat your exploration of them and the Ifa divination system with the respect that is due to them. In that case, you won't have any problem learning more about them.

The concept of fate and seeking a higher plane of consciousness are core aspects of Ifa, Voodoo, and Santería. Since everyone originally came from Olodumare, they are all destined to return to him. The primary focus people are meant to have while dwelling on Earth is to uncover their specific destiny and prepare their ori for its eventual reunion with their iponri. It's only when the spirit is made whole again that you truly comprehend the enormity of what has been achieved.

Of equal importance on the cosmic scale are the Orishas. Nearly every facet of life contains something connected to them. What people eat, how they behave, and their actions are all dictated by the reverence for the Orishas. This shouldn't be surprising, considering that most African diaspora religions maintain that part of the ori is the essence of a personal Orisha within their head. After reading about these beliefs, you might wonder which Orisha might belong to you. If you decide to continue following the path you set by picking up this guide, you may very well discover the answer and much more.

Here's another book by Silvia Hill that you might like

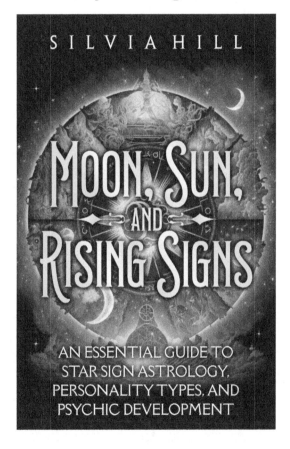

Free Bonus from Silvia Hill available for limited time

Hi Spirituality Lovers!

My name is Silvia Hill, and first off, I want to THANK YOU for reading my book.

Now you have a chance to join my exclusive spirituality email list so you can get the ebooks below for free as well as the potential to get more spirituality ebooks for free! Simply click the link below to join.

P.S. Remember that it's 100% free to join the list.

~~$27~~ FREE BONUSES

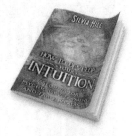

 9 Types of Spirit Guides and How to Connect to Them

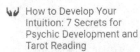 How to Develop Your Intuition: 7 Secrets for Psychic Development and Tarot Reading

Tarot Reading Secrets for Love, Career, and General Messages

Access your free bonuses here
https://livetolearn.lpages.co/african-spiritual-practices-paperback/

References

Barrett, O. (2022, January 23). Voodoo: The revolutionary roots of the most misunderstood religion. TheCollector. https://www.thecollector.com/voodoo-history-misunderstood-religion/

Beyer, C. (2010, February 1). An introduction to the basic beliefs of the Vodou (Voodoo) religion. Learn Religions. https://www.learnreligions.com/vodou-an-introduction-for-beginners-95712

Bjorling, J. (2013). Reincarnation: A Bibliography. Routledge. https://www.yogapedia.com/definition/5833/reincarnation

Chiorazzi, A. (2015, October 6). The spirituality of Africa. Harvard Gazette. https://news.harvard.edu/gazette/story/2015/10/the-spirituality-of-africa/

Coles, D. (2020, October 21). An introduction to hoodoo. Cosmopolitan. https://www.cosmopolitan.com/lifestyle/a34115081/hoodoo-vs-voodoo-facts-history/

Dev, B. (2016, February 4). Eight interesting facts about the Yoruba people. Bashiri. https://bashiri.com.au/eight-interesting-facts-yoruba-people/

Ekore, R. I., & Lanre-Abass, B. (2016). African cultural concept of death and the idea of advance care directives. Indian Journal of Palliative Care, 22(4), 369–372. https://doi.org/10.4103/0973-1075.191741

Knoetze, J. J. (2019). African spiritual phenomena and the probable influence on African families. In Die Skriflig/In Luce Verbi, 53(4), 1–8. https://doi.org/10.4102/ids.v53i4.2505

Obamwonyi, H. (2016, June 18). Life after death according to several African traditions. SwaliAfrica Magazine; SwaliAfrica. http://blog.swaliafrica.com/life-after-death-according-to-several-african-traditions/

Singh, C., & Bhagwan, R. (2020). African spirituality: Unearthing beliefs and practices for the helping professions. Social Work, 56(4), 403–415. https://doi.org/10.15270/56-4-882

The ancient roots of Yoruba. (2005, September 30). Tampa Bay Times. https://www.tampabay.com/archive/1997/01/07/the-ancient-roots-of-yoruba/

The Editors of Encyclopedia Britannica. (2022). reincarnation. In Encyclopedia Britannica.

The Santeria religion, a story. (2009, September 8). African American Registry. https://aaregistry.org/story/from-africa-to-the-americas-santeria/

What is Santeria? (n.d.). AboutSanteria. http://www.aboutsanteria.com/what-is-santeria.html

Wigington, P. (2011, November 15). What is the Santeria religion? Learn Religions. http://learnreligions.com/about-santeria-traditions-2562543

Wigington, P. (2019, November 29). Yoruba religion: History and beliefs. Learn Religions. https://www.learnreligions.com/yoruba-religion-4777660

Yoruba. (n.d.). Everyculture.com. https://www.everyculture.com/wc/Mauritania-to-Nigeria/Yoruba.html

Abisoye. (2021, August 11). Olodumare, the god with no images, shrines. Plus TV Africa. https://plustvafrica.com/olodumare-the-god-with-no-images-shrines/

Baggini, J. (2006, March 27). Why do we have creation myths? The Guardian. https://amp.theguardian.com/theguardian/2006/mar/28/features11.g21

Creation Myth. (n.d.). Nau.edu. https://www2.nau.edu/~gaud/bio301/content/crtm.htm

LibGuides: African traditional religions textbook: Ifa: Chapter 4. Olodumare is a gracious creator. (2021). https://research.auctr.edu/Ifa/Chap4Intro

Olodumare –. (n.d.). Eneke The Bird. https://enekethebird.wordpress.com/tag/olodumare/

OLODUMARE - the Yoruba Religious concepts. (n.d.). Google.com. https://sites.google.com/site/theyorubareligiousconcepts/olodumare

Olodumare, Olorun and Olofin: The names of God. (2022, February 7). Oshaeifa.com. https://en.oshaeifa.com/orisha/olodumare-olorun-olofin/

Olujobi, H. (2016, September 24). The lies of their forefathers: Yoruba myth of creation. Linkedin.com. https://www.linkedin.com/pulse/lies-forefathers-yoruba-myth-creation-hezekiah-olujobi/

Rodríguez, C. (2020, August 11). Who are Olofin Olorun and Olodumare? Ashé pa mi Cuba. https://ashepamicuba.com/en/quienes-son-olofin-olorun-y-olodumare/

Yoruba creation myth. (n.d.). Gateway-africa.com. https://www.gateway-africa.com/stories/Yoruba_Creation_Myth.html

Beyer, C. (2012, June 11). The Orishas. Learn Religions. https://www.learnreligions.com/who-are-the-orishas-95922

Brandon, G. (2018). orisha. In Encyclopedia Britannica.

Burton, N. (2020, July 31). How some Black Americans are finding solace in African spirituality. Vox. https://www.vox.com/2020/7/31/21346686/orisha-yoruba-african-spirituality-covid

Fields, K. (2020, January 18). The Seven African Powers for beginners (African spirituality & magic). Otherworldly Oracle; FIELDS CREATIVE CONSULTING. https://otherworldlyoracle.com/seven-african-powers/

Mark, J. J. (2021). Orisha. World History Encyclopedia. https://www.worldhistory.org/Orisha/

Murphy, J. M. (2022). Santería. In Encyclopedia Britannica.

Nigeria, G. (2019, August 11). The 5 most influential orishas. The Guardian Nigeria News - Nigeria and World News; Guardian Nigeria. https://guardian.ng/life/the-5-most-influential-orishas/

demo. (2016, September 20). Who are the Orishas? DJONIBA Dance Center. https://www.djoniba.com/who-are-the-orishas/

Konkwo, R. (2022, September 21). Yoruba gods and goddesses: their history explained in detail. Legit.Ng - Nigeria News; Legit.ng. https://www.legit.ng/1175618-yoruba-gods-goddesses.html

Mark, J. J. (2021). Orisha. World History Encyclopedia. https://www.worldhistory.org/Orisha/

Ogbodo, I. (2022, March 17). Yoruba mythology: The orishas of the Yoruba religion. African History Collections. https://medium.com/african-history-collections/yoruba-mythology-the-orishas-of-the-yoruba-religion-f411c3db389d

Orisha orunmila. (n.d.). Themythdetective.com. https://themythdetective.com/index.php/orisha-orunmila/

Ost, B. (2021). LibGuides: African traditional religions textbook: Ifa: Chapter 1. Orientation and overview. https://research.auctr.edu/Ifa/Chap1Intro

Wigington, P. (2019, November 29). Yoruba religion: History and beliefs. Learn Religions. https://www.learnreligions.com/yoruba-religion-4777660

Mark, J. J. (2021). Orisha. World History Encyclopedia. https://www.worldhistory.org/Orisha/

Alvarado, D. (2010). The Voodoo Doll Spellbook: A Compendium of Ancient and Contemporary Spells and Rituals, Part 1. Prescott Valley, AZ: Creole Moon Publications.

Bellegarde-Smith and Claudine, Michel. Haitian Vodou: Spirit, Myth & Reality. Indiana University Press, 2006.

Benedicty-Kokken, Alessandra (2014). Spirit Possession in French, Haitian, and Vodou Thought: An Intellectual History. Lexington. ISBN 978-0739184653.

Gamache, H. (1984). The Master Book of Candle Burning: Or, How to Burn Candles for Every Purpose. Original Publications.

Hurston, Z. N., Boas, F., Covarrubias, M., & Rampersad, A. (1935). Mules and men (p. 8). New York: Perennial Library.

Joseph, Celucien L.; Cleophat, Nixon S. (2016). Vodou in the Haitian Experience: A Black Atlantic Perspective. Lexington. ISBN 978-1498508346.

Joseph, Celucien L.; Cleophat, Nixon S. (2016). Vodou in Haitian Memory: The Idea and Representation of Vodou in Haitian Imagination. Lexington. ISBN 978-1498508346.

Cosentino, Donald. 1995. "Imagine Heaven" in Sacred Arts of Haitian Vodou. Edited by Cosentino, Donald, et al. Berkeley: University of California Press.

Daniel, Yvonne (2005). Dancing Wisdom: Embodied Knowledge in Haitian Vodou, Cuban Yoruba, and Bahian Candomblé. University of Illinois Press. ISBN 978-0252072079.

Herskovits, Melville J. (1971). Life in a Haitian Valley: Garden CITY, NEW YORK:

McAlister, Elizabeth. 2002. Rara! Vodou, Power, and Performance in Haiti and its Diaspora. Berkeley: University of California Press.

McAlister, Elizabeth. 1998. "The Madonna of 115th St. Revisited: Vodou and Haitian Catholicism in the Age of Transnationalism." In S. Warner, ed., Gatherings in Diaspora. Philadelphia: Temple Univ. Press.

Rey, Terry; Stepick, Alex (2013). Crossing the Water and Keeping the Faith: Haitian Religion in Miami. NYU Press. ISBN 978-0814777084.

Richman, Karen E. (2005). Migration and Vodou. University Press of Florida. ISBN 978-0813033259

"10 Mojo Bag Color Meanings Explained [+ How to Use Them]." Magickalspot.com, 19 Sept. 2020, https://magickalspot.com/mojo-bag-colors/

"A List of Powerful Herbs for Love Spells [+Zodiac Signs]." Magickalspot.com, 5 May 2020, https://magickalspot.com/herbs-for-love-spells/ .

americanadmin. "Facts about High John the Conqueror." American History for Kids, 24 July 2019, www.americanhistoryforkids.com/the-civil-war-high-john-the-conqueror/.

Ashley, Kelly. "10 Signs You Need to Clear Your Energy Now." Spiritual Awakening Signs, 19 Jan. 2019, https://spiritualawakeningsigns.com/spiritualawakening/10-signs-you-need-to-clear-your-energy-now/#:~:text=So%2C%20with%20that%20in%20mind%2C%20here%20are%2010

Bird, Stephanie Rose. "10 Tips to Help You Practice 365 Days of Hoodoo." Llewellyn Worldwide, 3 Dec. 2018, www.llewellyn.com/journal/article/2718 .

"Bottle Trees: A Beautiful Tradition with a Spiritual Past." HowStuffWorks, 5 Oct. 2022, https://history.howstuffworks.com/history-vs-myth/bottle-tree.htm .

Fertility Spells – Free Witchcraft Spells. https://freewitchspells.com/fertility-spells

fields. "Candle Magic for Beginners: Your ULTIMATE Guide." *Otherworldly Oracle*, 23 Oct. 2018, https://otherworldlyoracle.com/candle-magic-for-beginners/ .

"How to Connect with Your Ancestors in 10 EFFECTIVE Ways." *Otherworldly Oracle*, 13 Mar. 2019, https://otherworldlyoracle.com/how-to-connect-with-your-ancestors/ .

"Spiritual Cleansing: Your Guide to Cleansing Rituals and Methods." *Otherworldly Oracle*, 8 July 2019, https://otherworldlyoracle.com/spiritual-cleansing-rituals/ .

Hayford, Vanessa. "The Humble History of Soul Food • BLACK FOODIE." *Black Foodie*, 22 Jan. 2018, www.blackfoodie.co/the-humble-history-of-soul-food/ .

Hayn, Lyza. "Spiritual Meaning of the Kongo Cosmogram (Dikenga)." *OutofStress.com*, 14 Oct. 2022, www.outofstress.com/kongo-cosmogram-spiritual-meaning/#:~:text=The%20Kongo%20Cosmogram%20%28also%20known%20as%20Dikenga%20or .

Heckman, William. "12 Fun Mindfulness Exercises." *The American Institute of Stress*, 10 Feb. 2021, www.stress.org/12-fun-mindfulness-exercises .

"Hoodoo Formulas and Recipes." *Www.Hoodoo-Conjure.com*, www.Hoodoo-conjure.com/recipes/bitterbaths.htm .

Hoodoo Herbs - HoodooWitch. 24 Apr. 2016, https://Hoodoowitch.net/book-of-shadows/magickal-Hoodoo-herbs/ .

"Magical Days of the Week: Correspondences & Daily Energy." *Otherworldly Oracle*, 22 Apr. 2020, https://otherworldlyoracle.com/magical-days-of-the-week/ .

"Mojo Bags - What They Are and How to Make Them." *A Pagan Mess*, 27 Jan. 2019, https://apaganmess.com/mojo-bags/#:~:text=How%20to%20Make%2C%20feed%2C%20and%20charge%20mojo%20bags .

"Mood Food: 9 Foods That Can Really Boost Your Spirits." *Healthline*, 5 Feb. 2020, www.healthline.com/nutrition/mood-food#6.-Berries .

Patterson, Rachel. "Hoodoo Herbs and Roots." *Rachelpatterson*, 11 Aug. 2017, www.rachelpatterson.co.uk/single-post/2017/08/11/Hoodoo-Herbs-and-Roots .

"Reading Candle Wax | Divination." *Shirleytwofeathers.com*, https://shirleytwofeathers.com/The_Blog/divination/ceromancy-reading-candle-wax/#:~:text=Another%20way%20to%20observe%20and%20identify%20the%20messages .

"What Is Hoodoo-Conjure." *Theconjureman,* https://theconjureman.com/What_is_Hoodoo-Conjure.html#:~:text=Conjure%2FHoodoo%20is%20a%20form%20of%20folk%20magick%20and .

WiseWitch. "7 Steps for Making Magical Charms, Amulets, Talismans & Fetishes." *Wise Witches and Witchcraft,* 17 Apr. 2018, https://witchcraftandwitches.com/magic-magick/7-steps-for-making-magical-charms-amulets-talismans-fetishes/ .

"Hoodoo Witch (Rootworker)." *Wise Witches and Witchcraft,* 18 Feb. 2018, https://witchcraftandwitches.com/types-of-witches/Hoodoo-witch-rootworker/ .

Wright, Mackenzie Sage. "How to Cast a Jar Spell: Witchcraft for Beginners." *Exemplore,* https://exemplore.com/wicca-witchcraft/Witchcraft-for-Beginners-How-to-Cast-a-Jar-Spell .

"How to Make Your Own Hidden/Portable Shrine." *Exemplore,* exemplore.com/wicca-

Abiodun, R. (2014). Yoruba art and language: Seeking the African in African art. Cambridge University Press.

Adebanwi, With. (2016). Yoruba elites and ethnic politics in Nigeria: Obafemi Awolowo and corporate agency. Cambridge University Press.

Adeoye, C. L. (1985). Ìgbàgbọ́ àti èsìn Yorùba. Evans Brothers (Nigeria Publishers).

Adesoye, A. (2015). Scientific pilgrimage: "The life and times of emeritus professor V.a oyenuga ."D.sc, Fas, cfr Nigeria's first emeritus professor and Africa's first agriculture professor. Authorhouse.

Afrika, I. (2021, January 23). The Yoruba goddess of sensuality and prosperity: Oshun. Inside Afrika - Mother To All; Inside Afrika Store. https://insideafrika.store/2021/01/23/the-yoruba-goddess-of-sensuality-and-prosperity-oshun/

Agbo, N. (2018, May 7). Oro: A Yoruba festival that is anti-women. The Guardian Nigeria News - Nigeria and World News; Guardian Nigeria. https://guardian.ng/life/oro-a-yoruba-festival-that-is-anti-women/

Agbo, N. (2020, February 9). Significance of Egungun in Yoruba cultural history. The Guardian Nigeria News - Nigeria and World News; Guardian Nigeria. https://guardian.ng/life/significance-of-egungun-in-yoruba-cultural-history/

Ajayi, S. T. (2007). Moremi, the Courageous Queen. Rasmed Publications.

Asante, M. K., & Mazama, A. (Eds.). (2009a). Encyclopedia of African religion. SAGE Publications.

Asante, M. K., & Mazama, A. (Eds.). (2009b). Encyclopedia of African religion. SAGE Publications.

Asante, M., & Mazama, A. (2009). Encyclopedia of African religion. SAGE Publications, Inc.

Asiwaju, A. I. (1976). Western yorubaland under European rule, 1889-1945. Longman.

Awolalu, J. O. (1973). Yoruba sacrificial practice. Journal of Religion in Africa, 5(2), 81. https://doi.org/10.2307/1594756

Bascom, W. W. (1969). Ifa divination: Communication between gods and men in west Africa. Indiana University Press.

Bascom, William R. (1992). African folktales in the new world. Indiana University Press.

Bascom, William Russell. (1984). The Yoruba of southwestern Nigeria. Waveland Press.

Bata drumming :: Notations, discographies, Glossary. (n.d.). Scribd. https://www.scribd.com/doc/85753/Bata-Drumming-Notations-Discographies-Glossary

BBC News. (2017, August 23). Nigeria's Egungun festival: Colour, culture and community. BBC. https://www.bbc.com/news/world-africa-41026019

Beier, U. (1980). Yoruba Myths. Cambridge University Press.

Berger, H. A. (Ed.). (2005). Witchcraft and magic: Contemporary North America. University of Pennsylvania Press.

Biz, A. (2020, June 6). Elegua-god of crossroads. Augustine's; Augustines Spiritual Boutique Chicago. https://www.augustines.biz/elegua-lord-the-crossroads/

Blue basin – Orisha shrine – idakeda group ltd. (n.d.). Idakedagroup.com. https://idakedagroup.com/african-legacy-tours/sites-of-african-heritage-in-tt/blue-basin-orisha-shrine/

Bolaji Idowu, E. (2000). Olodumare: God in Yoruba Belief. Original Publications.

Bonaventure. (2018a). The life of Saint Francis. Franklin Classics.

Bonaventure. (2018b). The life of Saint Francis. Franklin Classics.

Books Group. (2012). The church missionary juvenile instructor volume 6, no. 6. Rarebooksclub.com.

Brown, D. H. (2003). Santería enthroned : art, ritual, and innovation in an Afro-Cuban religion: Art, ritual and innovation in an Afro-Cuban religion. University of Chicago Press.

Brown, K. M. (2011). Mama Lola: A vodou priestess in Brooklyn (3rd ed.). University of California Press.

Bullroarer. (2014, September 8). Science World. https://www.scienceworld.ca/resource/hummers/

By the gods! (n.d.). Tumblr. https://www.bythegods.net/post/506662684

Camara, L. (2015). Le Choix de l'Ori. Amalion Publishing.

Canson, P. E. (2014a). Yemonja. In Encyclopedia Britannica.

Canson, P. E. (2014b). Yemonja. In Encyclopedia Britannica.

Chemeche, G., Goncalves da Silva, V., & Cosentino, D. J. (2013). Eshu: The Divine Trickster. ACC Art Books.

Chesson, F. W. (2014). Twilight Tales. Createspace Independent Publishing Platform.

Clark, M. A. (2005). Where Men Are Wives And Mothers Rule: Santería Ritual Practices and their Gender Implications. University Press of Florida.

Clark, M. A. (2007). Santeria: Correcting the myths and uncovering the realities of a growing religion. Praeger.

Creating an Orisha Altar. (n.d.). Original Botanica. https://www.originalbotanica.com/blog/creating-an-orisha-altar-/

Cross, F. L., & Livingstone, E. A. (Eds.). (2005). The oxford dictionary of the Christian church. Oxford University Press.

Drewal, H. J. (Ed.). (2008). Sacred waters: Arts for Mami wata and other divinities in Africa and the diaspora. Indiana University Press.

Drewel, H., & Pemberton, J. (1990). Yoruba: Nine centuries of African art and thought. Harry N. Abrams.

Dundun Drum Family; used by Lagbaja. (2018, February 14). Lagbaja.com; Lagbaja - Ultimate Drum Reviews, Guides and Tutorials. https://www.lagbaja.com/drums/dundun.php

Eglash, R. (2007, November 29). The fractals at the heart of African designs.

Egun - Spirits of the Dead. (n.d.). Scribd. https://www.scribd.com/document/255134659/Egun-Spirits-of-the-Dead

Eleguá/eshu. (n.d.). AboutSanteria. http://www.aboutsanteria.com/eleguaacuteeshu.html

Elery, Y. J. (2016). Spiritual Cleansing. Tate Publishing & Enterprises.

Fairchild, M. (2021, March 22). How many religions are there in the world? Learn Religions. https://www.learnreligions.com/how-many-religions-are-there-in-the-world-5114658

Falola, T., & Amponsah, N. A. (2012). Women's roles in Sub-Saharan Africa. ABC-CLIO.

Made in United States
North Haven, CT
01 March 2025

66355044R00225